THE ARTISTIC ANATOMY COLORING BOOK

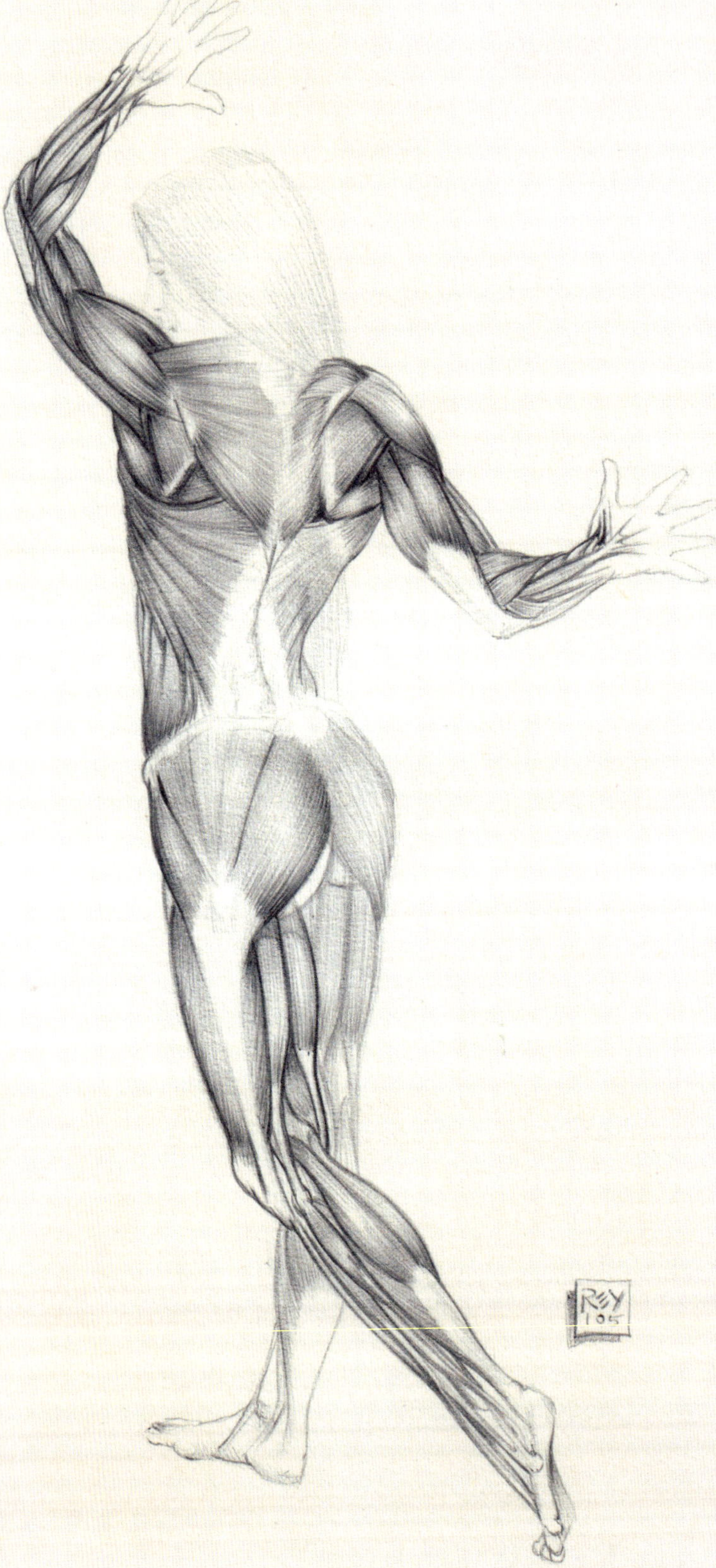
REY
105

REY BUSTOS

THE ARTISTIC ANATOMY COLORING BOOK

The Essential Muscles
Artists Need to Know

rockynook

The Artistic Anatomy Coloring Book:
The Essential Muscles Artists Need to Know
Rey Bustos

Editor: Jocelyn Howell
Project manager: Lisa Brazieal
Marketing manager: Koryn Olage
Graphic design and layout: John Calmeyer
Cover design: John Calmeyer

ISBN: 979-8-88814-326-1
1st Edition (1st printing)

Rocky Nook, Inc.
1010 B Street, Suite 350
San Rafael, CA 94901
USA
www.rockynook.com
info@rockynook.com
(415) 747-8756

Represented in the E.U. by:
Rheinwerk Verlag GmbH
Rheinwerkallee 4
53227 Bonn
Germany
service@rheinwerk-verlag.de

Distributed in the UK and Europe by Publishers Group UK
Distributed in the U.S. and all other territories by
Publishers Group West

Library of Congress Control Number: 2024943308

This book is printed on acid-free paper.
Printed in China

TABLE OF CONTENTS

FOREWORD

Of all artistic subjects, none are as demanding as the human figure. This is due not only to the complexity of the human form, but to the sensitivity we have when looking at one another. General drawing practice alone falls short. To draw, paint, model, or carve the figure with confidence and control, the artist must go further into a prolonged study of the subject matter we call artistic anatomy.

Of all the masters of artistic anatomy teaching students in recent times, from the great Eliot Goldfinger to the late Gottfried Bammes, Rey Bustos stands out uniquely. For decades Rey has been an inescapable name in the west coast art community of the United States. Through his famous blackboard demos, his écorché clay modeling, and his comparative anatomy classes, he has taught generations of artists at institutions such as ArtCenter in Pasadena and the Los Angeles Academy of Figurative Art. His classes are known for their challenge and rigor, but also for the enthusiasm, warmth, and generosity he brings to them. Rey's fascination with artistic anatomy is undeniable and infectious. Students cannot help but be drawn into the beauty of the subject through the force of his teaching, and few leave his classes without being deeply moved by the experience.

When New Masters Academy was founded, Rey was our natural choice to teach artistic anatomy. Through his courses at NMA, he has reached many thousands of students, and the love and loyalty they feel for him speaks volumes. That became especially clear after the Los Angeles fires of 2025, when Rey lost his home and all of his possessions. In a situation that would have broken many people, Rey's students stepped forward to help their beloved teacher rebuild his life, his home, his library, and his teaching resources. I am honored to call Rey an inspiration and a friend. This new volume is the continuation of a lifetime of devoted teaching, and I have no doubt it will become a staple in the libraries of serious art students for years to come.

—Joshua Jacobo
Founder, *New Masters Academy*

INTRODUCTION

Artistic anatomy has been a part of different cultures for millennia—from the ancient Egyptians to the Greeks to the Romans. The art that represents the cultures of these lands and people required those artists to become educated in the sciences of the arts, whether it be visual arts, literature, or performing arts.

As a teacher of figure drawing and artistic anatomy for over three decades, my love for the subject compelled me to make this book to help my students and others wanting to further their education. My hope has always been to make anatomy a more accessible and enjoyable experience for artists of all levels. Knowing even basic anatomy will facilitate drawing from imagination, and once an artist understands some of the fundamentals of anatomy covered in this book, it will allow for a more personal and dynamic quality in their figurative work. In this ever-changing, digital world, one thing will never cease to be necessary, and that is knowledge of the basics for artists.

That said, artistic anatomy is always heavily edited. Books on this subject vary from book to book and from author to author. Every artistic anatomist chooses which muscles to include, and the author of this book (that's me!) is no different. Medical anatomy books are great—I have many—but, unless one wants to teach anatomy or simply wants to know everything, few pages are necessary for artists. We do not need to know enervation or physiology to draw the human figure. This is by no means a "complete" book of anatomy, as it does not need to be—it is a fun way to learn the subject.

In this book, I have chosen not to include a number of muscles because they make little to no impact on the surface form of the body; however, I did include some muscles that are rarely or never seen because I thought they were interesting in one way or another. Many of the facial muscles, for example, are omitted in an effort to ensure the information is easy to take in. The facial muscles are fascinating, but they are rather hidden in our soft, chubby faces! Still, some of them are included because they may be seen on some lean or older people.

Another decision I made was to group certain muscles and bones in order to focus on the primary forms and structures that take precedence in figure drawing, rather than on the anatomical complexities of each group. For example, I decided to illustrate the sacrospinalis muscles as two major forms easily seen on the back torso rather than the many muscles and layers that make up the entire group of deep vertebral muscles. As for the bones, I grouped the eight wrist bones—the carpals—rather than naming each little bone. I did the same with the seven tarsal bones that make up the heel and ankle bones. These decisions were not made to diminish the importance of any of these areas of anatomy, but to remind us artists that it is best to first learn the basics, the things that are more readily seen on the living form, and to seek more in-depth anatomy as needed or desired.

There are also differences in the way artists and anatomists choose to interpret and visually represent muscles because "real" anatomy, the muscles of a flayed body in a cadaver lab, is not a pretty sight to most. My students who join me to draw from cadavers without skin are often confused when searching for specific muscles. In class, and in this and many artistic anatomy books, the muscles appear more like finely combed hair. This is not what muscle tissue looks like when you see it lying on a lab table. We often make the muscles neater and easier to identify for more clarity, and this book is no exception—I purposely "prettied up" the muscles for easier identification. I also eliminated the fat that we all have and pushed the muscles to the contour of every drawing to fill the gap that fat takes up in a real human body. Fat is an important part of anatomical learning, but in this book, it was eliminated as a shortcut. Again, this is not to diminish its importance but to keep this book more basic in approach. •

HOW TO APPROACH THIS BOOK

One of the first things I talk about at the beginning of every anatomy or figure drawing class is the importance of the skeleton. The skeleton is the structural support and the mechanical frame of the body, necessary for both movement and protection. To illustrate this, I like to show my students a picture of a chair with a white sheet over it. The sheet is formless until it is draped over something. If we think of this analogy in relation to the body, the chair is the skeleton and the sheet is the muscle, fat, and skin layers. In many areas, the skeleton is evident on the surface of the figure—we call these visible points "bony landmarks." Just as the sheet takes on the form of the chair, our muscles, fat, and skin take on the shape of the skeleton.

In this book, the skeleton serves as a prologue to what follows, which are the muscles as they lay on the skeleton. My main focus is to enhance the reader's understanding of the muscles that have the most impact on the surface of the body as we see it. For this reason, I've called the skeleton chapter The Foundation, and I've labeled the muscle chapters sequentially with the letters A–H, starting with A at the bottom (the lower leg and foot) and working my way up to H at the top (the head and face). For each muscle in this book, I have included information about its structure/shape, its origin (where it is anchored), its insertion (where it ends; usually, where it makes something move), and its action.

Note: I use the letters of the alphabet rather than numbers because I find it to be a clearer system. I have always had learning disabilities, so I've had to organize information in a way that makes it easier for me to learn. I've found that it is easier to differentiate between A.1, A.2, B.2, etc., than a bunch of numbers in a row, like 1.1, 1.2, 2.1, and so on. I hope this system works for you as well as it did for little Rey!

As you work your way through this book, start by coloring each muscle individually, and then color the same muscle within its muscle group. When you move on to the next muscle, color that muscle individually, and then color both the previous muscle and the new one in their group. Continue in this manner, building the group as you go.

Enjoy learning while relaxing as you color and absorb the information. This is an amazing way to learn this subject!

—Rey Bustos (a.k.a. Mr. Rey)

TIP FOR FURTHER EDUCATION

It is always important for anyone who wants to know more about the surface forms of the living figure to practice looking at art or photographs of art models and identifying the muscles, tendons, and skeletal landmarks. There are a couple of ways that I have my students do this:

1. Find a figure, print it out, and place tracing paper over it to draw in the muscles. You can add more of the muscles as you learn them.

2. You can also do this digitally (I use Photoshop) by placing a new layer over the image and bringing down the opacity so that it simulates tracing paper. Then use a fine brush to draw in the muscles on the new layer. This method is convenient since it is much easier to make corrections than when drawing on paper.

It is also a good idea to use one of these methods to practice drawing the skeleton. Drawing simplified skeletons is a great way to become familiar with this important framework of the body. •

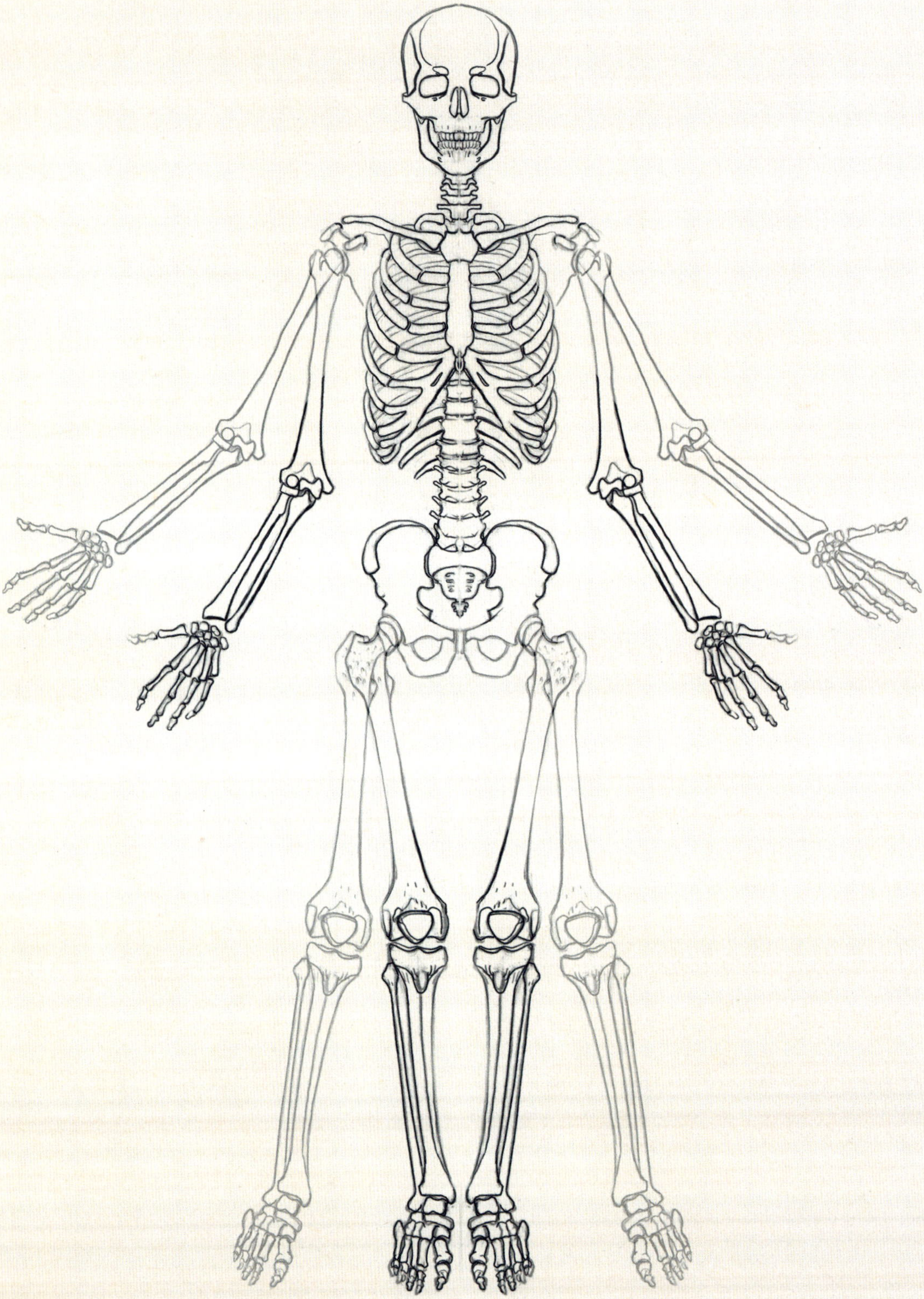

THE FOUNDATION

THE HUMAN SKELETON

When we are born, we have between 270 and 300 bones in our body. As we grow, some of these bones fuse together, typically resulting in 206 bones in an adult. These are divided into two main parts, the appendicular skeleton and the axial skeleton. The appendicular skeleton consists of 126 bones, which include the pelvis, shoulders, and upper and lower extremities (the arms, hands, legs, and feet). The axial skeleton consists of the skull, the entire vertebral column (spine and sacrum), the pelvis, and the thorax (rib cage).

The skeleton is the main support and protection for the body and it facilitates movement. It is the main frame of the body and is therefore critically important for an artist to know. Many parts of the skeleton poke through the surface and are often easily seen by the eye. In art, these points can create a more believable and structurally sound figure.

S.1. FOOT

The foot supports the body weight, enabling locomotion like walking, running, and jumping. The design of the human foot has two major arches, one from the heel to the big toe, and one from side to side across the midfoot. These arches provide shock absorption and weight distribution. This is all done through a complex combination of bones, joints, ligaments, tendons, and muscles working together to create stability, balance, and a lever system that would make the best engineers envious of its elegant design.

There are twenty-six bones that make up the human foot: seven tarsal bones (including the heel bone, or calcaneus), five metatarsals, and the fourteen bones that make up the toes, three for each toe except the big toe, which only has two bones.

The nervous system also provides critical feedback to the brain to adjust posture and balance.

The two little "jelly beans" that you see by the big toe in the bottom view are sesamoid bones. They give the big toe extra leverage. They are the same as the patella (knee cap), which is the largest sesamoid bone. Note that in the top and bottom views, the bones labeled with a 9 are called the distal phalanges. The big toe only has a proximal and distal phalanx; it does not have a medial section.

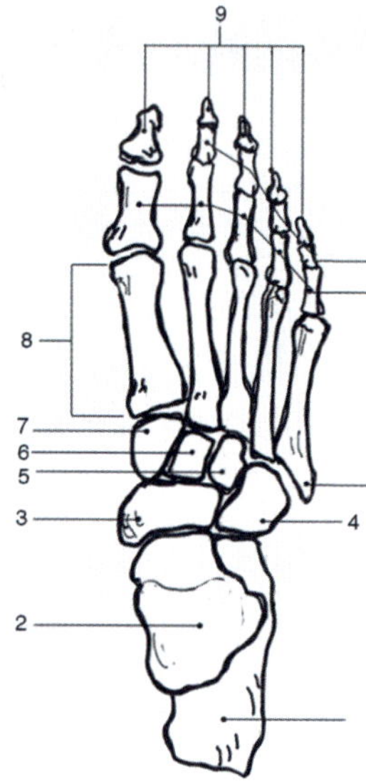

Top
(Right Foot)

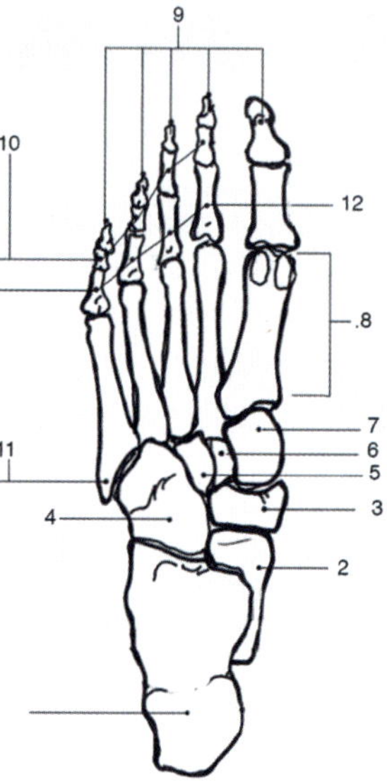

Bottom
(Right Foot)

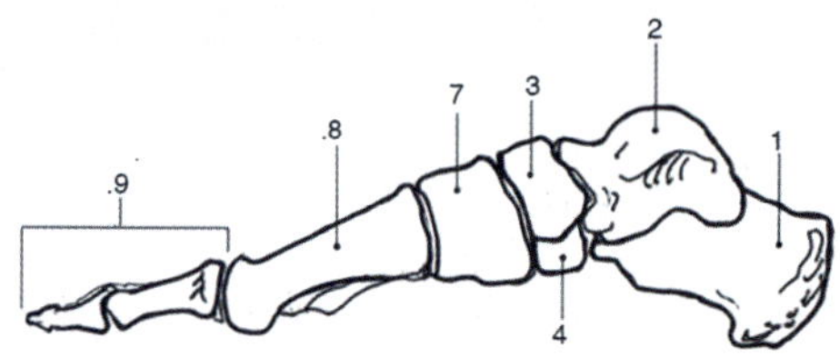

Medial (Inside) View

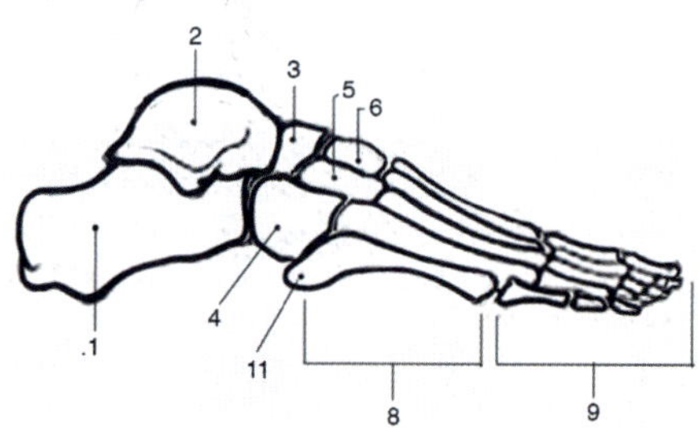

Lateral (Outside) View

CHECKLIST

- O 1. Calcaneus
- O 2. Talus
- O 3. Navicular
- O 4. Cuboid
- O 5. Third Cuneiform
- O 6. Second Cuneiform
- O 7. First Cuneiform
- O 8. Metatarsals
- O 9. Phalanges
- O 10. Medial Phalanges
- O 11. Tuberosity of Fifth Metatarsal
- O 12. Proximal Phalanges

TIBIA, FIBULA, AND PATELLA S.2.

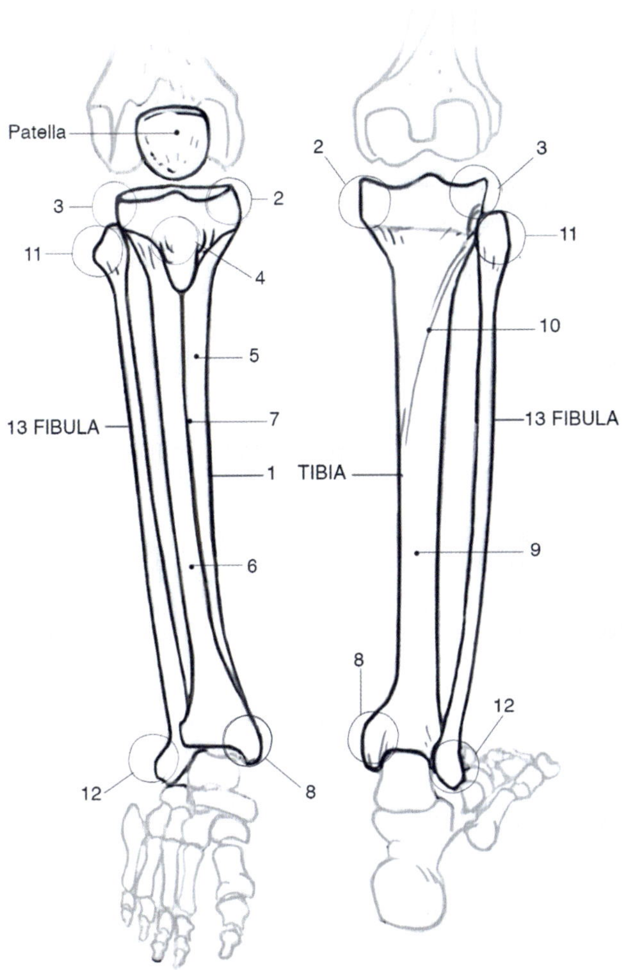

Anterior (Front) View

Posterior (Back) View

The tibia, or shin bone, is the second longest bone in the human body. Only the femur is longer. The tibia is a strong bone with a triangular cross-section design that gives it added strength—picture a prism with the edge facing forward. The main thing to remember as an artist is that the length of the tibia with the foot equals the length of the femur. This is very important when drawing anyone, even when making up a figure: The length of the thigh will equal the length of the shin and foot.

The inside lower part of the tibia is your inside ankle, the medial malleolus, which is higher than the outside ankle, the lateral malleolus of the fibula. It is also important to note that the patella, or kneecap, is attached to the tibia and the protruding bump called the tibial tuberosity by the patellar ligament. The space between the patella and the tibia is constant, as the patellar ligament does not stretch. The patella is a flat triangular bone embedded in the connective tissue of the knee. It gives the knee mechanical advantage that allows for easier extension of the entire leg.

The fibula is the thinner bone that flanks the tibia. It is the same length as the tibia, but it attaches lower on the back/side corner of the lateral condyle and becomes your outside ankle, the lateral malleolus, down by your foot. The lateral malleolus of the fibula is lower than the medial malleolus of the tibia.

CHECKLIST

- O 1. Tibia
- O 2. Medial Condyle
- O 3. Lateral Condyle
- O 4. Tibial Tuberosity
- O 5. Medial Surface
- O 6. Lateral Surface
- O 7. Anterior Crest
- O 8. Medial Malleolus
- O 9. Posterior Surface
- O 10. Soleal Line
- O 11. Head of Fibula
- O 12. Lateral Malleolus
- O 13. Fibula

S.2. TIBIA, FIBULA, AND PATELLA

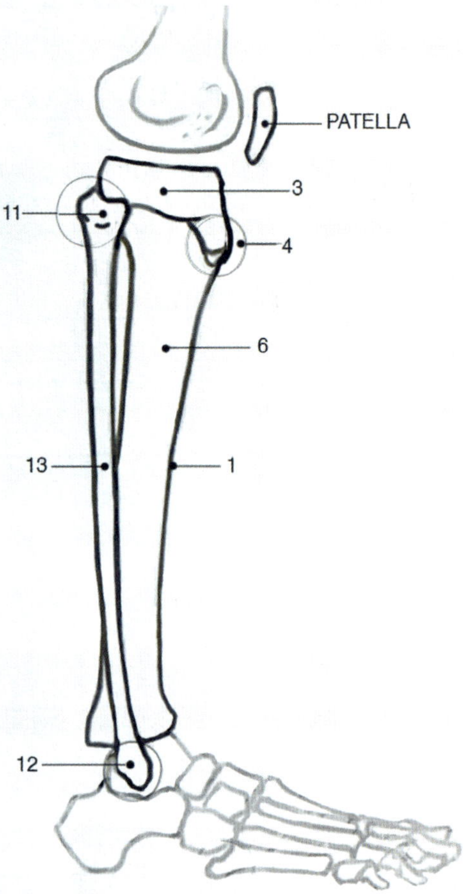

Lateral (Outside) View

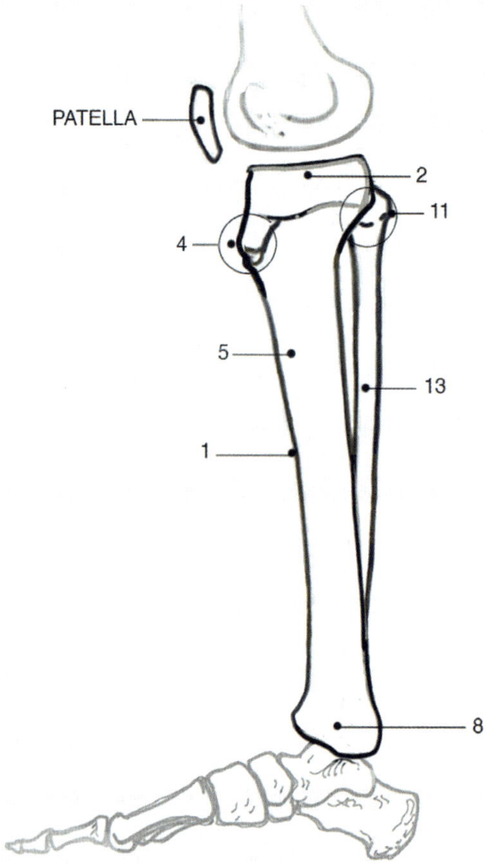

Medial (Inside) View

CHECKLIST

- O 1. Tibia
- O 2. Medial Condyle
- O 3. Lateral Condyle
- O 4. Tibial Tuberosity
- O 5. Medial Surface
- O 6. Lateral Surface
- O 7. Anterior Crest *(see p. 13)*
- O 8. Medial Malleolus
- O 9. Posterior Surface *(see p. 13)*
- O 10. Soleal Line *(see p. 13)*
- O 11. Head of Fibula
- O 12. Lateral Malleolus
- O 13. Fibula

FEMUR S.3.

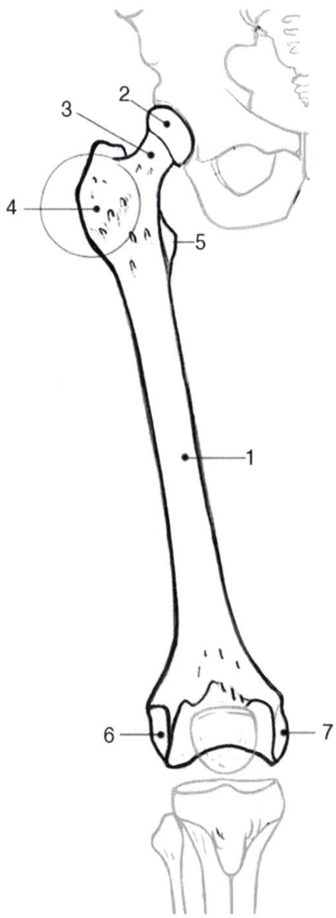

Anterior
(Front) View

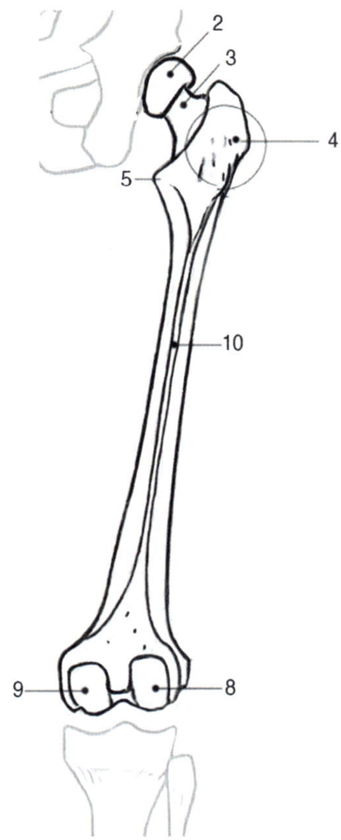

Posterior
(Back) View

The femur is the longest bone in the human body, comprising 26.74 percent, or roughly one-fourth, of the total height of a person. It is also extremely strong and thick. It has a ridge on the back called the linea aspera, which adds strength to the back of the shaft and serves as a flat attachment point for many of the inner-thigh adductor muscles.

The femur has a large, rounded head that articulates with the acetabulum, or socket, of the pelvis. It has a large, rocklike bony protrusion at the hip called the great (or greater) trochanter and a smaller protrusion on the inner, back part of the upper end called the lesser trochanter.

At the distal end, at the knee, the femur has two rounded, almost wheel-like forms that articulate with the top of the tibia. These forms fit into two hollow, indented forms of the tibia called condyles ("knuckles").

CHECKLIST

- O 1 Femur (Shaft)
- O 2 Head
- O 3 Neck
- O 4 Great Trochanter
- O 5 Lesser Trochanter
- O 6 Lateral Epicondyle
- O 7 Medial Epicondyle
- O 8 Lateral Condyle
- O 9 Medial Condyle
- O 10 Linea Aspera

5.3. FEMUR

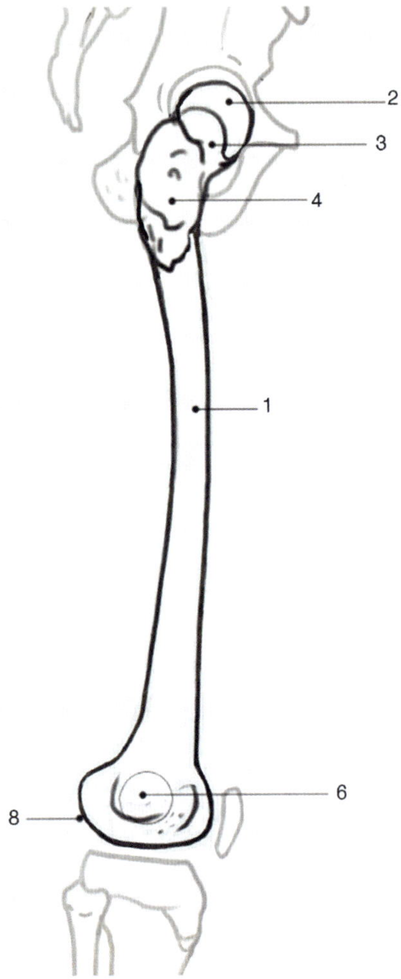

Lateral (Outside) View

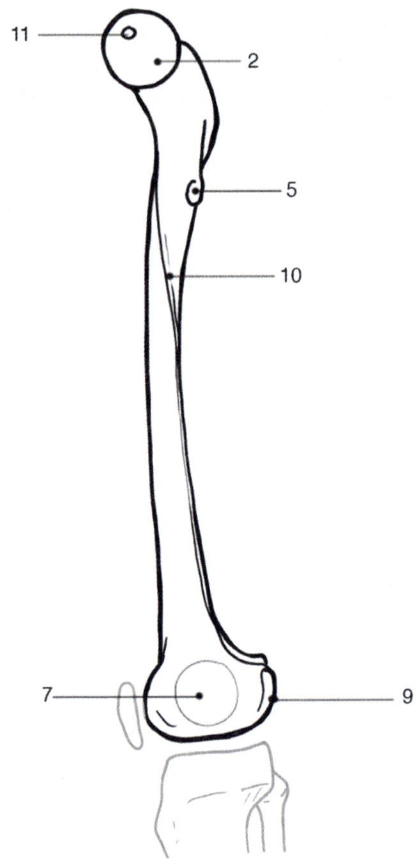

Medial (Inside) View

CHECKLIST

O 1. Femur

O 2. Head

O 3. Neck

O 4. Great Trochanter

O 5. Lesser Trochanter

O 6. Lateral Epicondyle

O 7. Medial Epicondyle

O 8. Lateral Condyle

O 9. Medial Condyle

O 10. Linea Aspera

O 11. Fovea (dimple for ligament)

PELVIS S.4.

Anterior (Front) View

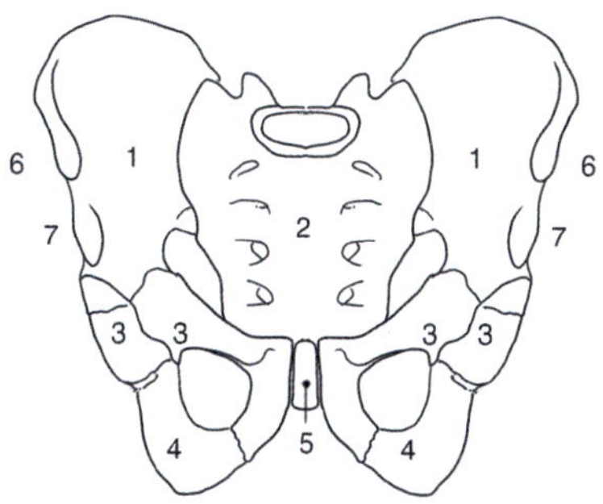

Posterior (Back) View

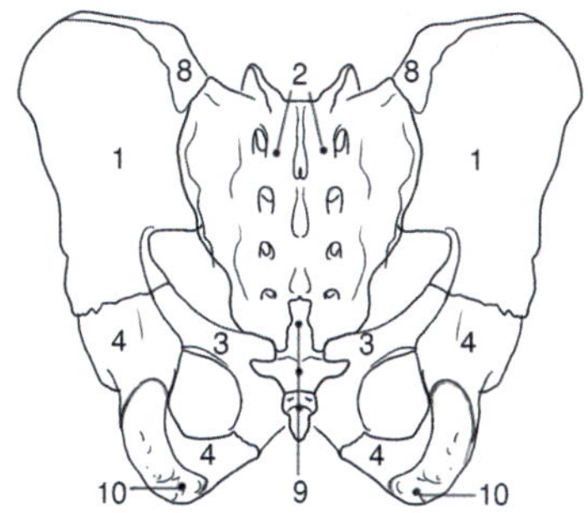

The two shapes represent the differences in the male (blue) and female (red). Basically, the male pelvis is narrower and taller than the female pelvis.

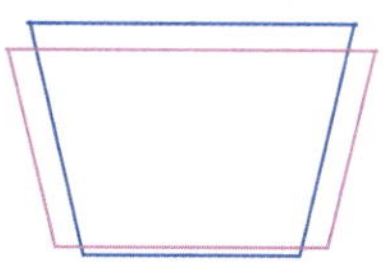

These five views of the pelvis are simply to show the pelvis from different angles, as it is a difficult shape to learn.

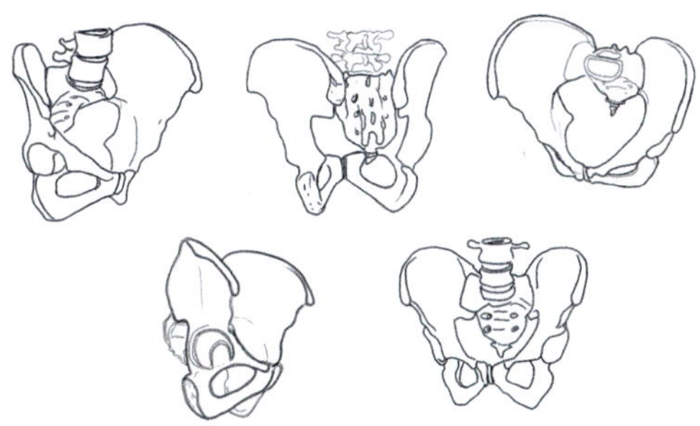

The male pubic arch is narrower than the female pubic arch, which is 90 degrees or wider. The male pelvis has the Anterior Superior Iliac Spine and Posterior Superior Iliac Spine on the same horizontal line. The female's are slanted, as shown here with the red lines.

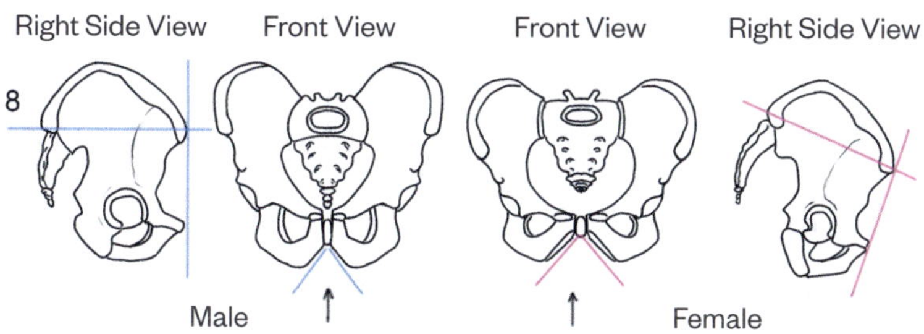

The pelvis is the lower part of the trunk of the human body. It consists of three fused bones on each side: the ilium, the pubis, and the ischium. These are separate at birth and fuse together as we grow. There is a gap at the front of the pubic bone that is made up of cartilage called the pubic symphysis. On women this cartilage softens during pregnancy and allows the pelvis to open a bit during childbirth. In humans the pelvis is bowl-shaped because we are bipedal, allowing for the reproductive organs and abdomen, as well as a developing baby, to be more easily supported. In quadrupeds or primates, such as chimps, the pelvis is more like a hammock.

The main pelvis landmarks for artists to know are the protruding parts of the ilia at the beltline. These are the anterior superior iliac spines (ASIS), and at the back, the posterior superior iliac spines (PSIS), which create the dimples on the back side. Note that generally all four of these landmarks are on the same horizontal belt line. The bottom of the ischium is sometimes referred to as the "sit bone" and it can easily be felt when sitting on a hard chair.

CHECKLIST

- O 1. Ilium
- O 2. Sacrum
- O 3. Pubis
- O 4. Ischium
- O 5. Pubic Symphysis
- O 6. Anterior Superior Iliac Spine (ASIS)
- O 7. Anterior Inferior Iliac Spine (ASIS)
- O 8. Posterior Superior Iliac Spine (PSIS)
- O 9. Coccyx
- O 10. Ischial Tuberosity ("Sit Bone")

S.5. SPINE (VERTEBRAL COLUMN)

The spine, or backbone, consists of approximately thirty-three spine bones, called vertebrae, which are categorized into five regions: seven cervical neck bones, twelve thoracic, five lower back lumbar, five fused sacral, and three to five fused coccygeal tail bones.

The spinal column protects the spinal cord and supports the head and upper body, allowing for an upright posture and weight distribution during movement. Many muscles and ligaments attach to the spine, facilitating stability and movement.

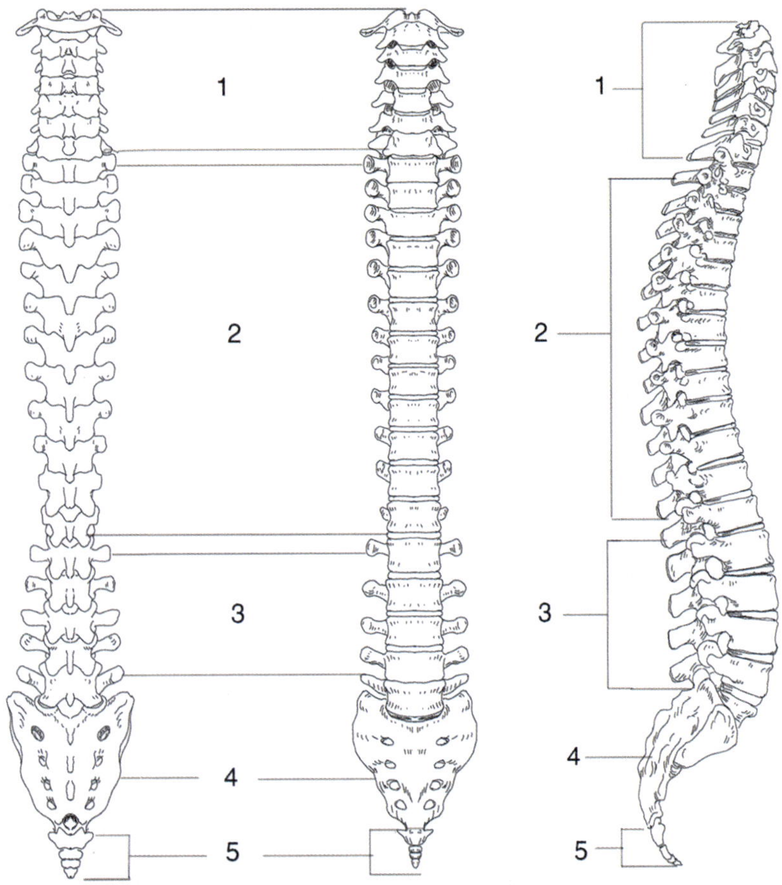

CHECKLIST

- O 1. Cervical Vertebrae (7)
- O 2. Thoracic Vertebrae (12)
- O 3. Lumbar Vertebrae (5)
- O 4. Sacrum (5 fused vertebrae)
- O 5. Coccyx (3–5 fused vertebrae)

THORACIC CAGE (RIB CAGE) S.6.

Anterior (Front) View

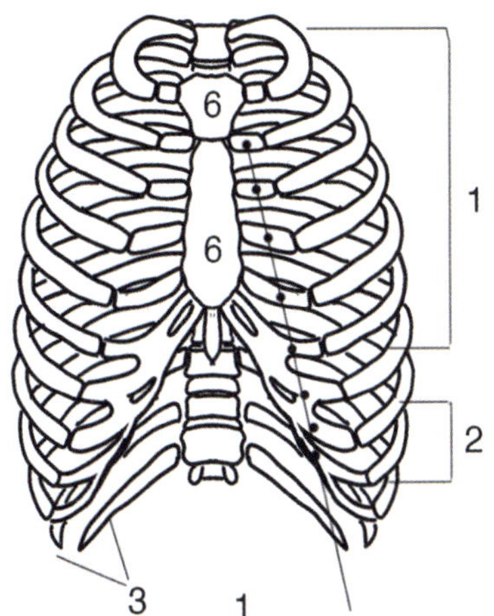

Posterior (Back) View

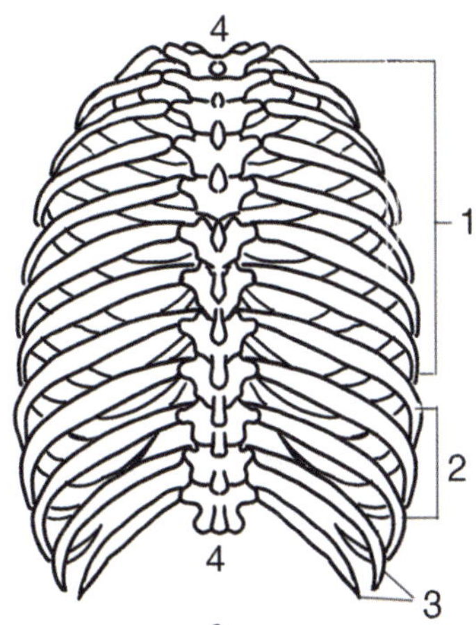

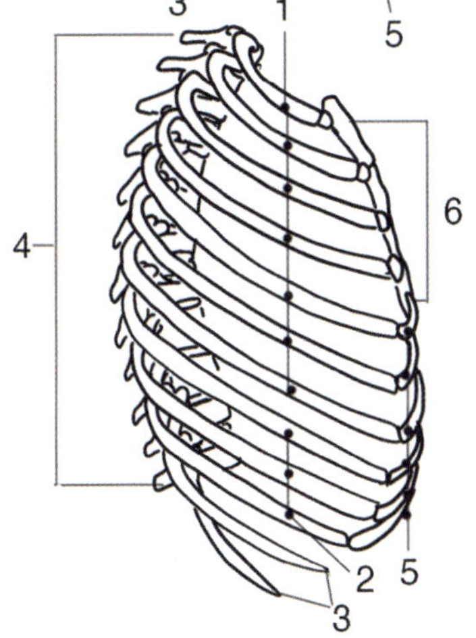

Right Lateral (Side) View

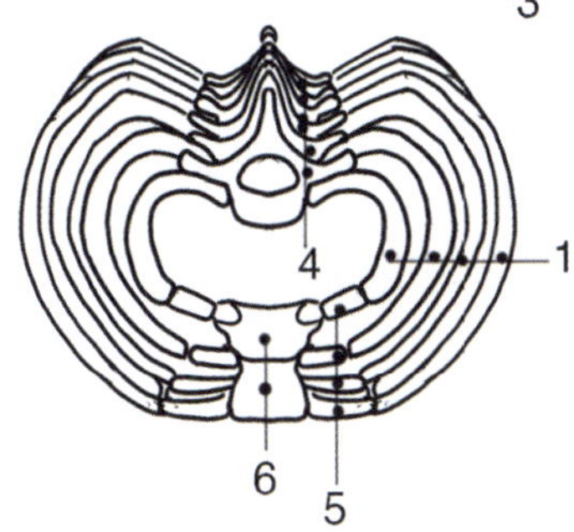

Top View
(front is facing down)

The thoracic cage (rib cage) protects the vital organs: the heart, lungs, and part of the liver and major blood vessels. There are twenty-four ribs total, twelve on each side of the thoracic vertebrae (spine). The thorax, which includes the thoracic cage, thoracic vertebrae, and sternum (breastbone), also provides support for the upper limbs. The ribs attach to the sternum by costal cartilage. There are seven true ribs, which attach to the sternum with their own individual costal cartilage. Ribs 8, 9, and 10 attach by combined cartilage that merge onto the sternum. Ribs 11 and 12 are called the floating ribs since they do not attach to the sternum at all. These primarily protect the kidneys.

CHECKLIST

- O 1. True Ribs (1–7)
- O 2. False Ribs (8, 9, and 10)
- O 3. Floating Ribs (11 and 12)
- O 4. Thoracic Vertebrae
- O 5. Costal Cartilage
- O 6. Sternum

S.7. SCAPULA/HUMERUS

The scapula (shoulder blade), in a way, is the first bone of the arm. This is because the humerus (upper arm bone) articulates with the scapula and the scapula glides around the thoracic cage, so when the arm moves up, down, forward, or backward, the scapula moves relative to the action of the arm. When the scapulae (plural of scapula) move back and closer together on the back, it is called retraction. When the scapulae move forward, it is called protraction. Moving up is called elevation, and moving down is called depression. They also rotate as the arms move outward.

The scapula is a flat, thin, and relatively triangular bone with complicated bony protrusions (tuberosities and processes) where important muscles attach. The scapula has a ridge that slopes at a slight diagonal angle, starting a quarter of the way from the top and ending at the top of the shoulder with a flat bony area called the acromion process. This is where the end of the clavicle (collarbone) attaches. There is a bony hook on the front of the scapula by the shallow socket (glenoid fossa) where the ball of the humerus articulates called the coracoid process. This is an important attachment point for ligaments and muscles.

The humerus is the upper arm bone. It has a head (ball) with two prominent bony bumps, the lesser and greater tubercles. In between these two bumps is the bicipital groove, into which one of the tendons of the biceps brachii fits snuggly, using it like a pulley. About halfway down the side of the humerus is a ridge called the deltoid tuberosity, which is where the deltoid attaches.

The amazing part about the lower part of the humerus is that it flares out and has two types of moveable joints: ball and socket (capitulum) and hinge (spool-shaped trochlea). This is the only area of the body where we have both types of moveable joints; usually there is only one type at a time. For example, we have a ball-and-socket joint where the femur fits into the socket of the pelvis (acetabulum) and where the top of the humerus fits into the shallow socket (glenoid fossa) of the scapula. At the knee, the condyles of the femur fit into the hollows of the tibia, which makes for a hinge-type joint. But the bend of the elbow has both: the ball and socket of the radius articulating with the capitulum of the humerus, and the ulna articulating with the trochlea of the humerus. This allows the radius to rotate over the ulna, a movement that is called pronation.

Back View (Right)

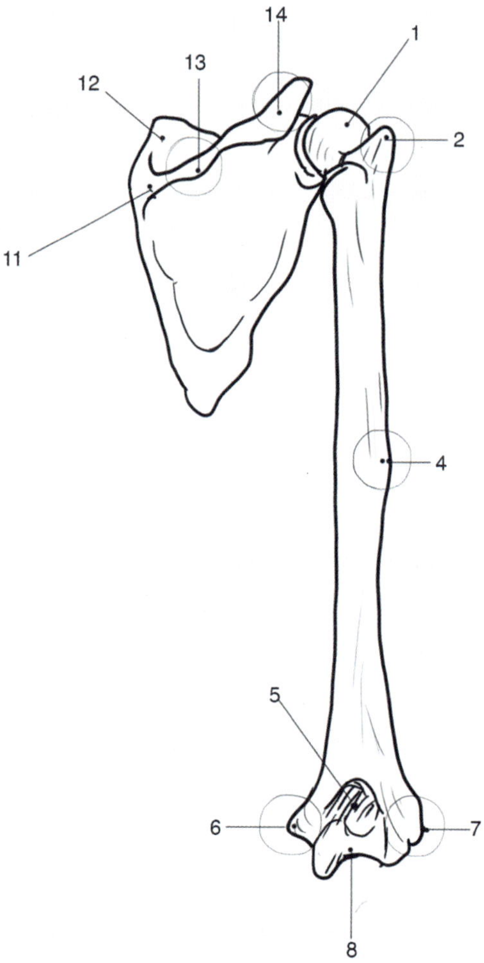

CHECKLIST

- O 1. Ball of Humerus
- O 2. Greater Tubercle
- O 3. Lesser Tubercle
- O 4. Deltoid Tuberosity
- O 5. Olecranon Fossa
- O 6. Medial Epicondyle
- O 7. Lateral Epicondyle
- O 8. Trochlea
- O 9. Capitulum
- O 10. Bicipital Groove

Side View (Right)

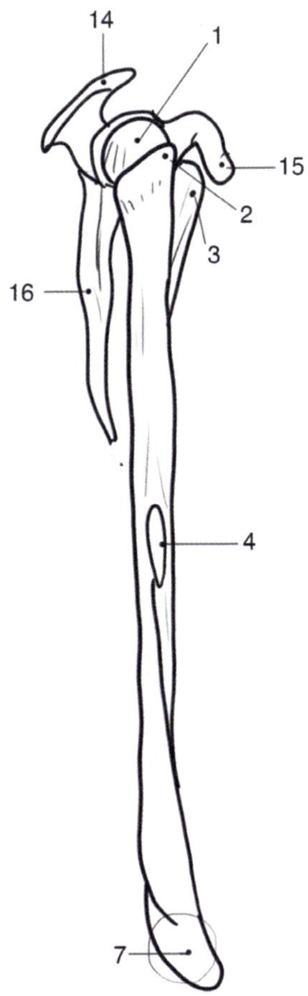

Front View (Right)

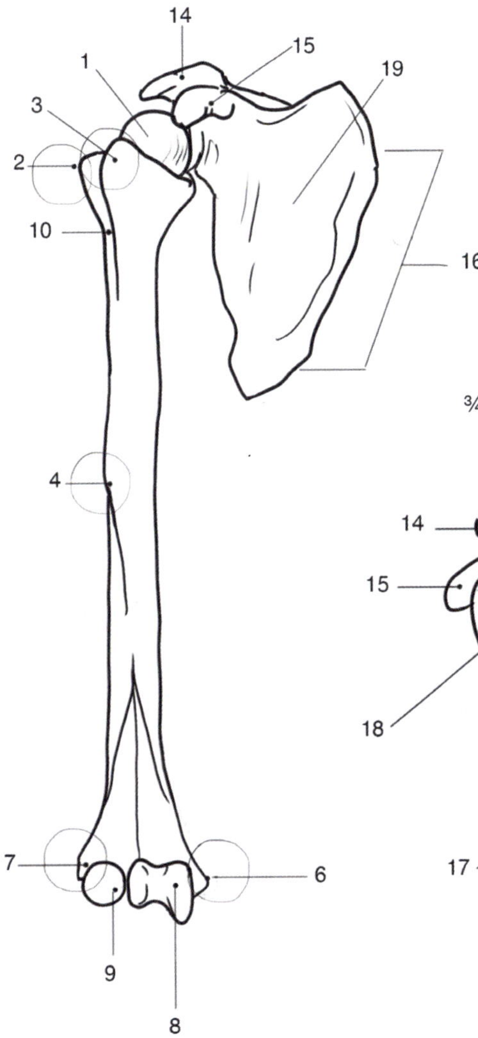

¾ View of Scapula (Left)

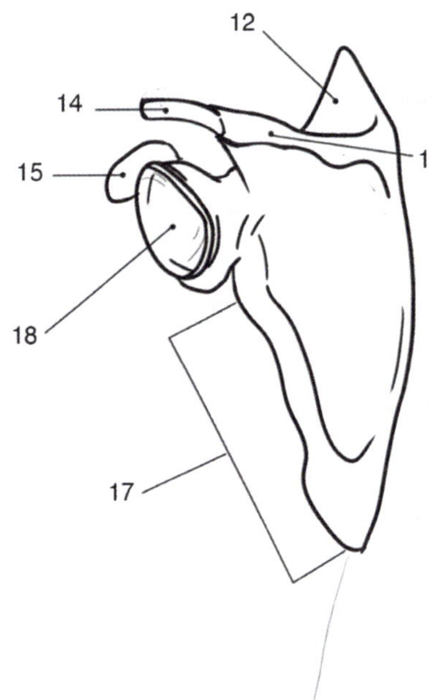

CHECKLIST

- O 11. Spine of Scapula
- O 12. Superior Aspect of Scapula
- O 13. Tubercle of Spine
- O 14. Acromion Process
- O 15. Coracoid Process
- O 16. Medial Border of Scapula
- O 17. Lateral Border of Scapula
- O 18. Glenoid Fossa
- O 19. Subscapular Fossa

S.8. RADIUS/ULNA

The lower limb consists of the femur, tibia, and fibula—one bone, then two bones, and then many (the foot). The upper limb is the same: one bone, the humerus, followed by two, the radius and ulna, and finally, the many bones of the wrist and hands.

The radius starts with a small socket, or fossa, and articulates with a head on the humerus, allowing it to pronate (turn the palm down) and supinate (turn the palm up). It ends with a prominent widening of the bone at the wrist. It is good to note that the radius always follows the thumb.

The proximal end of the ulna has a clawlike design that wraps around the spool (trochlea) of the humerus, creating a hinge joint that is stable and can only bend and straighten. At the back of it is the olecranon, a large bony structure that is commonly known as the elbow. The ulna ends narrowly with a bump of bone called the styloid process. The thing to remember here is that the ulna follows the pinky finger.

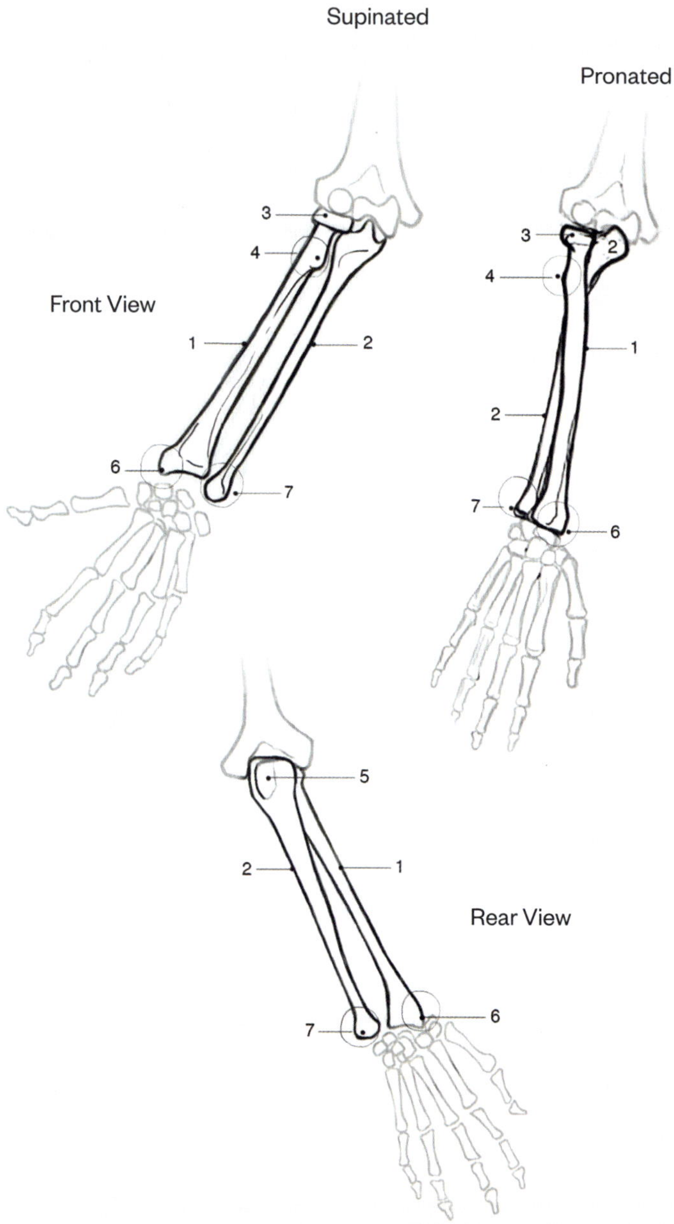

CHECKLIST

- O 1. Radius
- O 2. Ulna
- O 3. Head of Radius
- O 4. Radial Tuberosity
- O 5. Olecranon (Elbow)
- O 6. Styloid Process
- O 7. Head of Ulna

Back of Right Hand

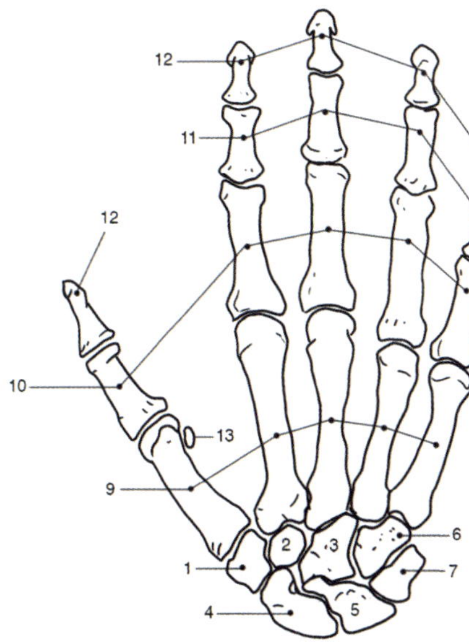

Palm of Right Hand

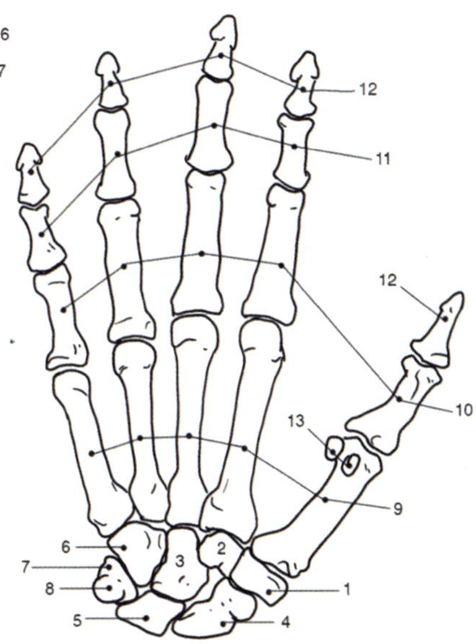

The human hand consists of twenty-seven bones, which includes the eight carpal (wrist) bones. The carpal bones create a combined shape that is semicircular as it articulates with the radius and ulna. These are followed by five bones that make up the body of the hand, the metacarpal bones (*meta* = beyond, *carpal* = wrist). There are fourteen finger bones: five proximal phalanges, five distal phalanges (where the nails are), and four intermediate or medial phalanges (middle bones), one for each finger except the thumb, which has only two segments of bone, proximal and distal.

CHECKLIST

CARPALS

O 1. Trapezium

O 2. Trapezoid

O 3. Capitate

O 4. Scaphoid

O 5. Lunate

O 6. Hamate

O 7. Triquetrum

O 8. Pisiform

HAND

O 9. Metacarpals

O 10. Proximal Phalanges

O 11. Medial Phalanges

O 12. Distal Phalanges

O 13.*Sesamoid Bones

**These little sesamoid bones are small versions of the patella. The patella of the knee is the largest sesamoid bone.*

S.10. SKULL

The skull is made up of twenty-two bones, not including the tiny ear bones. We do not go into each and every segment in this book, as I've reduced it down to larger areas for ease. The skull protects the brain like a helmet, though it is better to say that helmets mimic the skull. The skull bones also make up our faces, creating the individual look that each of us has. Our ancestry is often evident in our skulls.

There are two main portions of the skull, the cranium and the mandible (lower jaw). The mandible is the only part that is separate from the rest of the skull. The cranium is made up of six major segments: frontal (forehead), two temporal (temples), two parietal (upper and side parts of the skull), and occipital (back of the skull). The sphenoid bone sits between the frontal and temporal segments and the zygomatic bone of the cheek.

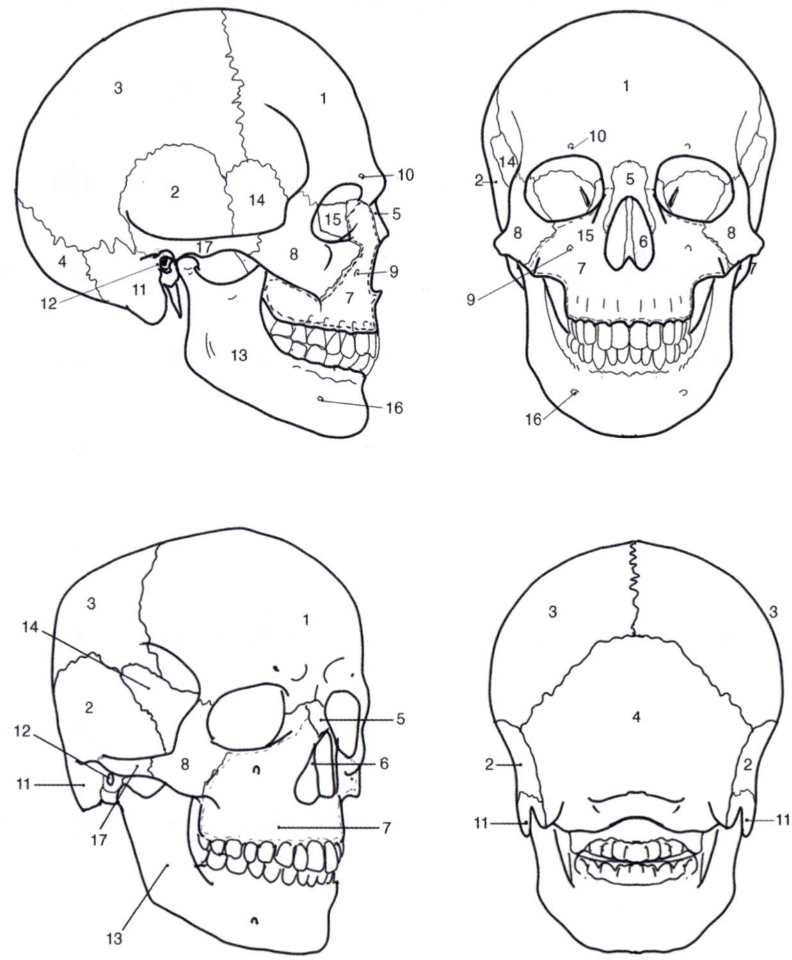

Posterior (Rear)View

CHECKLIST

- O 1. Frontal
- O 2. Temporal
- O 3. Parietal
- O 4. Occipital
- O 5. Nasal
- O 6. Vomer
- O 7. *Maxilla
- O 8. Zygomatic Bone
- O 9. Infraorbital Foramen
- O 10. Supraorbital Foramen
- O 11. Mastoid Process
- O 12. Acoustic Meatus
- O 13. Mandible
- O 14. Sphenoid Bone
- O 15. Lacrimal Bone
- O 16. Mental Foramen
- O 17. Zygomatic Arch

**Maxilla in dotted line*

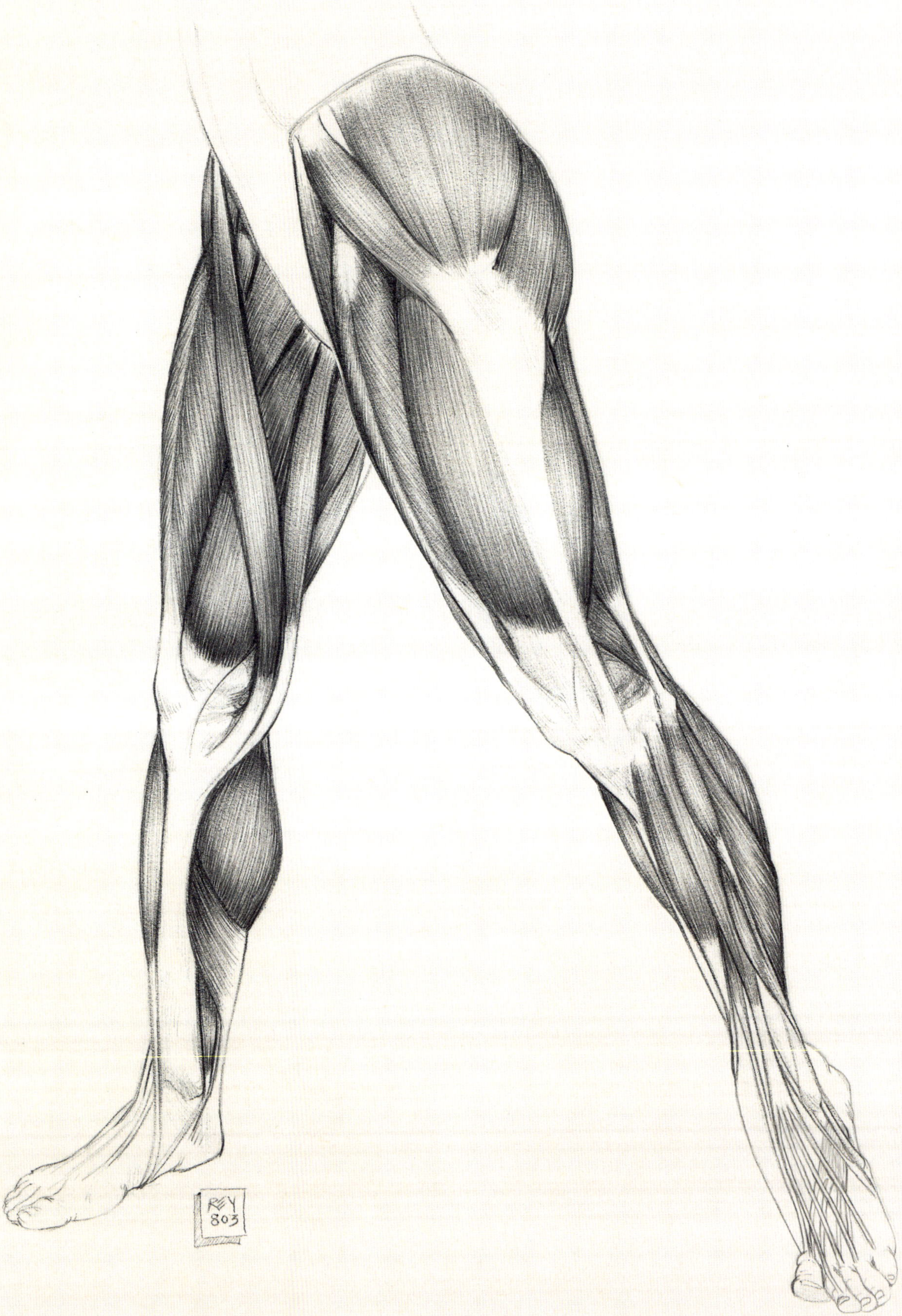
REY
803

CHAPTER A

THE LEG AND FOOT

Strictly speaking, in anatomy the leg refers to the area between the knee and the ankle. The area above it is the thigh and gluteals, and the area below it is the foot. The entire area—the glutes, thigh, leg, and foot—is referred to as the lower limb. For example, think of the terms we use for chicken parts: A chicken leg is different than a chicken thigh. The same is true in regard to human anatomy.

In this book, as in my classroom, I edit down the muscles as most artistic anatomists do to include only the muscles that make the most impact on the surface of the body.

Some muscles are included for their interesting job, such as the abductor digiti minimi, which abducts, or pulls outward, the little toe. The muscles on the leg generally activate the knee, ankle, or toes. In some cases, muscles activate more than one joint, such as the gastrocnemius (calf muscles) that attach to the lower back of the femur (thigh bone), cross over the knee joint, and insert into the calcaneus (heel), thus crossing over the ankle joint, allowing this muscle to bend the knee as well as lift the heel off the ground.

Even though I have included a few more muscles, the basic rule in my classroom is to remember the big six. These are the six essential muscles of the leg, which I organize neatly into three pairs for even more ease:

- **A.1.** Peroneus brevis and its partner, **A.2.** peroneus longus. Both of these run along the outside of the leg and both lay on the fibula, the smaller, thinner both of the leg.
- **A.3.** and **A.4.**, the extensor digitorum longus and the tibialis anterior, respectively.
- **A.5.** Soleus and **A.6.**, both heads of the gastrocnemius.

There is only one muscle on the foot itself that I give visual importance to: the extensor digitorum brevis, **A.9.**, which is a little bubble of muscle on the side of the foot by the outside ankle. The foot has many muscles, but I focus primarily on this one, and in this book, I included a few more. What is of major importance are the tendons of the foot, which are mainly the tendons of the six muscles that are highlighted here.

I will also remind the reader that artistic anatomists, myself included, tend to "pretty up" the anatomy that we know. I draw each muscle the same way I would draw a lock of hair. Muscle tissue, in reality, is not pretty to the average person. It is also dead. Artists like Leonardo da Vinci, Michelangelo, and others who studied cadavers were drawing what we look like without skin and its subcutaneous fat. The muscles are rather flat, as if deflated and loose, often hanging down onto the lab table. My students often have trouble discerning one muscle from another. Artists changed all of that for the world. I will use Leonardo as one example—his drawings of cadavers are sublime. They are almost alive, which is, in itself, a wonderful thing.

I bring to you a very reduced version of anatomy. I chose to do this to not overwhelm the reader with too much material that I deem not crucial for creating art. I've edited human anatomy down to the most important aspects of the human form that every artist needs to know.

A.1. PERONEUS BREVIS

STRUCTURE

The peroneus brevis from the side is a flat fish-shaped muscle. The tendon uses the lateral malleolus—the outside ankle bone (bottom of fibula)—like a pulley. The tendon, along with the tendon of the peroneus longus, is seen clearly by the outside ankle when the heel is off the ground.

ORIGIN

At around halfway down the fibula toward the outside ankle (the lateral malleolus).

INSERTION

The tuberosity of the fifth metatarsal, the bump on the side of the foot.

ACTION

Plantarflexes (lifts the heel off the ground or points the foot; 1 and 2) and everts (pulls the foot outward; 3) the foot.

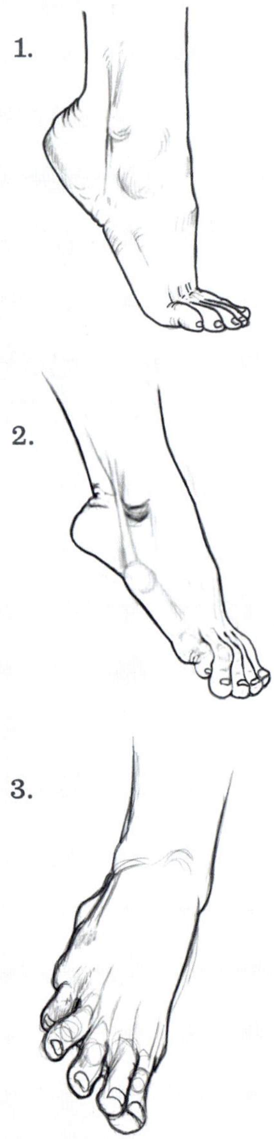

1. and 2. Plantarflexion; 3. Eversion

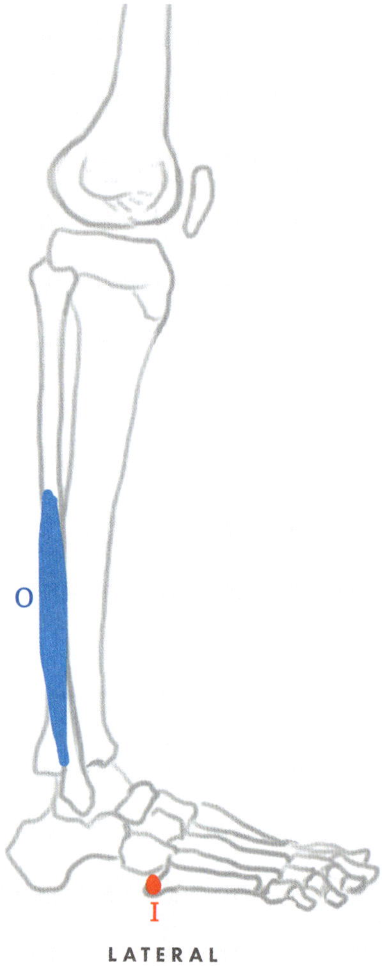

CHECKLIST

○ Peroneus brevis

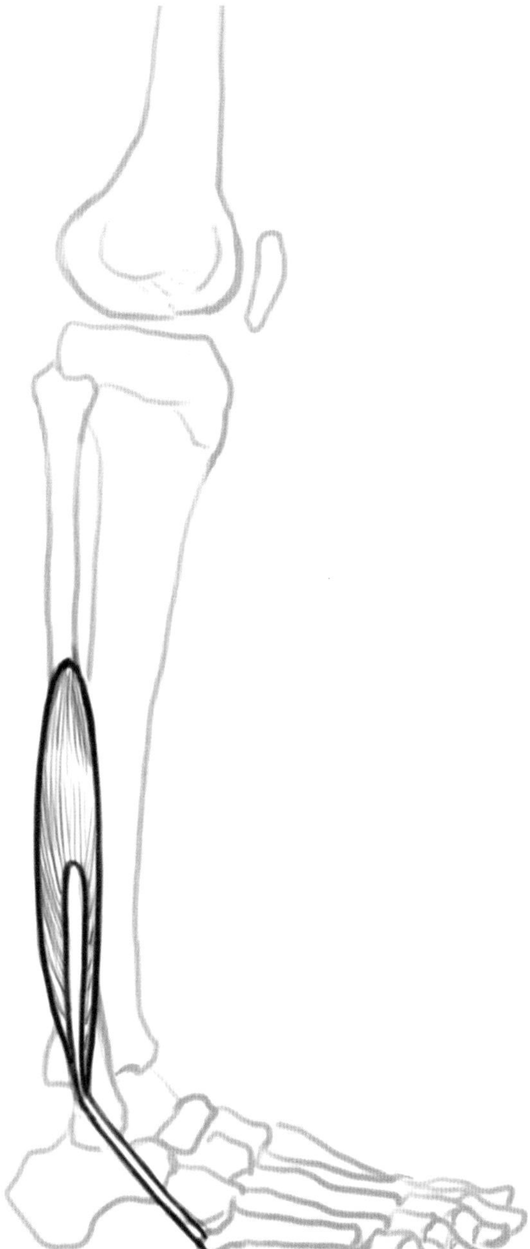

LATERAL

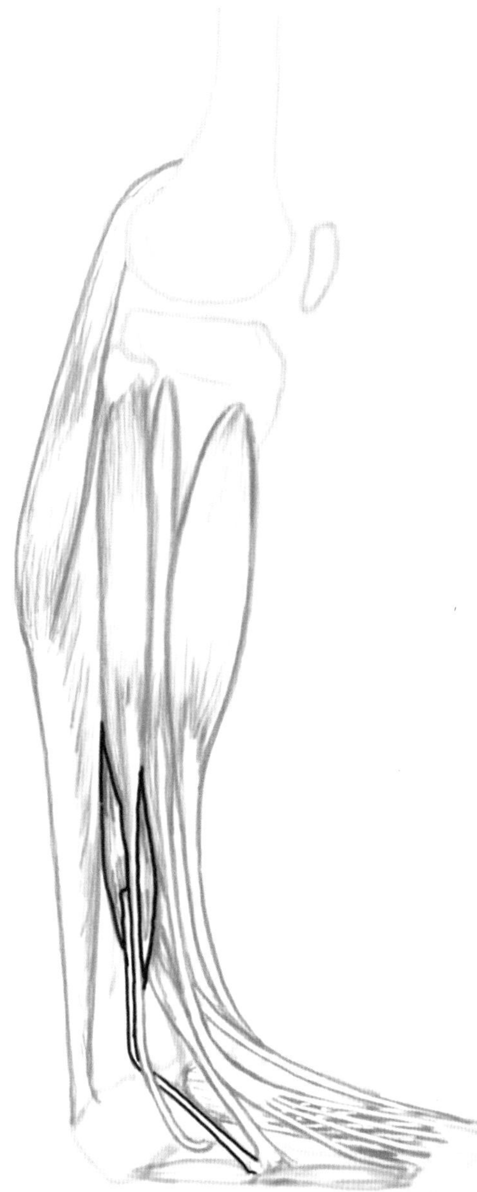

LATERAL

A.2. PERONEUS LONGUS

STRUCTURE

The peroneus longus is an elongated, flat muscle. It lays piggyback over the peroneus brevis. The tendon, along with the tendon of the peroneus brevis, is clearly visible at the ankle, especially when the heel is off the ground.

ORIGIN

Head of the fibula, upper part of the fibula about one-third of the way down the bone.

INSERTION

Under the foot toward the big toe at the medial cuneiform (tarsal), also at the first metatarsal.

ACTION

Plantarflexes (lifts the heel off the ground or points the foot; 1 and 2) and everts (pulls the foot outward; 3) the foot.

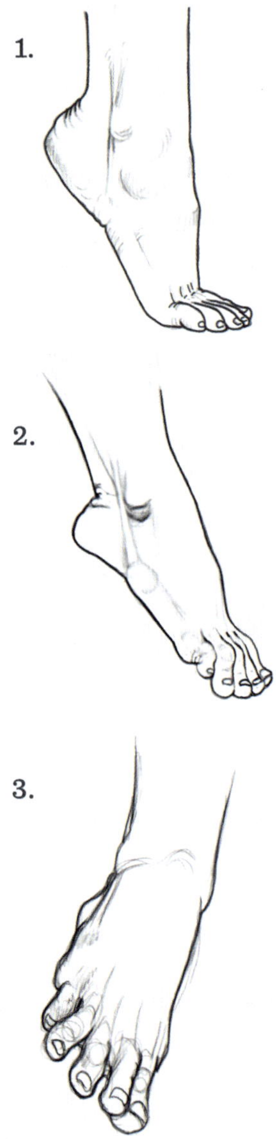

1. and 2. Plantarflexion; 3. Eversion

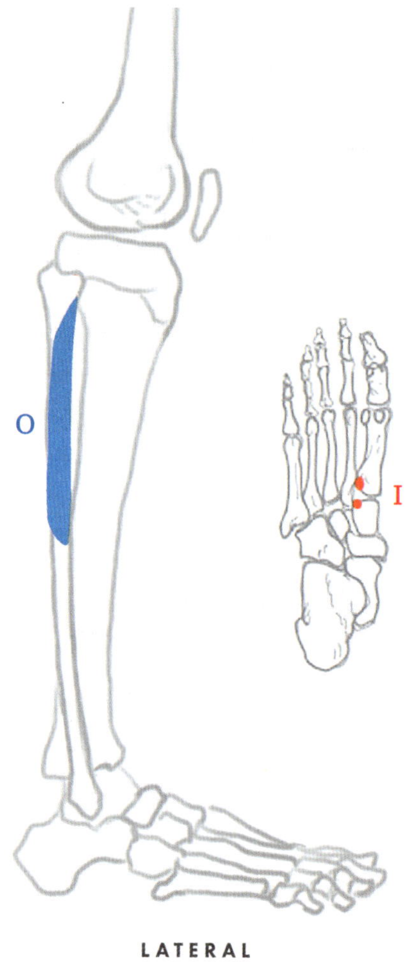

CHECKLIST

- O Peroneus brevis
- O Peroneus longus

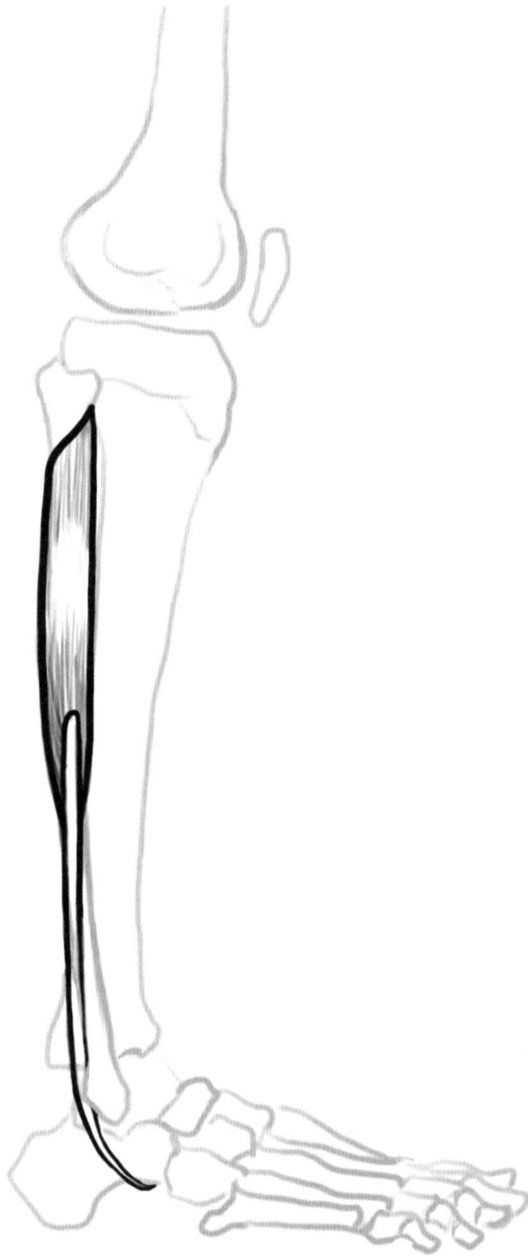

LATERAL

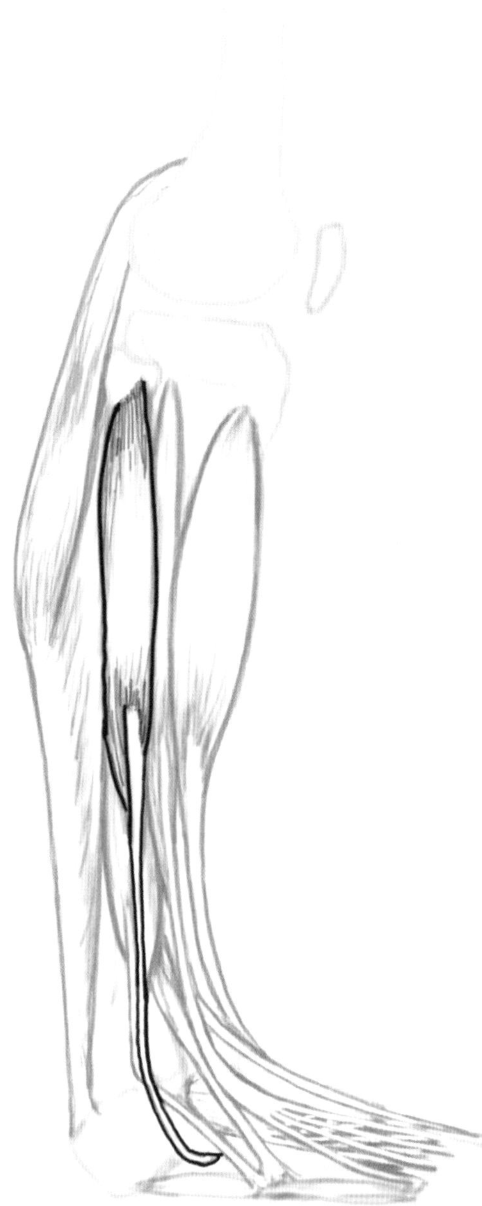

LATERAL

A.3. PERONEUS TERTIUS

STRUCTURE

The peroneus tertius is a small, somewhat elongated triangular muscle that aids in eversion, pulling the foot outward, and in dorsiflexion, pulling the foot upward toward the head. You will only see the tendon on the side of the foot; the muscle is well tucked in within the group.

ORIGIN

Low down on the anterior aspect of the fibula.

INSERTION

By the tuberosity of the fifth metatarsal.

ACTION

Dorsiflexes (pulls the foot upward; 1) and everts (pulls the foot outward; 2) the foot.

1.

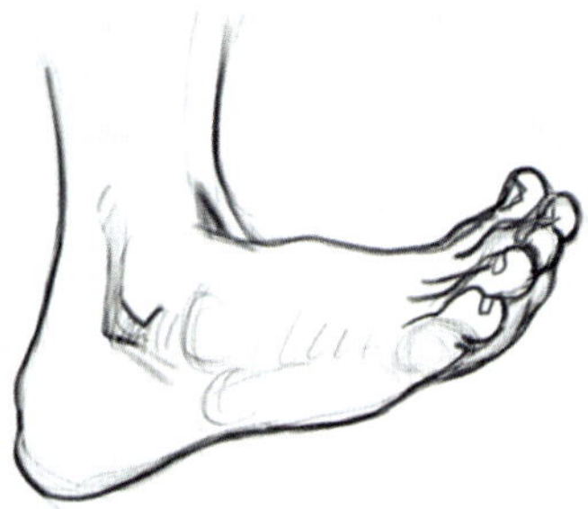

2.

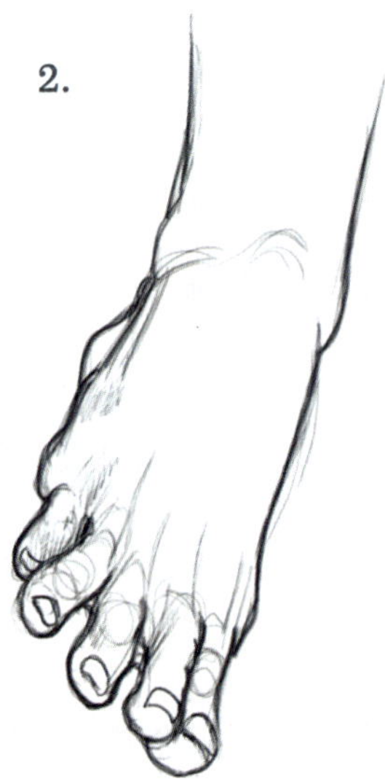

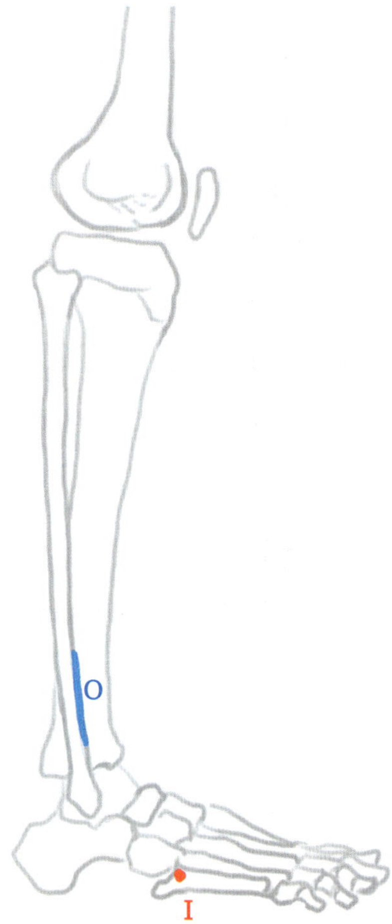

LATERAL

1. Dorsiflexion; 2. Eversion

CHECKLIST

- O Peroneus brevis
- O Peroneus longus
- O Peroneus tertius

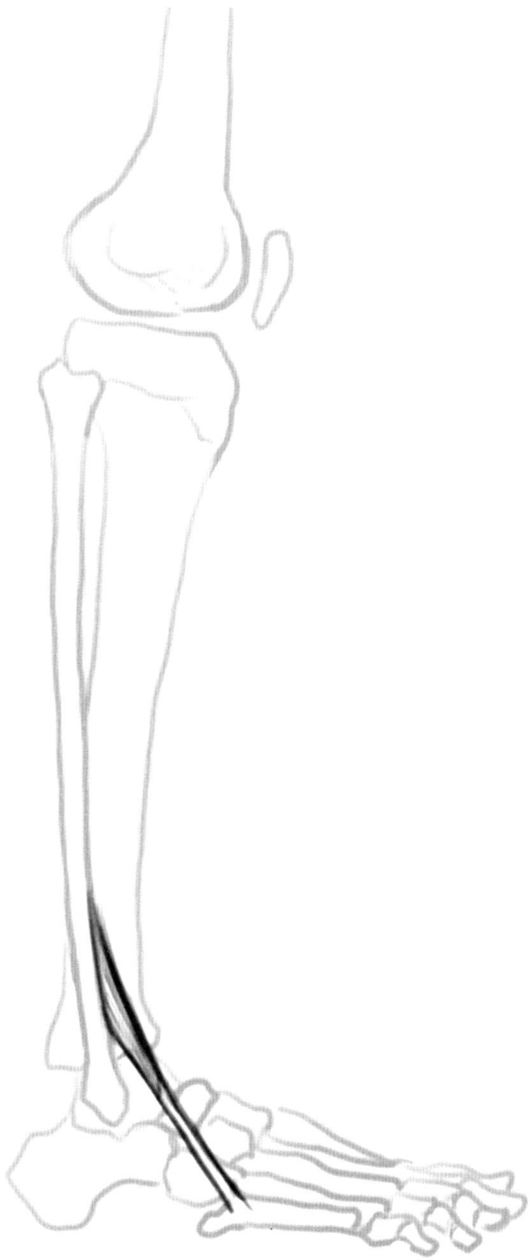

LATERAL

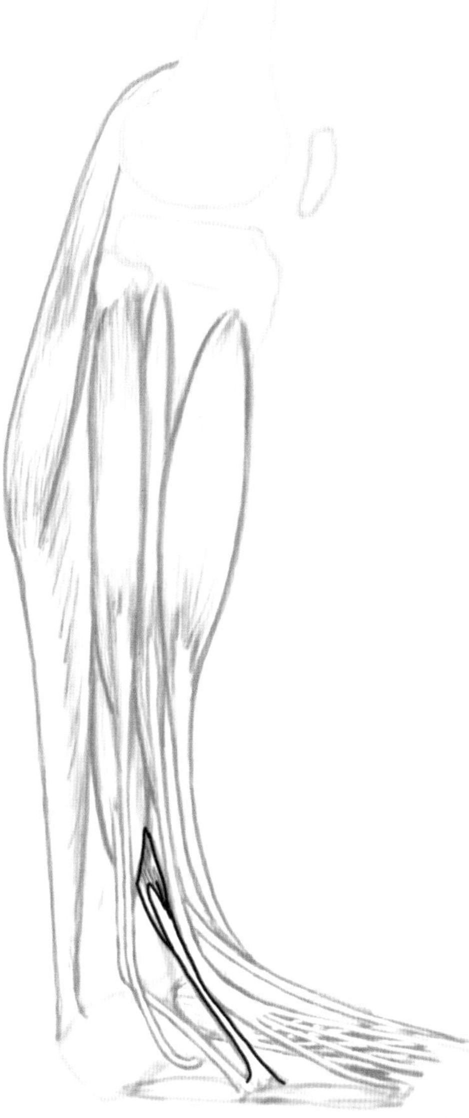

LATERAL

A4. EXTENSOR DIGITORUM LONGUS

STRUCTURE

The extensor digitorum longus is a long, thin muscle. It is actually four combined muscle bellies with four tendons that attach to four toes—all except the big toe. It is often seen as a blended muscle along with the tibialis anterior.

ORIGIN

A small portion touching the lateral condyle of the tibia, then a long portion down the fibula.

INSERTION

The middle and ends of four toes; not the big toe.

ACTION

Extends the toes (1) and pulls up on all toes except the big one (2).

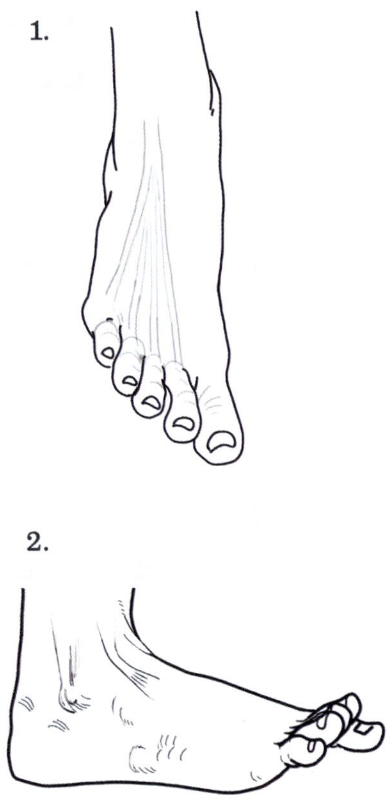

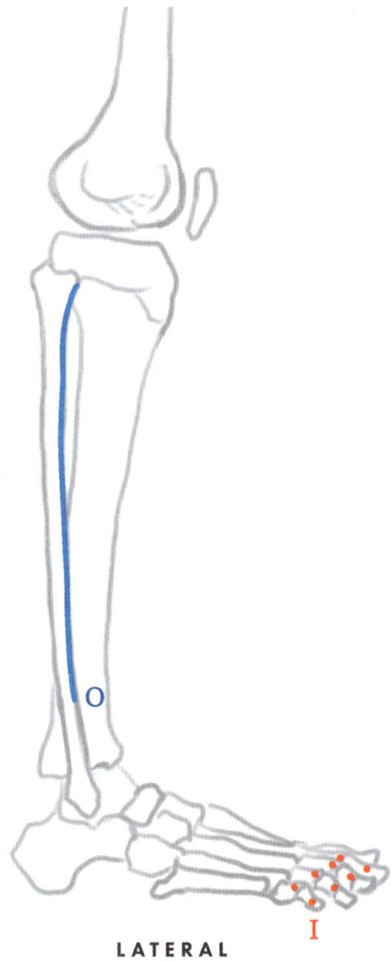

1. Toes extended; 2. Four toes pointing upward

CHECKLIST

- O Peroneus brevis
- O Peroneus longus
- O Peroneus tertius
- O Extensor digitorum longus

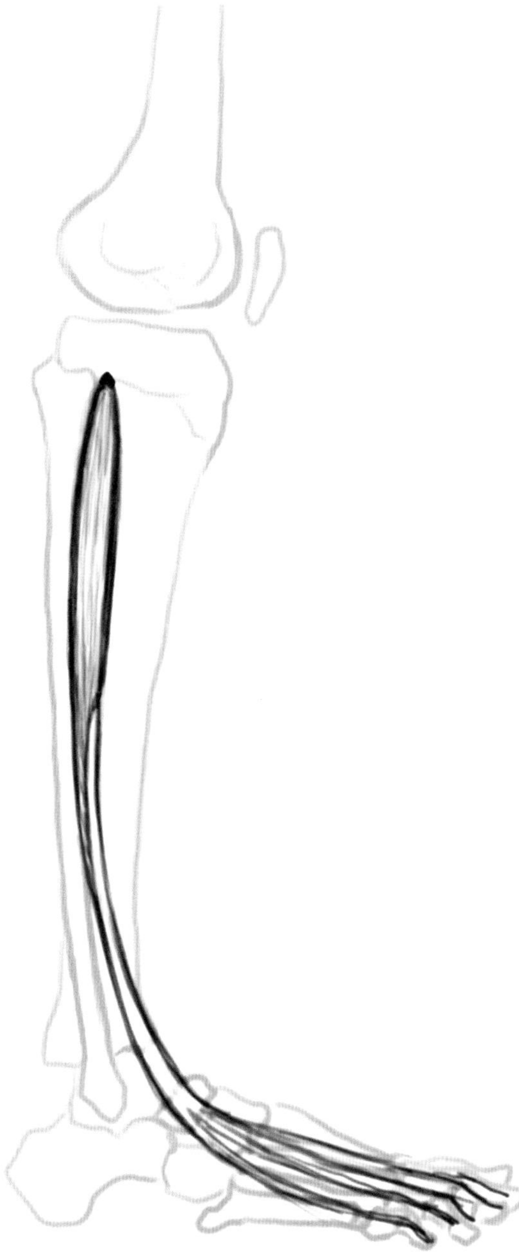

LATERAL

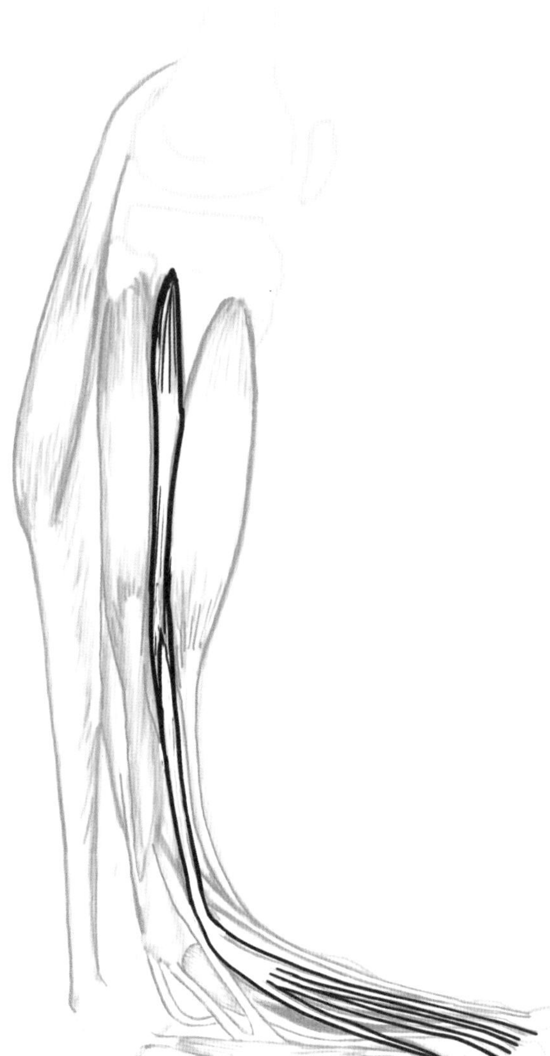

LATERAL

A.5. TIBIALIS ANTERIOR

STRUCTURE

The tibialis anterior muscle is a rather large muscle that tapers at the bottom, becoming a strong, thick tendon very visible at the top of the foot. It then disappears into the arch of the foot. It is an important muscle in that it creates the contour of the leg when seen from the side.

ORIGIN

Lateral condyle of the tibia, lateral surface of the upper half of the shaft of the tibia.

INSERTION

The tendon of the tibialis anterior goes down the arch and underneath the foot and is attached to the medial cuneiform bone and into the base of the metatarsal bone toward the big toe.

ACTION

Dorsiflexes (pulls the foot upward; 1) and inverts (pulls the foot inward; 2) the foot. In walking, the tibialis anterior keeps your toes from hitting the ground, lifting your foot and toes up toward the face.

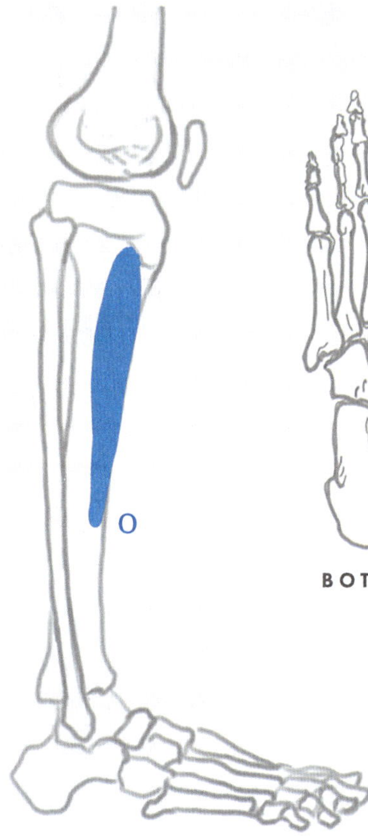

LATERAL

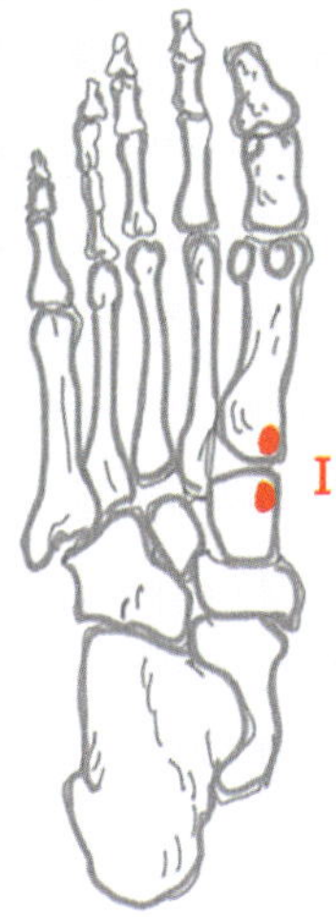

BOTTOM

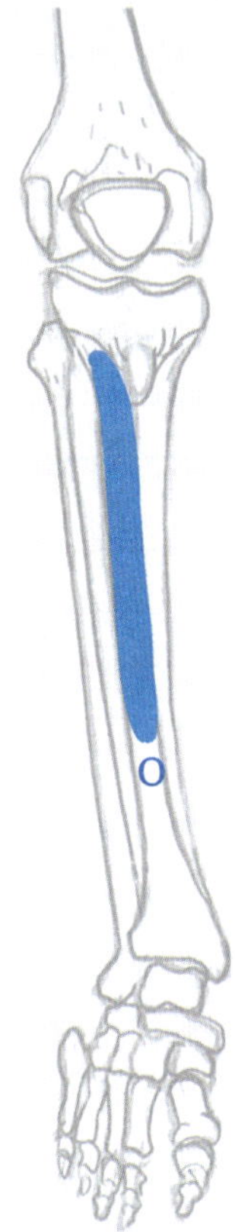

ANTERIOR

1.

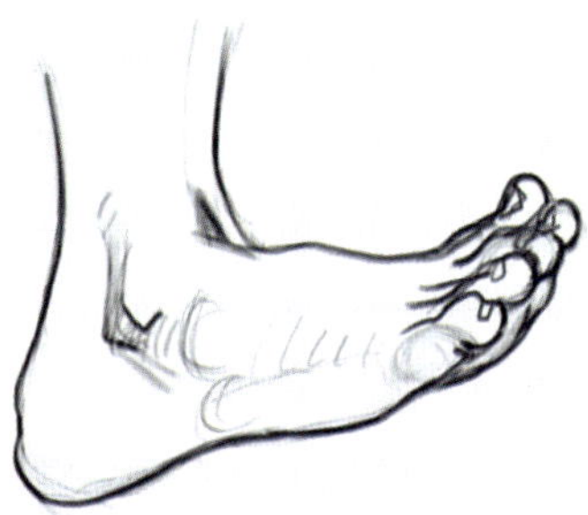

2.

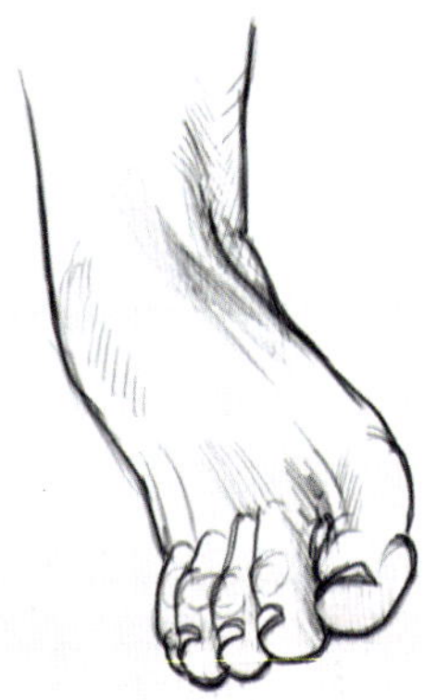

1. Dorsiflexion; 2. Inversion

CHECKLIST

- O Peroneus brevis
- O Peroneus longus
- O Peroneus tertius
- O Extensor digitorum longus
- O Tibialis anterior

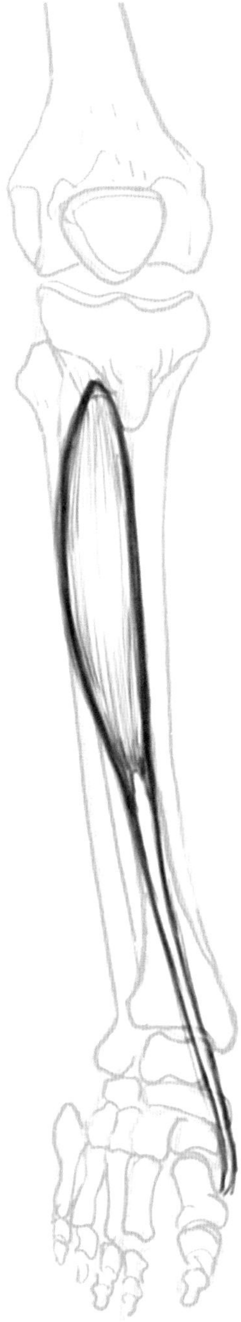

ANTERIOR

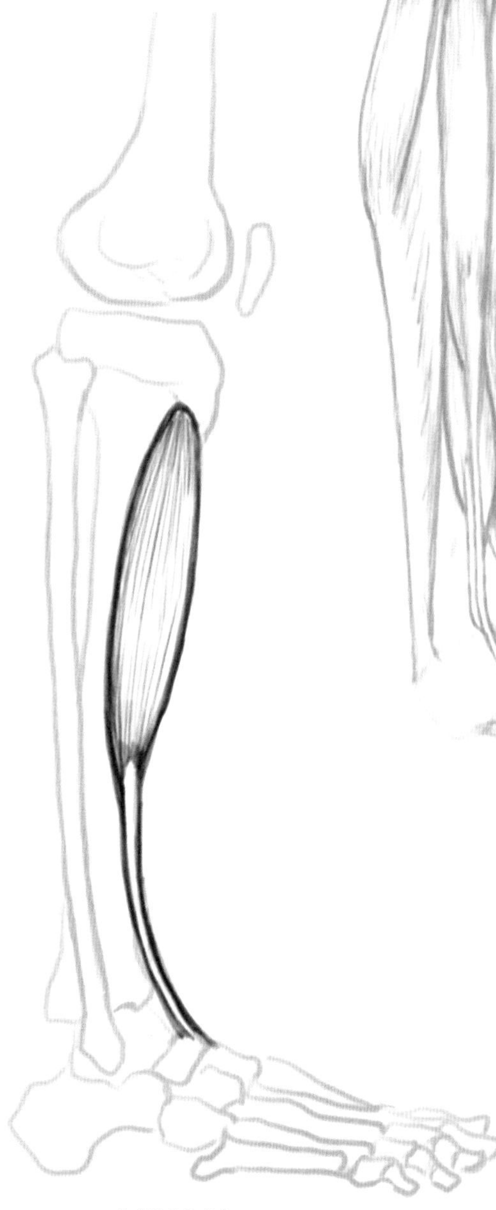

LATERAL

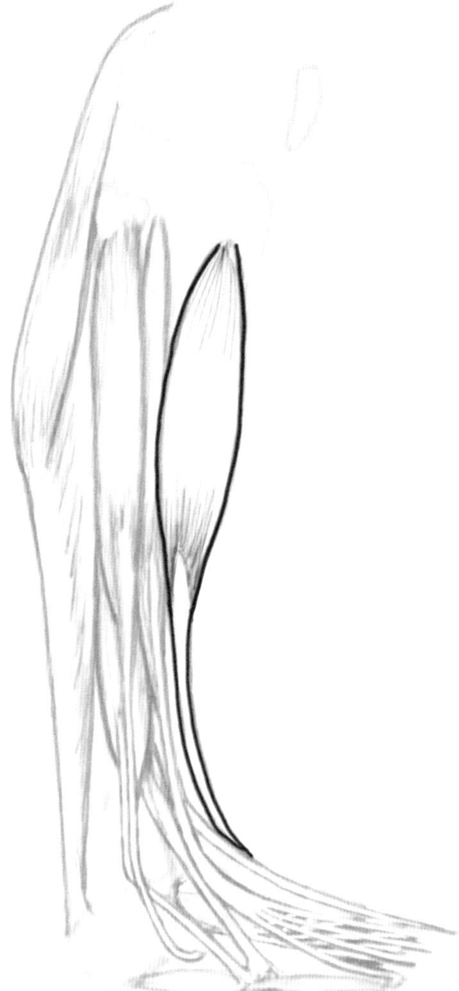

LATERAL

A.6. FLEXOR DIGITORUM LONGUS

STRUCTURE

The flexor digitorum longus muscle is deep inside the muscle group underneath the soleus and gastrocnemius on the posterior (backside) of the tibia. The bottom part can sometimes be seen. What you will see on some individuals is the tendon that uses the medial malleolus, or ankle bone of the tibia, as a pulley and it will go underneath the arch of the foot, attaching underneath the foot.

ORIGIN

The back of the shaft of the tibia at about a quarter of the way down from the knee joint to about the three-quarter mark of the length of the tibia.

INSERTION

Underneath the ends of each toe except the big toe.

ACTION

Curls the toes (1) and helps raise the heel (2).

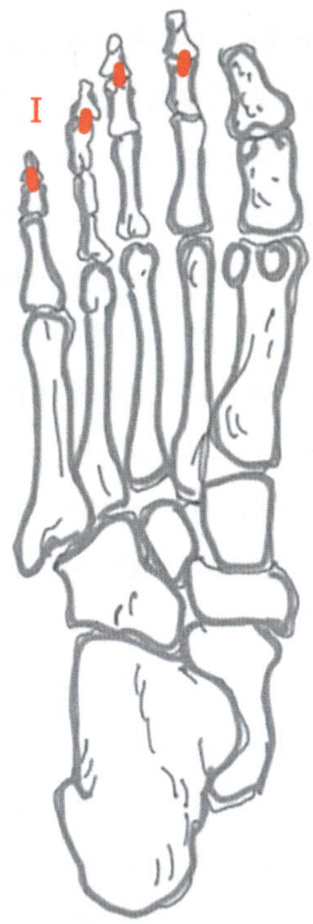

BOTTOM

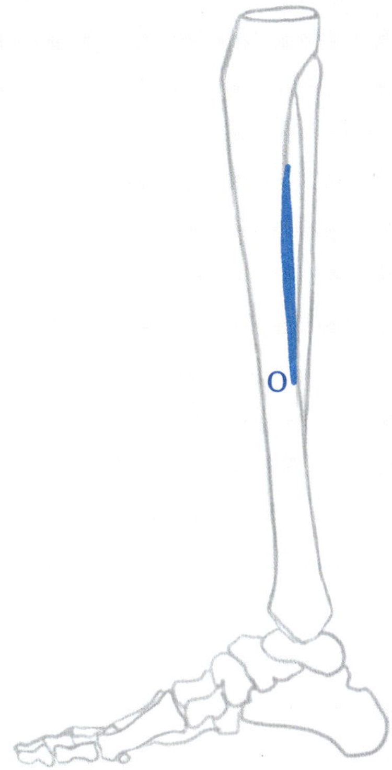

MEDIAL

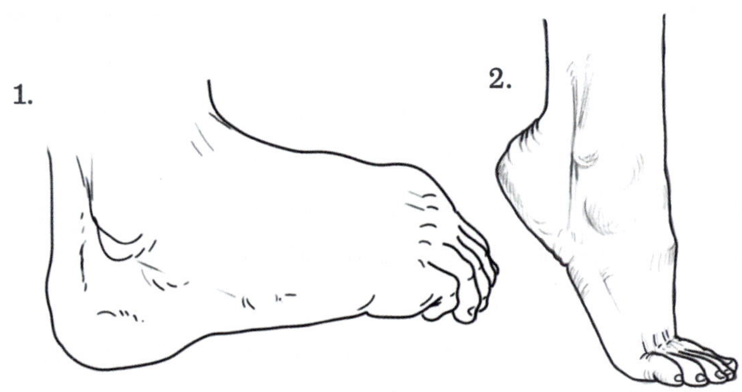

1. Curled toes; 2. Raised heel

CHECKLIST

- O Peroneus brevis
- O Peroneus longus
- O Peroneus tertius
- O Extensor digitorum longus
- O Tibialis anterior
- O Flexor digitorum longus

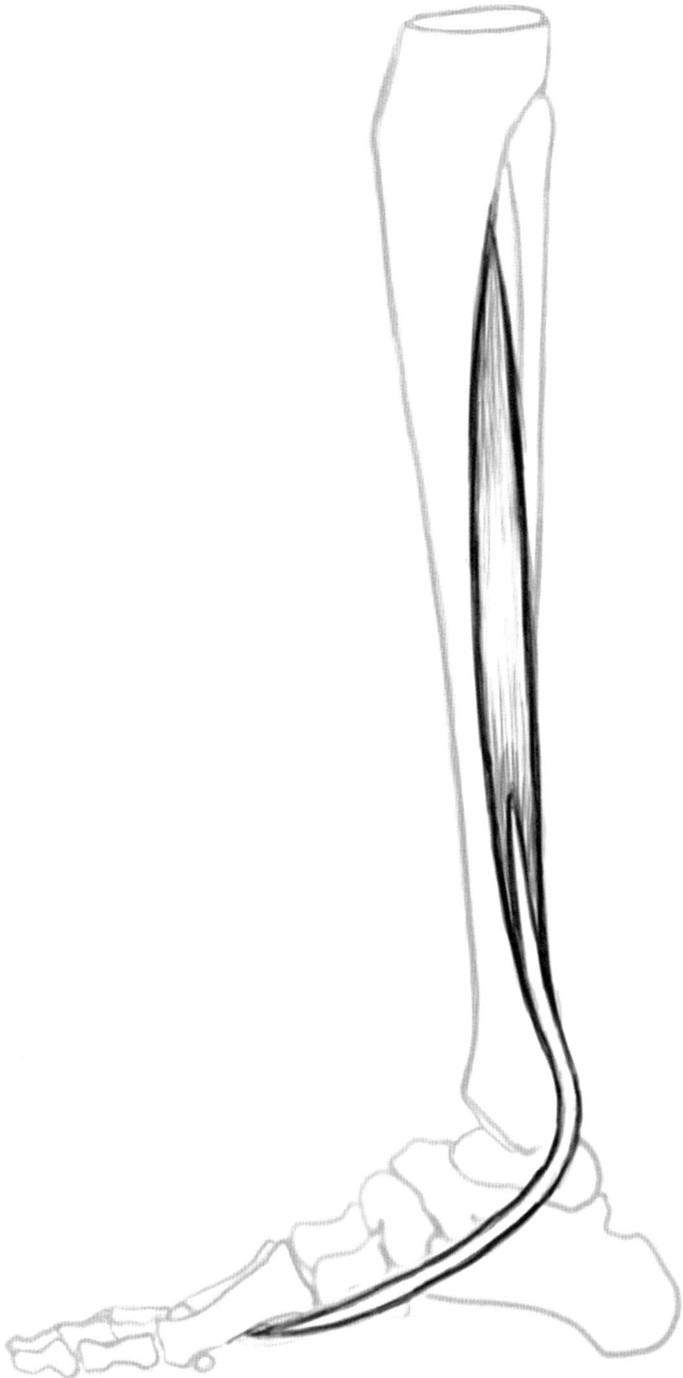

MEDIAL

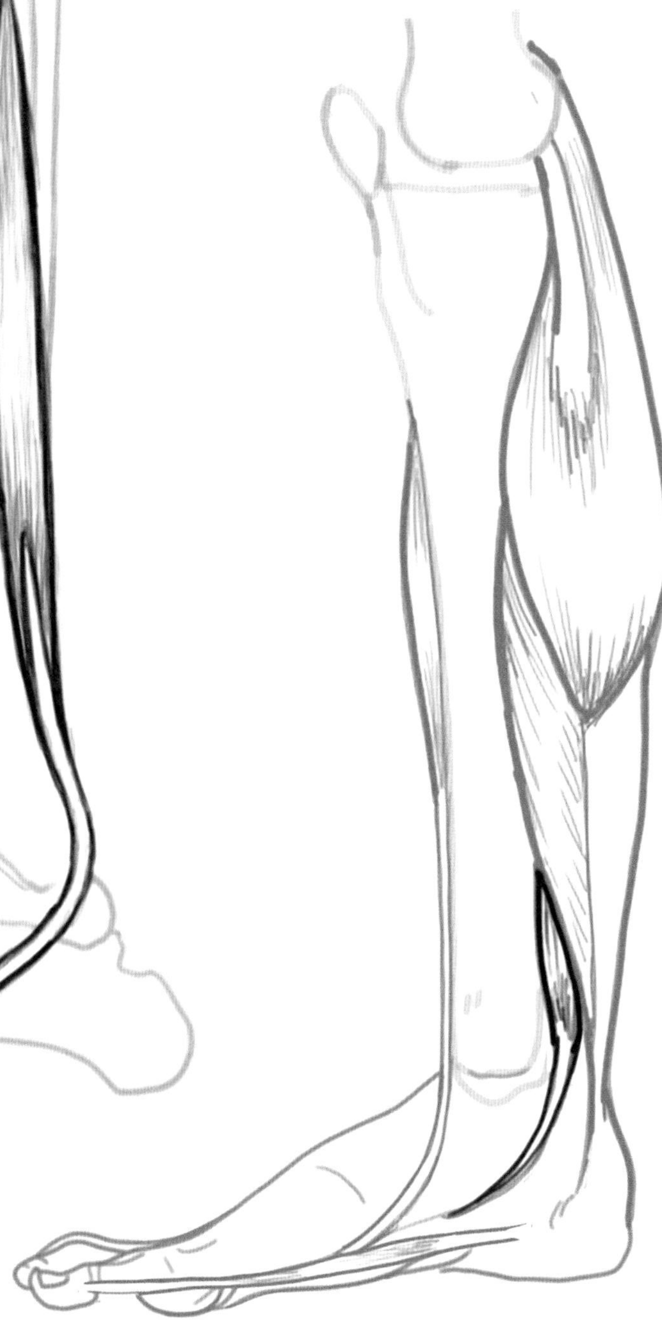

MEDIAL

A.7. SOLEUS

STRUCTURE

The soleus is a very large muscle, almost like a bed of muscle underneath the gastrocnemius heads. From the inside and outside view, it almost looks like a wedge.

ORIGIN

On the posterior, or rear view, the soleus attaches to the head of the fibula, a quarter of the way down the shaft of the fibula and on the upper part of the tibia posteriorly.

INSERTION

On the calcaneus. Shares a common tendon, the Achilles tendon, with the gastrocnemius heads.

ACTION

Points and plantarflexes the foot (1), lifts the heel off the ground (2).

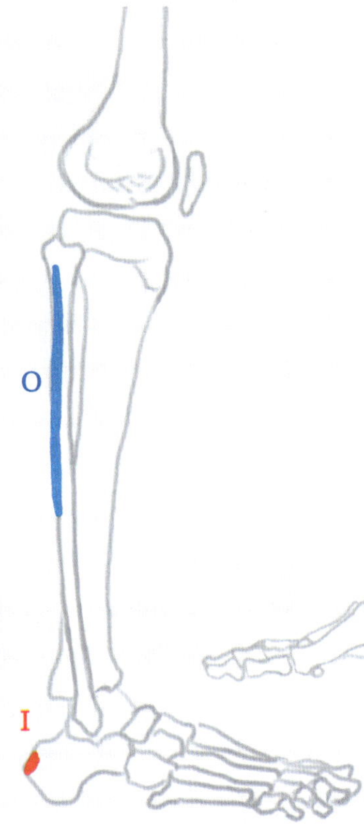

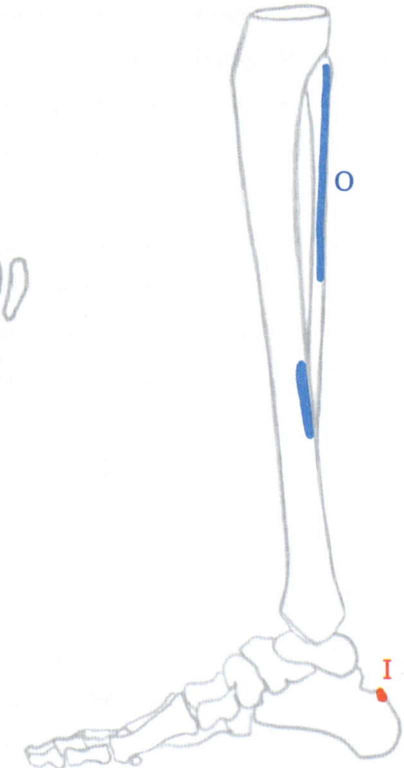

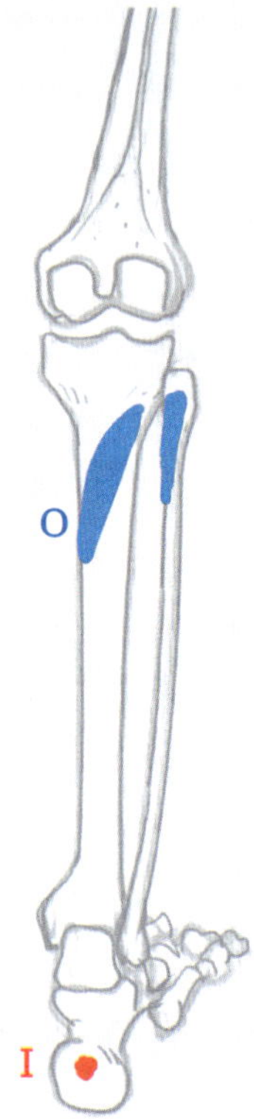

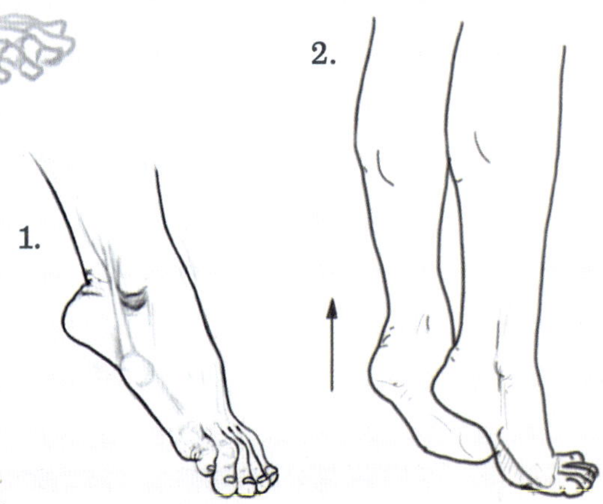

1. Plantarflexion; 2. Heel lifted

CHECKLIST

- O Peroneus brevis
- O Peroneus longus
- O Peroneus tertius
- O Extensor digitorum longus
- O Tibialis anterior
- O Flexor digitorum longus
- O Soleus

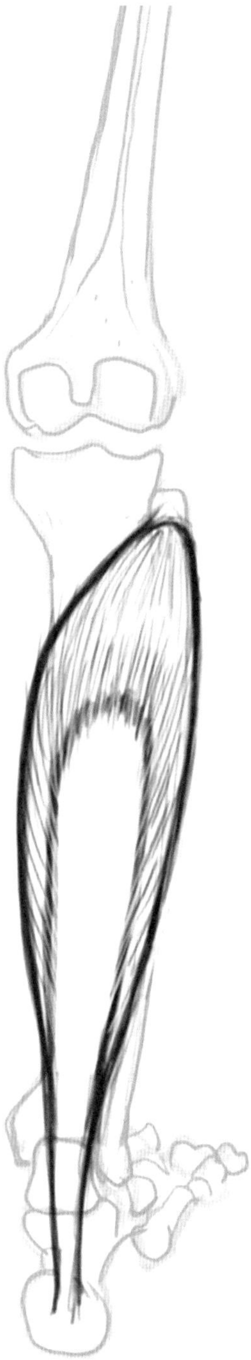

POSTERIOR

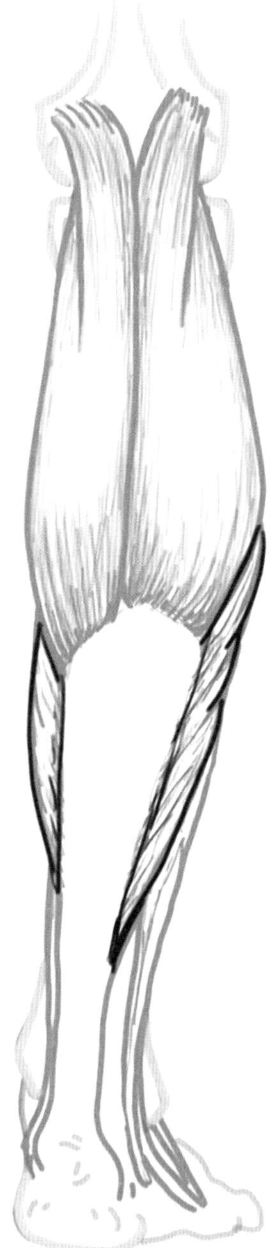

POSTERIOR

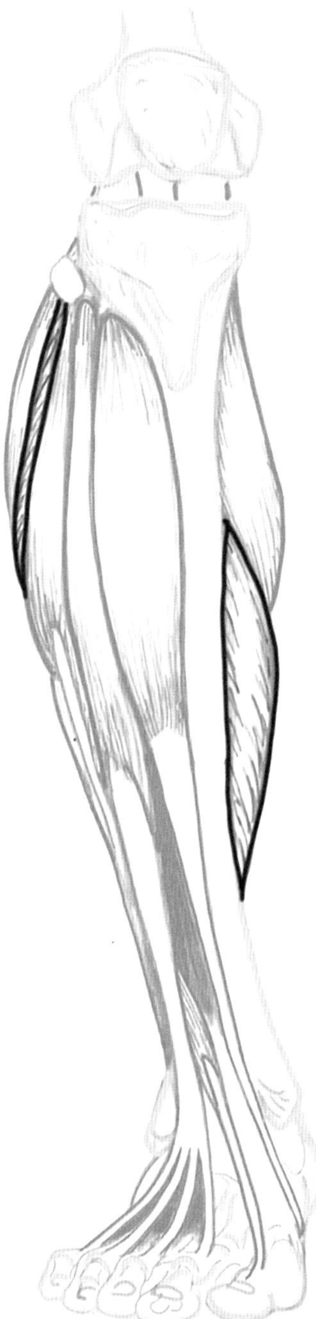

ANTERIOR

A.7. SOLEUS

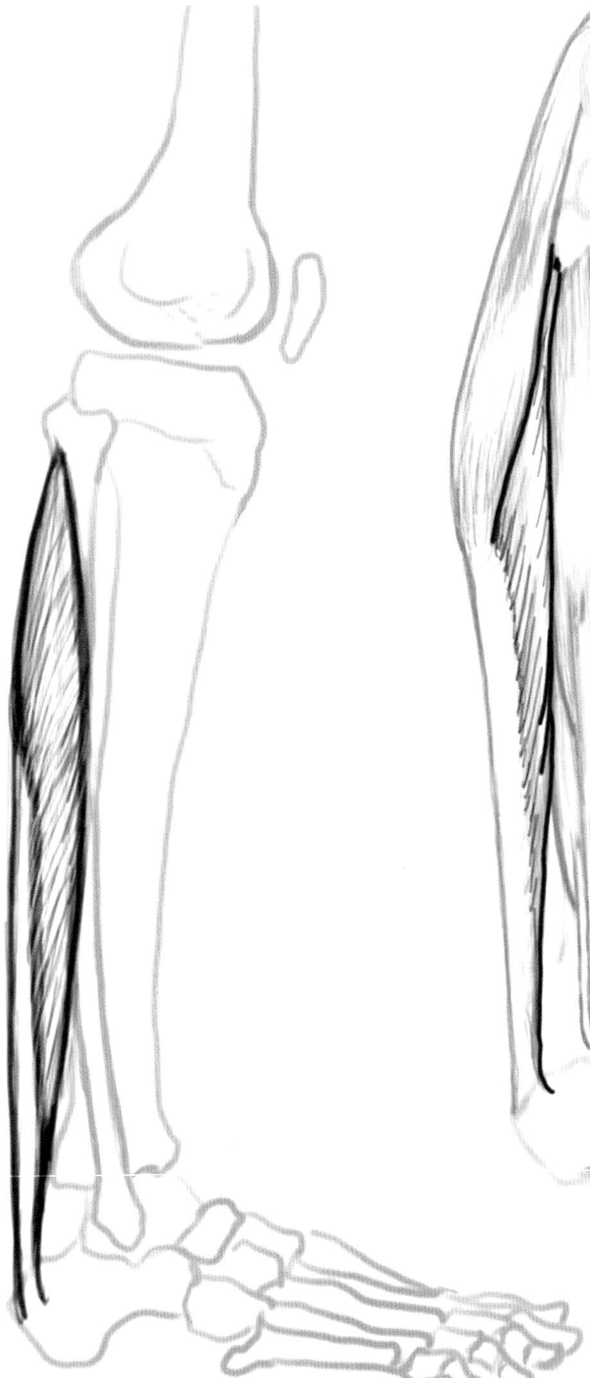

LATERAL

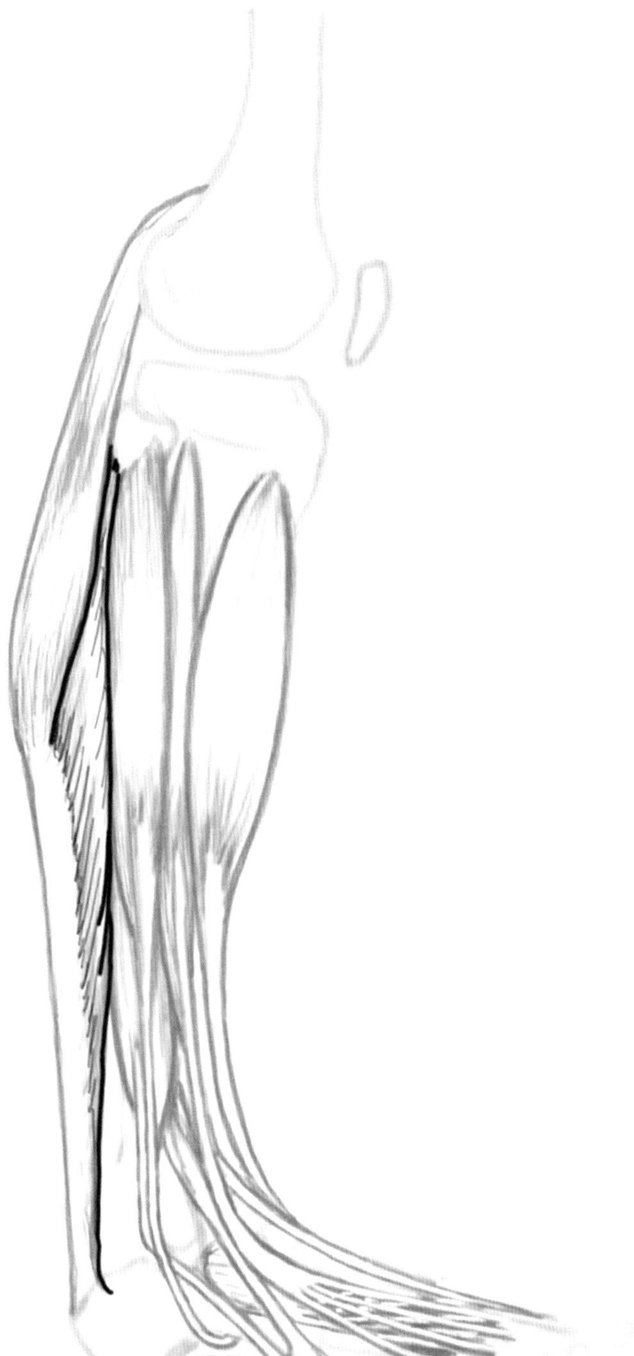

LATERAL

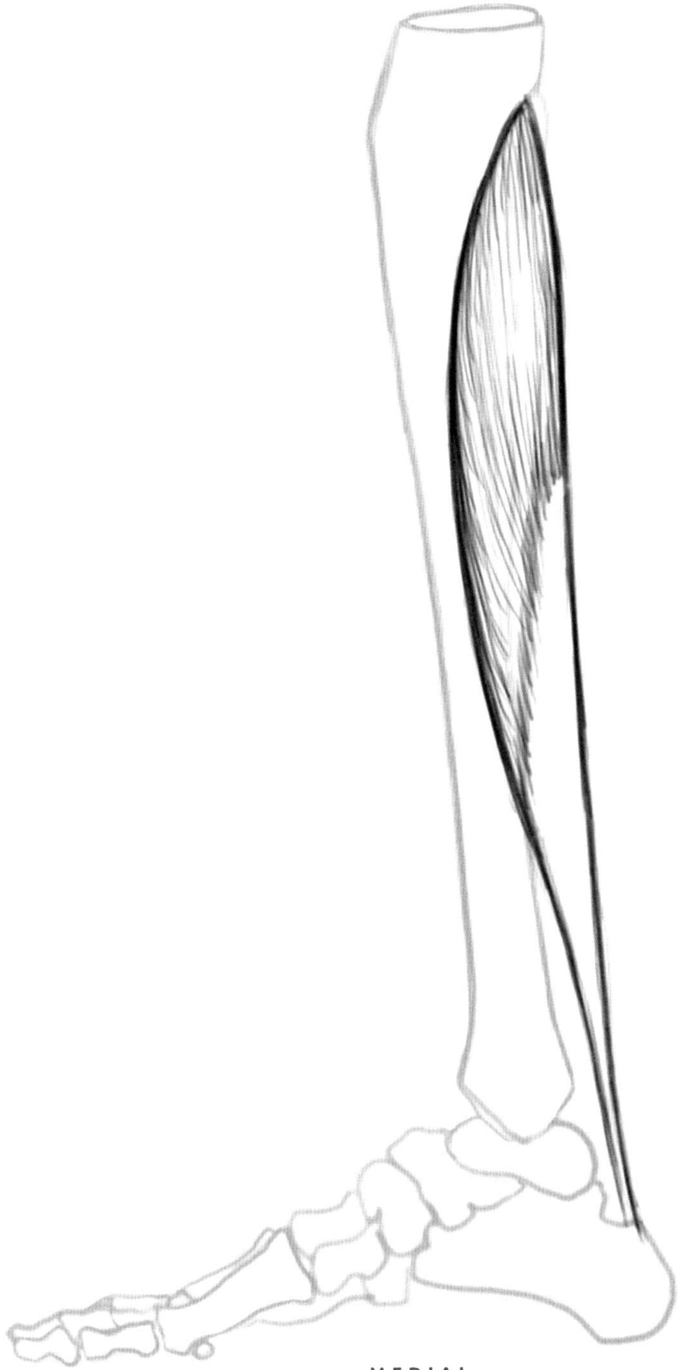

MEDIAL

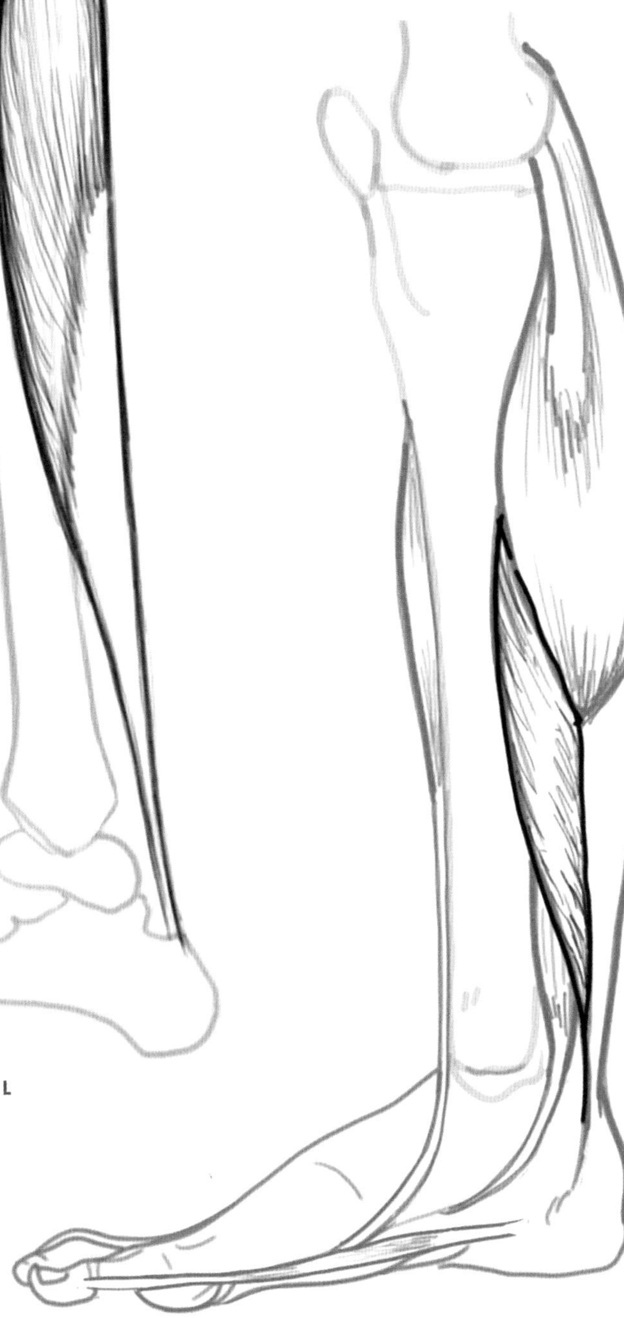

MEDIAL

A.8. GASTROCNEMIUS

STRUCTURE

The gastrocnemius consists of two heads, a medial head and a lateral head. The medial head is lower and larger than the lateral head and is easily seen on the medial (inside) view, along with the soleus.

ORIGIN

Just above the medial condyle of the femur on the flat surface facet of the lower end of the femur. The lateral head is just above the lateral condyle of the femur on the facet at the lower end of the femur on the fibular side.

INSERTION

On the calcaneus along with the soleus, their common tendon, the Achilles tendon.

ACTION

Plantarflexes the foot (1), lifts the heel off the ground (2).

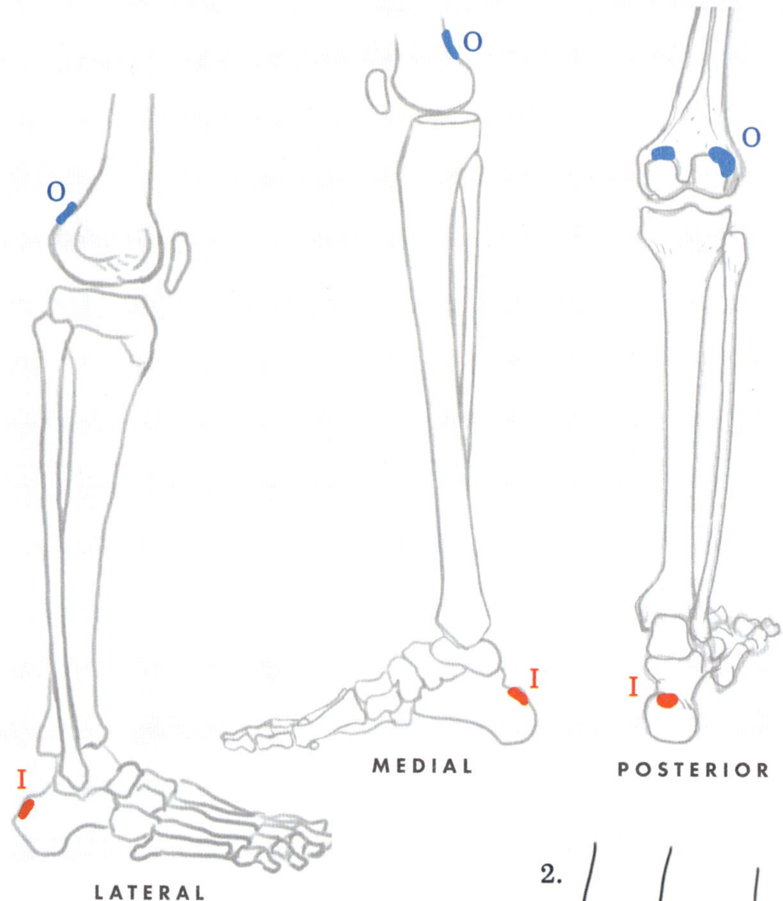

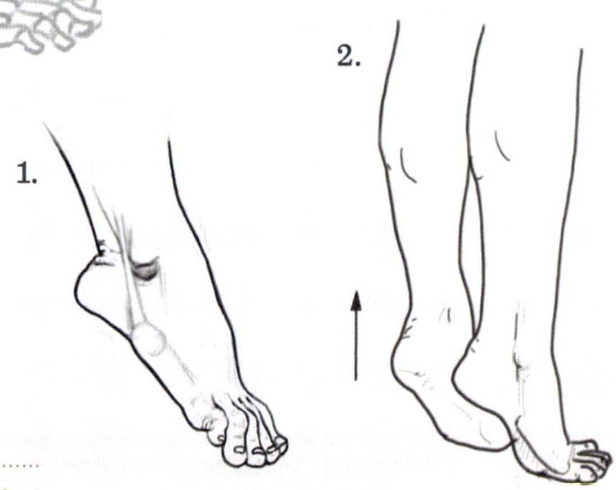

1. Plantarflexion; 2. Heel lifted

CHECKLIST

- O Peroneus brevis
- O Peroneus longus
- O Peroneus tertius
- O Extensor digitorum longus
- O Tibialis anterior
- O Flexor digitorum longus
- O Soleus
- O Gastrocnemius

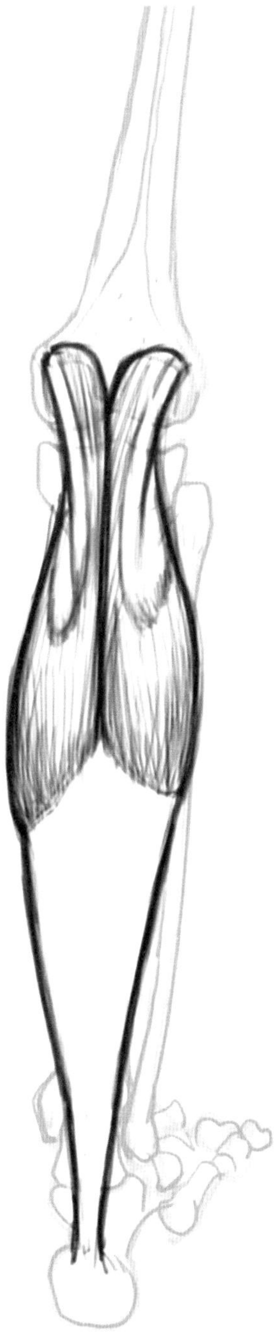

POSTERIOR

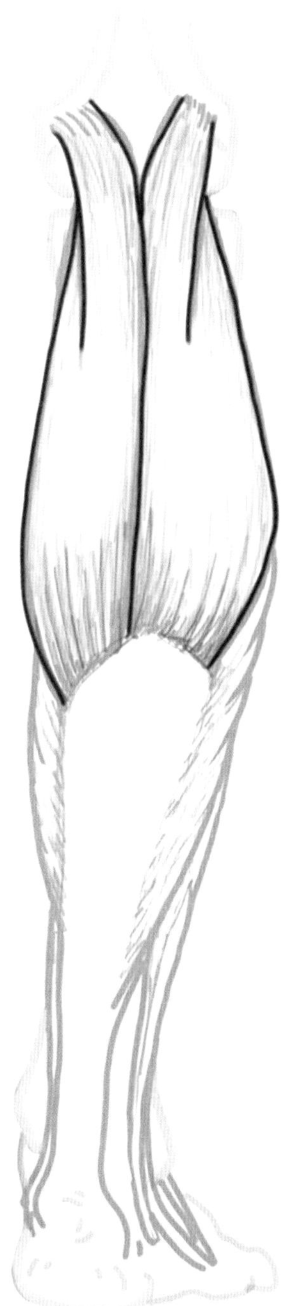

POSTERIOR

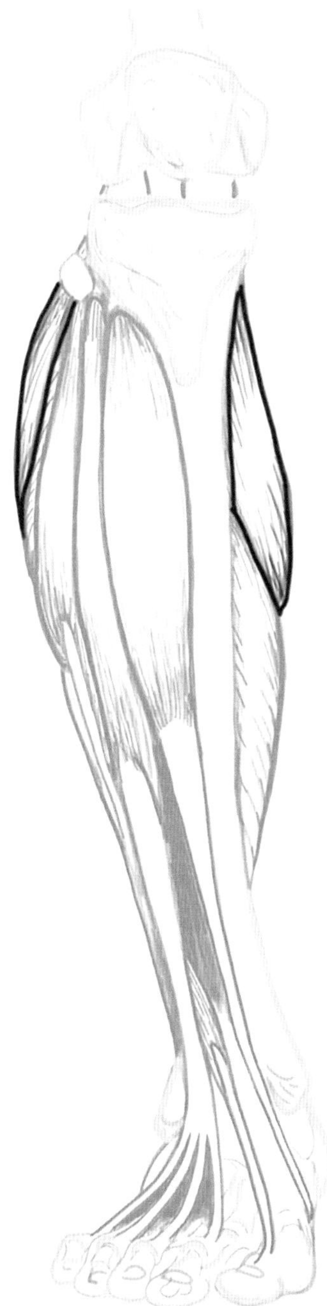

ANTERIOR

A.8. GASTROCNEMIUS

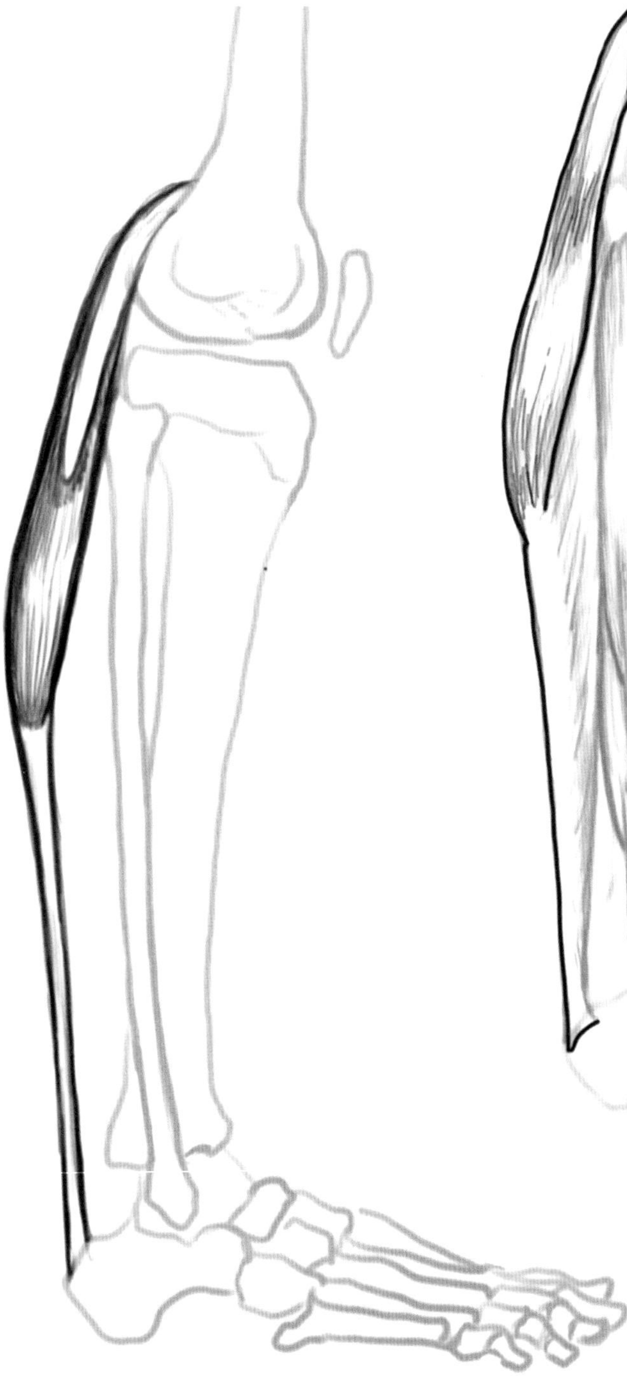

LATERAL

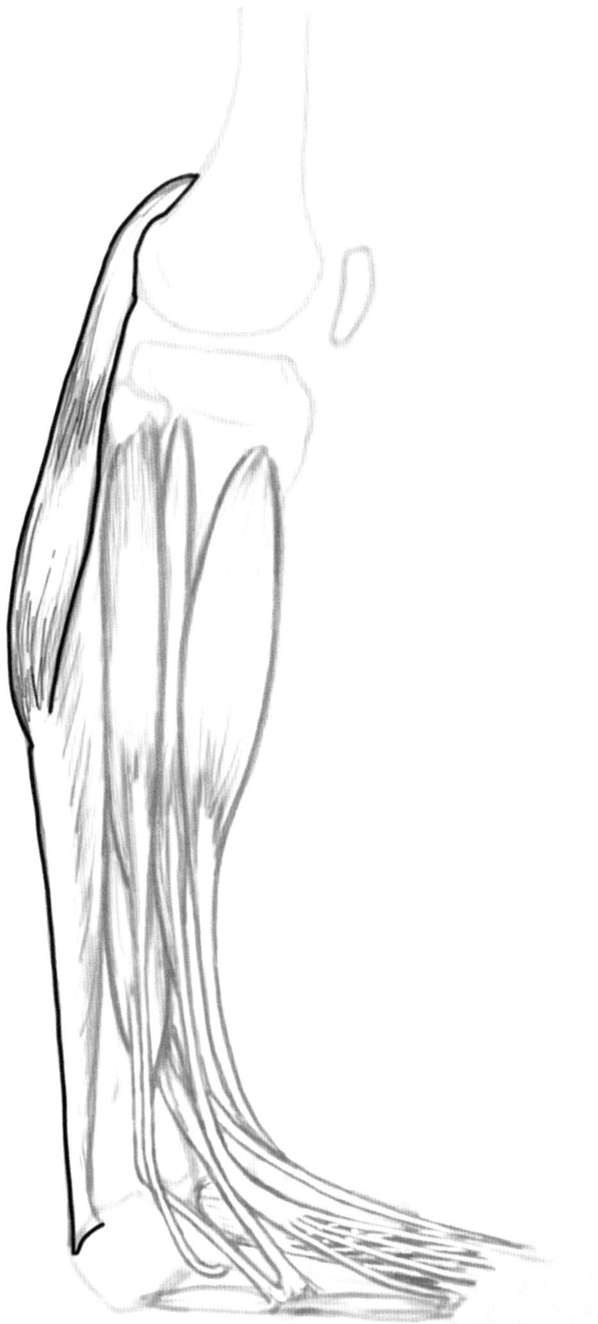

LATERAL

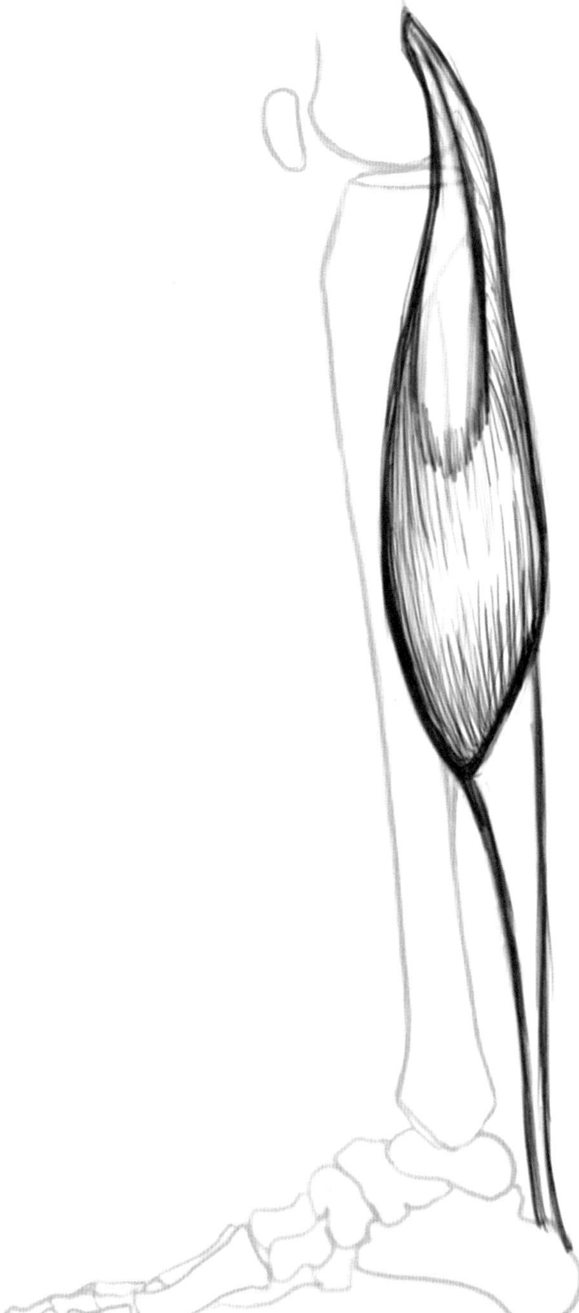

MEDIAL

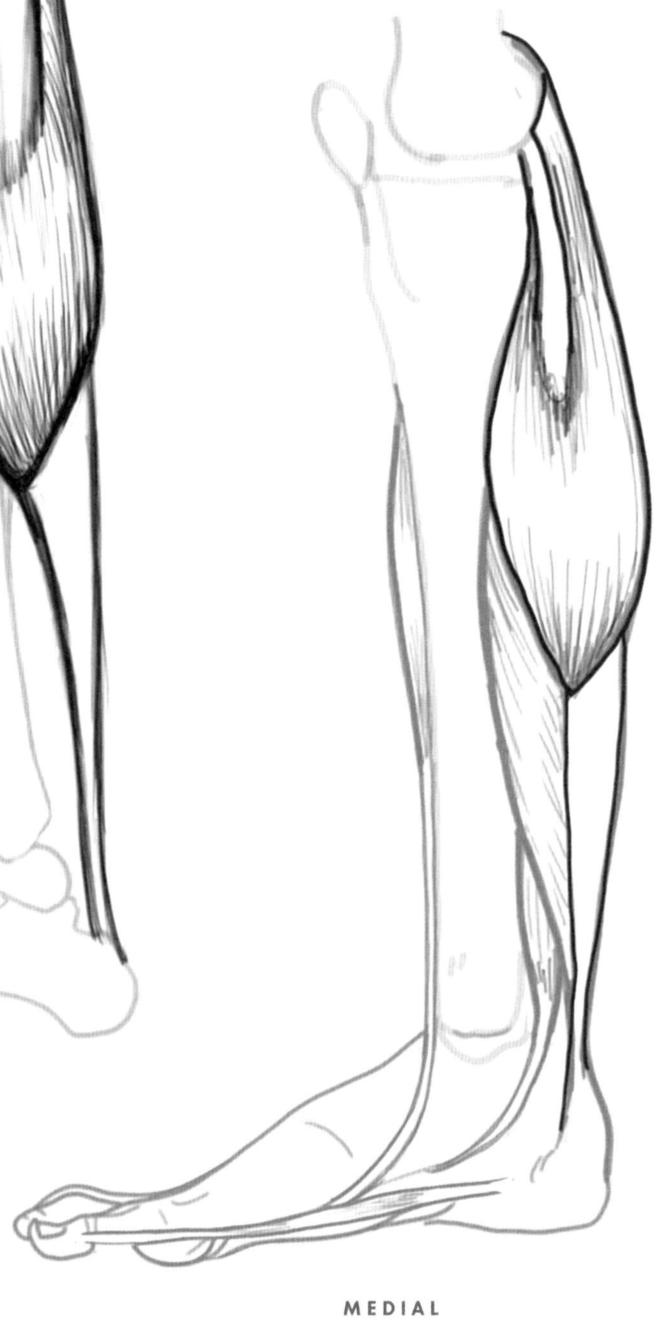

MEDIAL

A.9. EXTENSOR DIGITORUM BREVIS

STRUCTURE

The extensor digitorum brevis consists of four slender, flat bellies that pass forward medially over the top of the foot. One of them, the one that goes to the big toe, is actually called the extensor hallucis brevis, but I grouped it as part of the four for simplicity. The combined bellies create a noticeable bulge on the side of the foot, roughly between the lateral malleolus (outside ankle) and the tuberosity of the fifth metatarsal. The belly that goes to the big toe, the extensor hallucis brevis, attaches to bone, and the others attach to other tendons on the second, third, and fourth toes, leaving the little (fifth) toe alone. But remember that the extensor digitorum longus attaches to all except the big toe.

ORIGIN

The upper front portion of the calcaneus.

INSERTION

To the four toes, not the little toe, as follows: The extensor hallucis brevis attaches to the big toe onto the base of the proximal phalanx. This is the only one that attaches to bone. The others attach to the sides of the tendons of the extensor digitorum longus.

ACTION

Extends the toes (1). The extensor hallucis brevis helps the extensor hallucis longus pull up on the big toe (2). Hallux refers to the big toe.

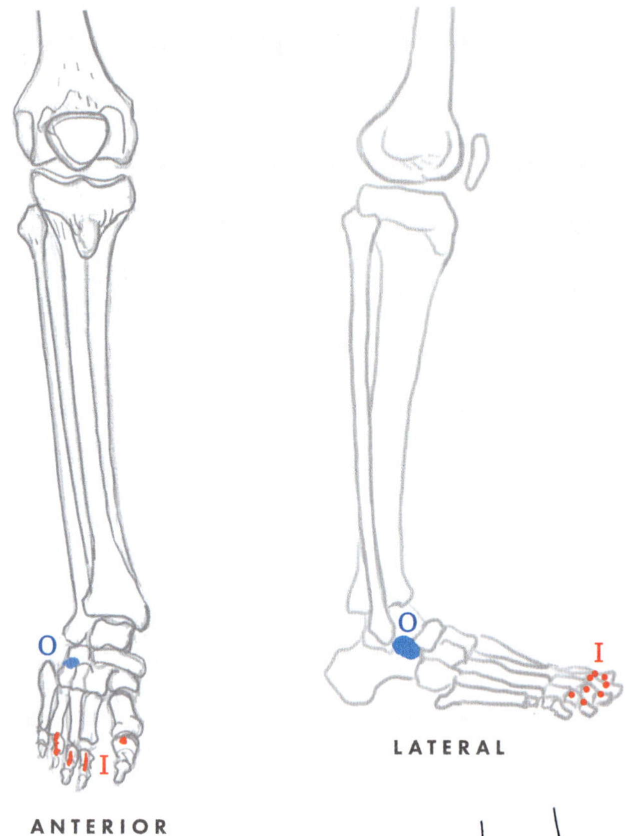

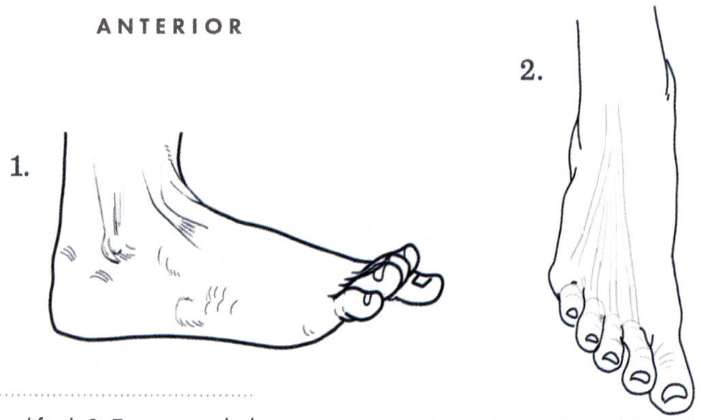

1. Toes lifted; 2. Toes extended

CHECKLIST

- O Peroneus brevis
- O Peroneus longus
- O Peroneus tertius
- O Extensor digitorum longus
- O Tibialis anterior
- O Flexor digitorum longus
- O Soleus
- O Gastrocnemius
- O Extensor digitorum brevis

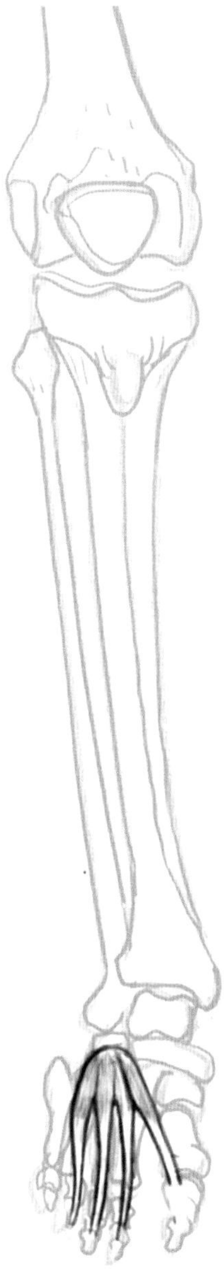

ANTERIOR

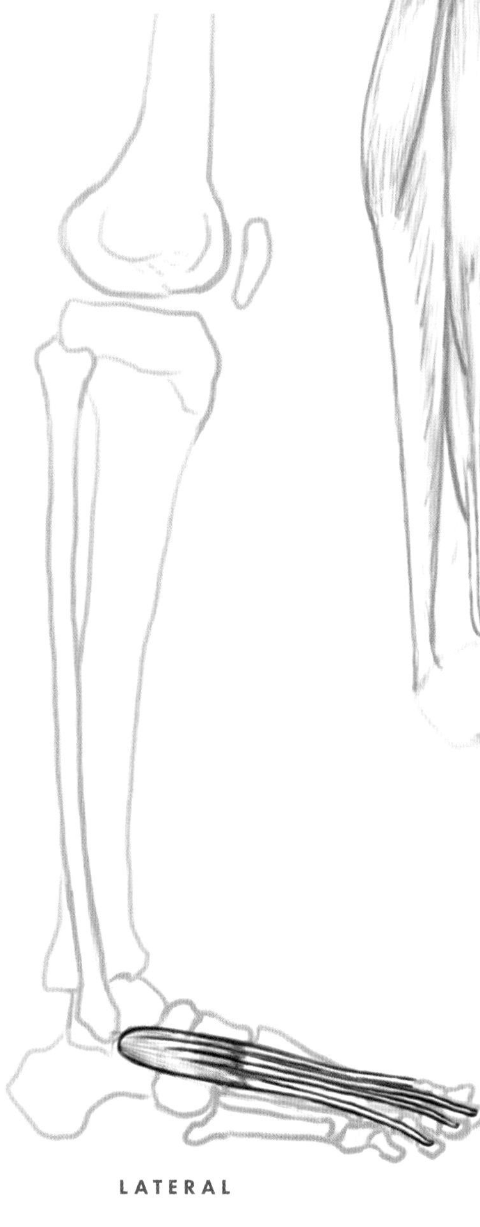

LATERAL

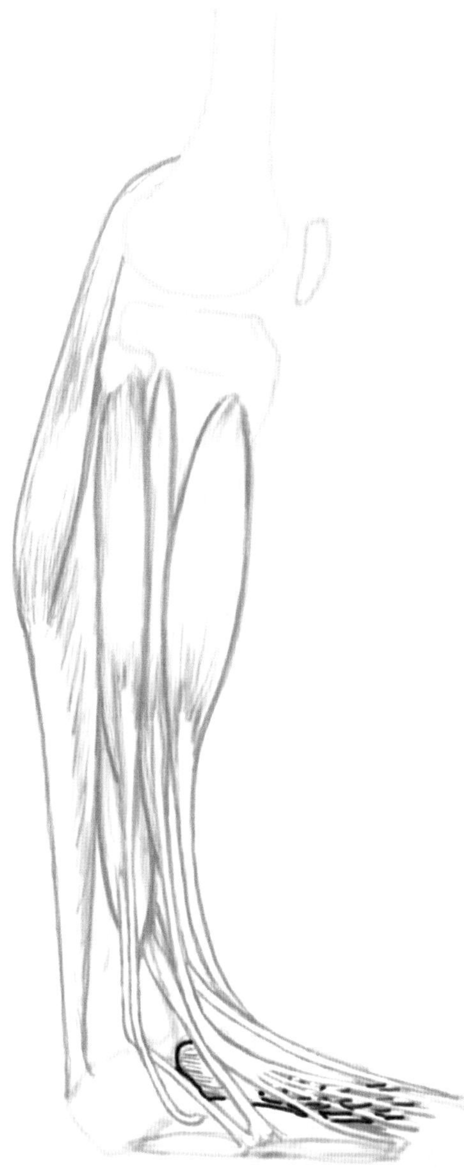

LATERAL

A.10. EXTENSOR HALLUCIS LONGUS

STRUCTURE

The extensor hallucis (big toe) is long and flat but is unseen. What is important for the artist is its tendon, which attaches to the big toe.

ORIGIN

Center section of the shaft of the fibula.

INSERTION

The distal (furthest toe bone) phalanx of the big toe.

ACTION

Lifts the big toe upward (1).

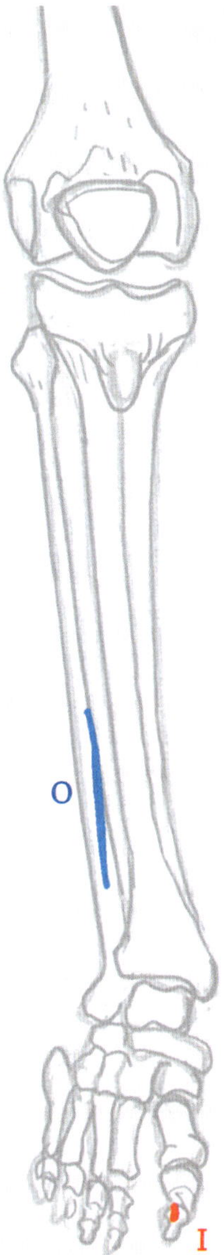

ANTERIOR

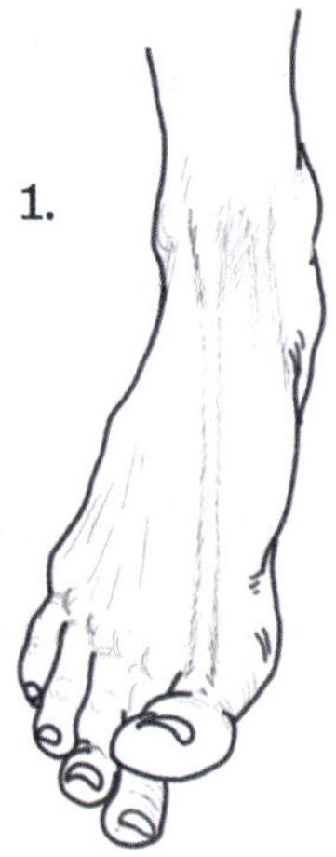

1. Big toe lifted

CHECKLIST

- O Peroneus brevis
- O Peroneus longus
- O Peroneus tertius
- O Extensor digitorum longus
- O Tibialis anterior
- O Flexor digitorum longus
- O Soleus
- O Gastrocnemius
- O Extensor digitorum brevis
- O Extensor hallucis longus

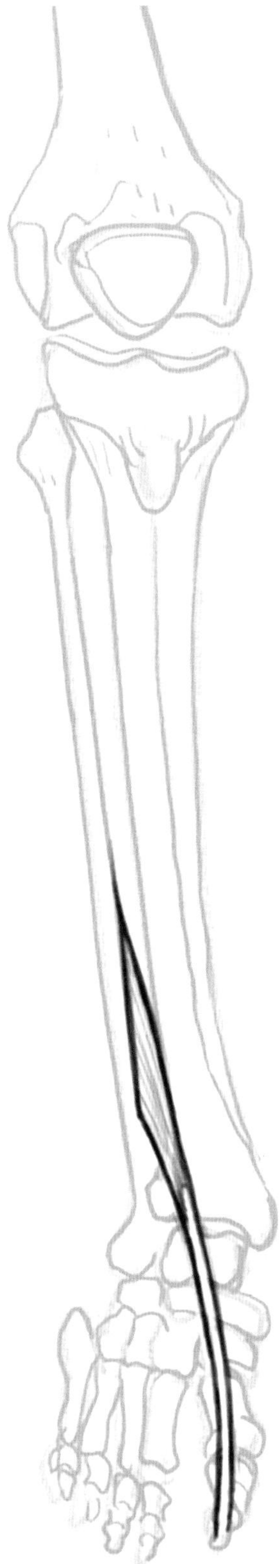

ANTERIOR

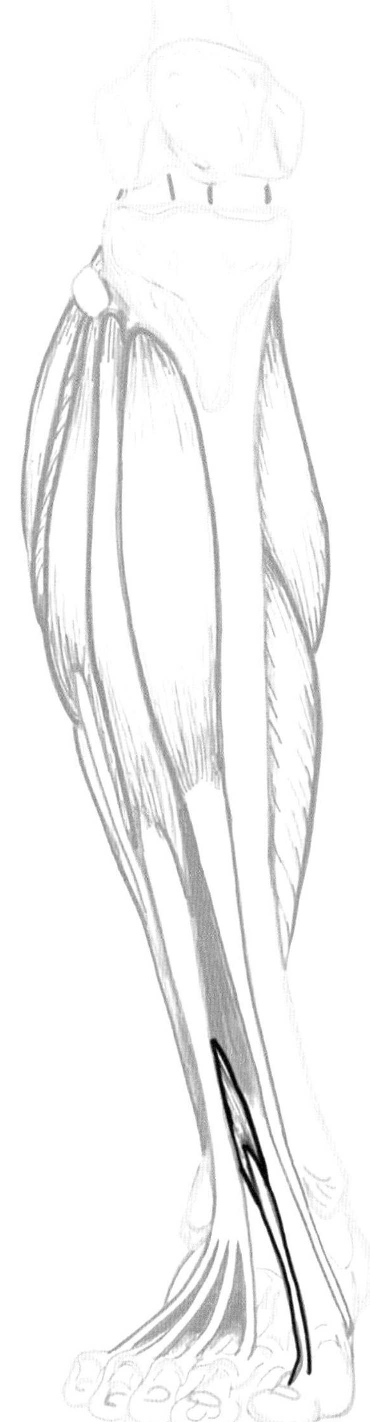

ANTERIOR

A.11. ABDUCTOR DIGITI MINIMI

STRUCTURE

The abductor digiti minimi is an elongated, thin muscle that is not seen due to the fatty pad of the side of the foot. However, it is important to know since it pulls the little toe outward.

ORIGIN

Bottom left aspect of the calcaneus.

INSERTION

The proximal phalanx of the little toe.

ACTION

Abducts, or pulls away, the little toe (1).

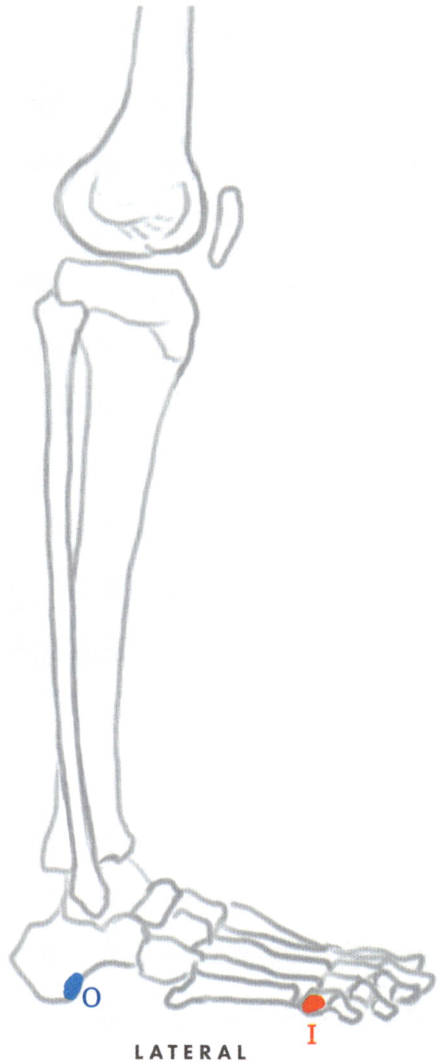

1.

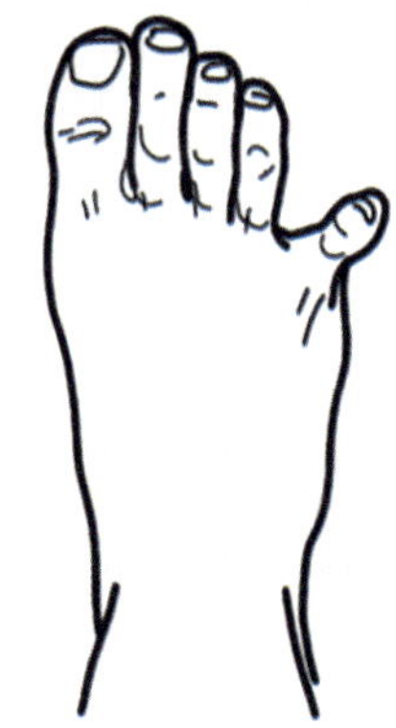

1. *Little toe abducted*

CHECKLIST

- O Peroneus brevis
- O Peroneus longus
- O Peroneus tertius
- O Extensor digitorum longus
- O Tibialis anterior
- O Flexor digitorum longus
- O Soleus
- O Gastrocnemius
- O Extensor digitorum brevis
- O Extensor hallucis longus
- O Abductor digiti minimi

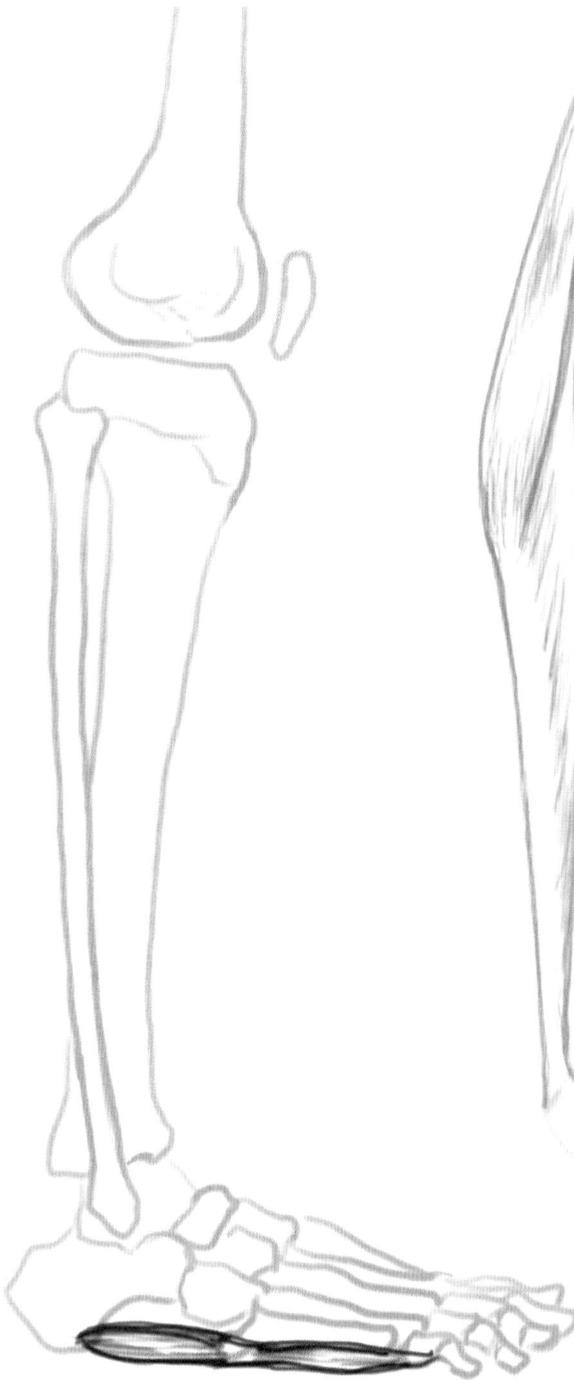

LATERAL

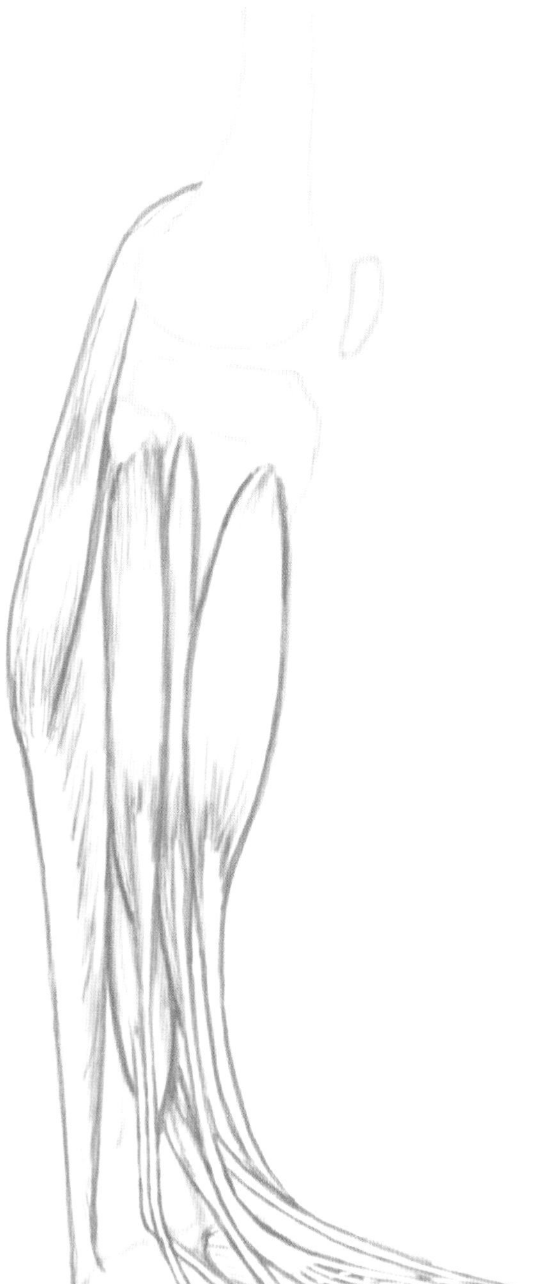

LATERAL

A.12. ABDUCTOR HALLUCIS

STRUCTURE

The abductor hallucis (big toe) starts wide and then tapers toward the big toe.

ORIGIN

On the inside aspect of the calcaneus.

INSERTION

The side of the proximal phalanx of the big toe.

ACTION

Abducts, or pulls away, the big toe (1).

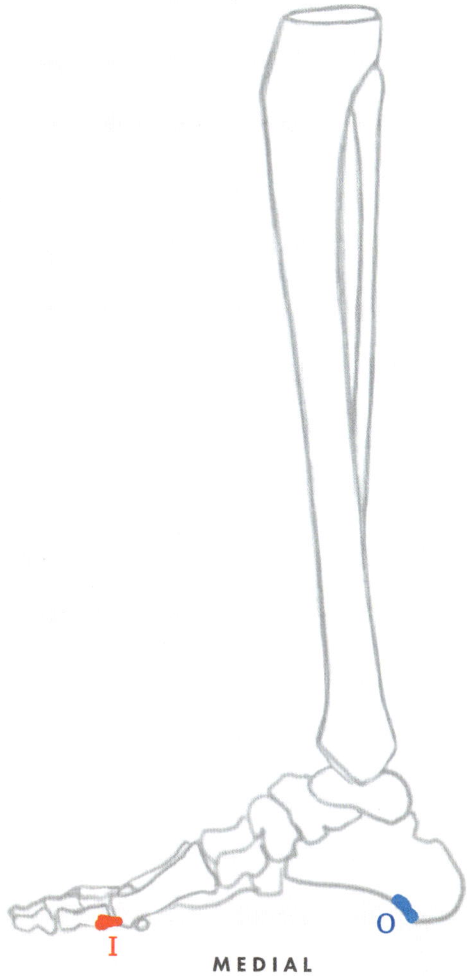

1.

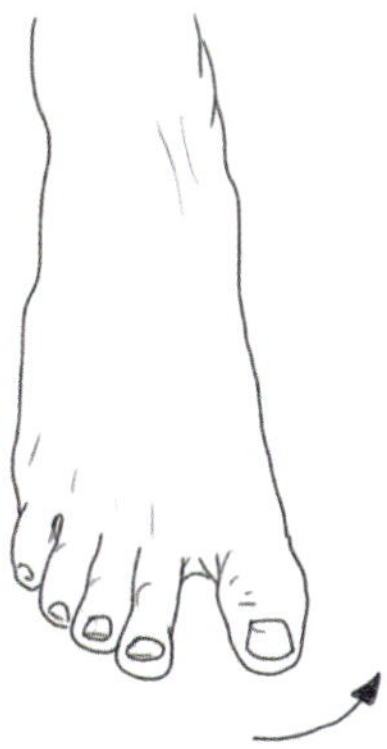

1. Big toe abducted

CHECKLIST

- O Peroneus brevis
- O Peroneus longus
- O Peroneus tertius
- O Extensor digitorum longus
- O Tibialis anterior
- O Flexor digitorum longus
- O Soleus
- O Gastrocnemius
- O Extensor digitorum brevis
- O Extensor hallucis longus
- O Abductor digiti minimi
- O Abductor hallucis

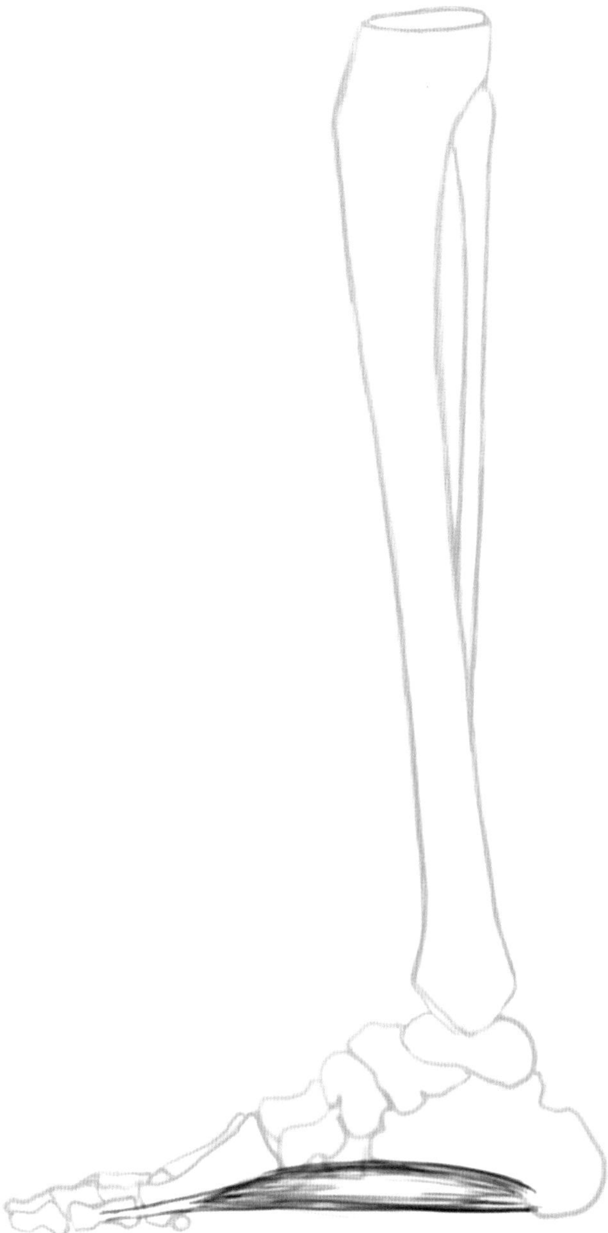

MEDIAL

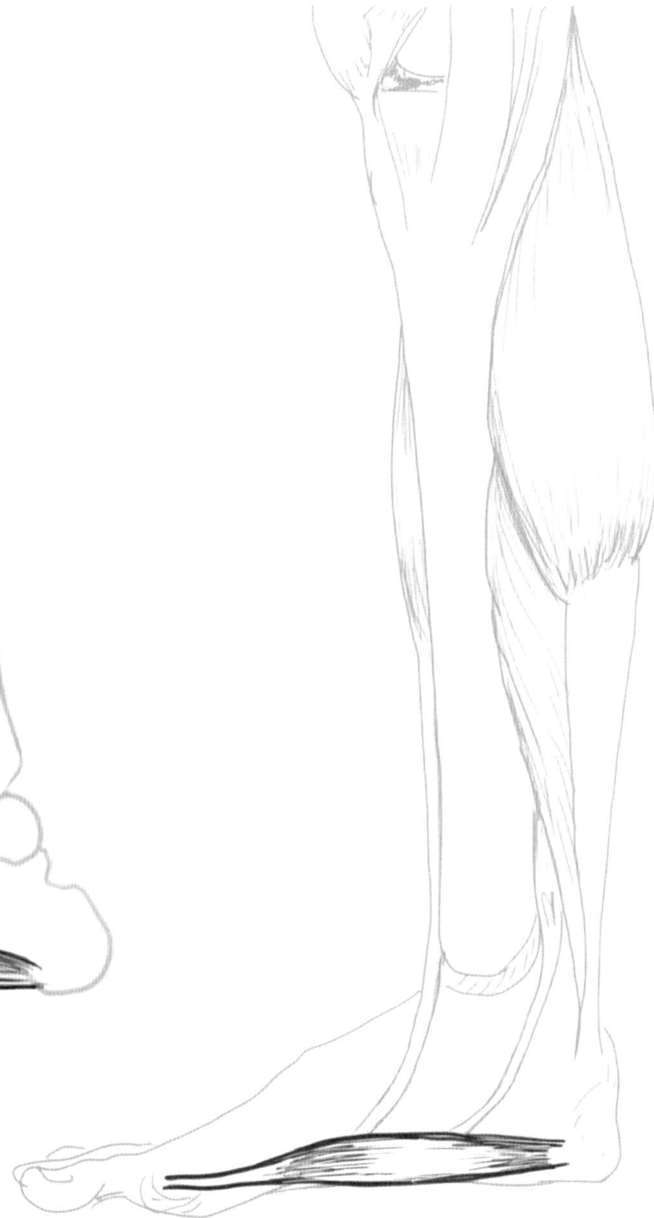

MEDIAL

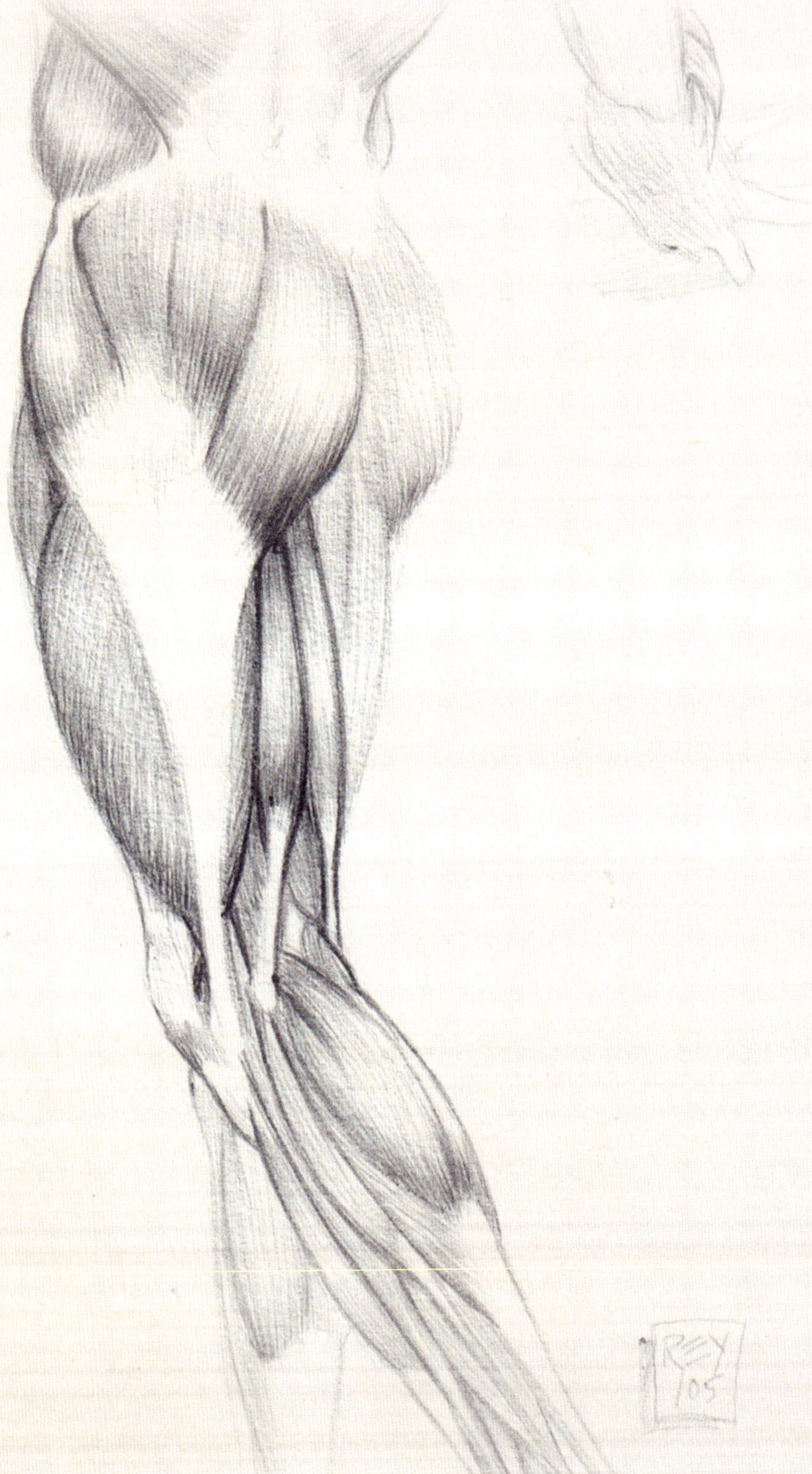
REY
'05

CHAPTER B

THE THIGH

The thigh muscles are comprised of four—five, if you include the glutes—areas of the upper portion of the lower limb. These include: In this book, as in my classroom, I edit down the muscles as most artistic anatomists do to include only the muscles that make the most impact on the surface of the body.

- **Quadriceps:** The quadriceps covered in this book are the vastus medialis (**B.7.**), vastus lateralis (**B.6.**), and rectus femoris (**B.8.**). The vastus intermedius was purposely left out since it is underneath the rectus femoris and is therefore not seen. Of the quadriceps, only the rectus femoris flexes your hip, such as in squatting. All of the quadriceps work together to extend your knee, as in standing at attention.
- **Adductors:** The adductors are on the inside of the thigh. As stated in the name, they adduct the legs, allowing you to bring your knees together.
- **Abductors:** In this book, the main abductors are the gluteus medius (**B.13.**) and the tensor fasciae lata (**B.15.**). The gluteus minimus is not seen superficially (on the surface).
- **Hamstrings:** These muscles allow you to bring your thigh behind you, like in walking, bring your foot back toward your rear, and bend your knee.
- **Glutes:** These are the large rear-end muscles, mainly the gluteus maximus (**B.14.**). Stair stepping is a good way to exercise this area. Once we became bipedal, the gluteus maximus became very large compared to other animals. The gluteus medius (**B.7.**) abducts your thigh, meaning it moves it away from the body, along with the tensor fasciae lata (**B.15.**).

B.1. ILIOPSOAS

STRUCTURE

The iliopsoas is comprised of two muscles: the iliacus and the psoas major. (There is also a third muscle, the psoas minor, not included.) The iliacus is flat and pressed up against the ilium of the pelvis and tapers toward the common insertion with the psoas major. The psoas major is conical and tapers toward the same insertion as the iliacus.

ORIGIN

The psoas major attaches to the five transverse processes of the five lumbar vertebrae. The iliacus attaches to the ilium and a bit to the top corner of the sacrum.

INSERTION

Both parts of the iliopsoas attach to the lesser trochanter of the femur.

ACTION

Very strong flexor of the hip joint and a powerful flexor of the trunk, such as in doing a sit-up (1).

1.

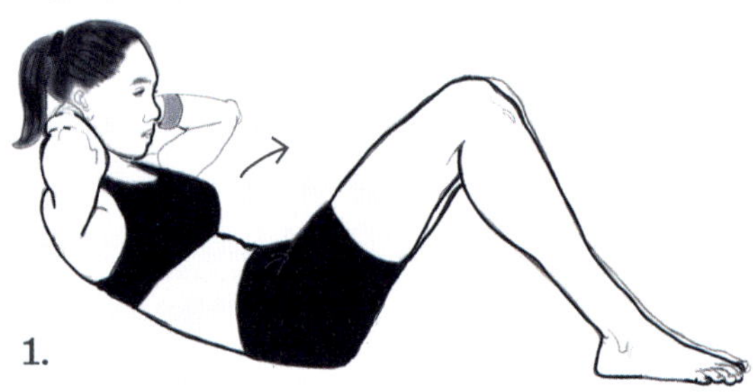

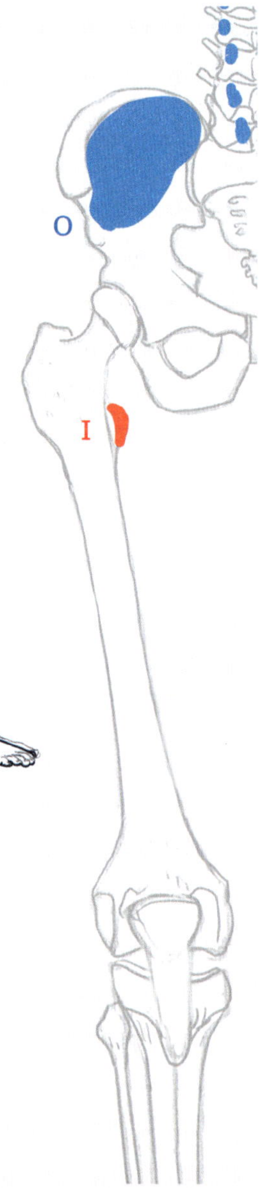

ANTERIOR

1. Flexor of hip joint and trunk

CHECKLIST

O Iliopsoas

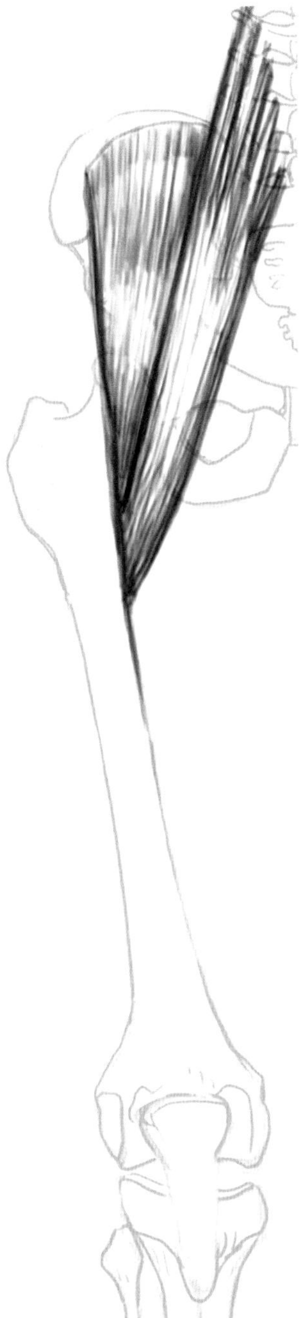

ANTERIOR

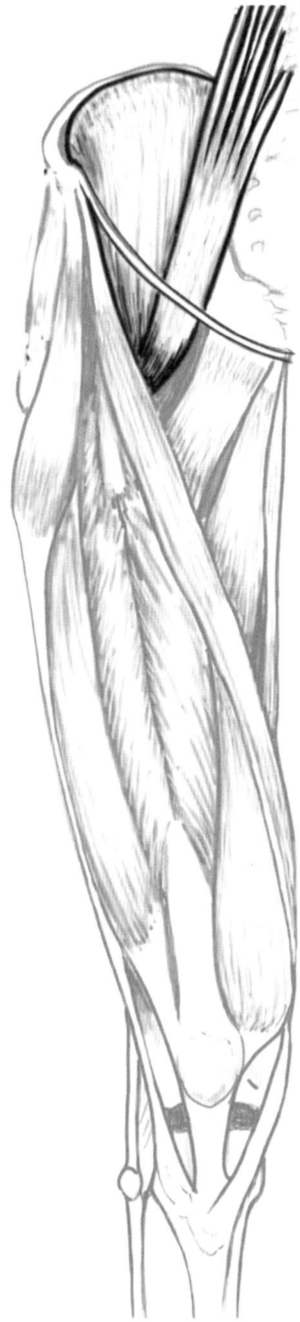

ANTERIOR

B.2. PECTINEUS

STRUCTURE

The pectineus is a flattened rectangular muscle.

ORIGIN

The pectineal line of the pubis.

INSERTION

The posterior (back) midline of the femur.

ACTION

Adducts (helps to bring the knees together; 1) and flexes the hip joint.

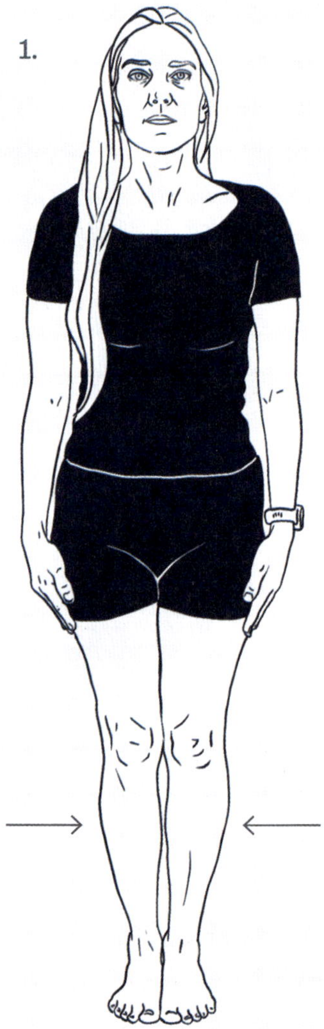

1. Adducted hip joint

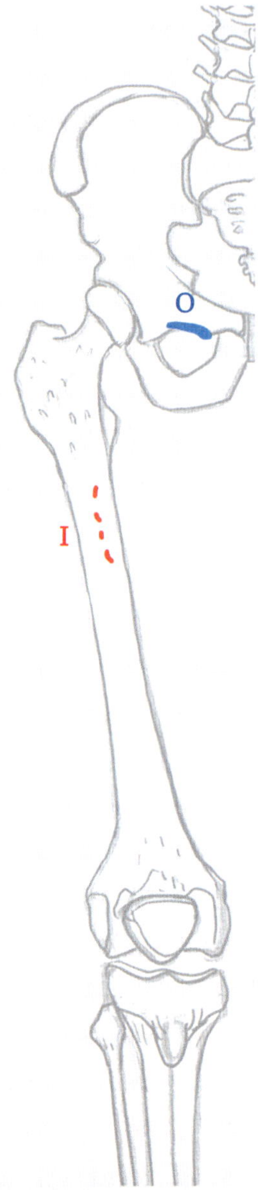

ANTERIOR

CHECKLIST

- O Iliopsoas
- O Pectineus

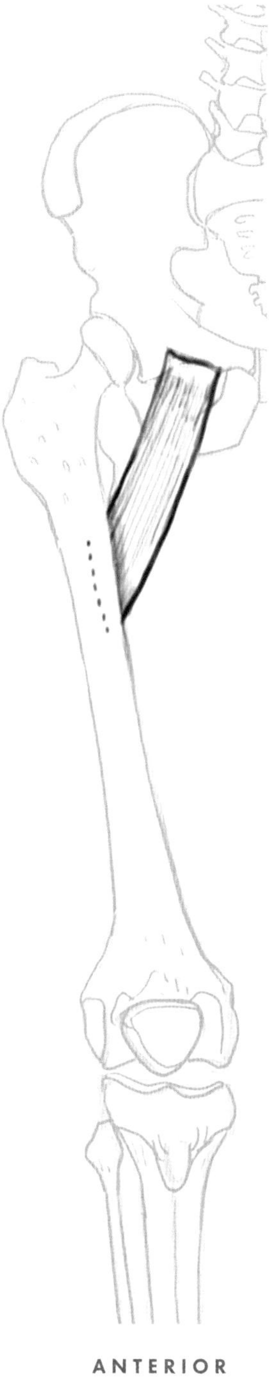

ANTERIOR

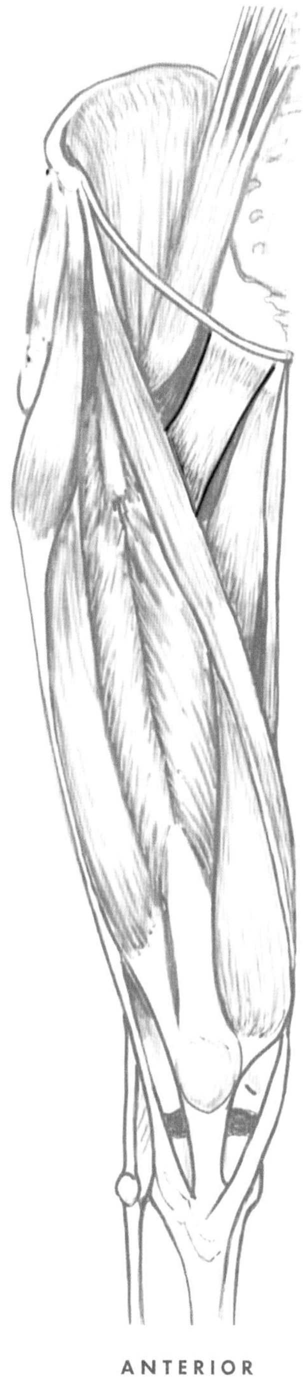

ANTERIOR

B.3. ADDUCTOR LONGUS

STRUCTURE

The adductor longus is a long triangular muscle with a very strong tendon at the groin area.

ORIGIN

At the front of the pubic bone.

INSERTION

At a long area at the center line (linea aspera) of the back of the femur.

ACTION

Adducts (1) and flexes the thigh.

1.

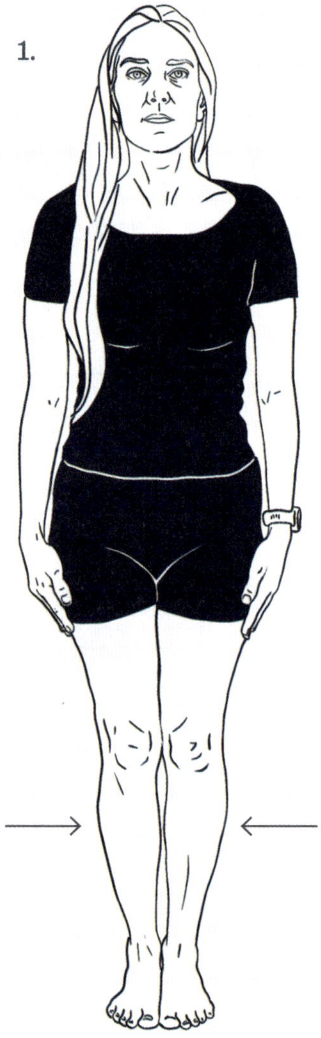

1. Adducts and flexes the thigh

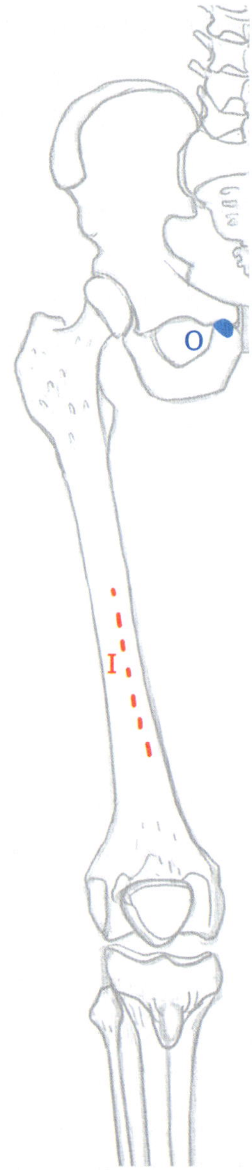

ANTERIOR

CHECKLIST

- O Iliopsoas
- O Pectineus
- O Adductor longus

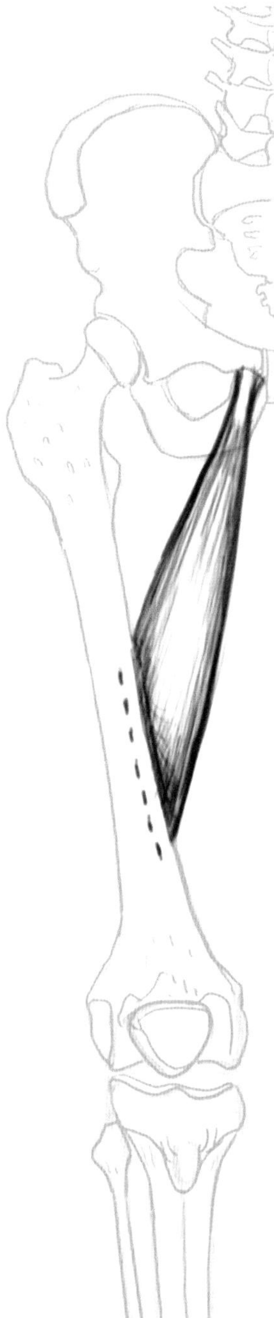

ANTERIOR

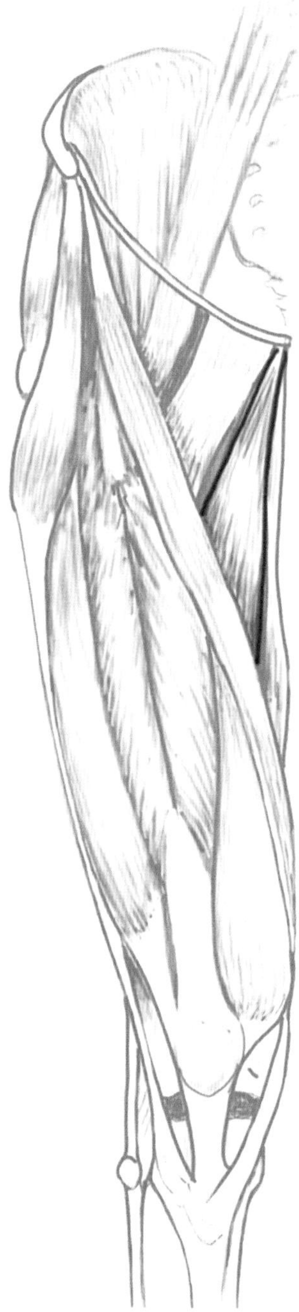

ANTERIOR

B4. ADDUCTOR MAGNUS

STRUCTURE

The adductor magnus is a huge muscle, but only one form shows, and that is on the rear inside of the thigh, high up by the butt cheek. It is broad at the top and pointier at the bottom. The bottom splits, with one section attaching to the back of the femur and the other, shaped like a sharp cone, tapering and becoming a strong tendon.

ORIGIN

Ischial tuberosity ("sit bone") of the pelvis and a portion toward the medial edge.

INSERTION

Down the midline of the femur on the back by the linea aspera (linear ridge on the back of the femur) and another section that splits and attaches to the medial edge of the femur.

ACTION

A strong adductor, it pulls the thighs and knees together (1).

1.

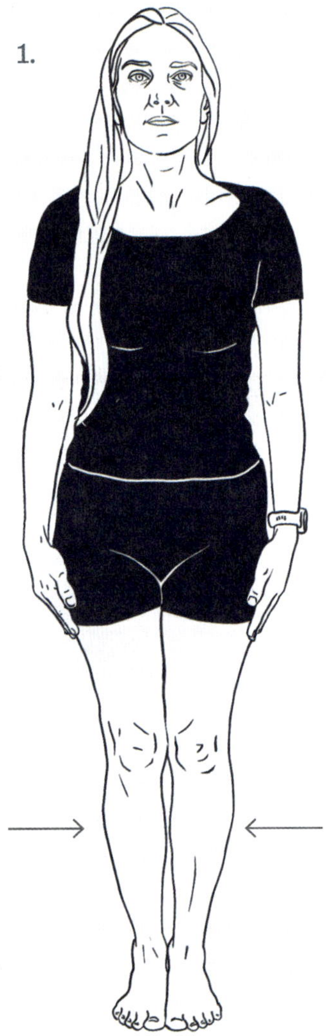

1. *Adducts thighs and knees*

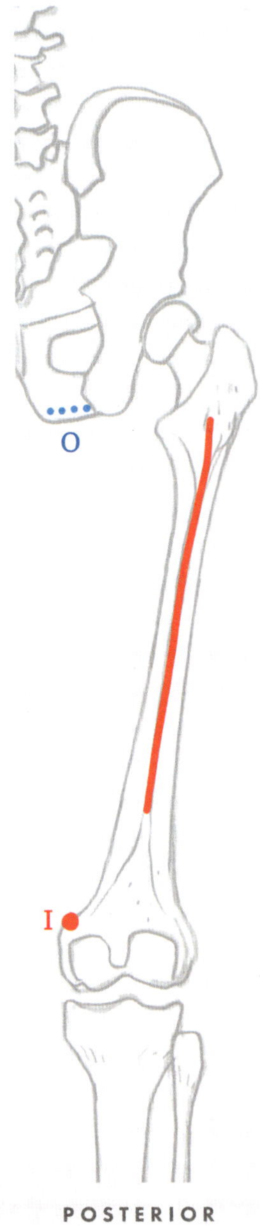

CHECKLIST

- O Iliopsoas
- O Pectineus
- O Adductor longus
- O Adductor magnus

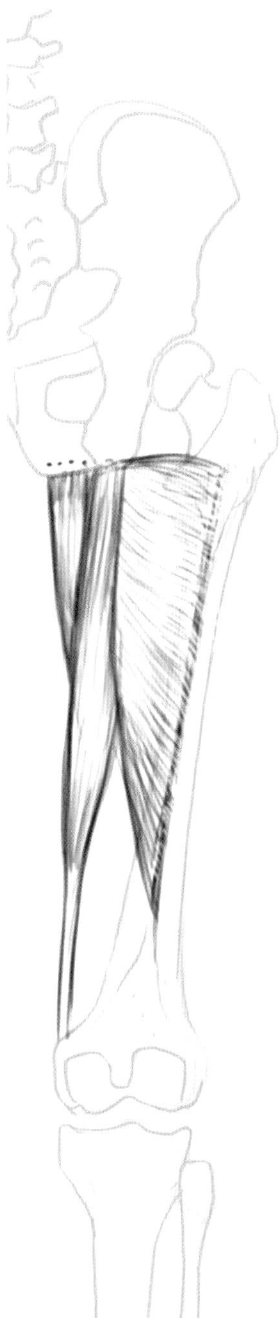

POSTERIOR

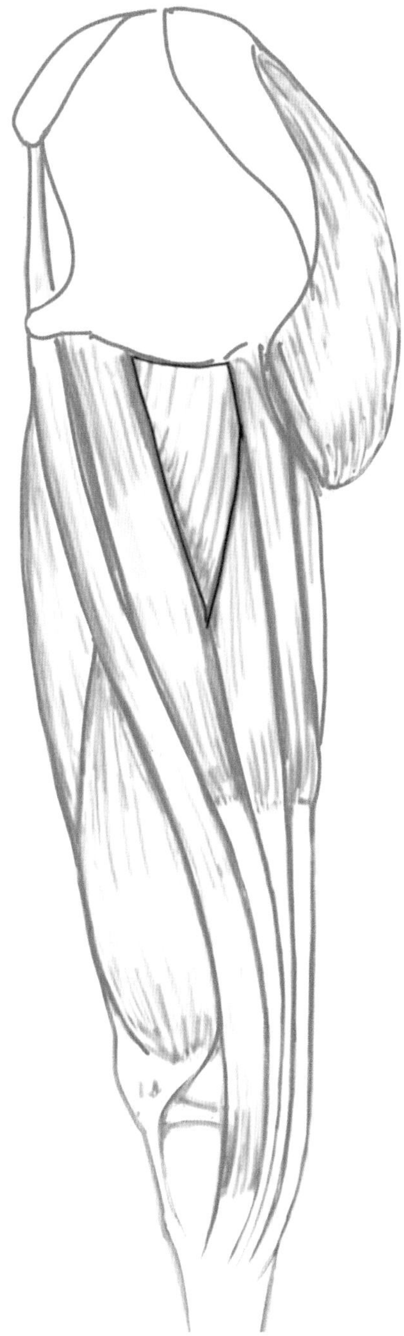

MEDIAL

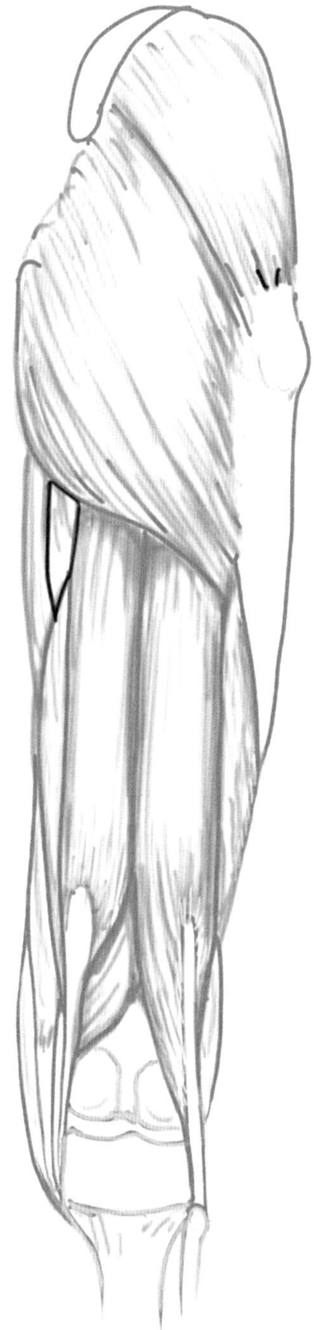

POSTERIOR

B.5. GRACILIS

STRUCTURE

The gracilis is a long, belt-like muscle that is flat and broad at the top and tapered at the bottom. It is located by the inside of the knee, close to the back of the knee, with a long tendon that attaches at the inside of the tibia. I call it the "inseam" muscle because it approximates where the inseam of a pair of pants would be.

ORIGIN

Ischium by the pubic arch.

INSERTION

Top, medial surface of the tibia.

ACTION

Adducts the thighs (1) and helps flex and medially rotate the leg (2).

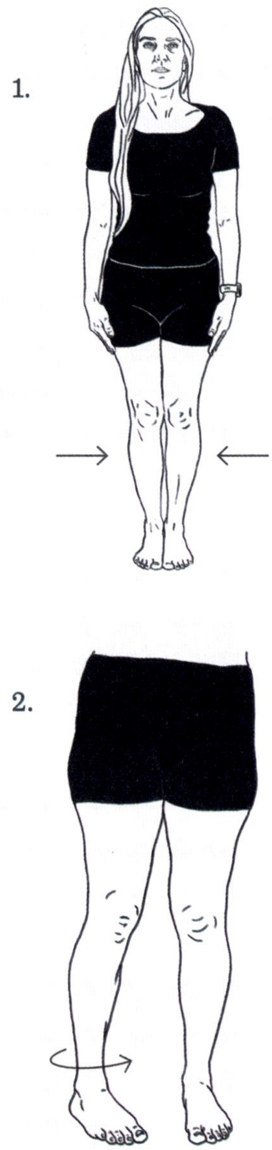

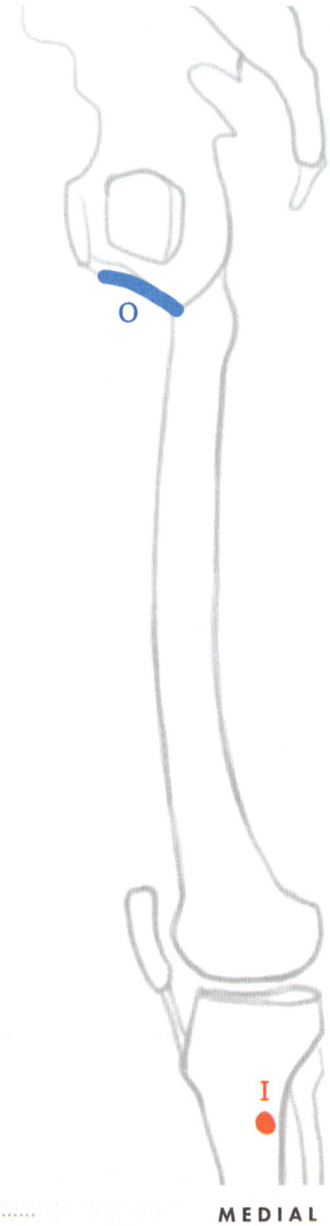

1. Adducts thighs; 2. Flexes and medially rotates leg

CHECKLIST

- O Iliopsoas
- O Pectineus
- O Adductor longus
- O Adductor magnus
- O Gracilis

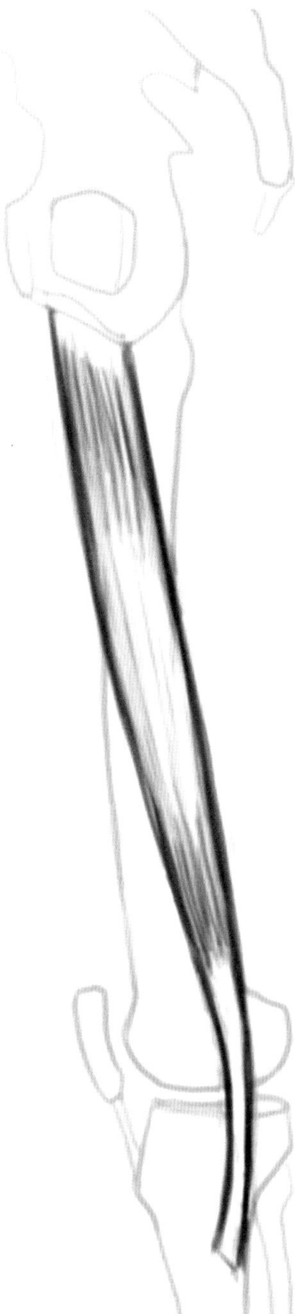

MEDIAL

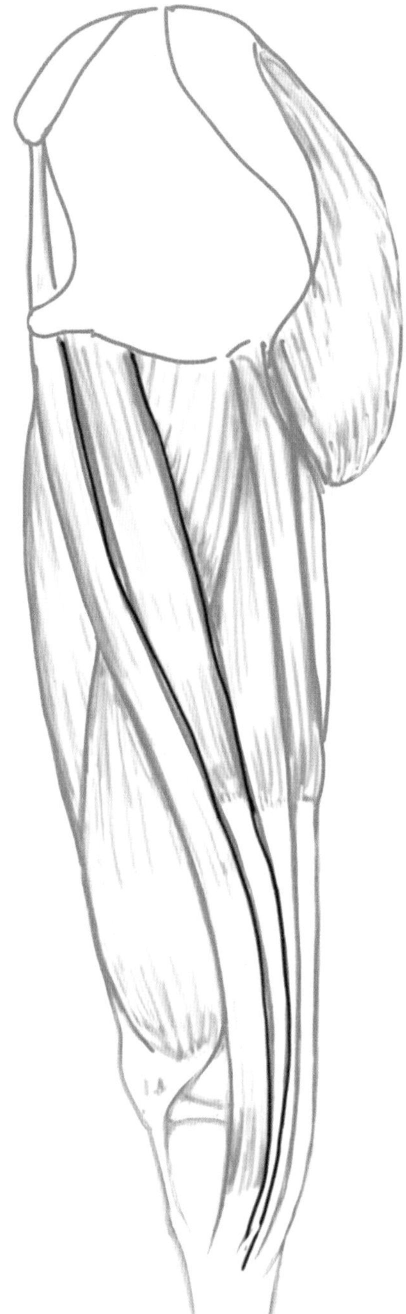

MEDIAL

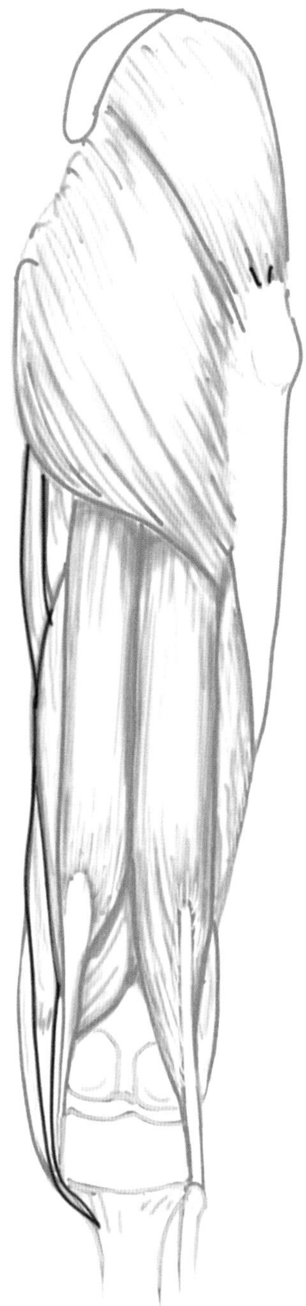

POSTERIOR

B.6. VASTUS LATERALIS

STRUCTURE

The vastus lateralis is a very large quadricep muscle that is shaped like a large fish. It is on the side of the thigh but also wraps around to the front above the knee.

ORIGIN

The greater trochanter of the femur and the linea aspera on the back of the femur.

INSERTION

The quadriceps tendon, which covers the patella. This is the common tendon for the quadriceps. (The rectus femoris and vastus medialis are the other two quadriceps muscles shown in the following sections. The vastus internus has been left out of this book since it is not seen.) Below the patella, the quadriceps tendon becomes known as the patellar ligament. This is because a tendon connects muscle to bone, and a ligament connects bone to bone. The patellar ligament inserts at the tibial tuberosity.

ACTION

Extends the leg at the knee (1).

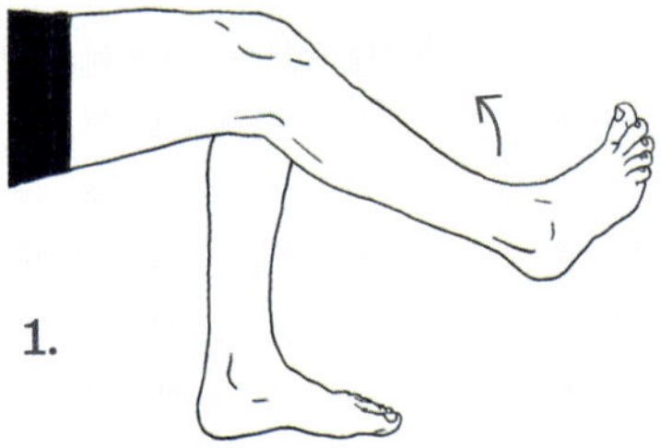

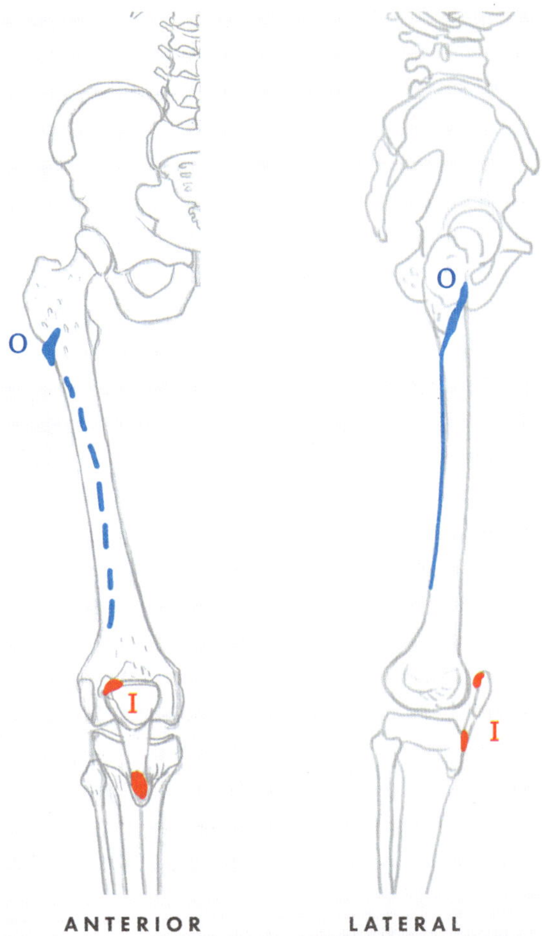

1. Extends leg at knee

CHECKLIST

- O Iliopsoas
- O Pectineus
- O Adductor longus
- O Adductor magnus
- O Gracilis
- O Vastus lateralis

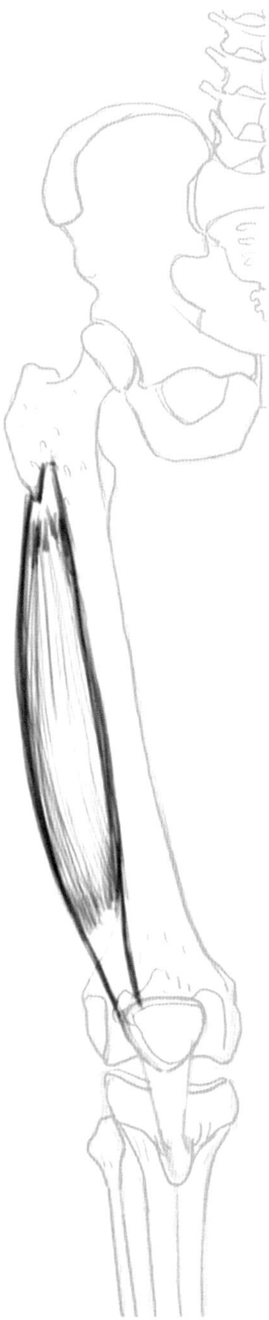

ANTERIOR

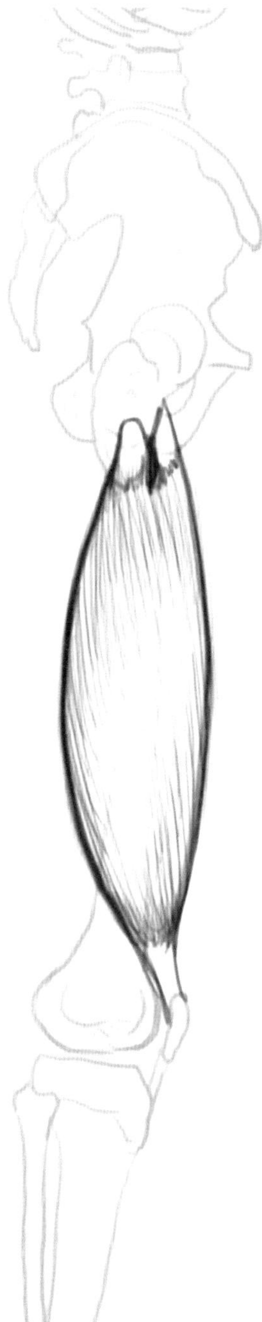

LATERAL

B.6. VASTUS LATERALIS

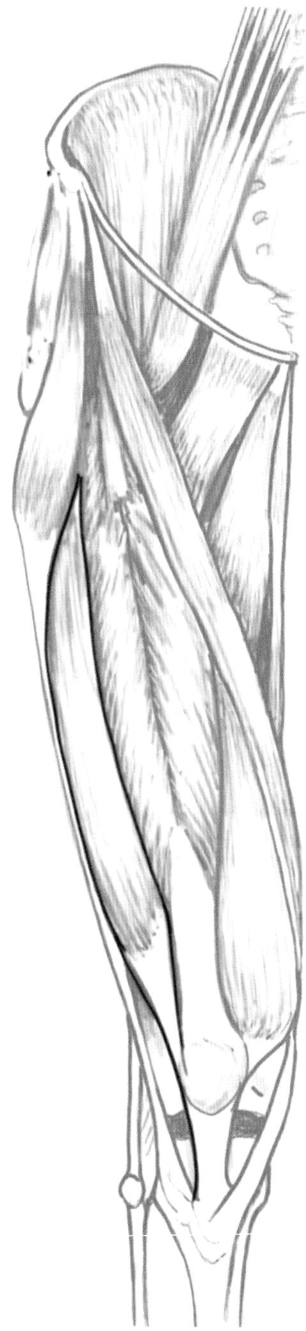

ANTERIOR

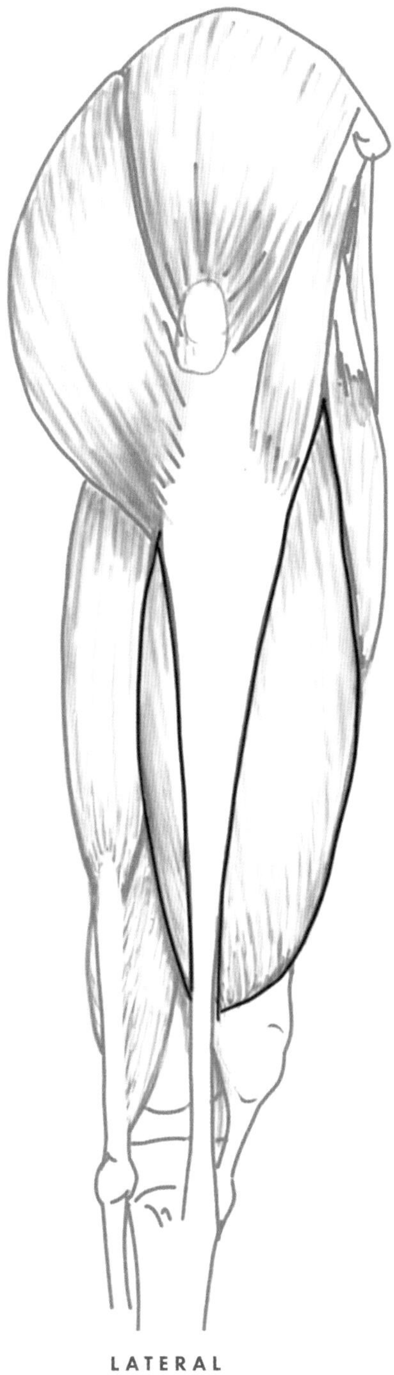

LATERAL

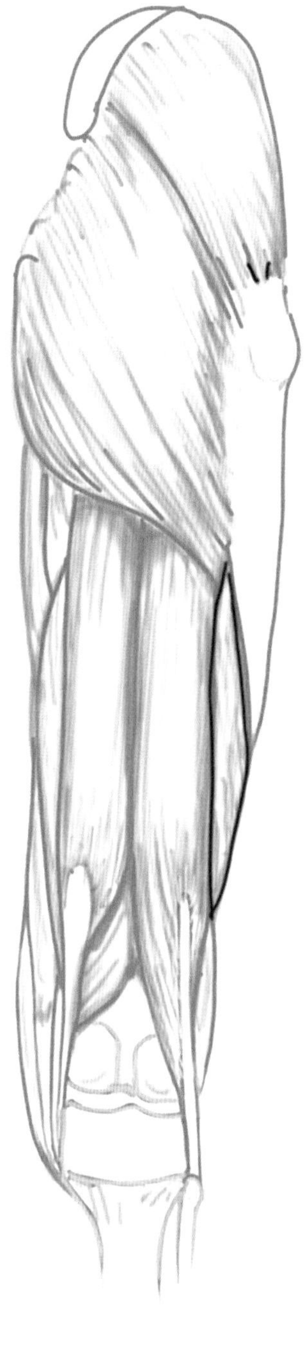

POSTERIOR

B.7. VASTUS MEDIALIS

STRUCTURE

The vastus medialis is a large teardrop-shaped muscle. It is the lowest of the quadriceps and it rests on the patella.

ORIGIN

By the linea aspera, the midline on the back of the femur, and a small section on the top-front of the femur.

INSERTION

The tibial tuberosity by way of the quadriceps tendon along with the other "quads."

ACTION

Extends the leg at the knee (1) and helps balance the action of the vastus lateralis.

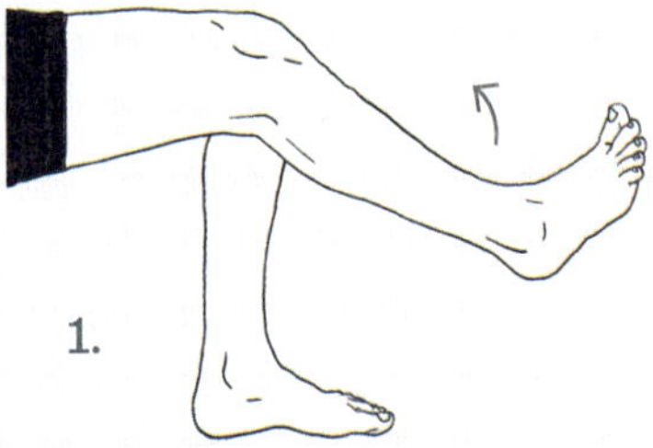

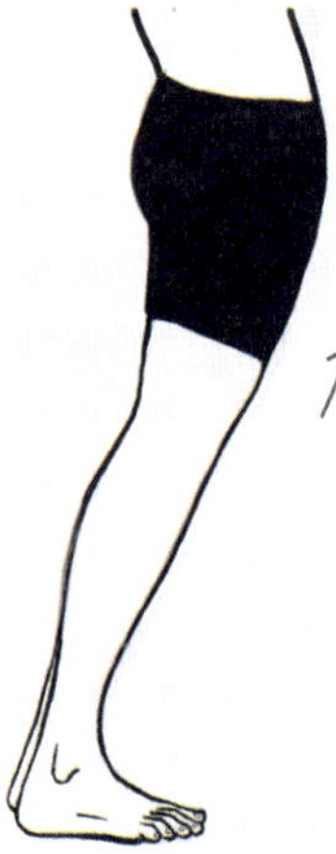

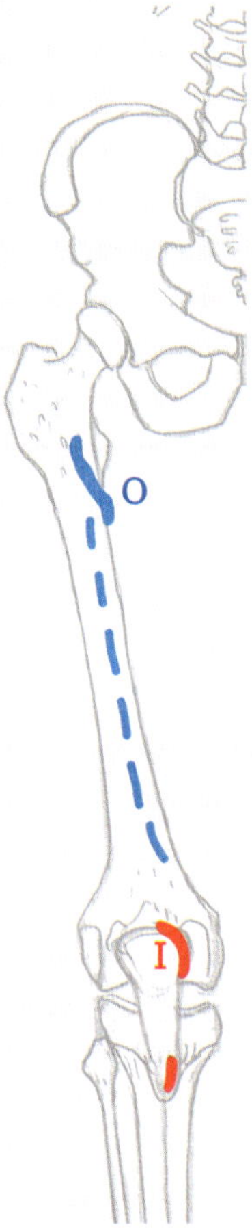

1. Extends leg at knee

CHECKLIST

- O Iliopsoas
- O Pectineus
- O Adductor longus
- O Adductor magnus
- O Gracilis
- O Vastus lateralis
- O Vastus medialis

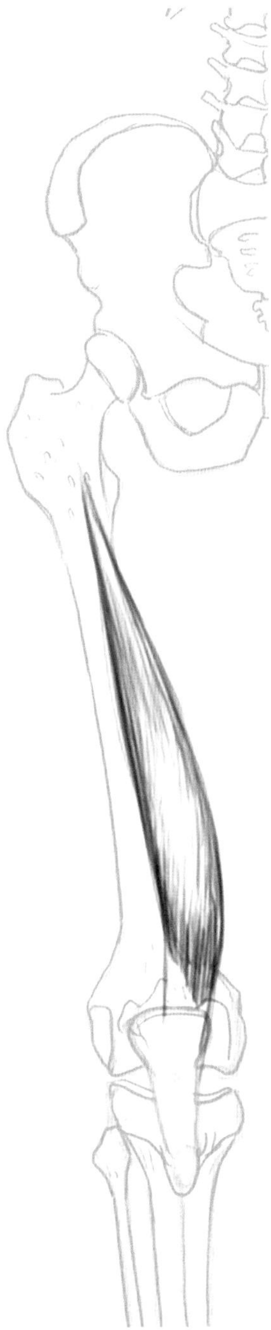

ANTERIOR

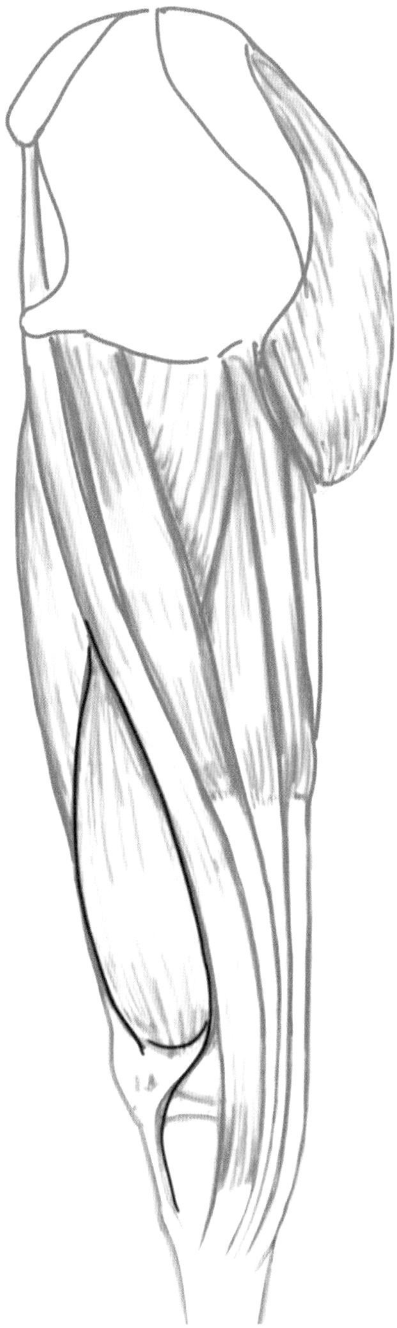

MEDIAL

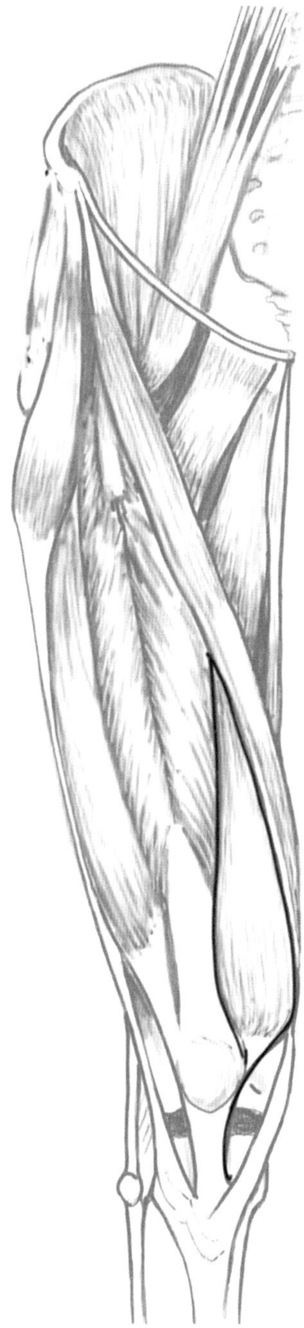

ANTERIOR

B.8. RECTUS FEMORIS

STRUCTURE

The rectus femoris is a strong, straight (rectus means straight) muscle that has a noticeable groove down the center with muscle fibers that look like arrowheads pointing upward. It is tapered at the top and bottom, making it look like a trout on the top of the front of the thigh. It is also the only quadricep that crosses over two joints: the hip, since it is attached to the pelvis, and the knee, since it attaches to the tibia along with the other quadriceps.

ORIGIN

The anterior inferior iliac spine of the pelvis.

INSERTION

At the tibial tuberosity along with the other "quads."

ACTION

Extends the knee (1) and flexes the hip (2).

1.

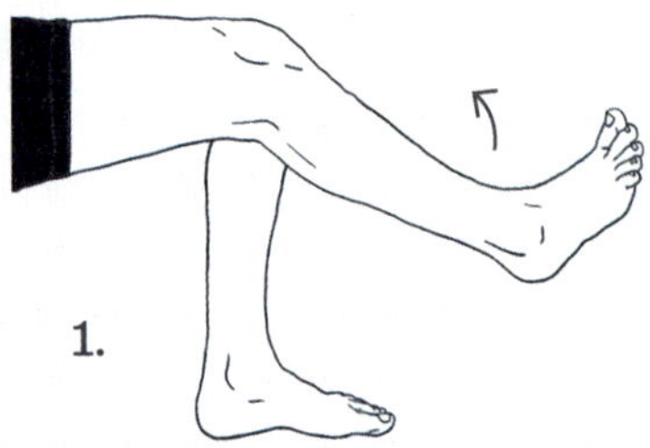

2.

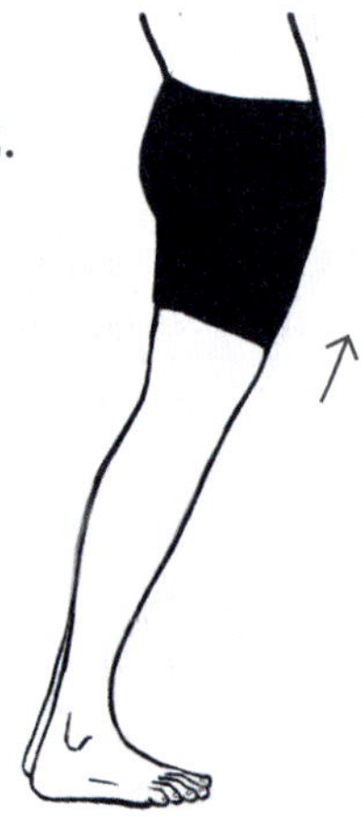

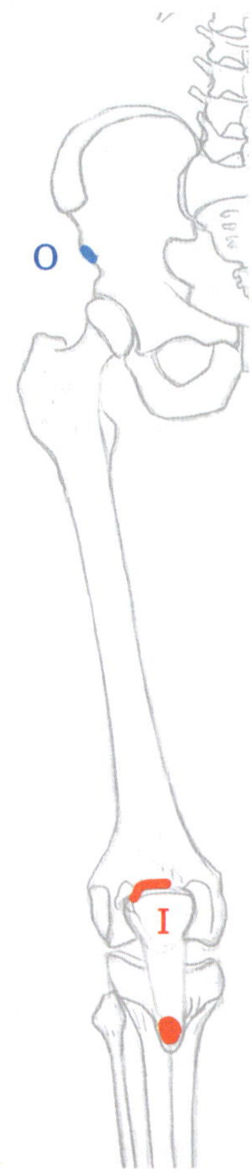

ANTERIOR

1. Extends leg at knee; 2. Flexes the hip

CHECKLIST

- O Iliopsoas
- O Pectineus
- O Adductor longus
- O Adductor magnus
- O Gracilis
- O Vastus lateralis
- O Vastus medialis
- O Rectus femoris

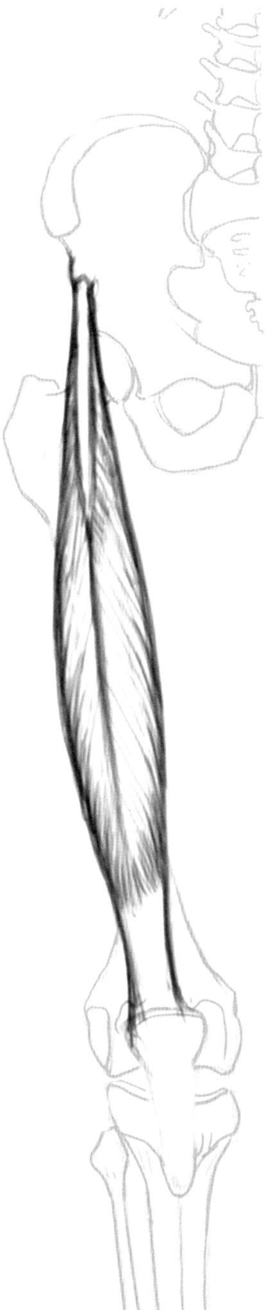

ANTERIOR

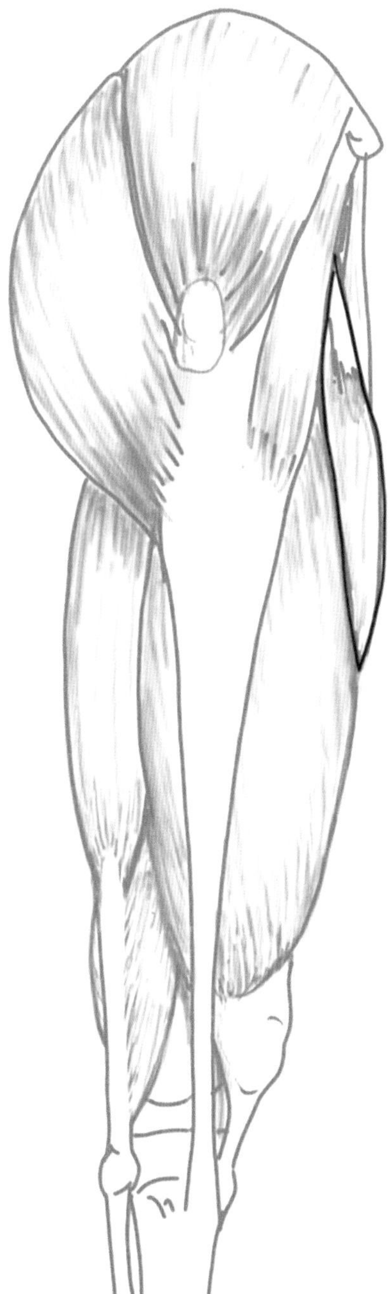

LATERAL

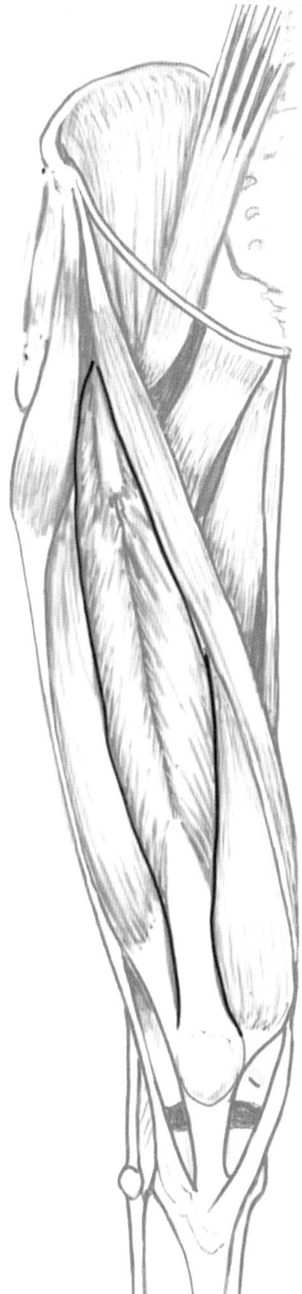

ANTERIOR

B.9. SEMIMEMBRANOSUS

STRUCTURE

The semimembranosus is large and full and has an interesting shape. The tendon at the top is more off to the side, and the lower one is at the inside of the knee, so it almost zigzags. The semimembranosus muscle is one of the three muscles that make up the hamstrings. The other two are the biceps femoris long head and the semitendinosus. The hamstrings all originate at the ischial tuberosity of the pelvis.

ORIGIN

At the ischial tuberosity ("sit bone") of the pelvis.

INSERTION

The top of the tibia, at the top inside corner.

ACTION

Flexes (1) and medially rotates the knee joint (points the foot inward). Extends the thigh at the hip joint.

1.

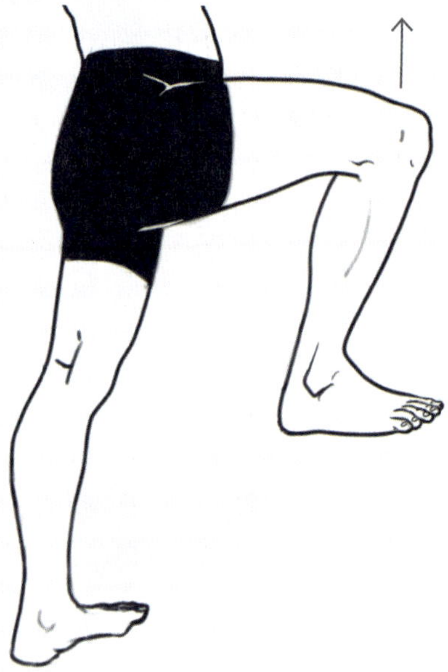

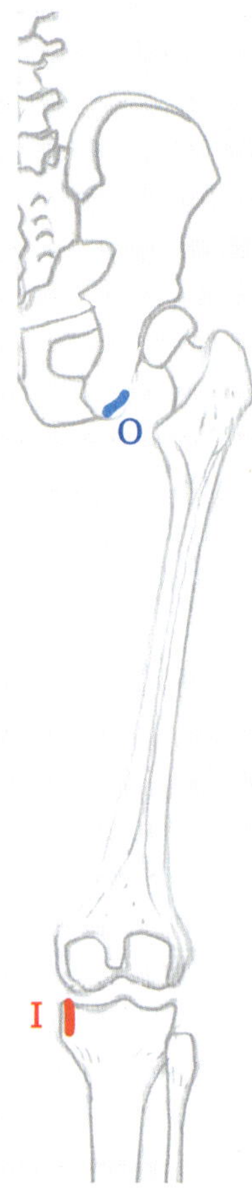

POSTERIOR

1. Flexes and medially rotates knee joint

CHECKLIST

- O Iliopsoas
- O Pectineus
- O Adductor longus
- O Adductor magnus
- O Gracilis
- O Vastus lateralis
- O Vastus medialis
- O Rectus femoris
- O Semimembranosus

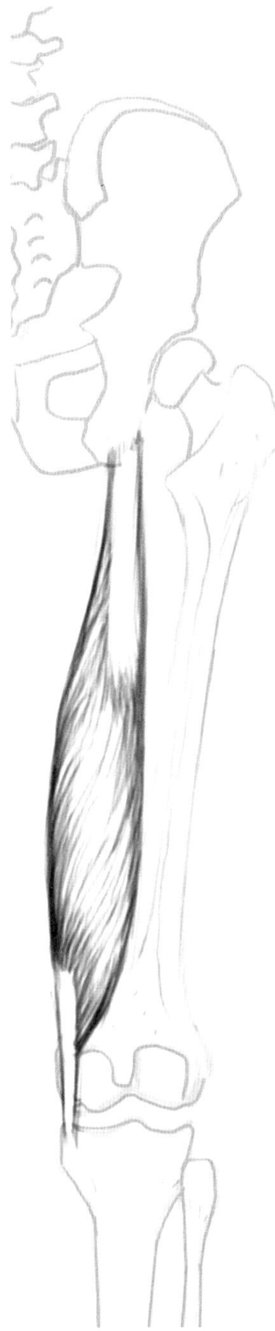

POSTERIOR

B.9. SEMIMEMBRANOSUS

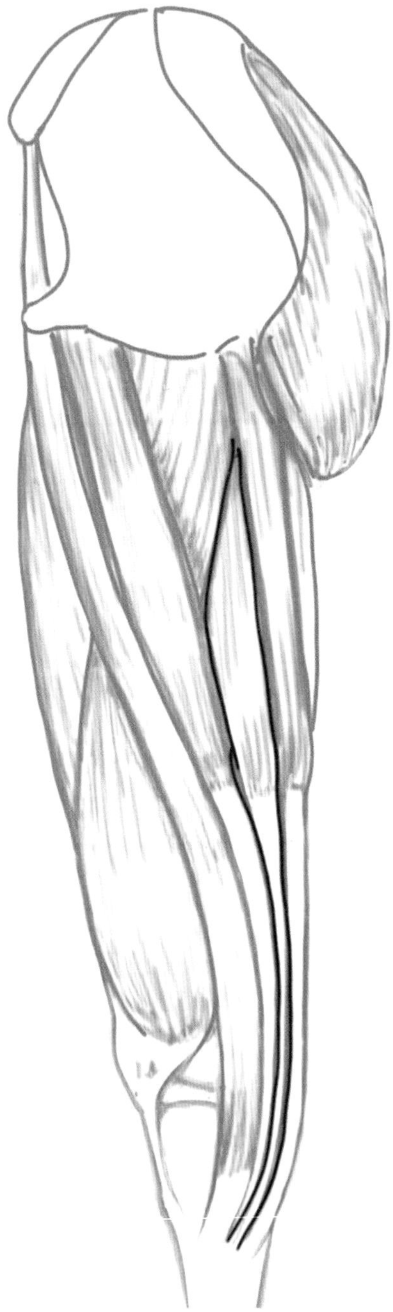

MEDIAL

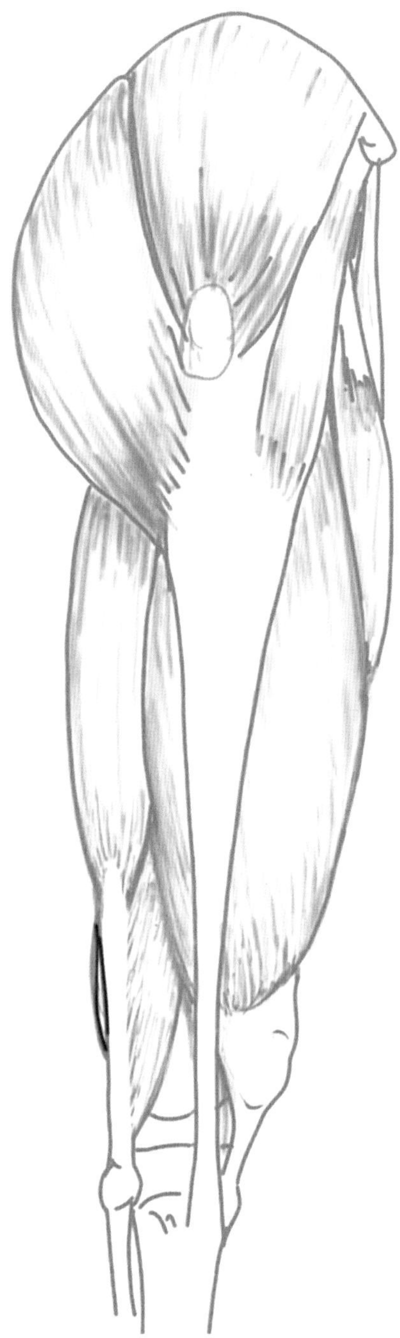

LATERAL

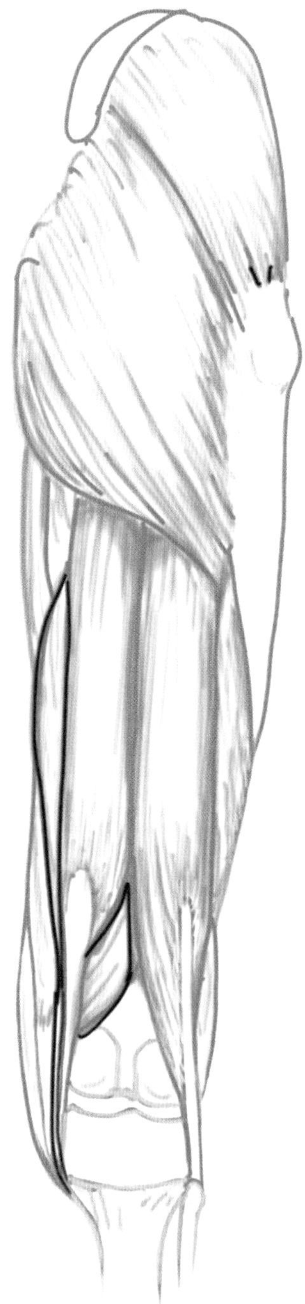

POSTERIOR

B.10. SEMITENDINOSUS

STRUCTURE

The semitendinosus is a long muscle tapered at both its origin and insertion. It is one of the three muscles that make up what is called the hamstrings. The other two muscles are the semimembranosus and the biceps femoris long head.

ORIGIN

The ischial tuberosity of the pelvis.

INSERTION

The upper medial aspect of the tibia.

ACTION

Flexes (1) and medially rotates the lower leg (points the foot inward). Extends the thigh at the hip joint.

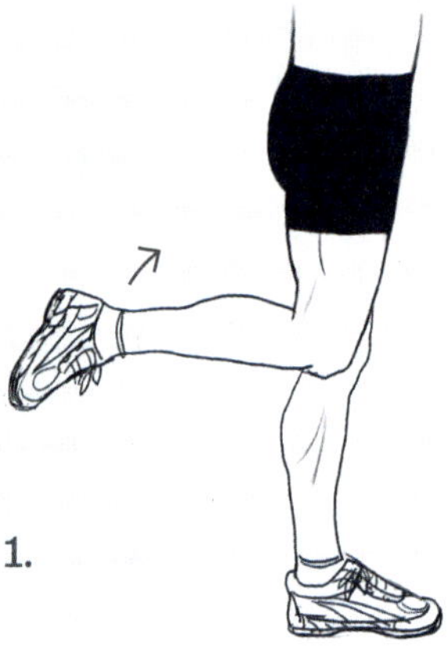

1.

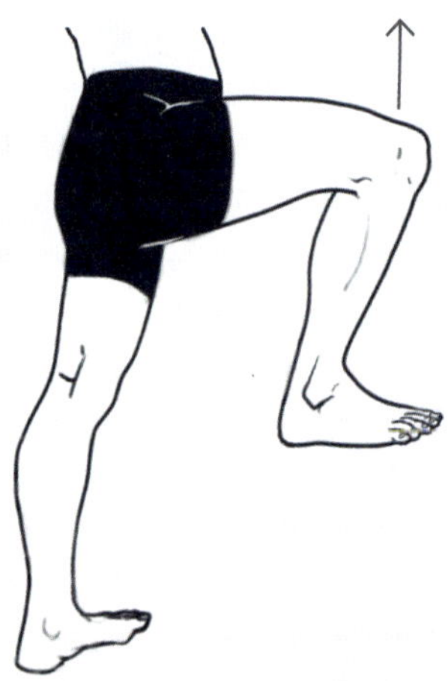

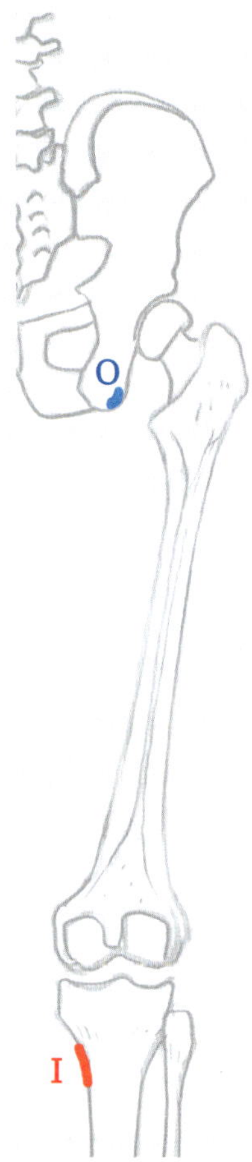

POSTERIOR
(REAR)

1. *Flexes and medially rotates lower leg*

CHECKLIST

- O Iliopsoas
- O Pectineus
- O Adductor longus
- O Adductor magnus
- O Gracilis
- O Vastus lateralis
- O Vastus medialis
- O Rectus femoris
- O Semimembranosus
- O Semitendinosus

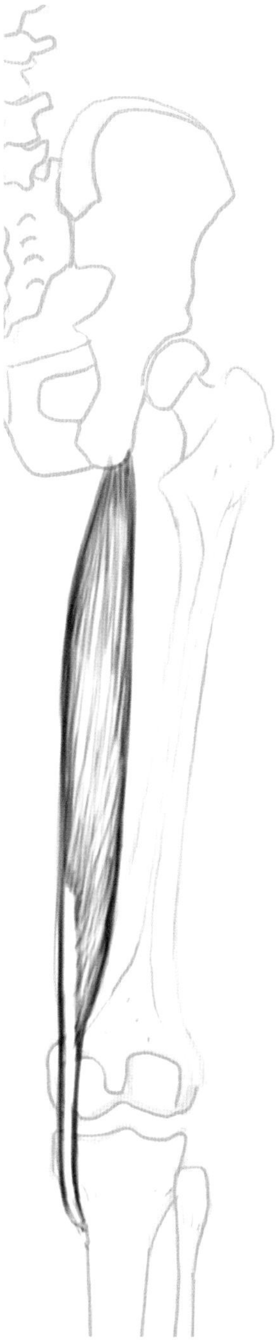

POSTERIOR

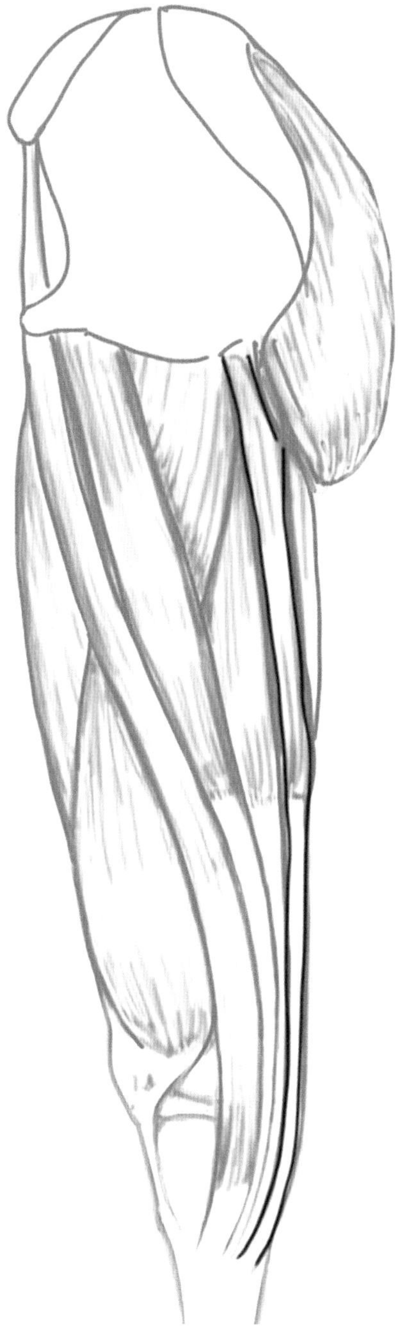

MEDIAL

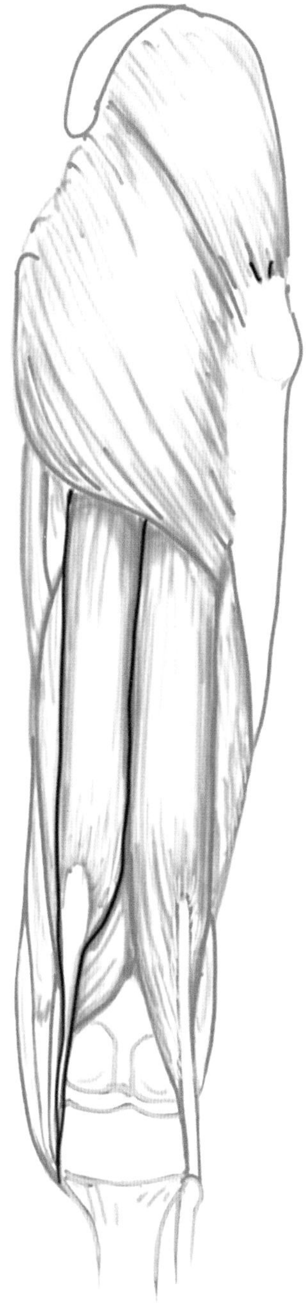

POSTERIOR

B.11. BICEPS FEMORIS, LONG AND SHORT HEADS

STRUCTURE

The biceps femoris has two heads. One is long and tapered at both ends, and the other is like a flat knife blade.

ORIGIN

The long head attaches on the ischial tuberosity. It is the third of the three hamstring muscles. The short head attaches on the back of the femur at the linea aspera.

INSERTION

Both heads insert at the head of the fibula with a common tendon, the biceps femoris tendon, which is very prominent on the lateral side of the leg when bent. It becomes a groove when the leg is straight, like the semitendinosus.

ACTION

Both heads flex the knee joint (1) and rotate it laterally, pointing the foot outward. The long head extends the thigh at the hip joint.

1.

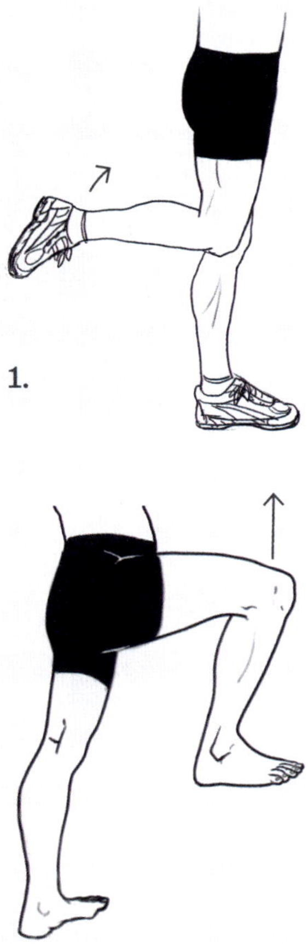

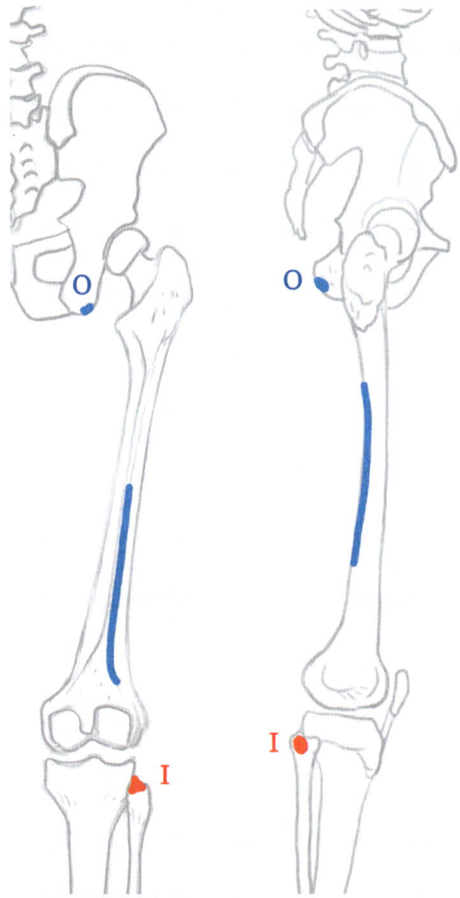

1. Flexes and laterally rotates knee joint

CHECKLIST

- O Iliopsoas
- O Pectineus
- O Adductor longus
- O Adductor magnus
- O Gracilis
- O Vastus lateralis
- O Vastus medialis
- O Rectus femoris
- O Semimembranosus
- O Semitendinosus
- O Biceps femoris, *long and short heads*

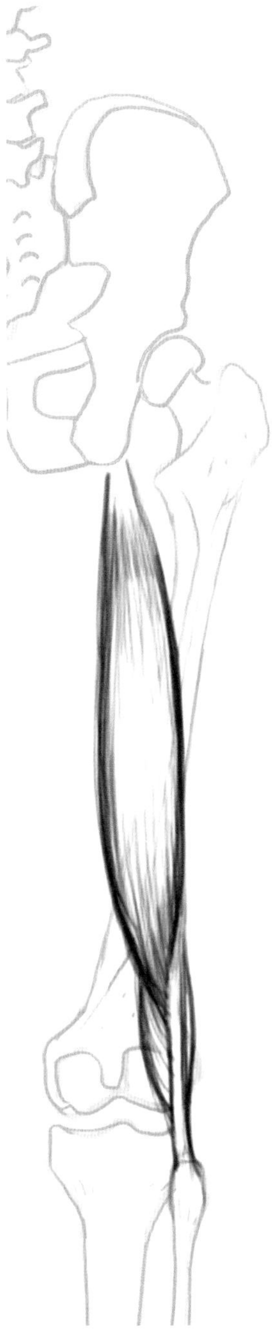

POSTERIOR

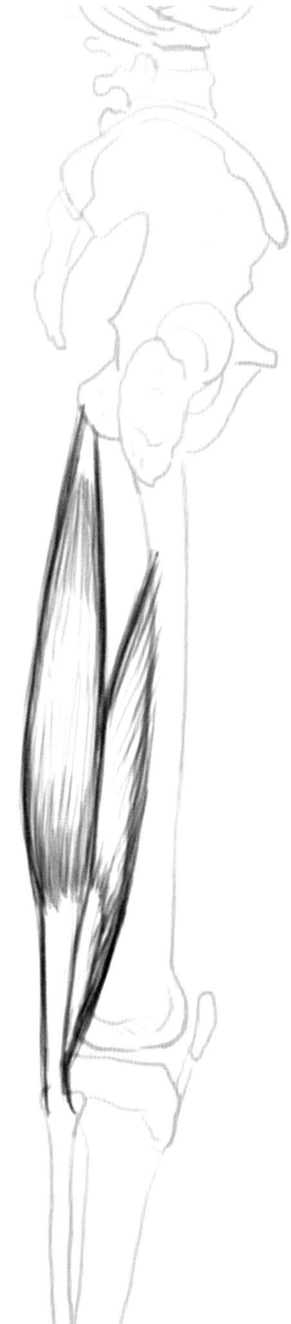

LATERAL

B.11. BICEPS FEMORIS, LONG AND SHORT HEADS

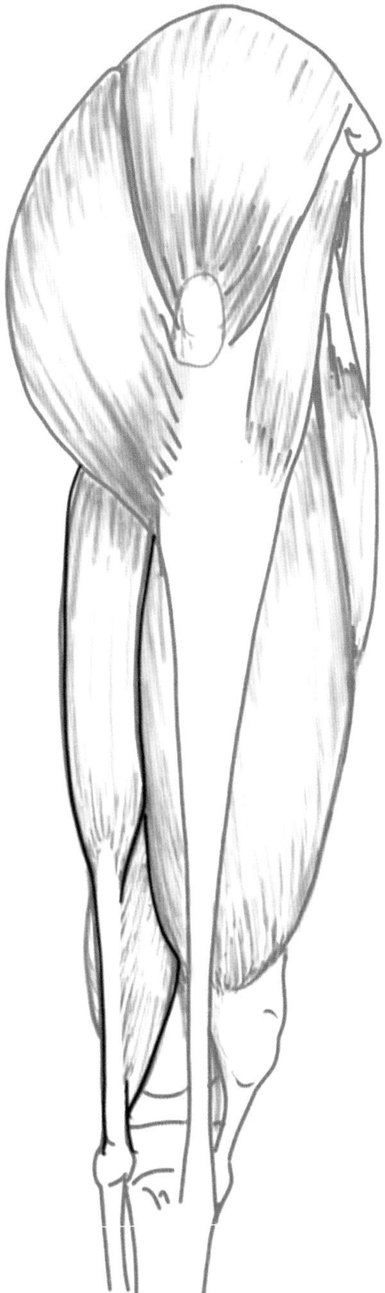

LATERAL

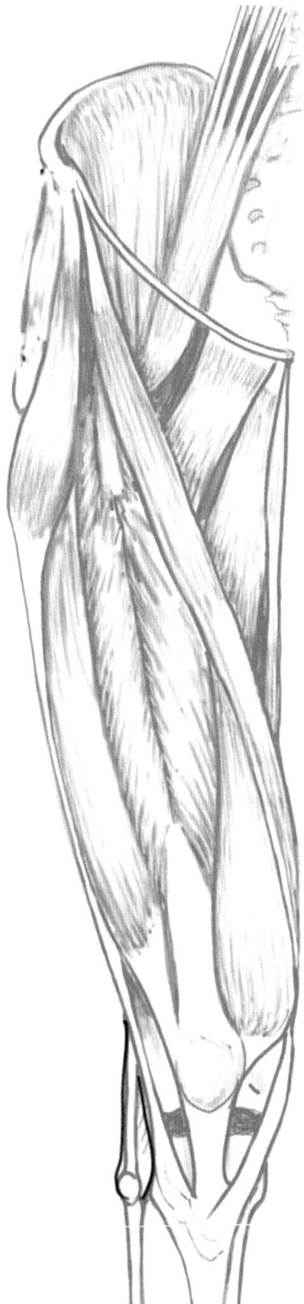

ANTERIOR

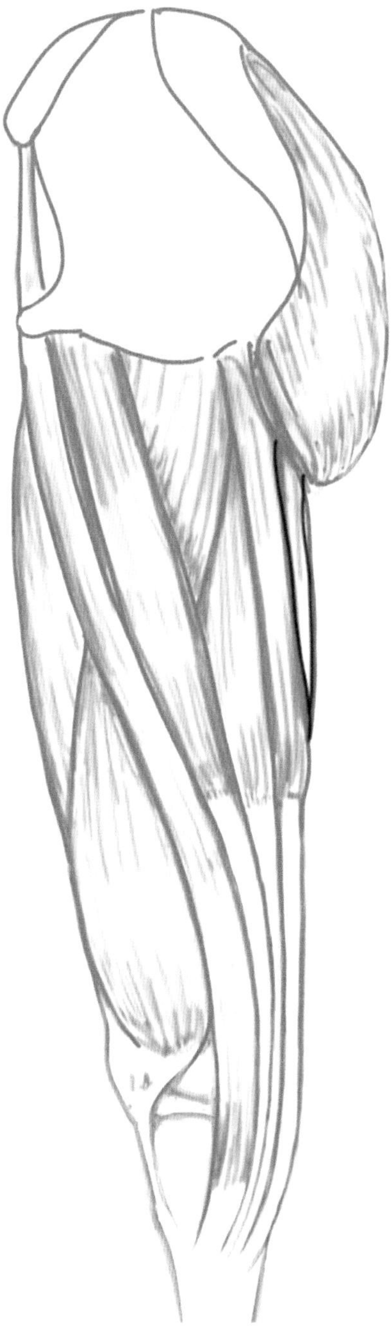

MEDIAL

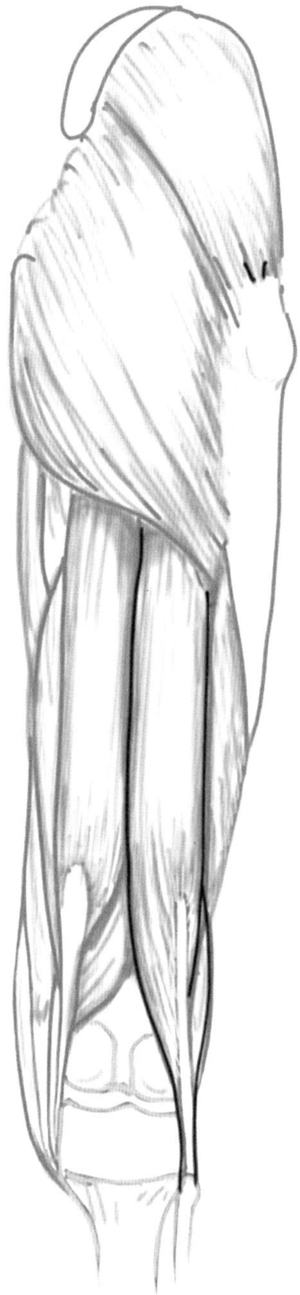

POSTERIOR

B.12. SARTORIUS

STRUCTURE

The sartorius is the longest muscle of the human body. It resembles a belt that spirals from the pelvis point to the inside of the knee and it separates the adductors from the quadriceps. It creates an indentation on the inside of the leg, but when the leg is contracted or scissored, it can pop out and can be seen as a convex form. It's called the "tailor's muscle," from the Latin root word for tailor, or "one who patches." Tailors often sat in lotus position when hemming garments and used this muscle to make all of the movements listed to be in that position.

ORIGIN

Just below the anterior superior iliac spine (ASIS) of the pelvis, the pointy, protruding part of the pelvis just under one's beltline.

INSERTION

On the top inside of the tibia, close to the tibial tuberosity, the "nose" of the tibia.

ACTION

The sartorius is rather weak, but it helps other muscles do a variety of things. It flexes, abducts, and laterally rotates the hip at the ball of the femur/acetabulum. It is a relatively strong flexor of the lower leg. When someone sits in "lotus" position, the sartorius is responsible for all of those actions.

1.

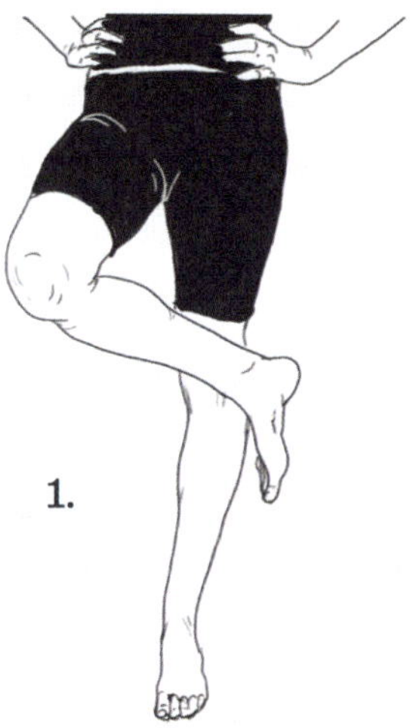

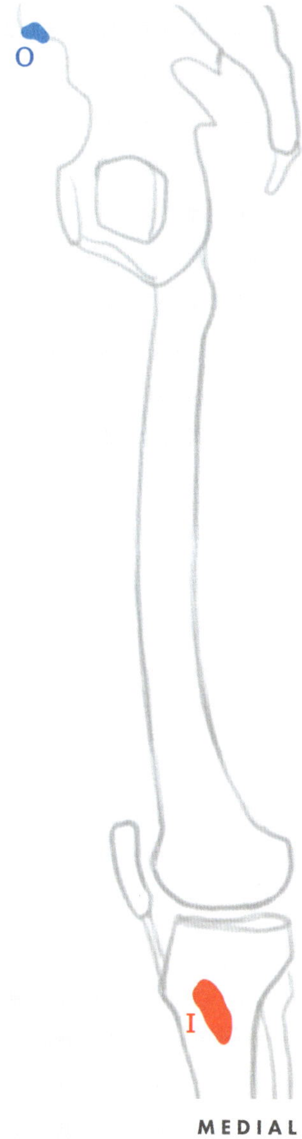

1. Flexes, abducts, and laterally rotates the hip at the ball of the femur/acetabulum

CHECKLIST

- O Iliopsoas
- O Pectineus
- O Adductor longus
- O Adductor magnus
- O Gracilis
- O Vastus lateralis
- O Vastus medialis
- O Rectus femoris
- O Semimembranosus
- O Semitendinosus
- O Biceps femoris, *long and short heads*
- O Sartorius

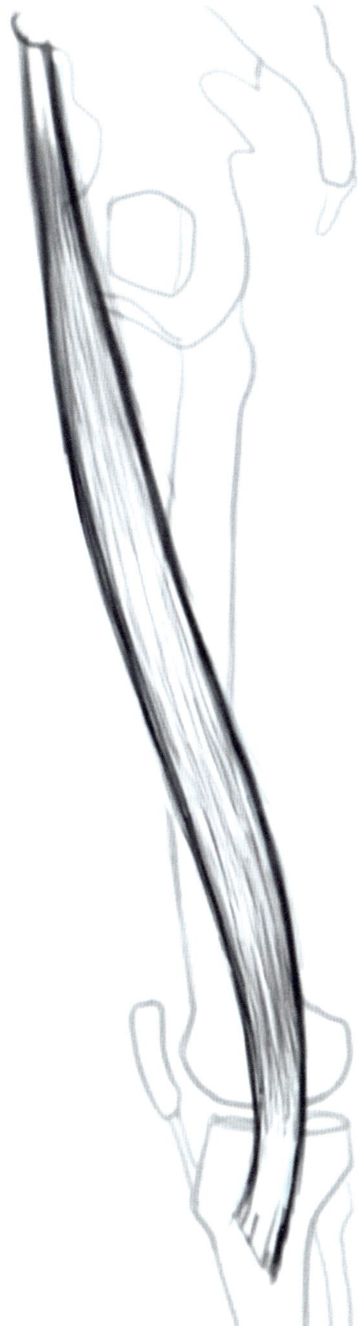

MEDIAL

B.12. SARTORIUS

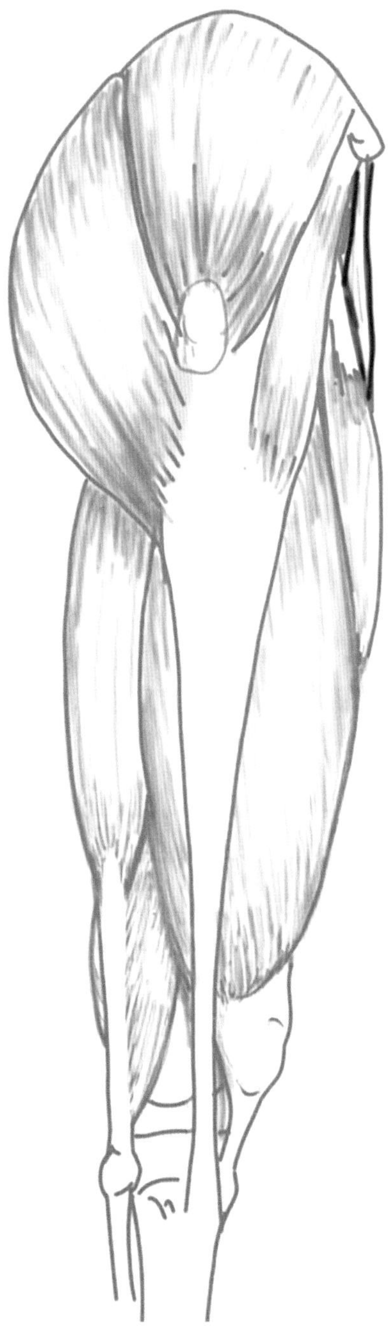

LATERAL

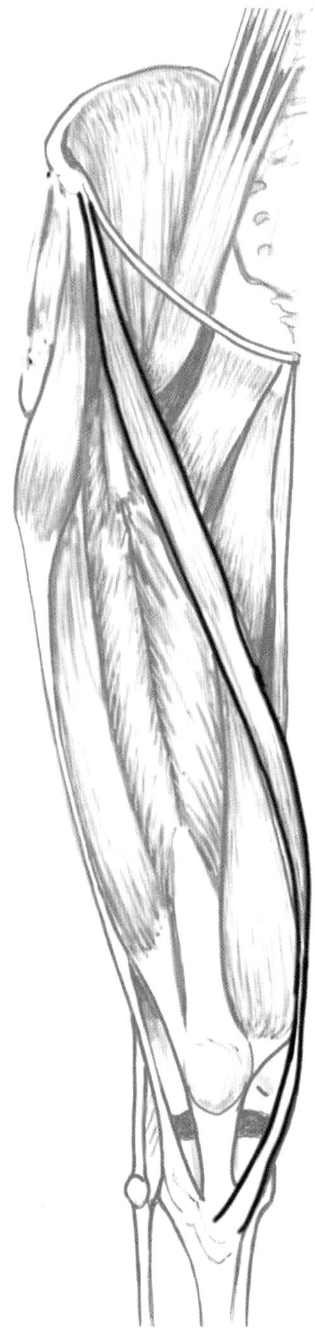

ANTERIOR

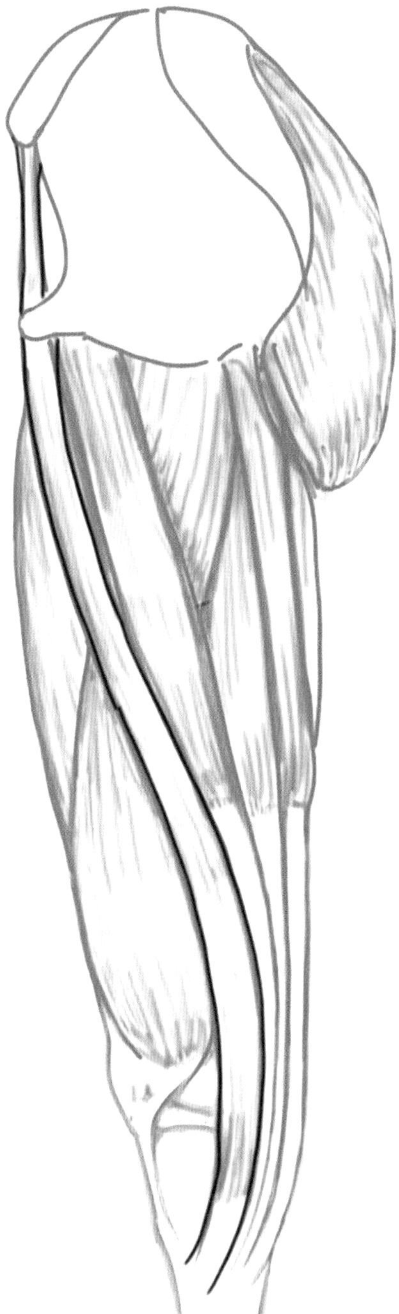

MEDIAL

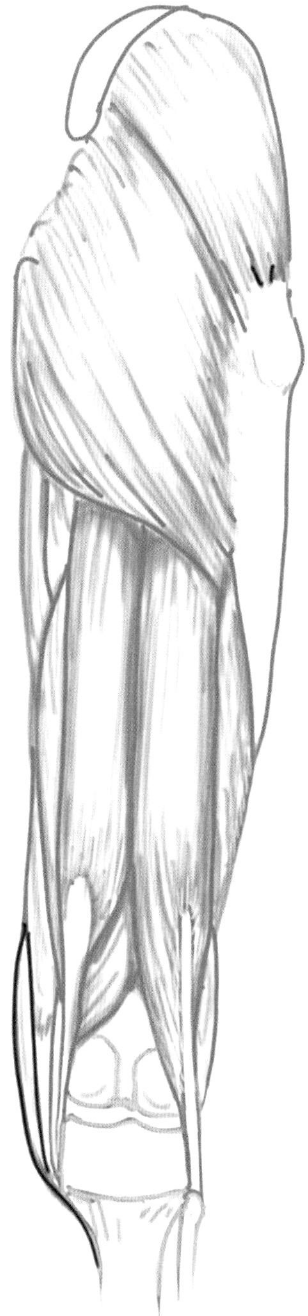

POSTERIOR

B.13. GLUTEUS MEDIUS

STRUCTURE

The gluteus medius is a large fanlike muscle.

ORIGIN

The ilium of the pelvis.

INSERTION

The greater trochanter of the femur.

ACTION

A strong abductor, it pulls the thigh outward (1), such as when doing the splits.

1.

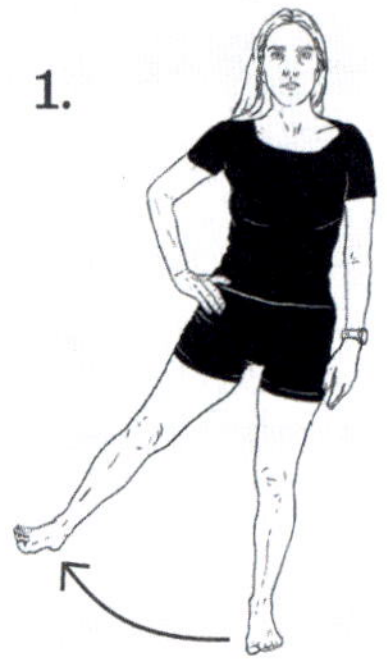

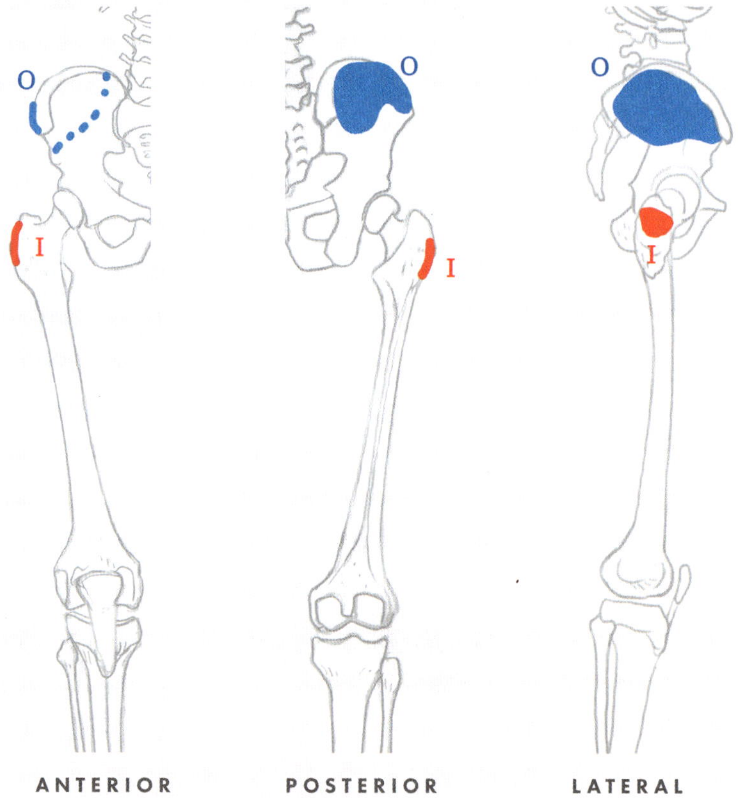

1. Pulls thigh outward

CHECKLIST

- O Iliopsoas
- O Pectineus
- O Adductor longus
- O Adductor magnus
- O Gracilis
- O Vastus lateralis
- O Vastus medialis
- O Rectus femoris
- O Semimembranosus
- O Semitendinosus
- O Biceps femoris, *long and short heads*
- O Sartorius
- O Gluteus medius

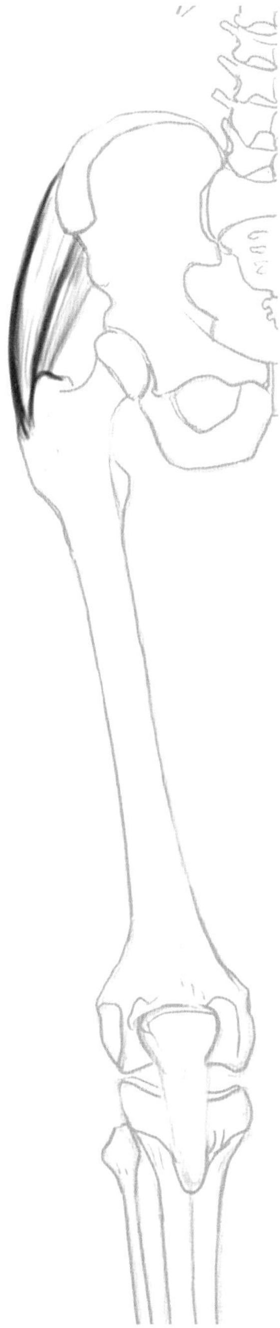

ANTERIOR

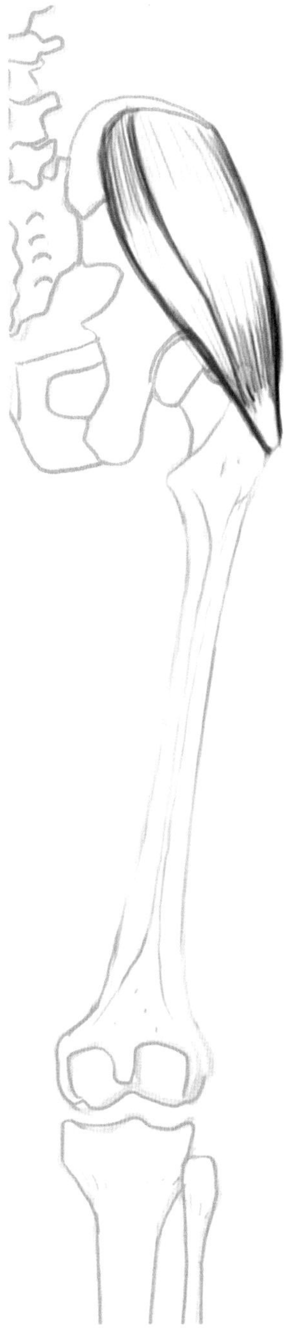

POSTERIOR

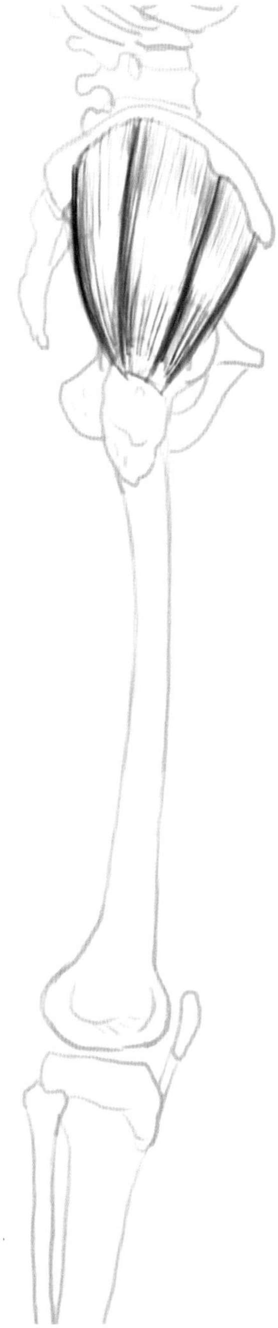

LATERAL

B.13. GLUTEUS MEDIUS

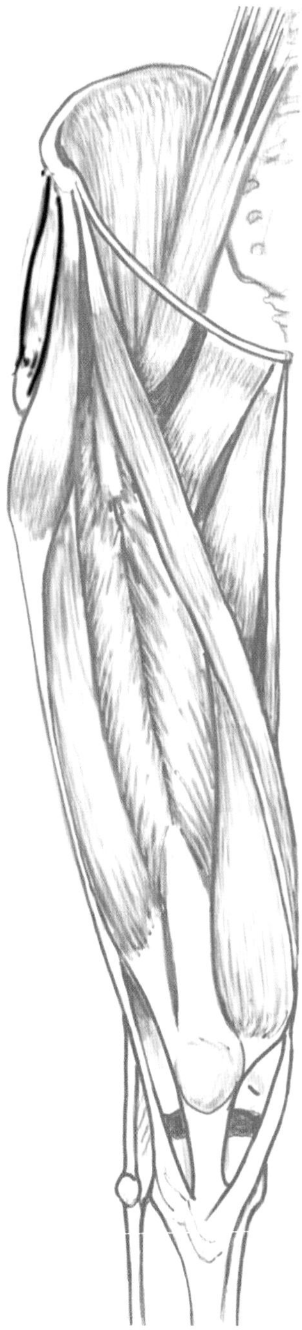

ANTERIOR

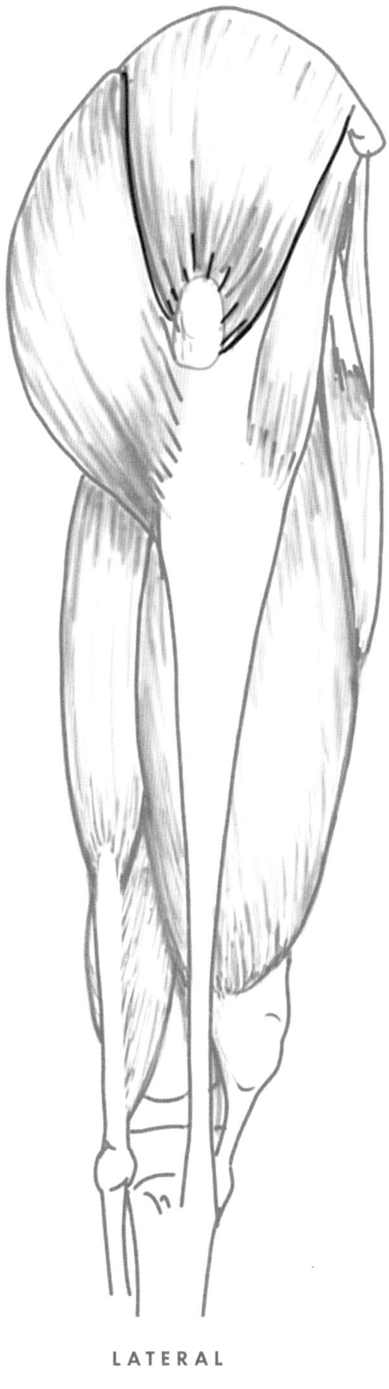

LATERAL

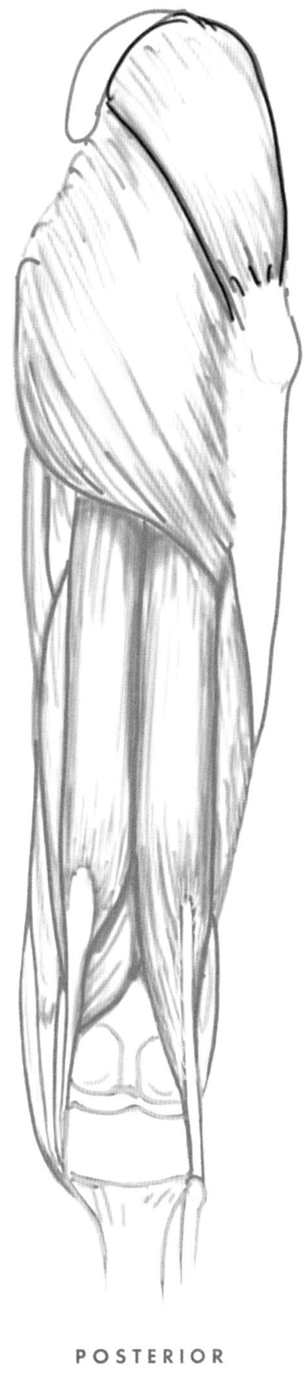

POSTERIOR

B.14. GLUTEUS MAXIMUS

STRUCTURE

The gluteus maximus is a huge, strong muscle that has almost a tire-like shape surrounding the side of the hip.

ORIGIN

Part of the ilium and sacrum.

INSERTION

The bottom border blends into the iliotibial (IT) band, which inserts into the side of the tibia. There is a small part that inserts into the upper back side of the femur, just below the greater trochanter.

ACTION

Extends the thigh (1) and laterally rotates it as well. The upper fibers help abduct the thigh, and the lower fibers of the muscle help in adduction.

1.

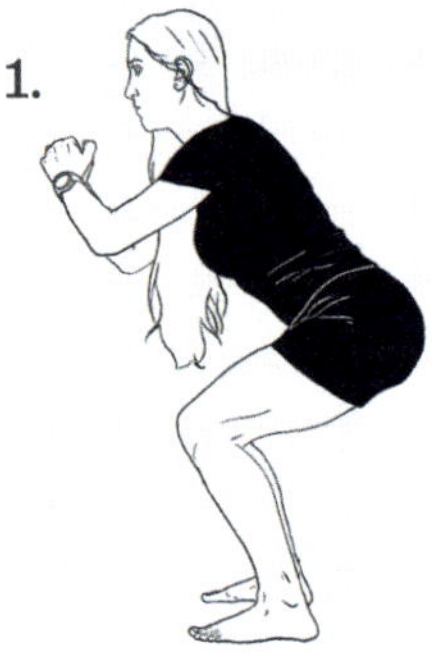

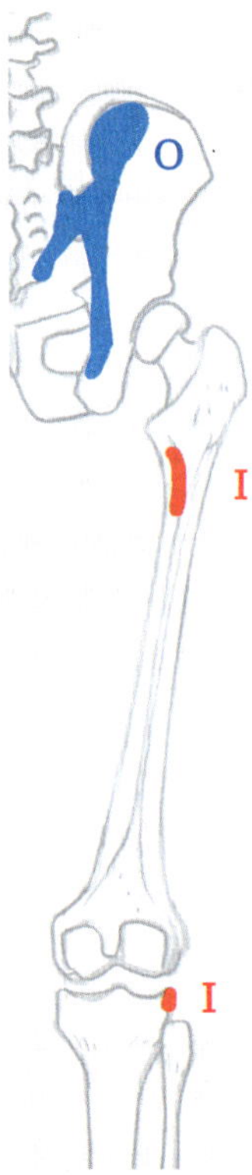

POSTERIOR

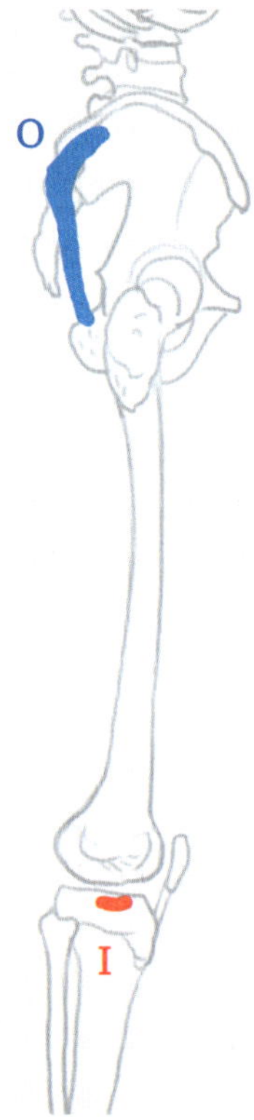

LATERAL

1. Extends and laterally rotates thigh

CHECKLIST

- O Iliopsoas
- O Pectineus
- O Adductor longus
- O Adductor magnus
- O Gracilis
- O Vastus lateralis
- O Vastus medialis
- O Rectus femoris
- O Semimembranosus
- O Semitendinosus
- O Biceps femoris, *long and short heads*
- O Sartorius
- O Gluteus medius
- O Gluteus maximus

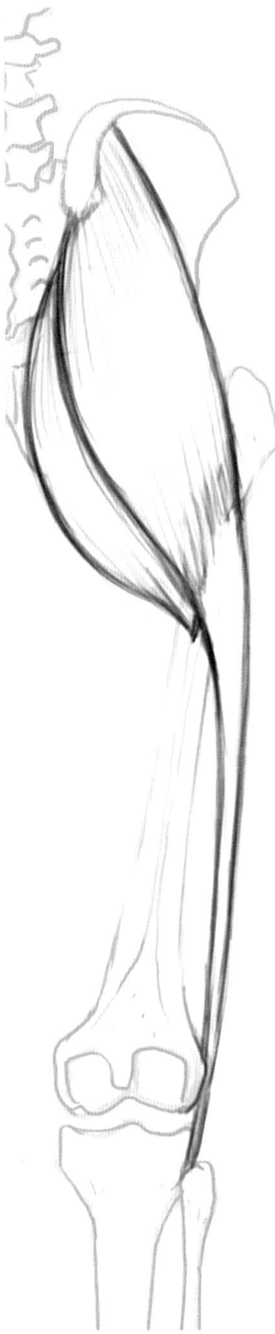

POSTERIOR

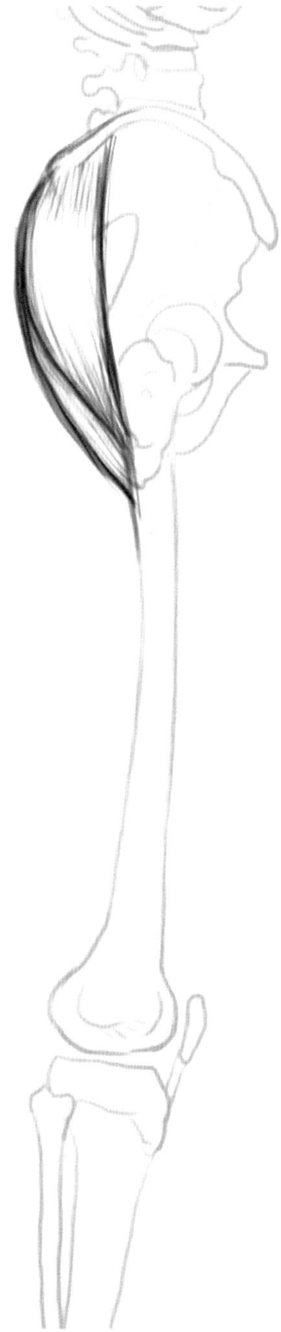

LATERAL

B.14. GLUTEUS MAXIMUS

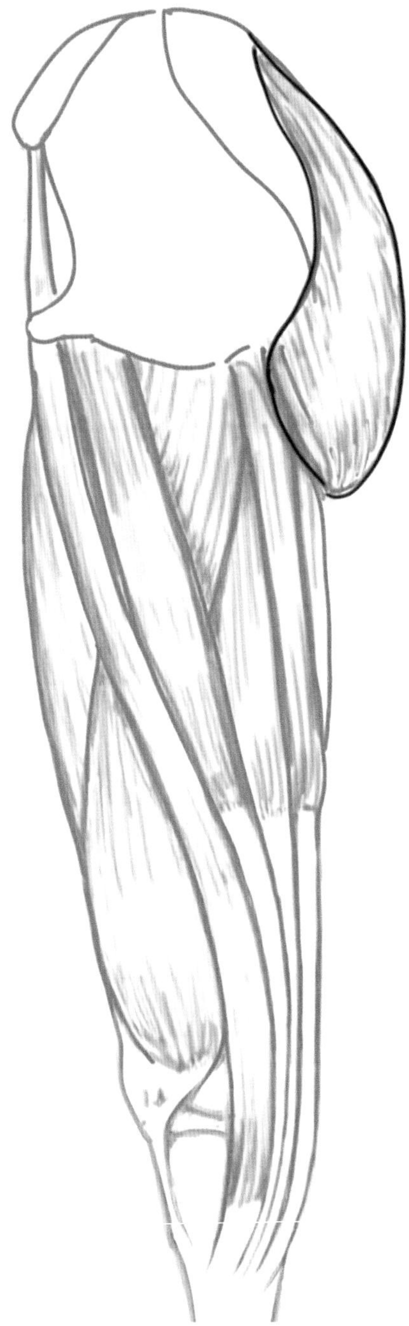

MEDIAL

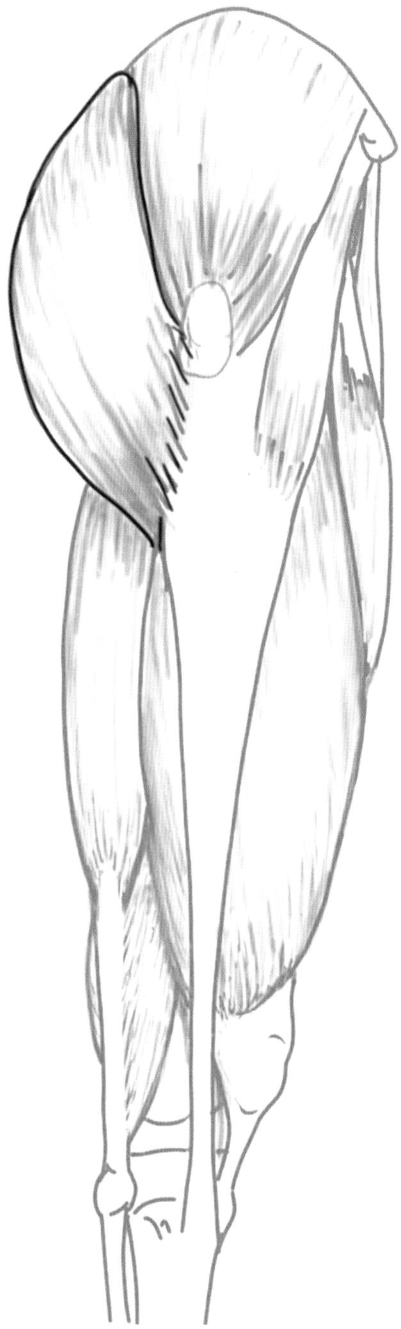

LATERAL

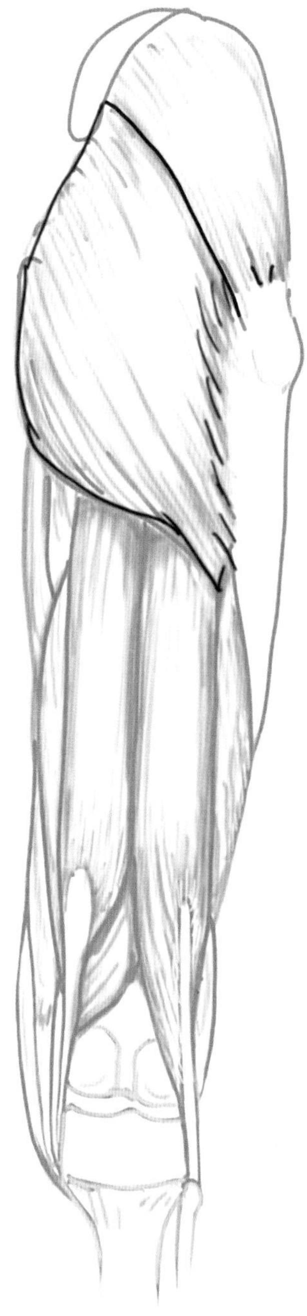

POSTERIOR

B.15. TENSOR FASCIAE LATA (PLURAL: LATAE)

STRUCTURE

The tensor fasciae lata (often referred to as the TFL) is a teardrop-shaped muscle inside the fascia (thin sheet of connective material) that is part of the iliotibial (IT) band. The iliotibial band is a strong, thick sheet of connective tissue that surrounds the thigh, but on the side it is so much thicker than the rest of the sheath (like a sausage casing) that it is the only important part for the artist to know. It's broad at the top, attaches to the ilium of the pelvis, and narrows toward the outside of the tibia, thus its name: ilio = ilium, and tibial = tibia.

ORIGIN

By the anterior superior iliac spine (ASIS).

INSERTION

Attached to the iliotibial band (IT band), which inserts on the lateral side of the upper part of the tibia.

ACTION

Flexes (1), abducts, and medially rotates the thigh (turns the thigh inward). It pulls strongly on the iliotibial band and can often make the band appear to be stringy and tight on the side of the thigh (on top of the vastus lateralis) like tight tape.

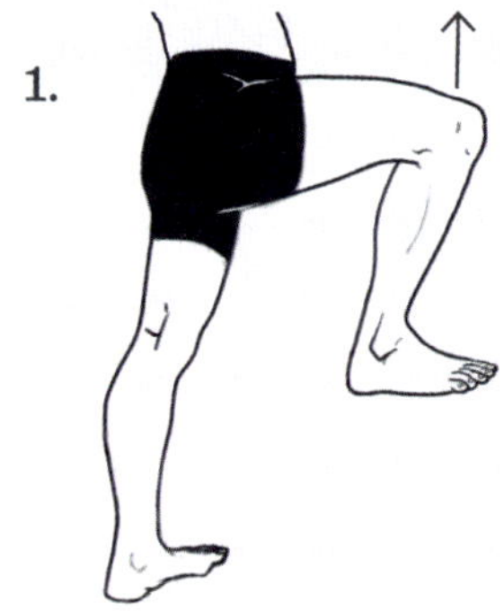

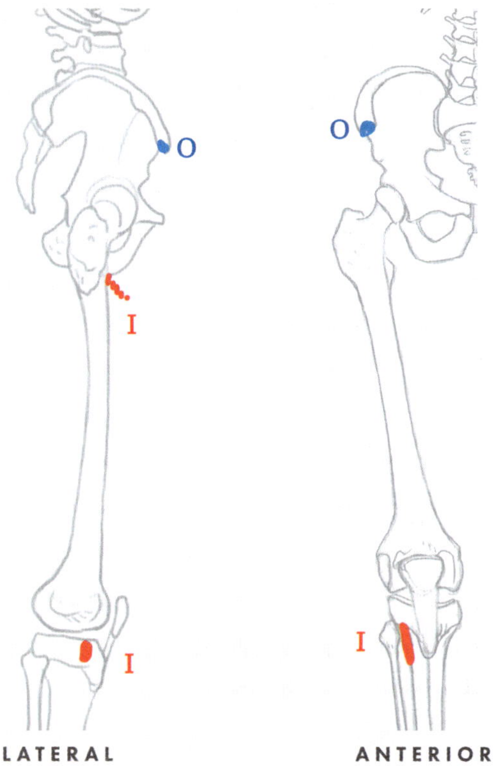

1. Flexes, abducts, and medially rotates thigh

CHECKLIST

- O Iliopsoas
- O Pectineus
- O Adductor longus
- O Adductor magnus
- O Gracilis
- O Vastus lateralis
- O Vastus medialis
- O Rectus femoris
- O Semimembranosus
- O Semitendinosus
- O Biceps femoris, *long and short heads*
- O Sartorius
- O Gluteus medius
- O Gluteus maximus
- O Tensor fasciae lata

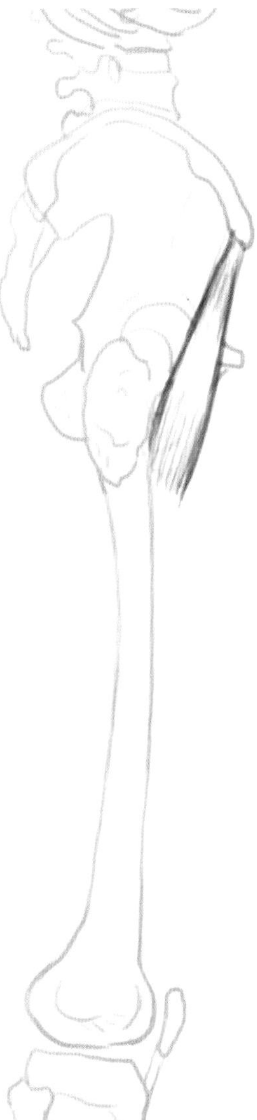

LATERAL

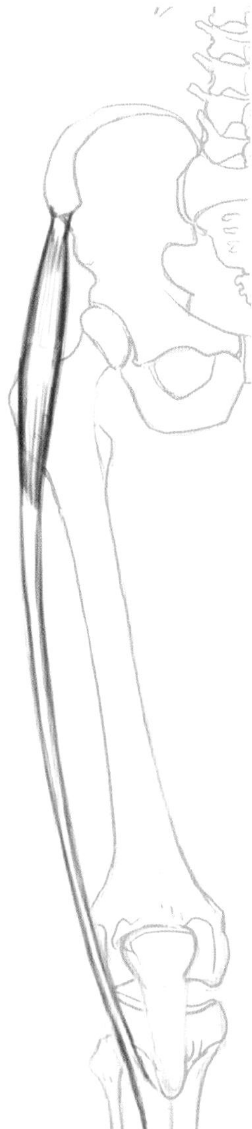

ANTERIOR

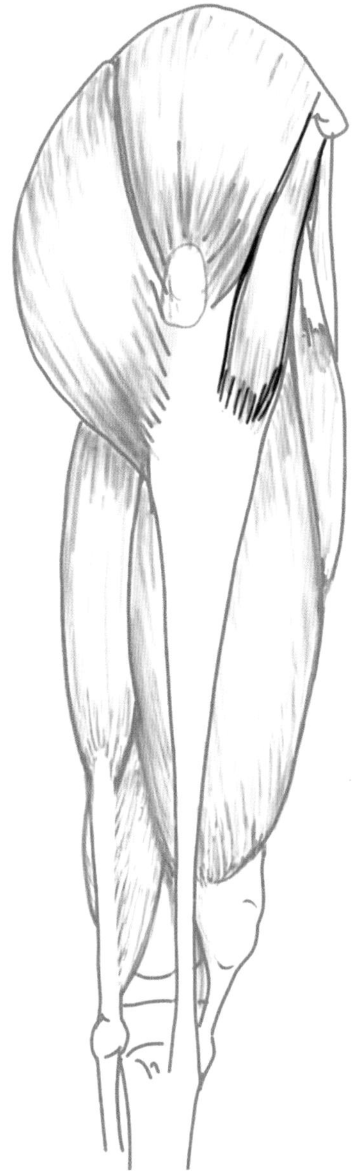

LATERAL

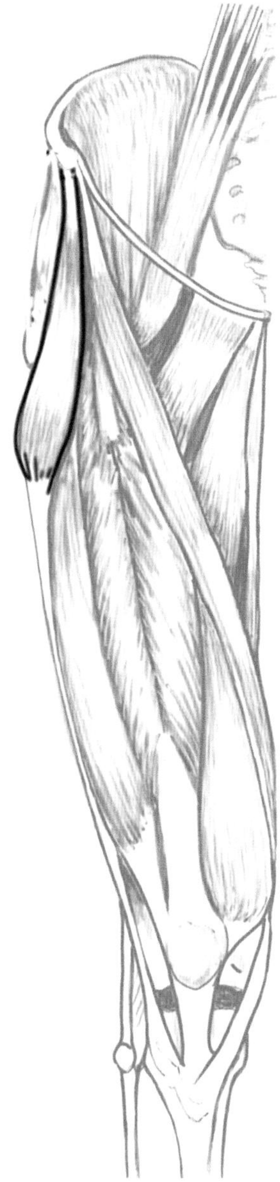

ANTERIOR

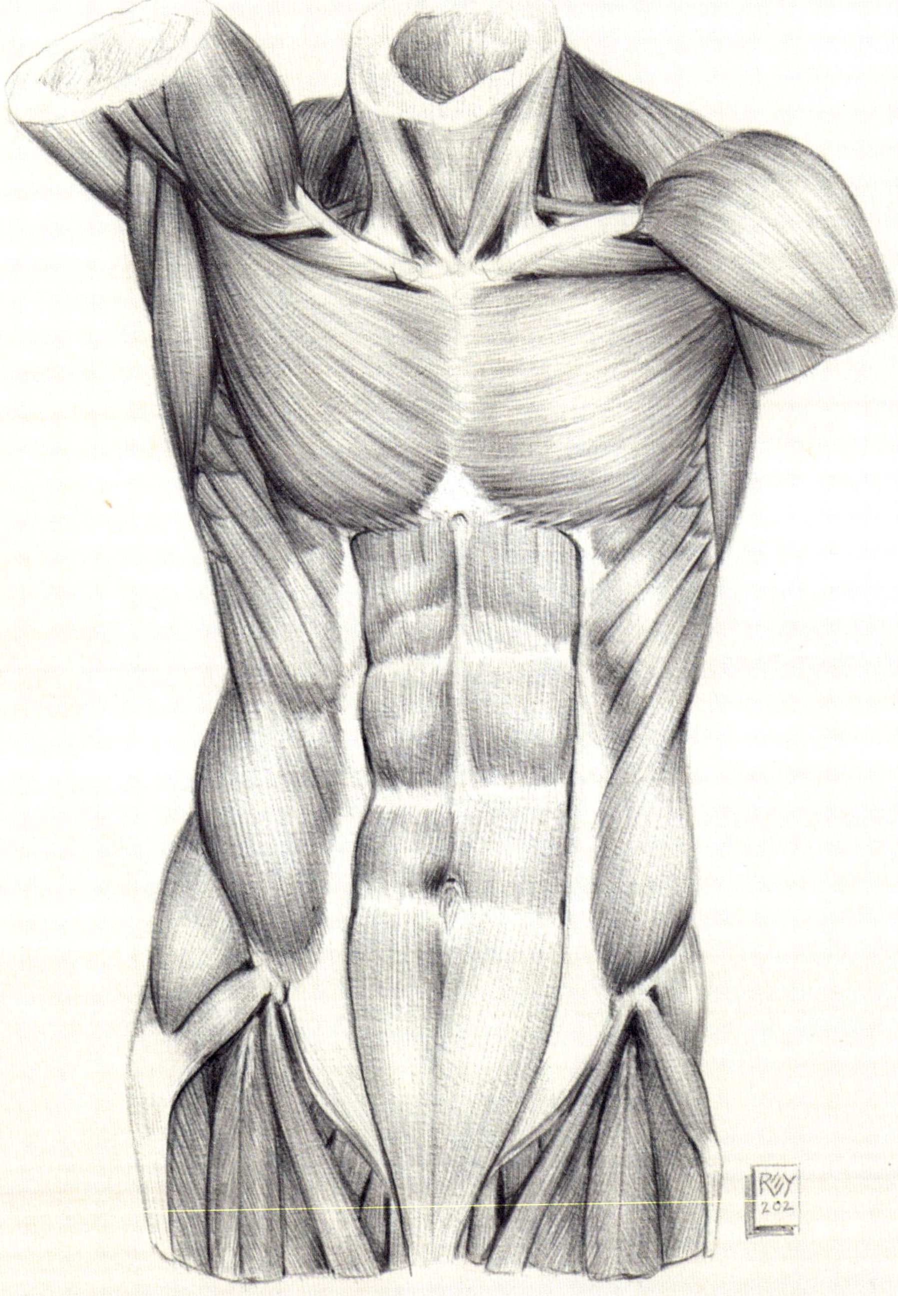

CHAPTER C

THE FRONT TORSO

The torso contains all the organs of the body except the brain. The front torso muscles enable the spine to flex forward, like when you bow and bend side to side, and they allow you to twist. The thorax (rib cage) and the torso muscles also protect the vital organs. The pectoral muscles control arm and shoulder actions, such as pushing, lifting, and adducting or hugging. One of the more interesting aspects of the front torso is that the pectoral muscles (**C.4.**) and the external oblique muscles (**C.3.**) are both attached to the center of the torso by a thin sheet of tendon called an aponeurosis, which covers the rectus abdominis (**C.1.**). The reason this is important is that when the body twists, this tendon can pull the external obliques over the rectus abdominis, creating what I call "transparency of form." As an example, imagine there is a sock lying on a bed, and then you place a sheet over the bed—you would still see a form under the sheet. That sock and the sheet over it creates the transparency of form.

C.1. RECTUS ABDOMINIS

STRUCTURE

The rectus abdominis is shaped like the front half of a surfboard. It is flat and has sections of tendinous, fibrous bands that segment into six pads of muscle (a "six pack"). Sometimes there is one or two segments below the navel. Each half of the muscle meets at the center line of the abdomen called the linea alba ("white line").

ORIGIN

The pubic bone and over the pubic symphysis (the cartilage at the pubic area in between both halves of the pelvis).

INSERTION

The cartilage of the ribs at the fifth, sixth, and seventh ribs and the xiphoid process (the small "arrow-head" at the bottom of the sternum, or breastbone).

ACTION

Flexes the trunk (1), the vertebral column, such as when bowing or doing sit ups.

1.

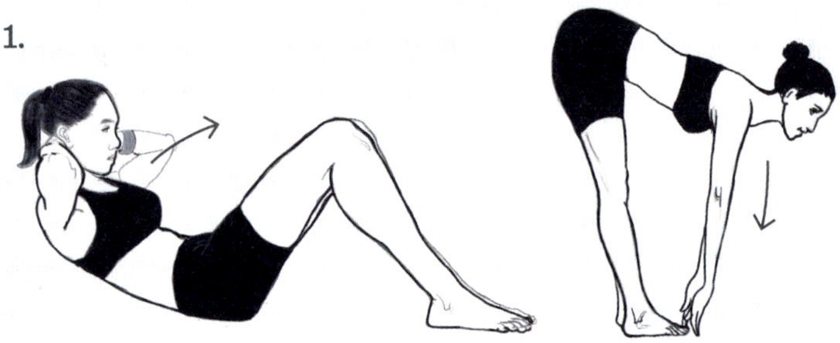

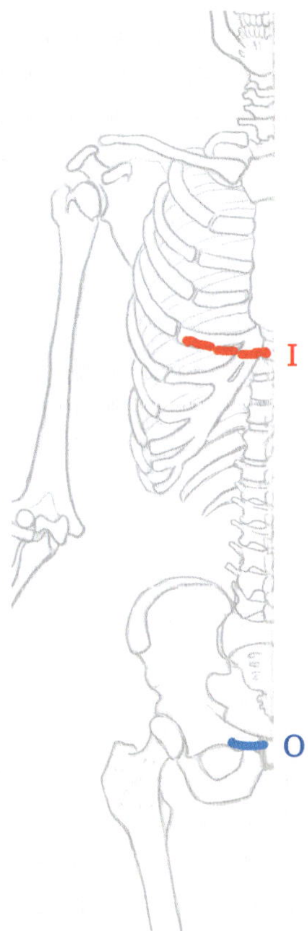

ANTERIOR

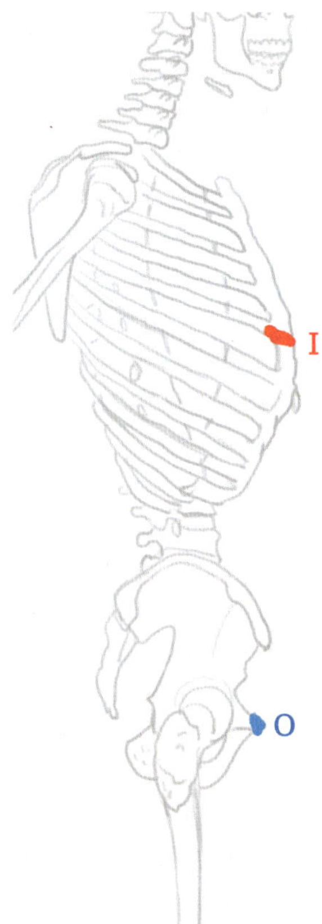

LATERAL

1. Flexes trunk

CHECKLIST

○ Rectus abdominis

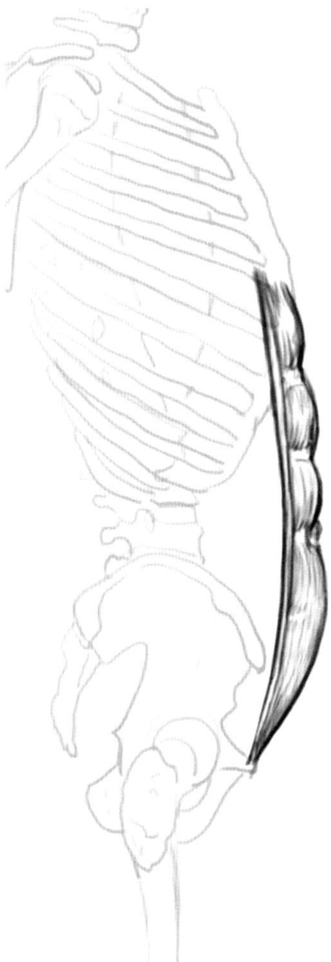

LATERAL

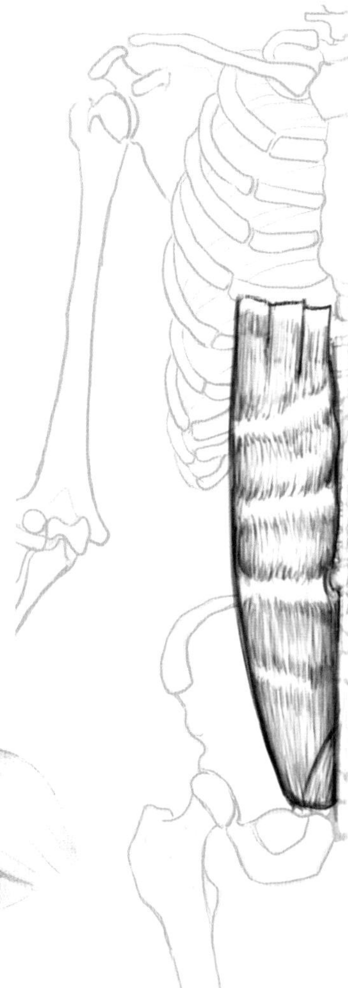

ANTERIOR

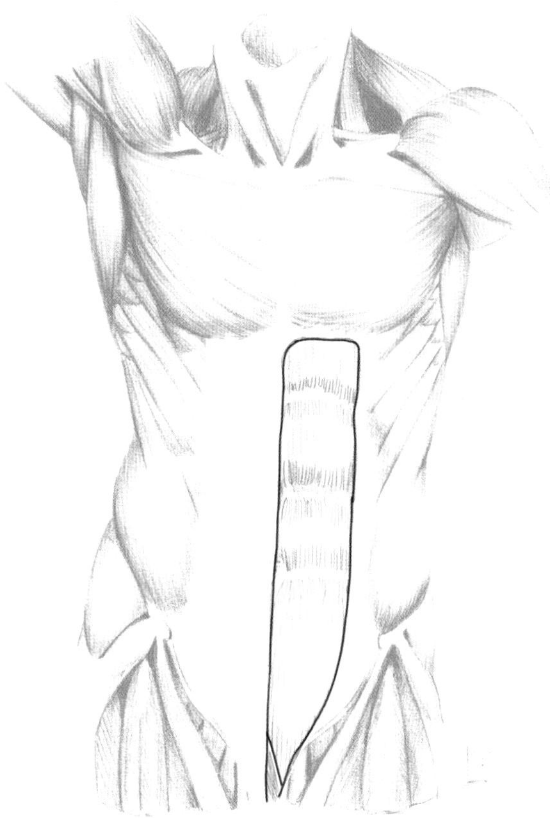

ANTERIOR

(with the aponeurosis cut to show the rectus abdominis underneath)

C.2. SERRATUS ANTERIOR

STRUCTURE

The serratus anterior muscle is made up of nine "fingers" called digitations. The serratus anterior has two sections. The first three digitations are the superior (higher) forms, which are flatter than the inferior (lower) forms, which are fuller. The upper forms are not seen, as they are deep under larger muscles. You can see some of the lower forms, four or five at the most, pop out from under the latissimus dorsi. On a muscular figure they can be quite plump and fanlike, especially when the arms are up.

ORIGIN

Each "finger" attaches to a rib, one through nine. The muscle is fanlike and hugs the rib cage as if holding it up. The serratus anterior meshes (interlocks) with the external oblique.

INSERTION

The front edge (underneath) of the scapula by the medial border, the border that roughly parallels the spine. The muscle is completely underneath the scapula, between it and the rib cage.

ACTION

It protracts the scapula (moves the scapula forward) and helps lift the arm (1).

1.

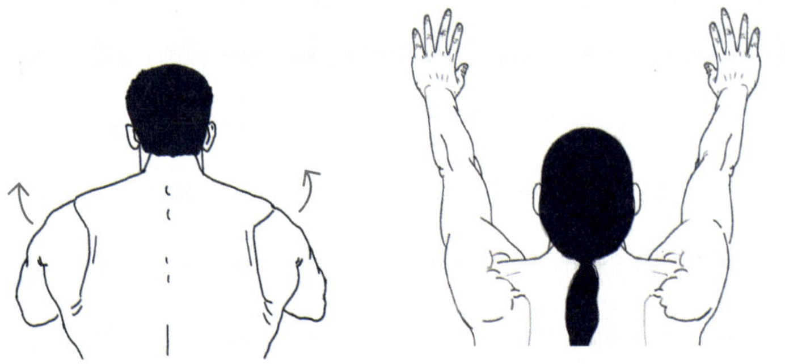

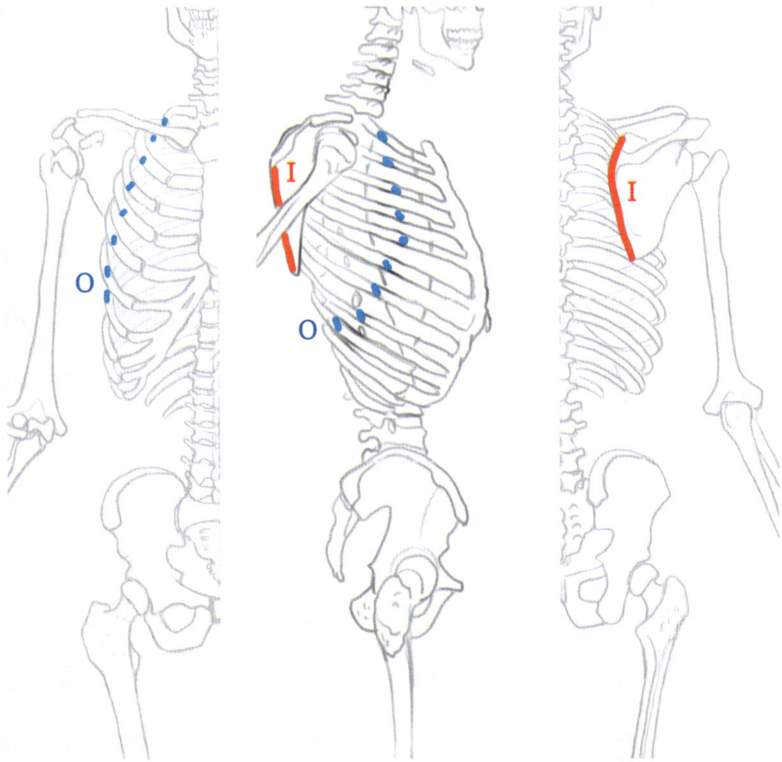

1. Protracts scapula and lifts arm

CHECKLIST

- O Rectus abdominis
- O Serratus anterior

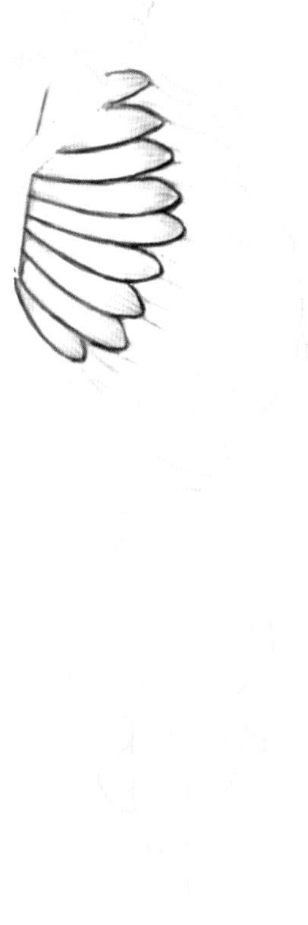

LATERAL

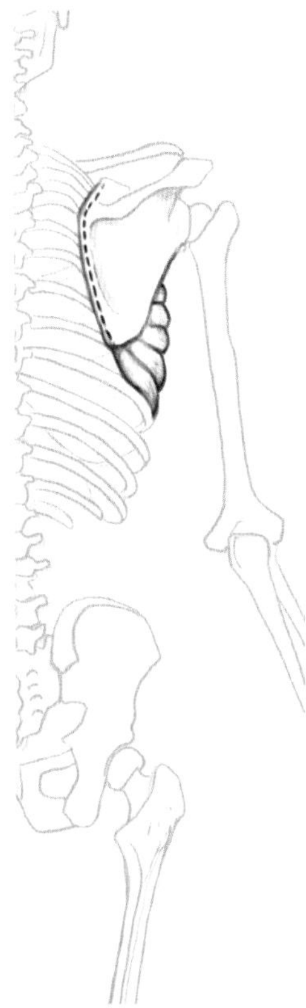

POSTERIOR

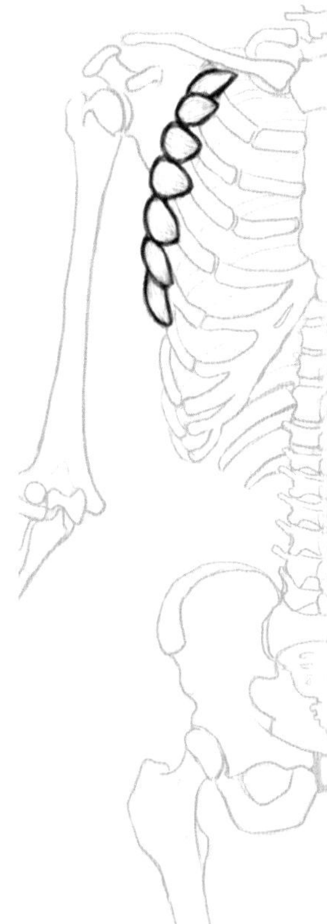

ANTERIOR

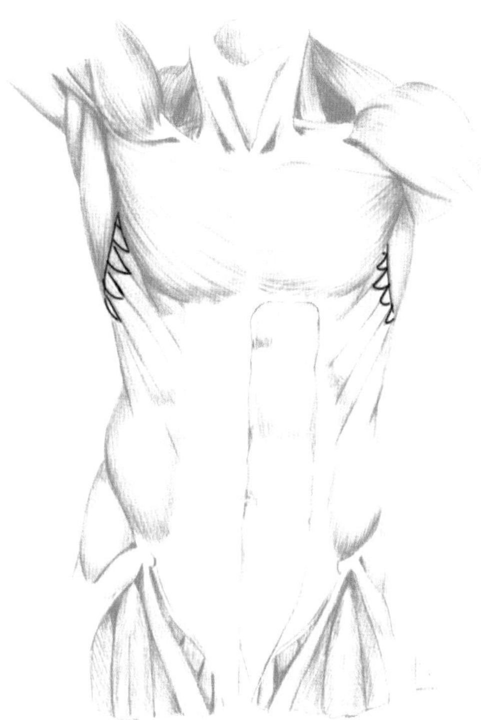

ANTERIOR

C.3. EXTERNAL OBLIQUE

STRUCTURE

The external oblique is a large, slat-like muscle that interdigitates (meshes) with the serratus anterior. There is a fuller, fleshier portion on the ilium (the "love handle").

ORIGIN

The slat-like points (almost like the points of a picket fence) of the muscle attach to ribs five through twelve.

INSERTION

About two-thirds of the front portion of the crest of the ilium, the abdominal aponeurosis (flat sheet of tendon), and the linea alba (center line of the torso), the inguinal ligament that spans from the anterior superior iliac spine (ASIS) of the pelvis and the pubic bone.

ACTION

Bends the trunk laterally (1), side to side, and twists the trunk.

1.

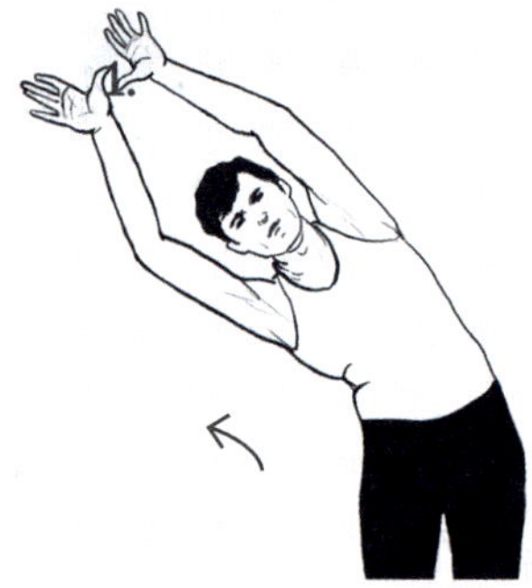

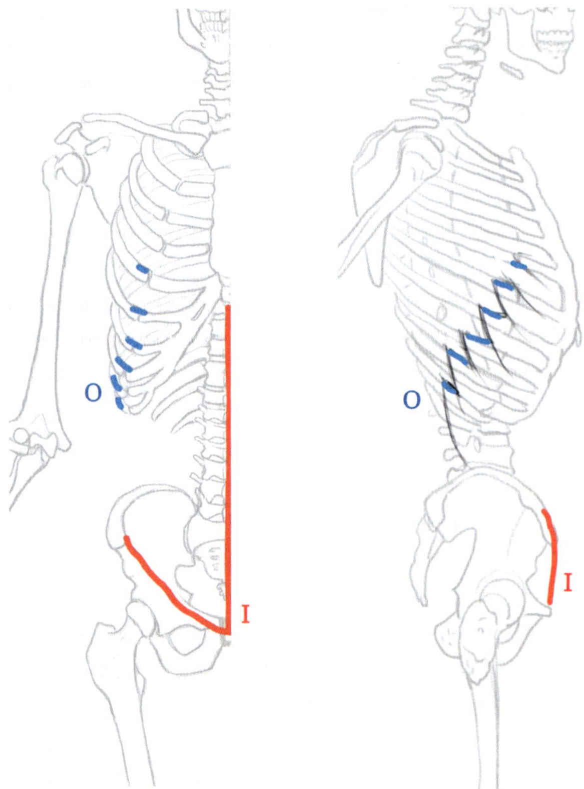

ANTERIOR LATERAL

1. Bends truck laterally and twists trunk

CHECKLIST

O Rectus abdominis

O Serratus anterior

O External oblique

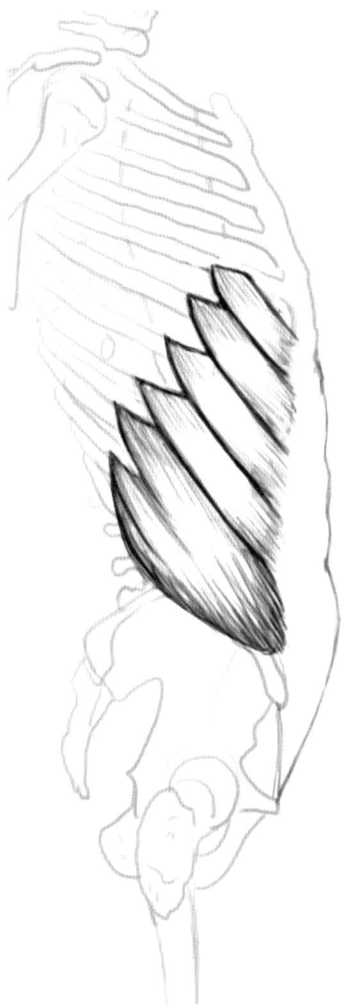

LATERAL

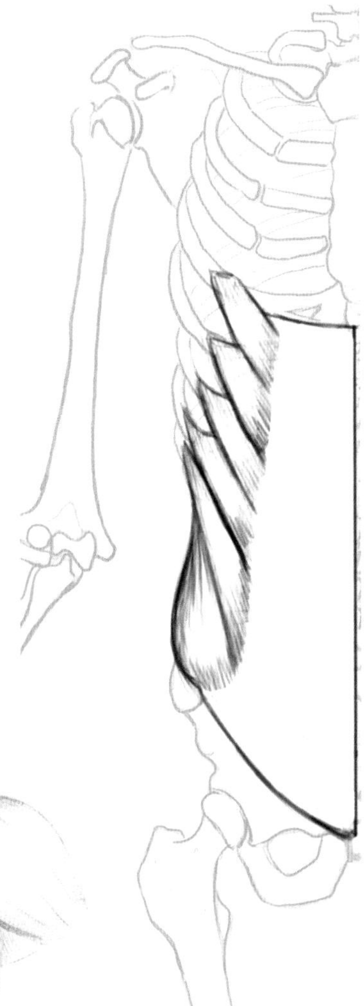

ANTERIOR

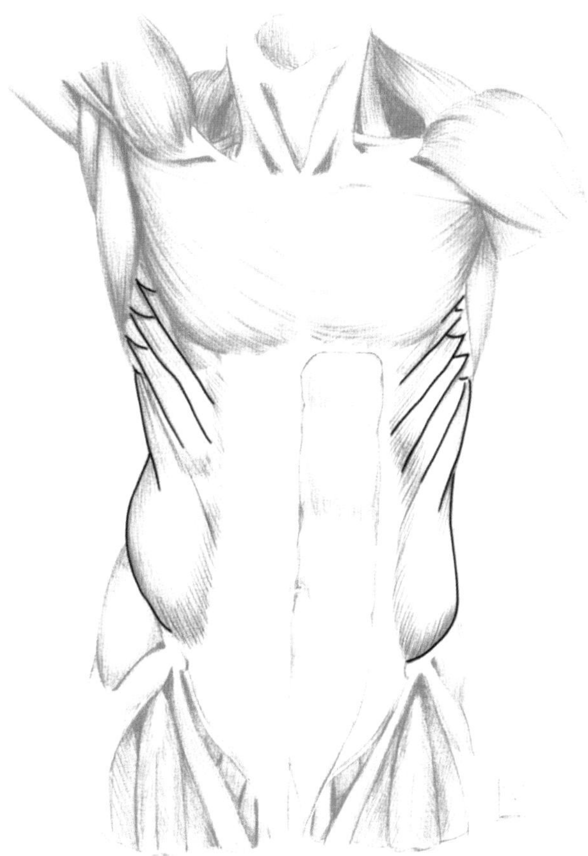

ANTERIOR

C.4. PECTORALIS MAJOR

STRUCTURE

The pectoralis major has three sections. The sternal section is broad and shaped like a home plate in baseball, or like a house. The clavicular portion looks like a kitchen knife and crosses over the sternal portion from the clavicle to the humerus (upper arm bone). There is a smaller portion that is an extension of the sternal portion that is lower and slanted toward the abdominal muscles.

ORIGIN

The sternal portion attaches to the sternum, and the lower portion is attached to the abdominal aponeurosis, just like the external oblique. The clavicular portion attaches to the clavicle from the area close to the pit of the neck to two-thirds on the distal (further) end of the clavicle.

INSERTION

On the humerus close to the lateral area of the bone, below the head of the humerus.

ACTION

Adducts the arms, like in a bear hug, and medially rotates the arms. The clavicular portion helps raise the arms. The lower portion of the sternal section and the abdominal portion help in pulling down the arms (1).

1.

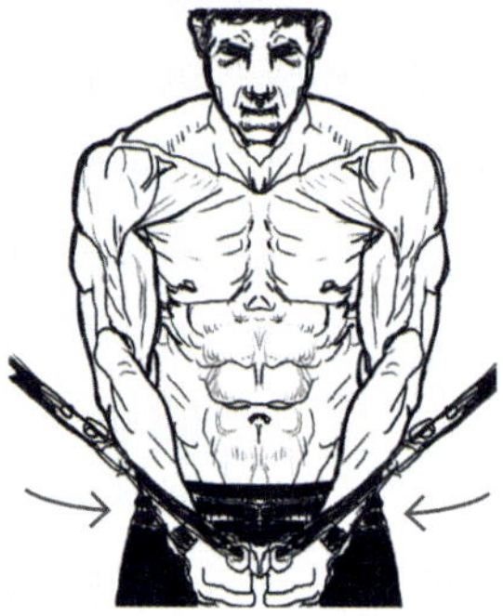

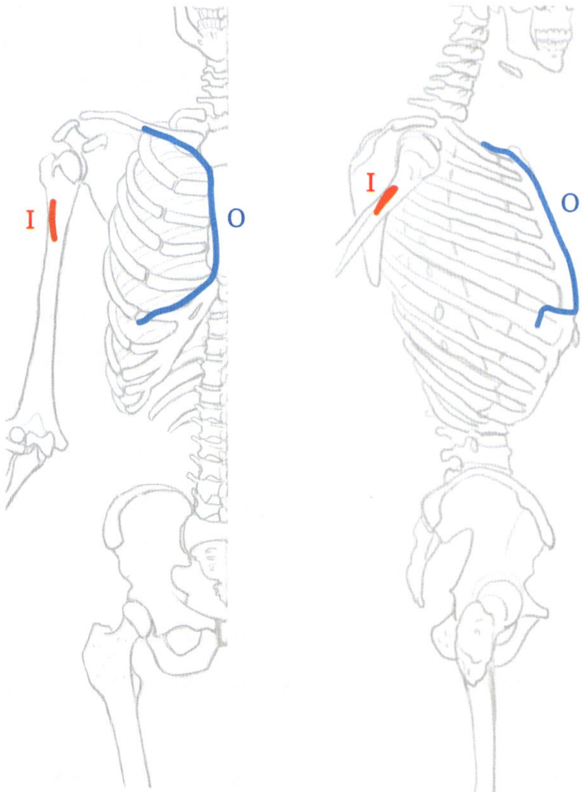

ANTERIOR LATERAL

1. Adducts, medially rotates, raises, and lowers arms

CHECKLIST

- O Rectus abdominis
- O Serratus anterior
- O External oblique
- O Pectoralis major

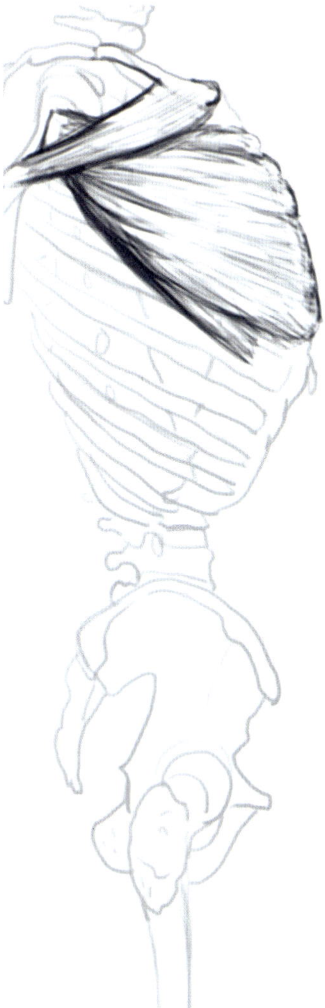

LATERAL

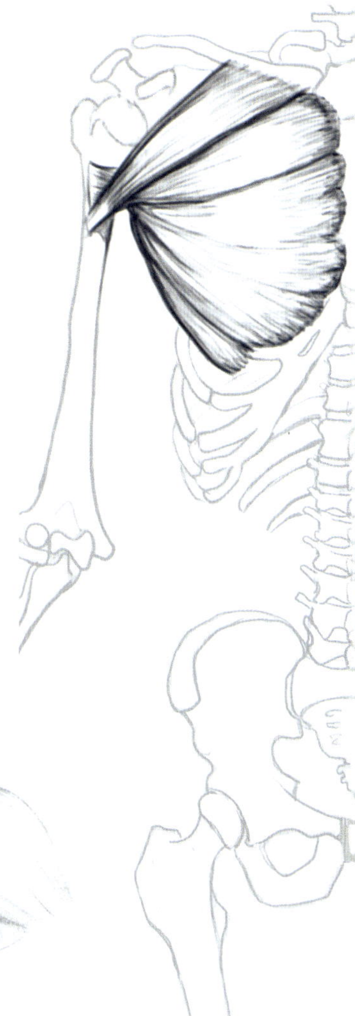

ANTERIOR

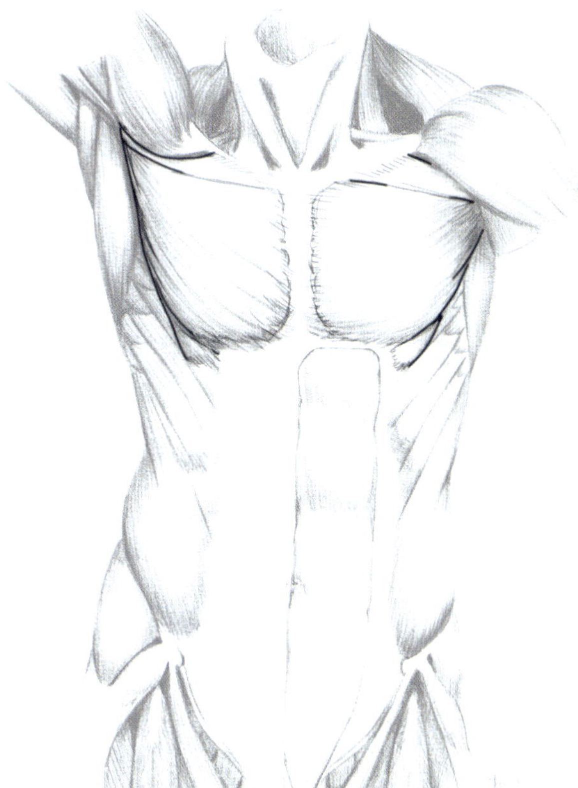

ANTERIOR

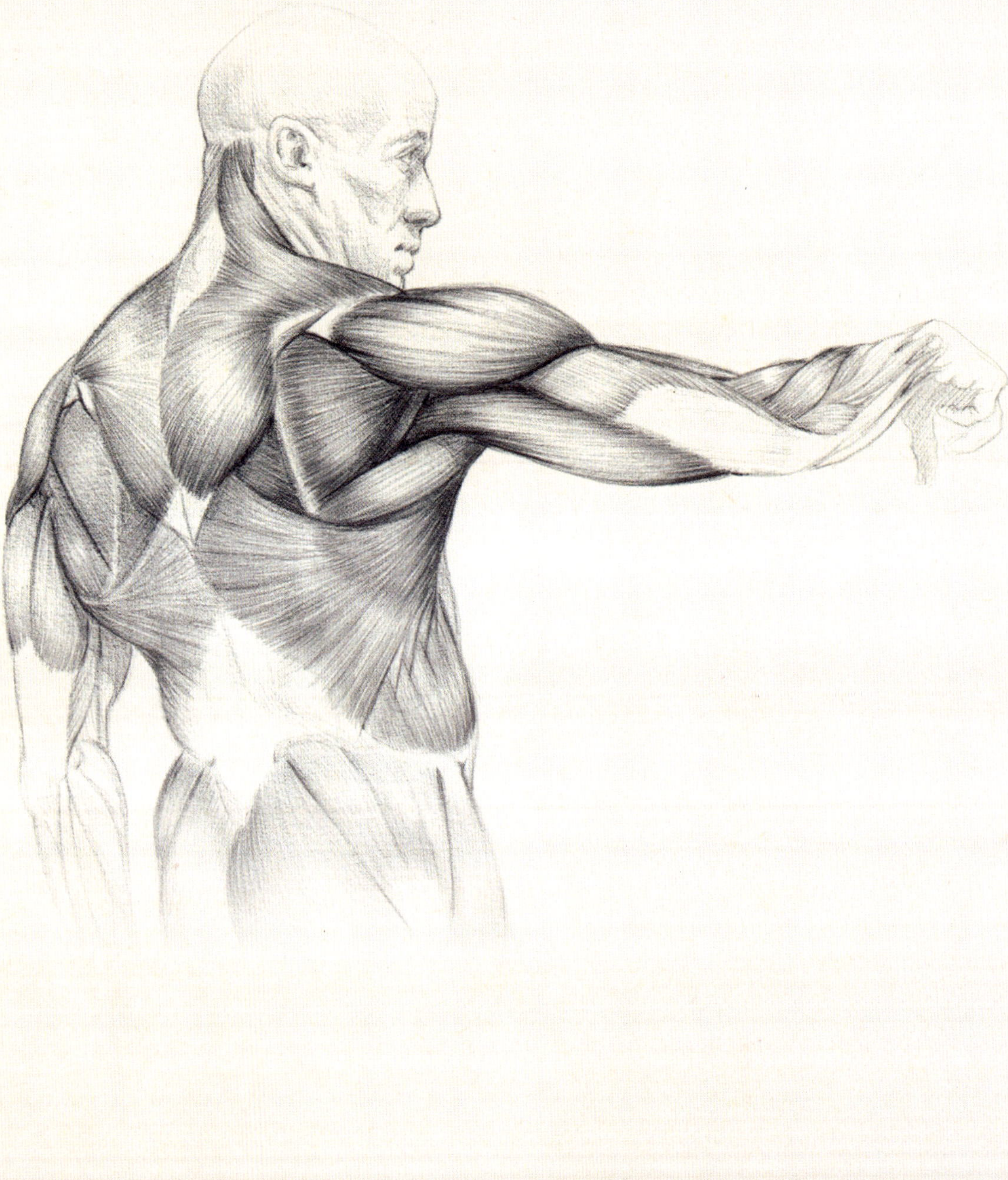

CHAPTER D

THE BACK TORSO

The back muscles, mainly the very deep group of muscles called the sacrospinalis group (**D.1.**), support the spine and extend it as in standing at attention. The muscles of the back torso attach the shoulders to the pelvis, providing stability and mobility. They maintain posture and provide shoulder and arm movements and assist in breathing. The trapezius (**D.8.**) is the largest of the back muscles, and because of the large area that it covers, the muscle fibers pull from different directions. The upper portion helps lift the shoulders, as in a shrug, helps move the neck side to side, and pulls the head back. The center portion helps stabilize the scapula and can bring them closer to the spine. The lower portion pulls the scapulae down as well as the shoulders. The rhomboids (**D.6.**) retract (bring together) the scapulae, and the serratus anterior (**C.2.**) protract (pull forward) the scapulae. Together, I call these two sets of muscles the "rowing" muscles.

D.1. SACROSPINALIS GROUP (ERECTOR SPINAE GROUP)

STRUCTURE

I decided to keep this complicated group of muscles simple. In the classroom I do this by dividing these deep back muscles into two basic forms: the medial form, which is lower and closer to the spine, and the lateral form, which is higher and fuller. I call the medial form the baguette, like the long, narrow loaf of bread at the bakery. It is tight and easily seen on a lean figure, especially when the arms are extended upward. The lateral form is more like a big French loaf, plump and seen easily on most figures.

ORIGIN

The sacrospinalis group (also called the erector spinae group) starts at the ilium by the posterior superior iliac spine (PSIS) (the protruding bumps on the pelvis that create the dimples on your backside) and continues to the lateral edge of the sacrum, to the midline, and all the way up the spine.

INSERTION

The lateral border of the larger form of the muscle has many tendons that attach to many points, including all twelve ribs, and then it narrows upward to the cervical transverse processes (the protruding spines on the neck bones that point outward), then to the mastoid process of the base of the skull (the bump behind the ear).

ACTION

These muscles extend the spine (1), the opposite action of the rectus abdominus.

1.

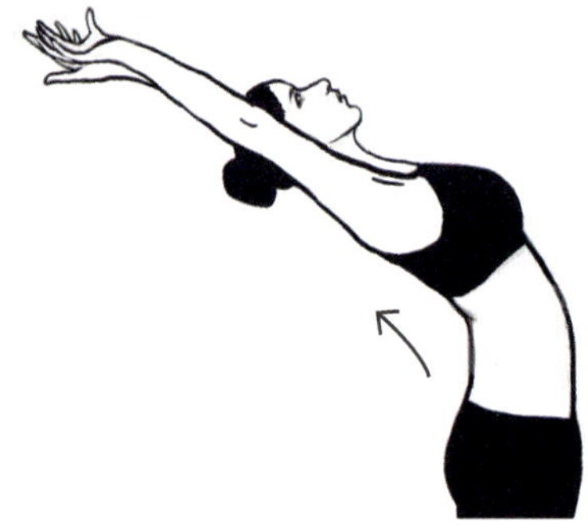

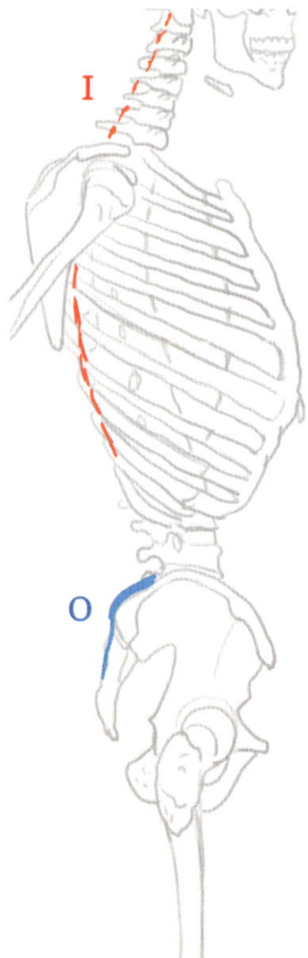

LATERAL

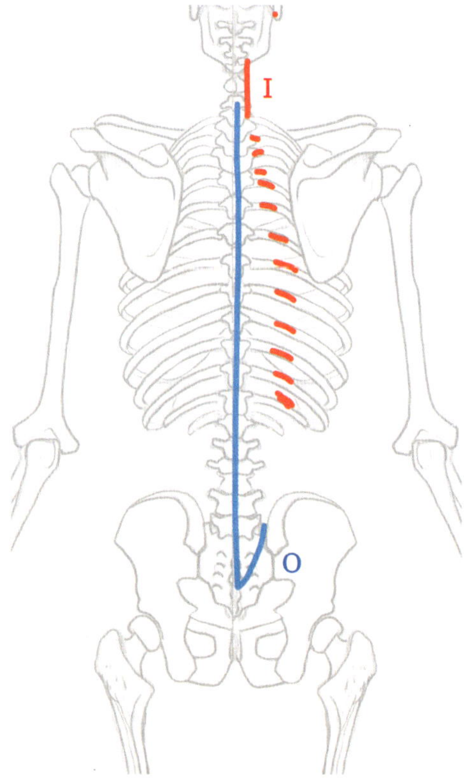

POSTERIOR

1. Extends the spine

CHECKLIST

○ Sacrospinalis group

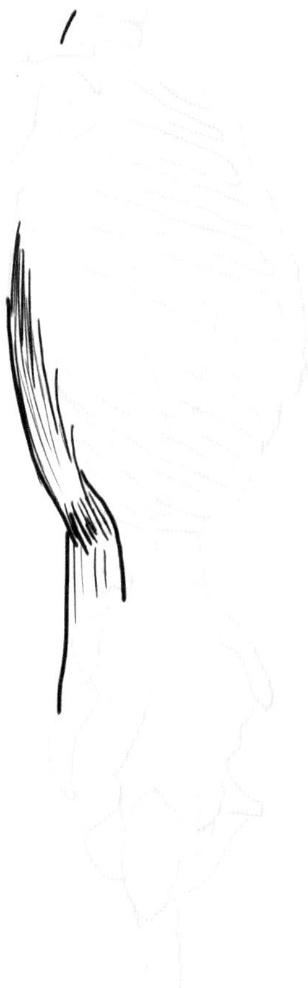

LATERAL

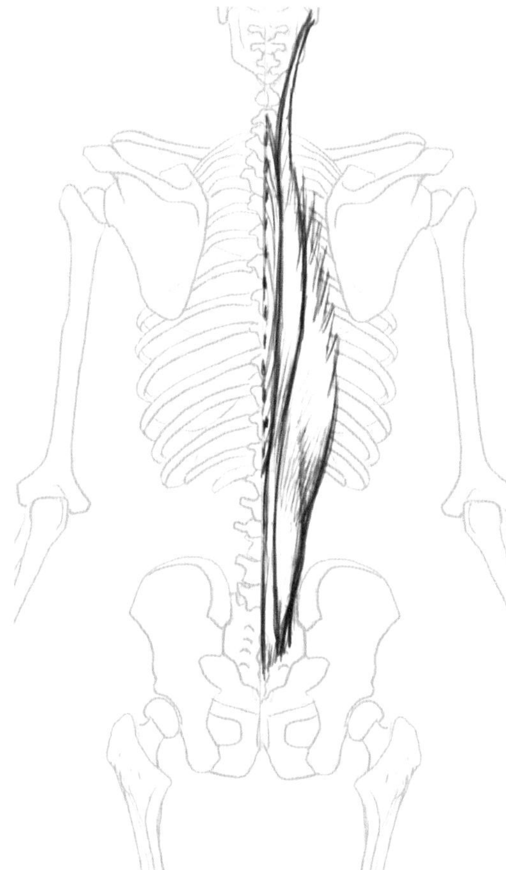

POSTERIOR

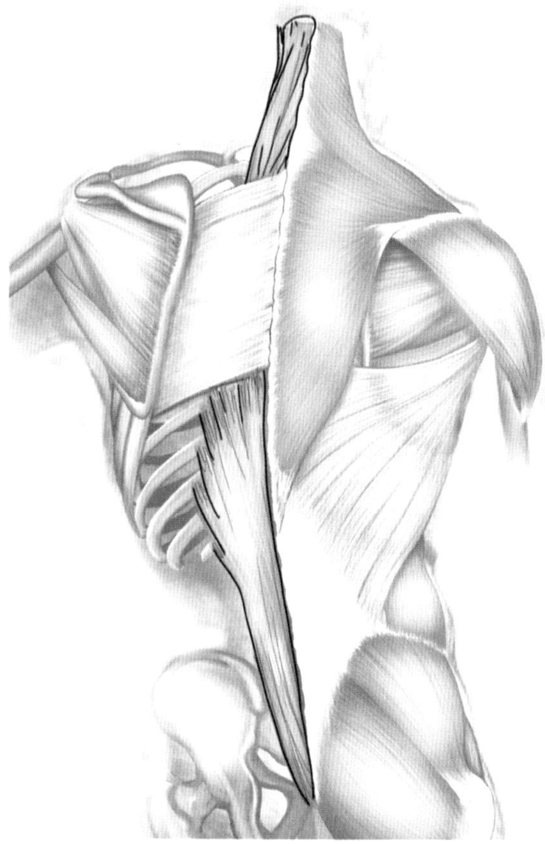

POSTERIOR

D.2. SUPRASPINATUS

STRUCTURE

The supraspinatus (literally "above the spine") is a teardrop-shaped muscle that lies on its side on the superior aspect of the scapula over the spine of the scapula (the spine resembles a shelf).

ORIGIN

The posterior surface of the scapula, over the spine of the scapula (the shelf), resting on the canoe-shaped furrow of the spine of the scapula.

INSERTION

The top of the humerus on the greater tubercle (bony protrusion) that you can see on this individual. The supraspinatus is one of four muscles that hold the head of the humerus into the glenoid fossa of the scapula (the shallow socket).

ACTION

Helps abduct the arm (moves the arm away from the side of the body; 1), which is the position where it might be seen. Since it is under the large trapezius muscle, it is often hidden.

1.

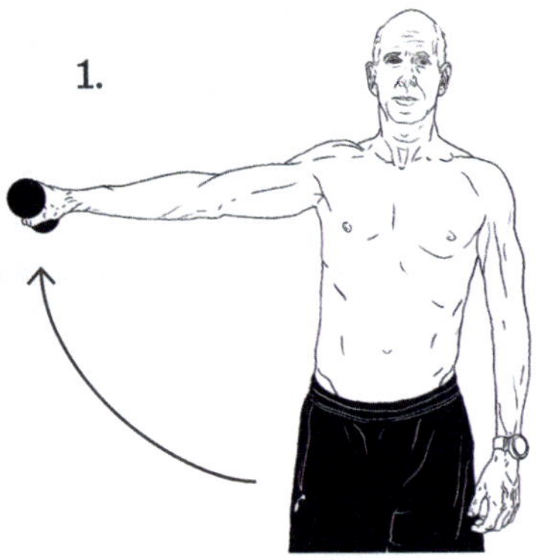

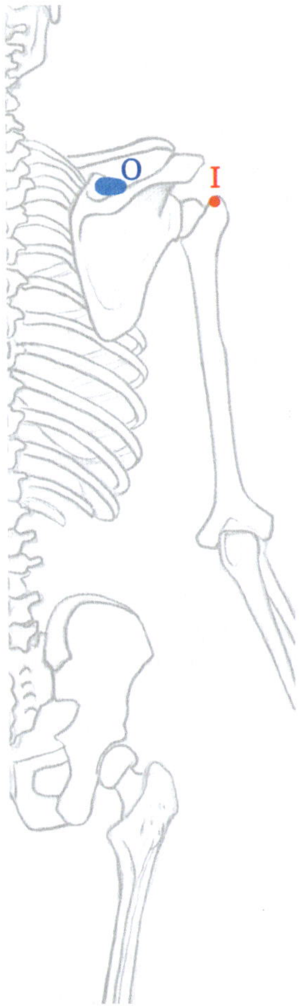

POSTERIOR

1. Abducts the arm

CHECKLIST

- O Sacrospinalis group
- O Supraspinatus

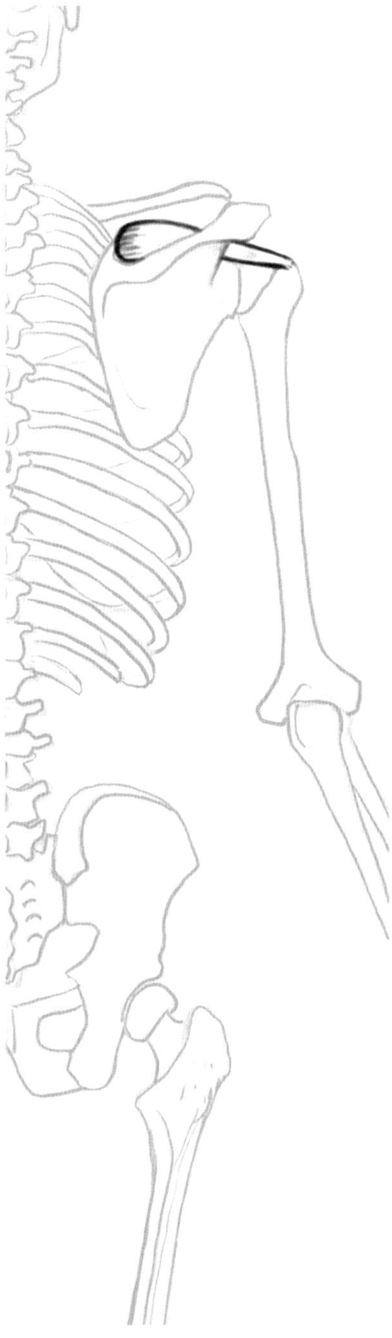

POSTERIOR

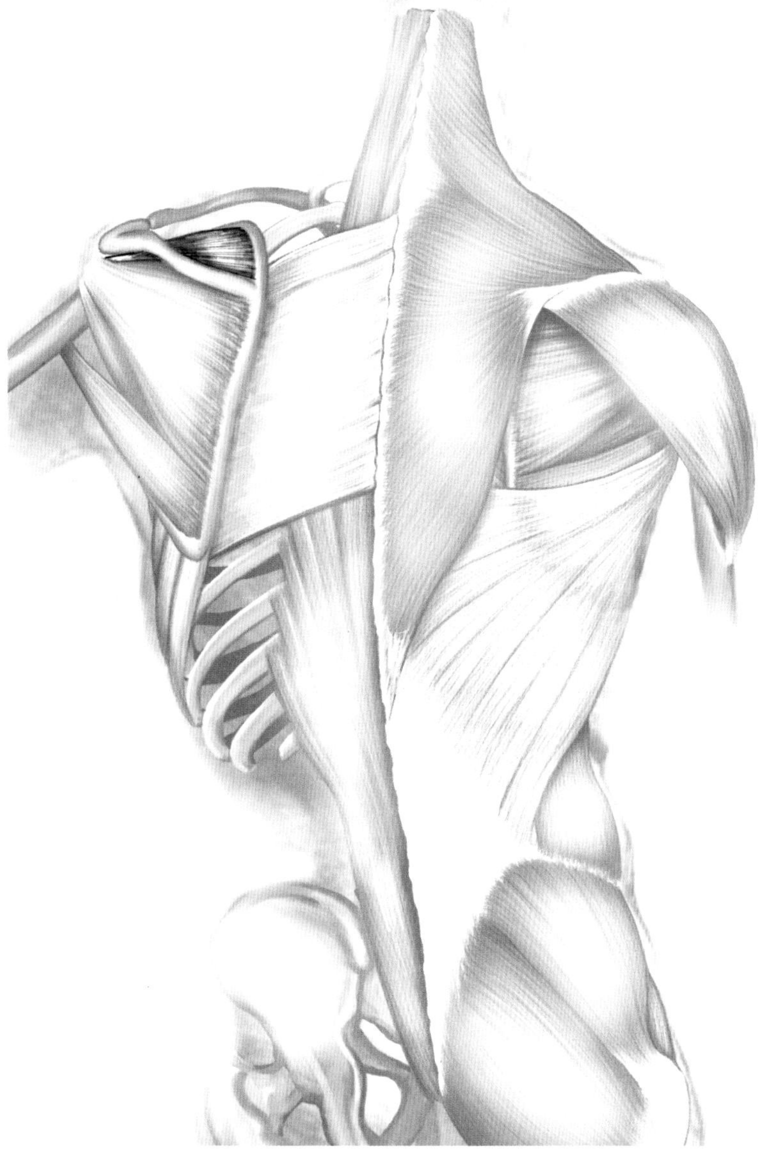

POSTERIOR

D.3. TERES MINOR

STRUCTURE

The teres minor is a small, thin, cigar-shaped muscle that is mostly hidden under the other, larger shoulder muscles. It is also one of the four rotator cuff muscles that hold the ball of the humerus in the glenoid fossa of the scapula, its shallow socket.

ORIGIN

Small strip on the lateral border of the scapula close to the glenoid fossa (shallow socket).

INSERTION

On the lateral side of the head of the humerus, but lower than the head of the humerus.

ACTION

A weak little muscle, but it helps hold the head of the humerus in the socket and helps rotate the humerus laterally (1).

1.

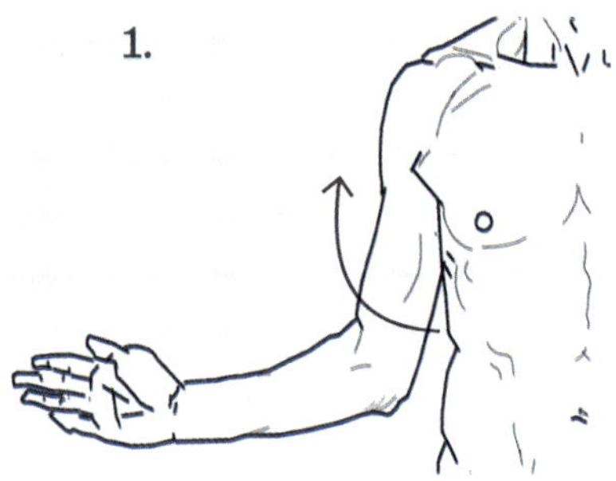

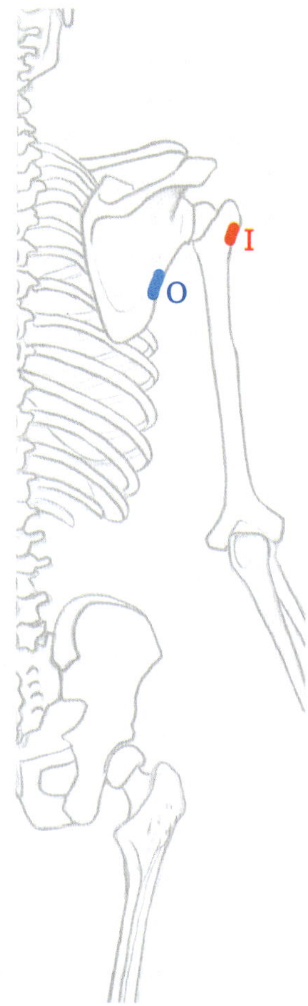

POSTERIOR

1. Rotates the humerus laterally

CHECKLIST

- O Sacrospinalis group
- O Supraspinatus
- O Teres minor

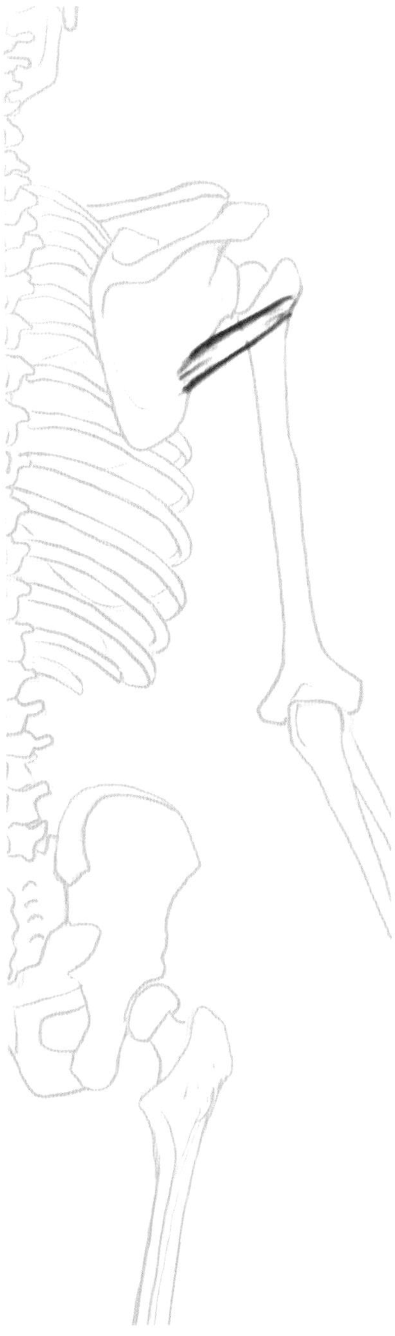

POSTERIOR

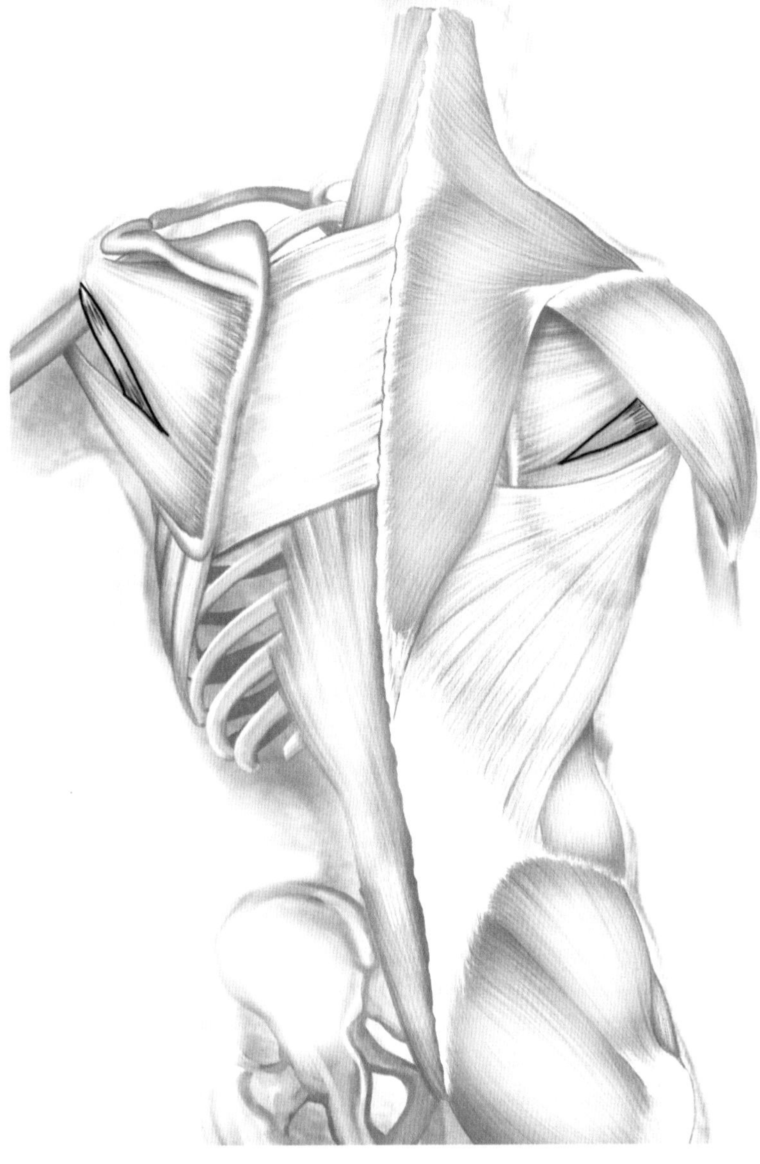

POSTERIOR

D4. INFRASPINATUS

STRUCTURE

The infraspinatus (*infra* meaning below/lower; *spinatus* referring to its placement under the spine of the scapula) is a triangular muscle that fits neatly on the shallow depression on the scapula.

ORIGIN

Most of the scapula.

INSERTION

By the greater tubercle (bump) of the humerus.

ACTION

The infraspinatus is the third of four muscles that make up the rotator cuff. The fourth, the subscapularis, is hidden under the scapula and is not visible, therefore it is not included in this chapter. The infraspinatus holds the ball of the humerus into the glenoid fossa of the scapula and it rotates the upper arm laterally (1).

1.

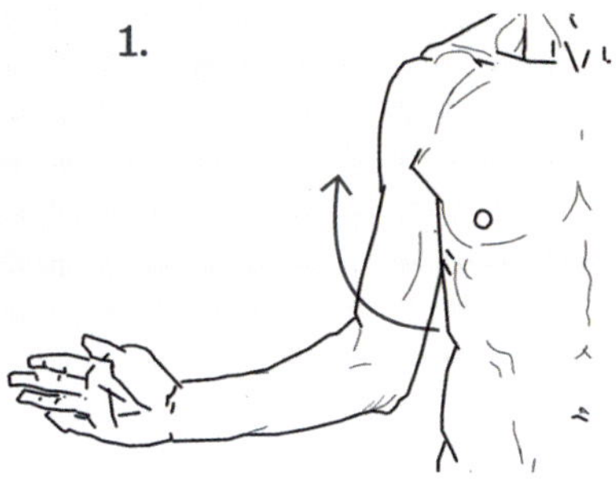

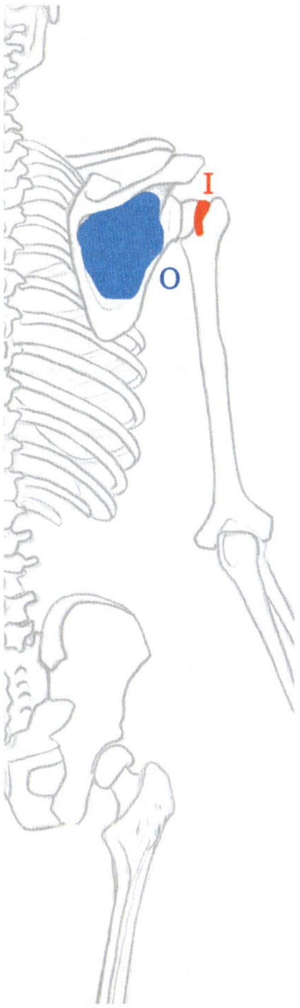

POSTERIOR

1. Rotates the humerus laterally

CHECKLIST

- O Sacrospinalis group
- O Supraspinatus
- O Teres minor
- O Infraspinatus

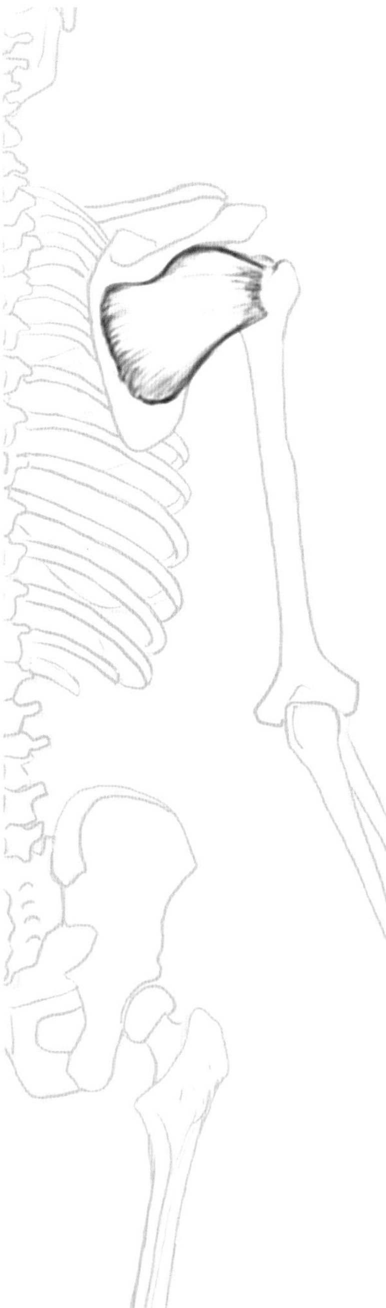

POSTERIOR

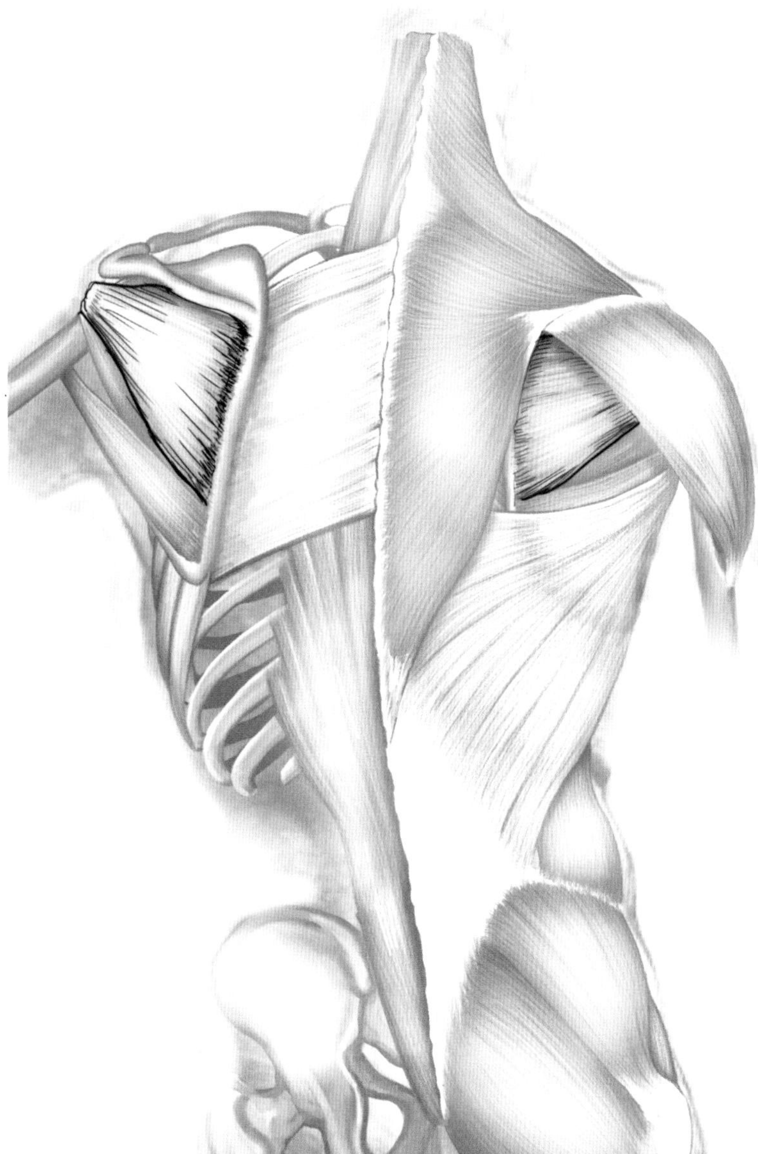

POSTERIOR

D.5. TERES MAJOR

STRUCTURE

The teres major, meaning round and large, is a tubular muscle that can be clearly seen on most figures in many poses.

ORIGIN

The bottom part of the scapula. The scapula looks like South America, so I named this lower section the "Tierra del Fuego" of the scapula, the area at the bottom of the continent.

INSERTION

On the front of the humerus not too far down from the head of the humerus.

ACTION

The teres major complements the other muscles that rotate the arm laterally (outward), the teres minor and the infraspinatus. The teres major rotates the humerus medially (inward; 1). It also adducts the arm, pulling it toward the body.

1.

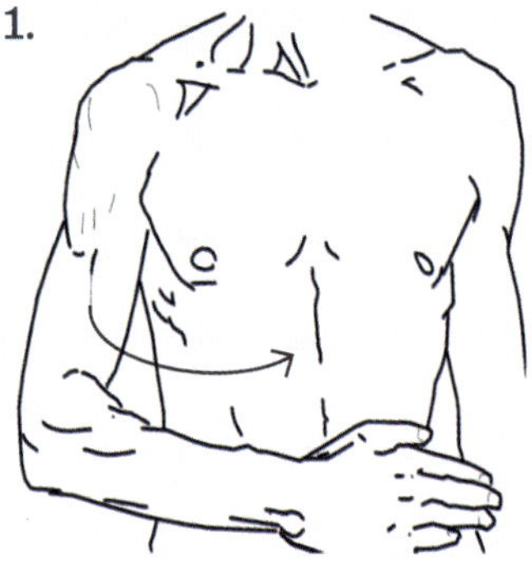

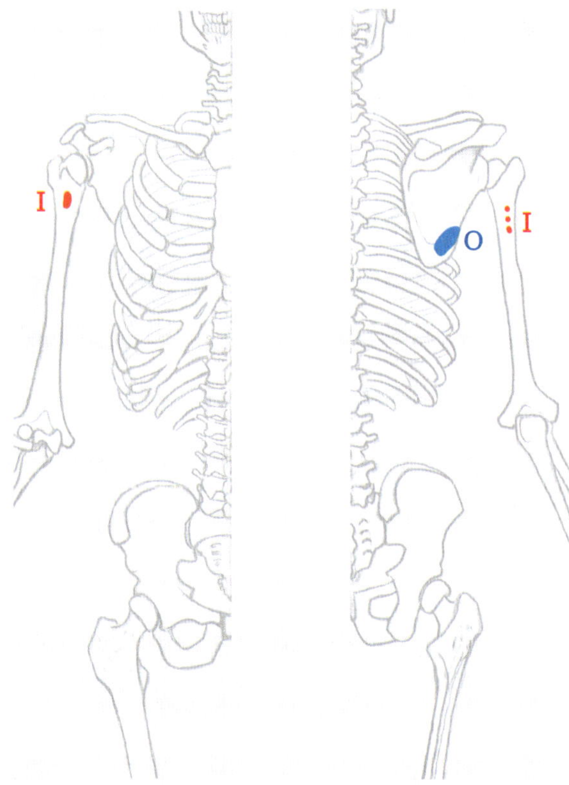

1. Rotates the humerus medially and adducts the arm

CHECKLIST

- O Sacrospinalis group
- O Supraspinatus
- O Teres minor
- O Infraspinatus
- O Teres major

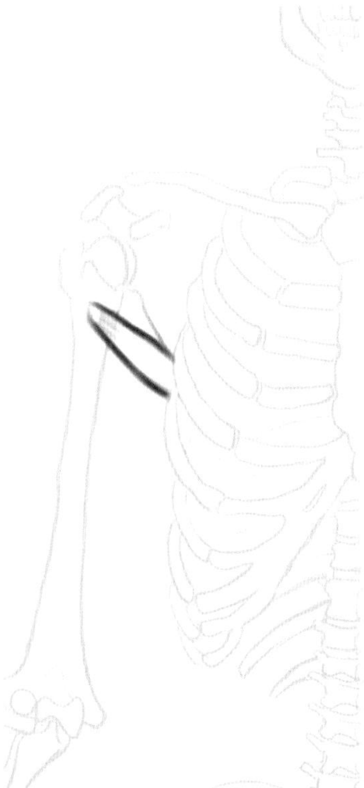

ANTERIOR

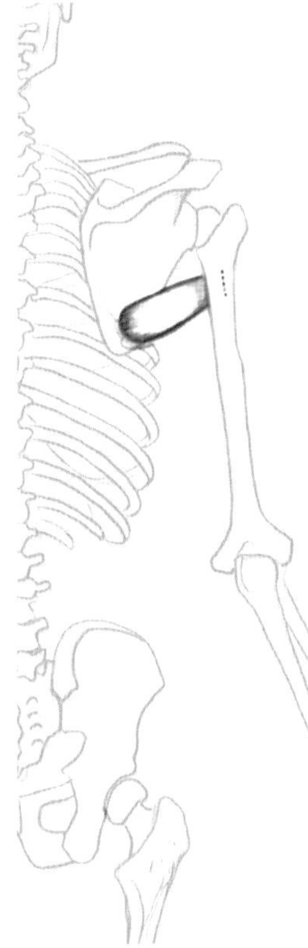

POSTERIOR

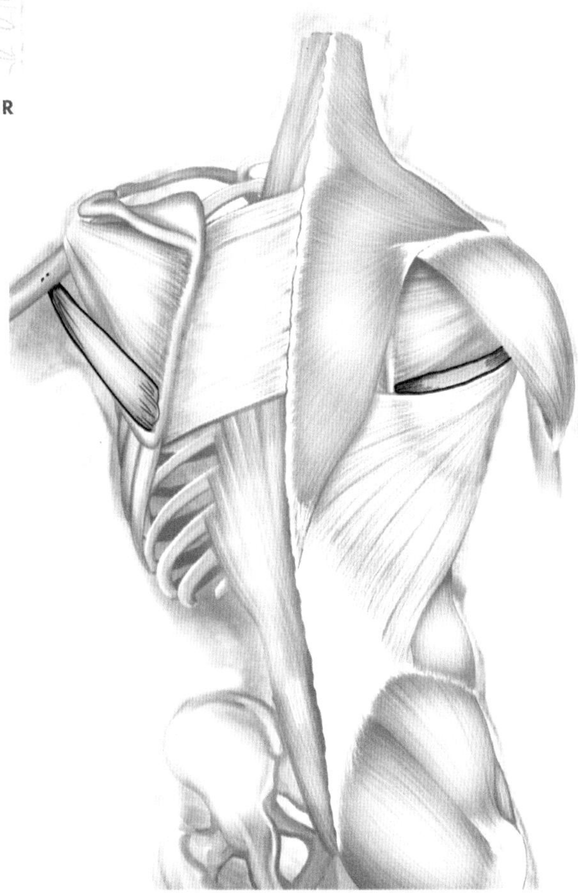

POSTERIOR

D.6. RHOMBOIDS (MAJOR AND MINOR COMBINED)

STRUCTURE

Both parts of the rhomboids are seen as one, which is why they are referred to as plural. They resemble a rhombus shape. Together with the ones on the other side of the spine, they resemble a chevron.

ORIGIN

Roughly on the seventh cervical vertebra (the protruding neck bone on your back) down to around the seventh thoracic (rib cage) vertebra.

INSERTION

The lateral edge of the scapula, from where the spine of the scapula is located down to the bottom of the edge (by the "Tierra del Fuego").

ACTION

The rhomboids adduct, retract, the scapula (brings the scapula closer to the spine; 1). They also help rotate the scapula.

1.

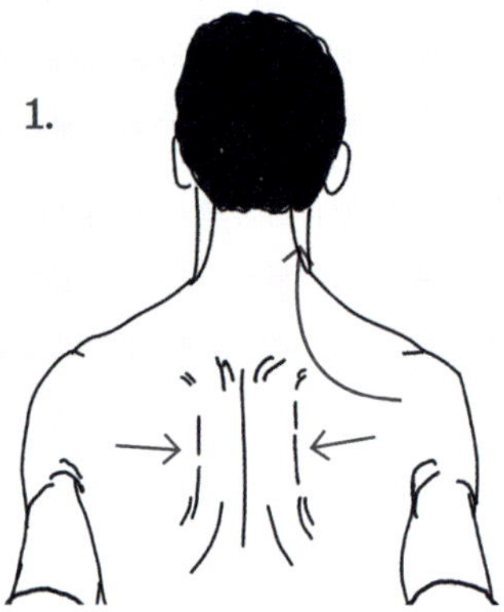

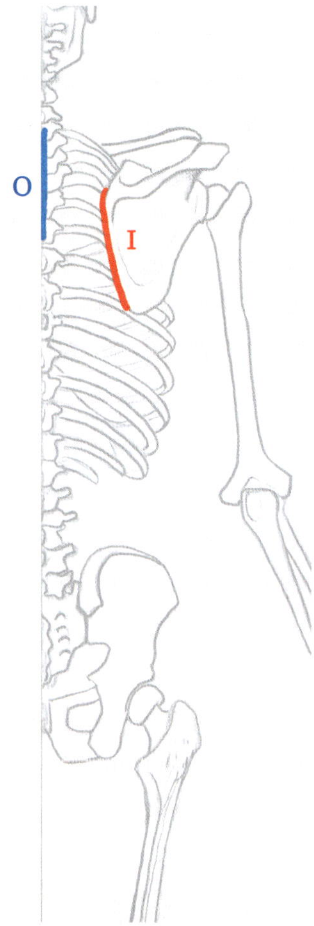

POSTERIOR

1. Adduct and retract the scapula

CHECKLIST

- O Sacrospinalis group
- O Teres minor
- O Teres major
- O Supraspinatus
- O Infraspinatus
- O Rhomboids

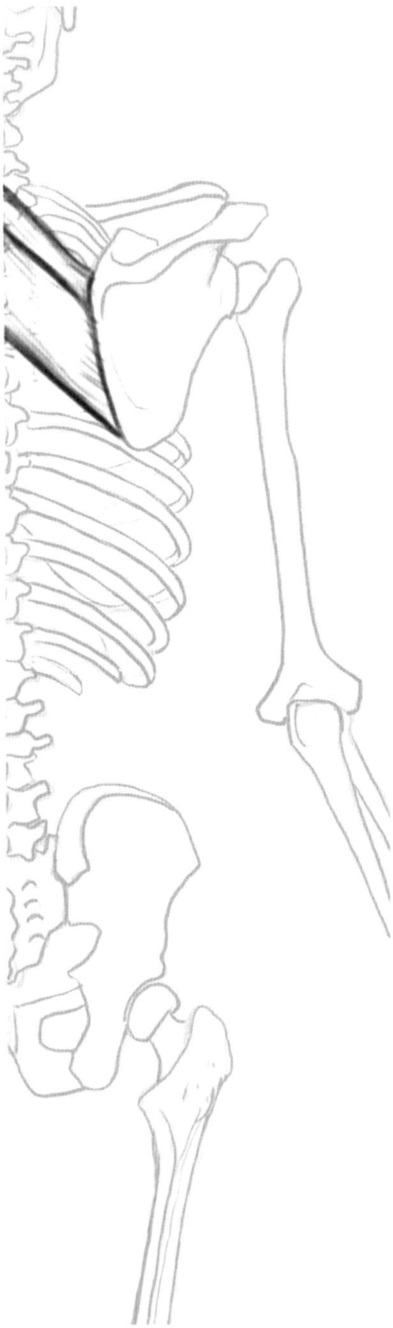

POSTERIOR

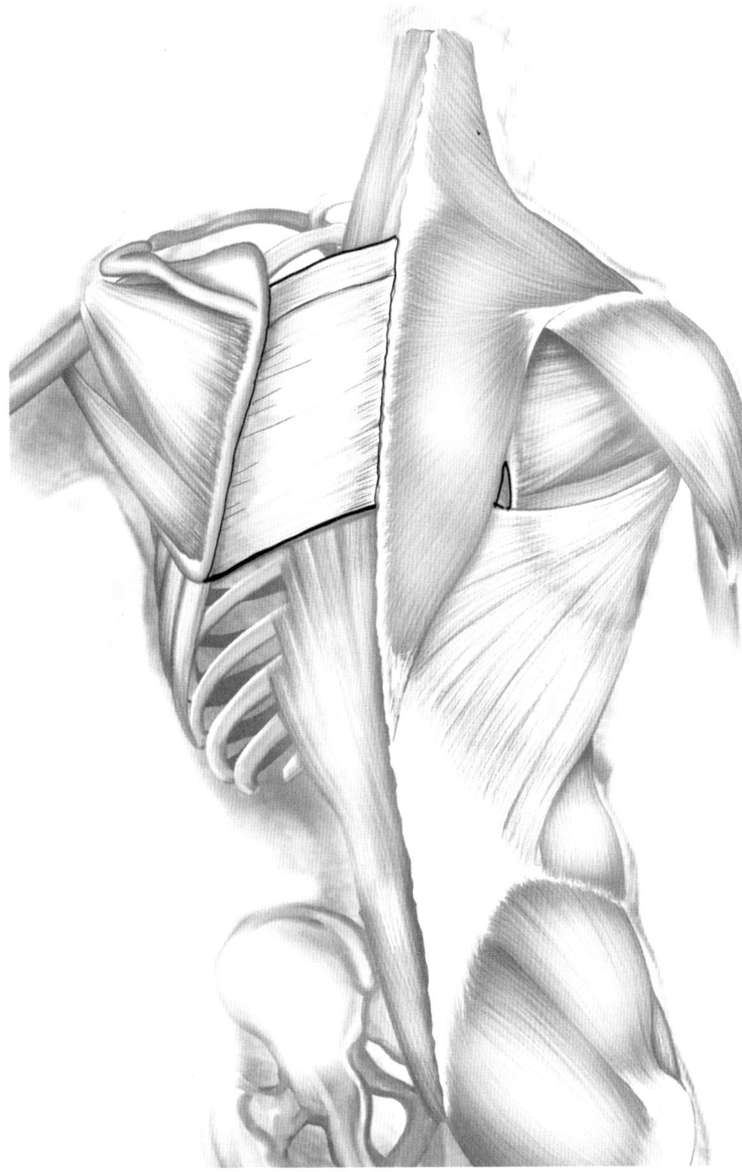

POSTERIOR

D.7. LATISSIMUS DORSI

STRUCTURE

The latissimus dorsi is a huge, triangular sheet of muscle with an extended band for attachment to the humerus.

ORIGIN

The lumbar aponeurosis that it is attached to runs along the spine and all the way down into the sacrum and to around a third of the rear of the ilium of the pelvis.

INSERTION

The front of the humerus by the insertion of the teres major, but a bit closer to the head of the humerus. When the arm is up and you're viewing the model from the front, this muscle often blends in with the teres major, but on more muscular figures you can easily see them as separate forms. There is a little piece of the latissimus dorsi that attaches to the lower part of the scapula.

ACTION

Adducts (moves inward), extends, and medially rotates (rotates inward) the humerus (1). It also depresses (pulls down) the scapula and helps rotate it as well.

1.

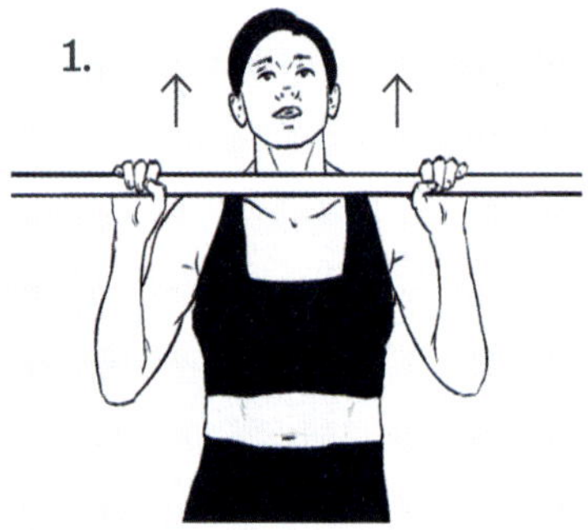

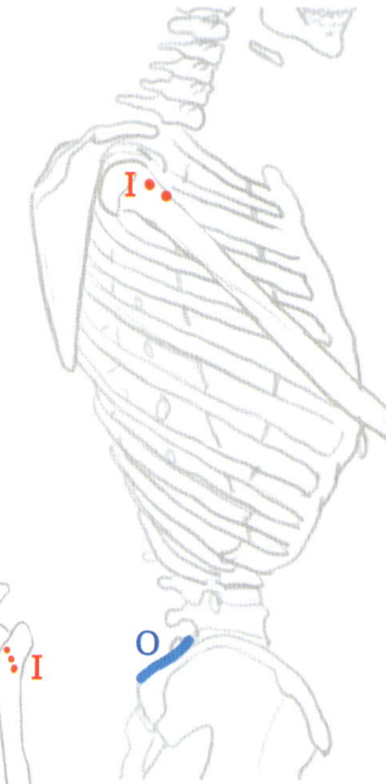

LATERAL

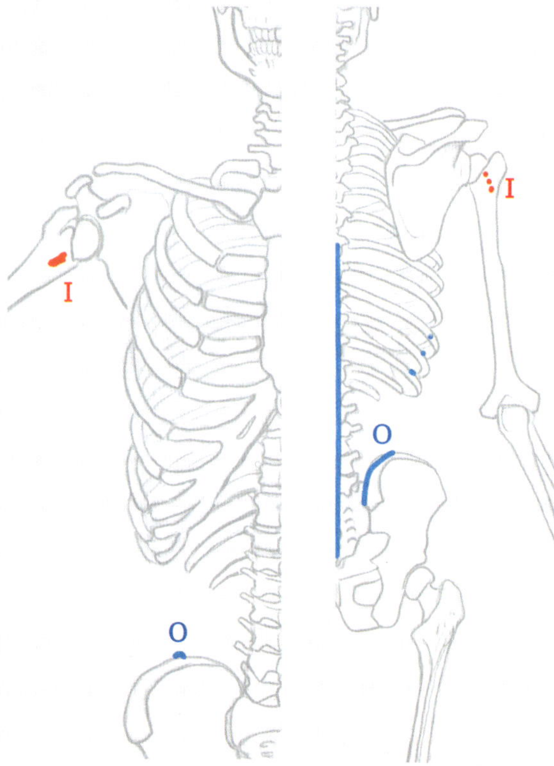

ANTERIOR POSTERIOR

1. Adducts, extends, and medially rotates the humerus; depresses and helps rotate the scapula

CHECKLIST

- O Sacrospinalis group
- O Supraspinatus
- O Teres minor
- O Infraspinatus
- O Teres major
- O Rhomboids
- O Latissimus dorsi

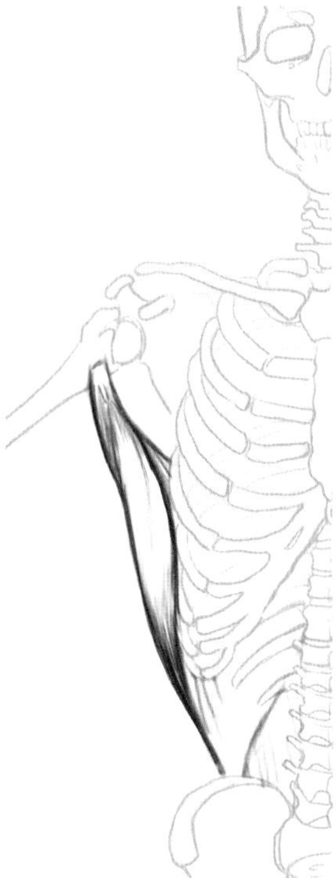

ANTERIOR

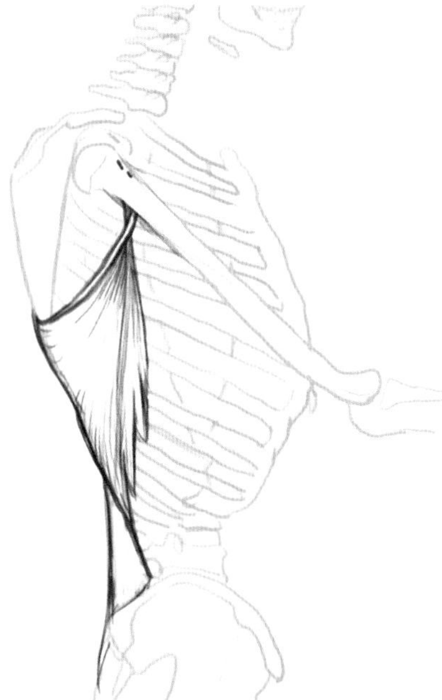

LATERAL

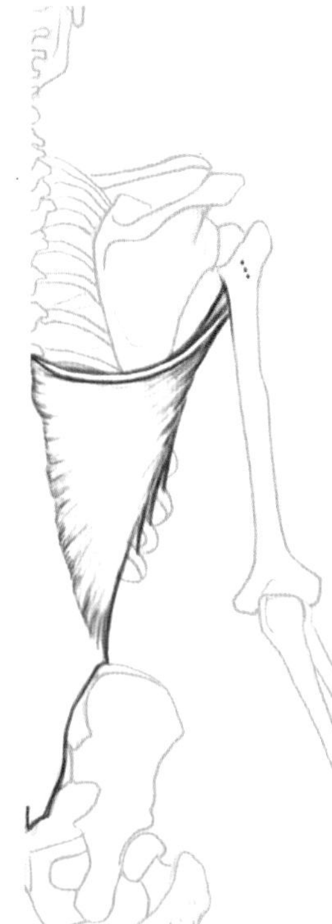

POSTERIOR

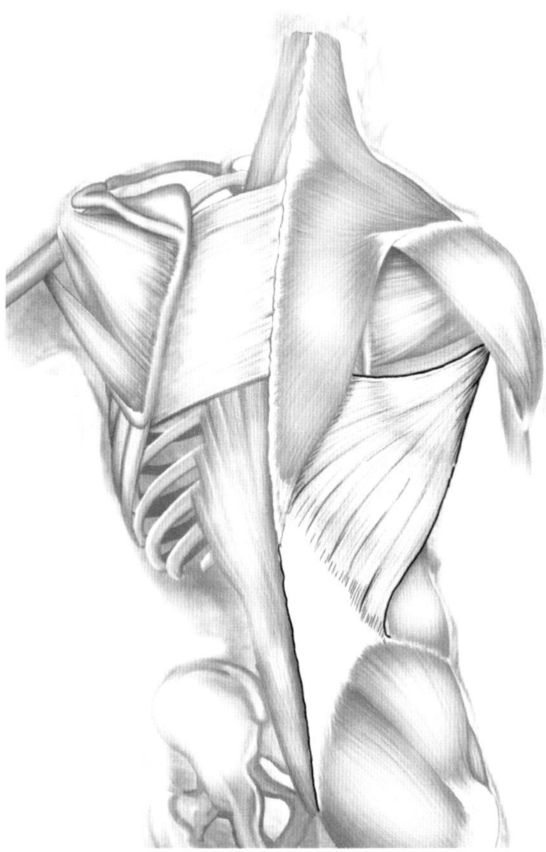

POSTERIOR

D.8. TRAPEZIUS

STRUCTURE

The trapezius is so large and has so many muscle fibers that radiate out in different directions that it is almost a group of muscles. Because of that, it performs a variety of actions.

ORIGIN

From the base of the skull, it descends down the spine to the twelfth thoracic (rib cage) vertebra. Some individuals have this attachment higher, making the bottom point of the trapezius closer to the bottom of the scapula. The tendon at the bottom can be at the twelfth vertebra, but the muscle bellies can be higher.

INSERTION

On the front it inserts onto the end of the clavicle about a third of the way in from the shoulder. It then wraps around the acromion process of the scapula onto the spine of the scapula. The tendon then wraps underneath the spine by the tubercle (bony bump) of the spine of the scapula.

ACTION

Lifts the scapula (1), like when holding a suitcase and then shrugging, while the lower fibers of the muscle pull the scapula downward. The center fibers bring together the scapulae along with the rhomboids.

1.

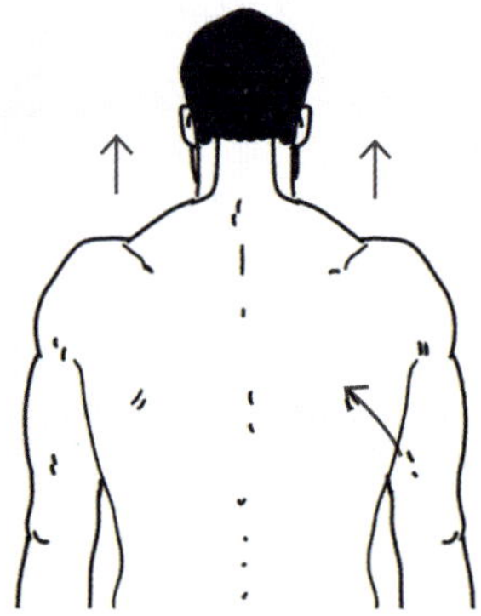

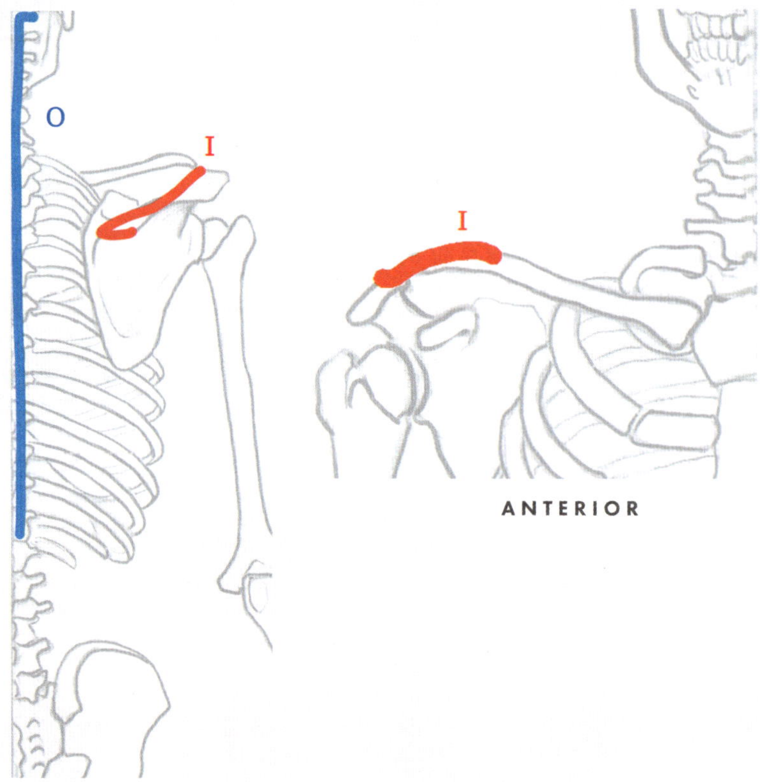

1. Lifts scapula, pulls scapula downward, pulls scapulae together

CHECKLIST

- O Sacrospinalis group
- O Supraspinatus
- O Teres minor
- O Infraspinatus
- O Teres major
- O Rhomboids
- O Latissimus dorsi
- O Trapezius

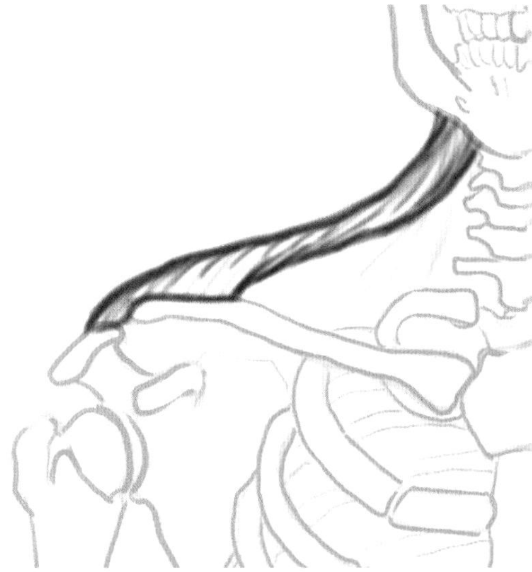

ANTERIOR

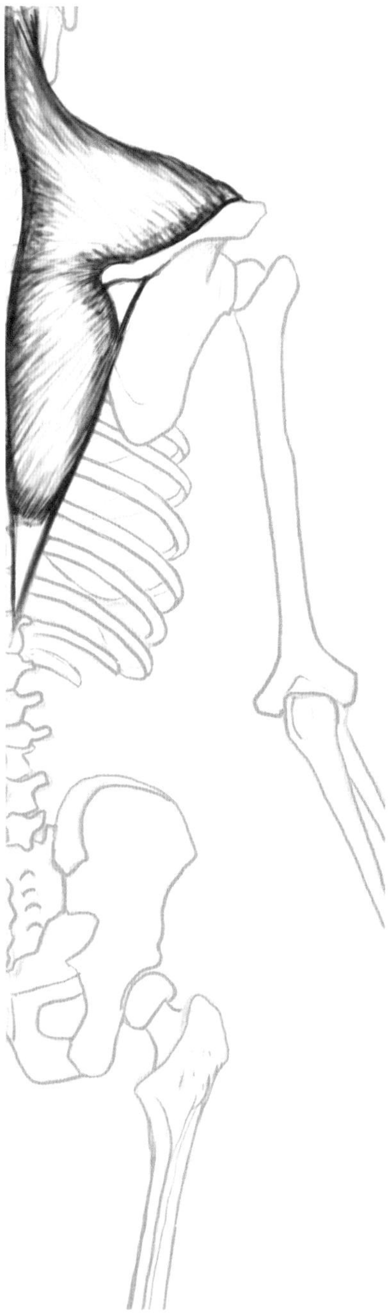

POSTERIOR

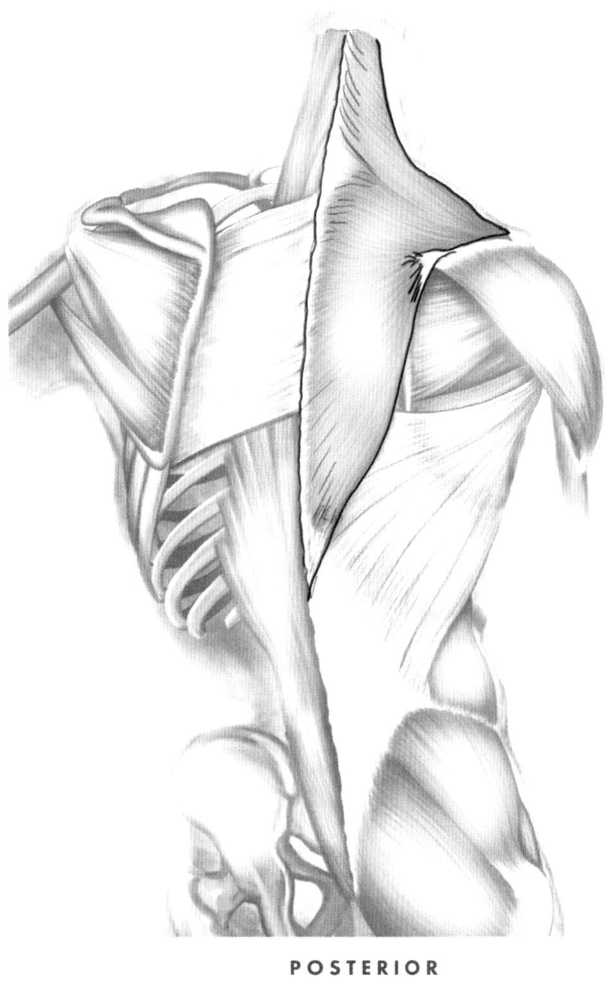

POSTERIOR

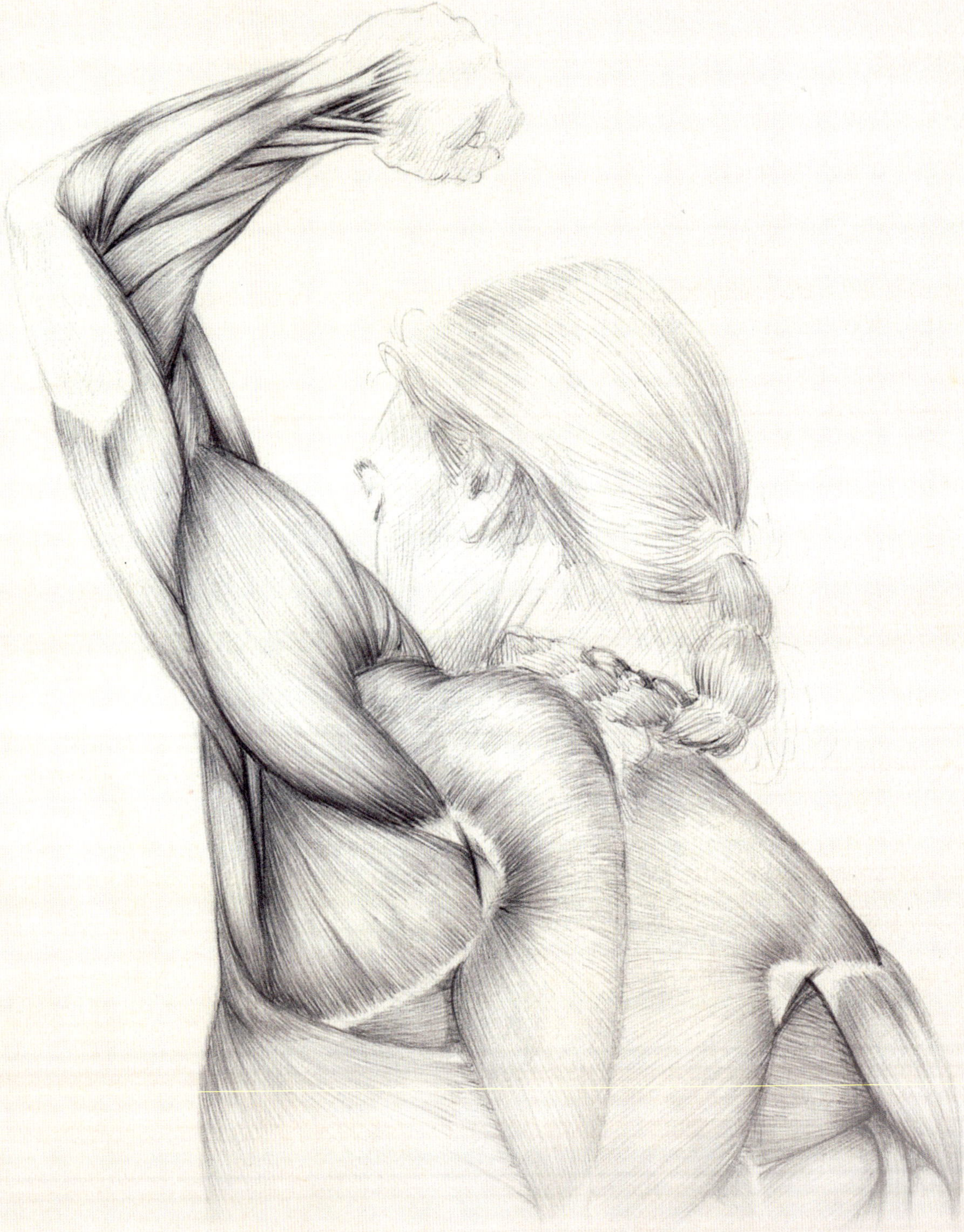

CHAPTER E

THE UPPER ARM

The upper arm muscles allow you to move your arms. In artistic anatomy we focus on the superficial muscles up against the skin. These muscles—the biceps and triceps—along with the deltoid allow for powerful motions, such as lifting a heavy weight or throwing a ball.

E.1. BRACHIALIS

STRUCTURE

The brachialis lies under the biceps brachii like a bed on the outside and front of the humerus where the bend of the elbow is. It can be seen on lean or very muscular people on the lateral side of the arm just below the deltoid. Basically, where the deltoid ends, the brachialis starts. When the elbow is straightened, the brachialis can also be seen right by the medial epicondyle, or the "funny bone" on the medial (inside) side of the arm. It is easily seen and felt as a soft form by the bend of the elbow and just lateral to the biceps brachii. In this section of the upper arm, many muscles have *brach* in their names because *brachium* means "upper arm" in Greek.

ORIGIN

At the deltoid tuberosity and down the front of the humerus, almost to the bend of the elbow.

INSERTION

At the front, upper part of the ulna.

ACTION

Flexes the arm (1).

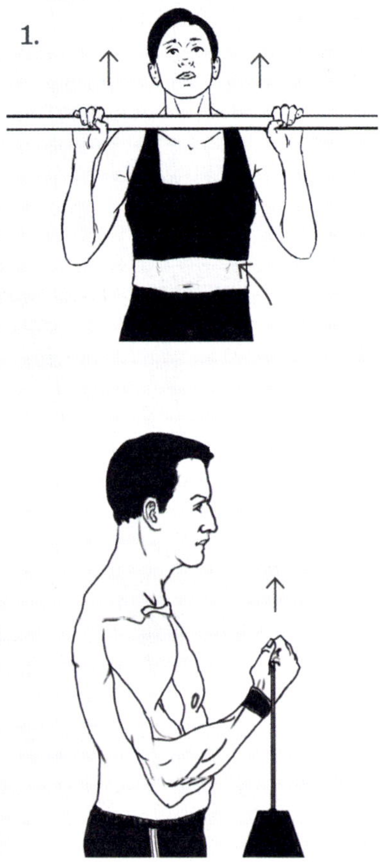

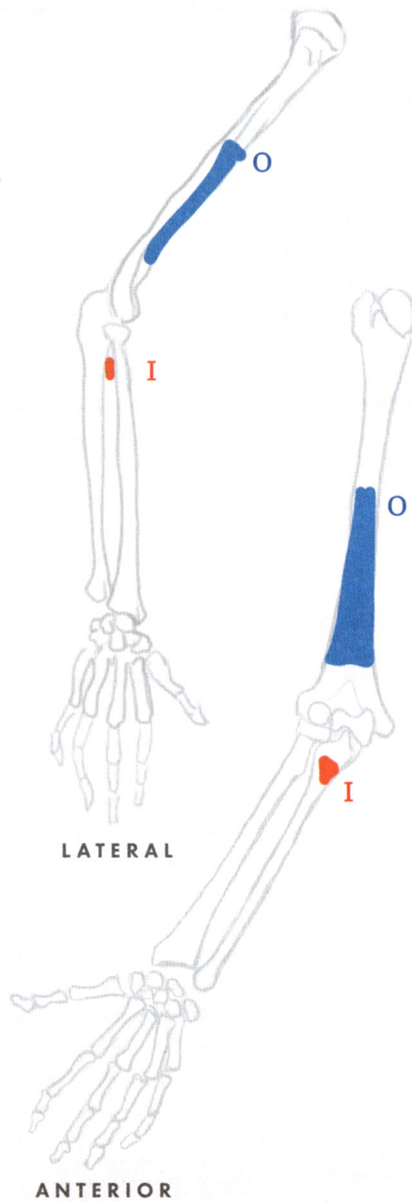

1. Flexes the arm

CHECKLIST

○ Brachialis

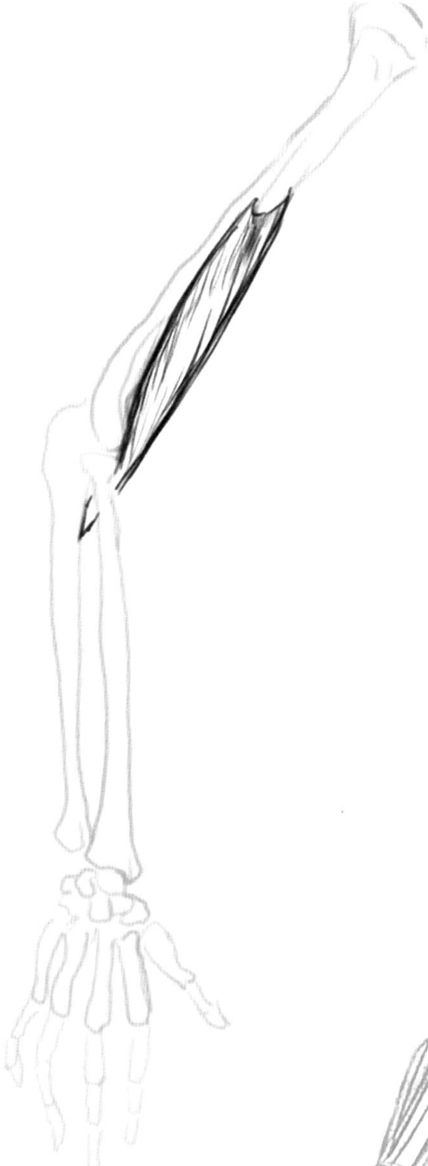

MEDIAL

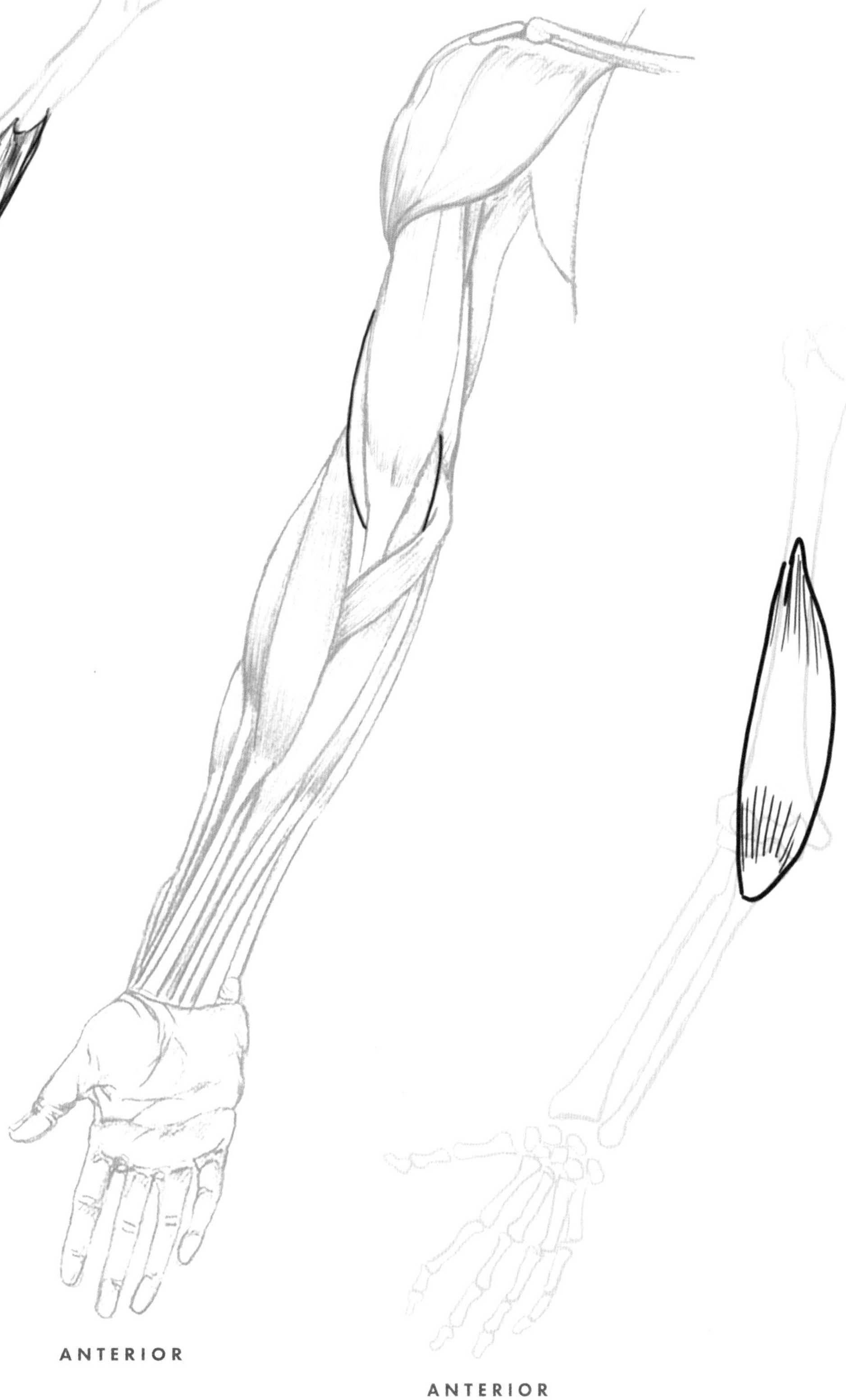

ANTERIOR

ANTERIOR

E.2. BICEPS BRACHII

STRUCTURE

The biceps brachii is made up of two heads, a long head that is lateral, further outward, and a short head that is more medial, inward. They are spilt at the top, the origin, and blend together as one at the bottom, the insertion. The biceps brachii is large and tubular. It comes out from under the pectoral muscles and deltoid.

ORIGIN

The long head originates over the glenoid fossa (shallow socket of the scapula). The short head originates at the tip of the coracoid process of the scapula (the beaklike bone on the front of the scapula; *coracoid* means "bird's beak").

INSERTION

The radial tuberosity (the bony bump) of the radius.

ACTION

Flexes (1) and supinates (2) the forearm.

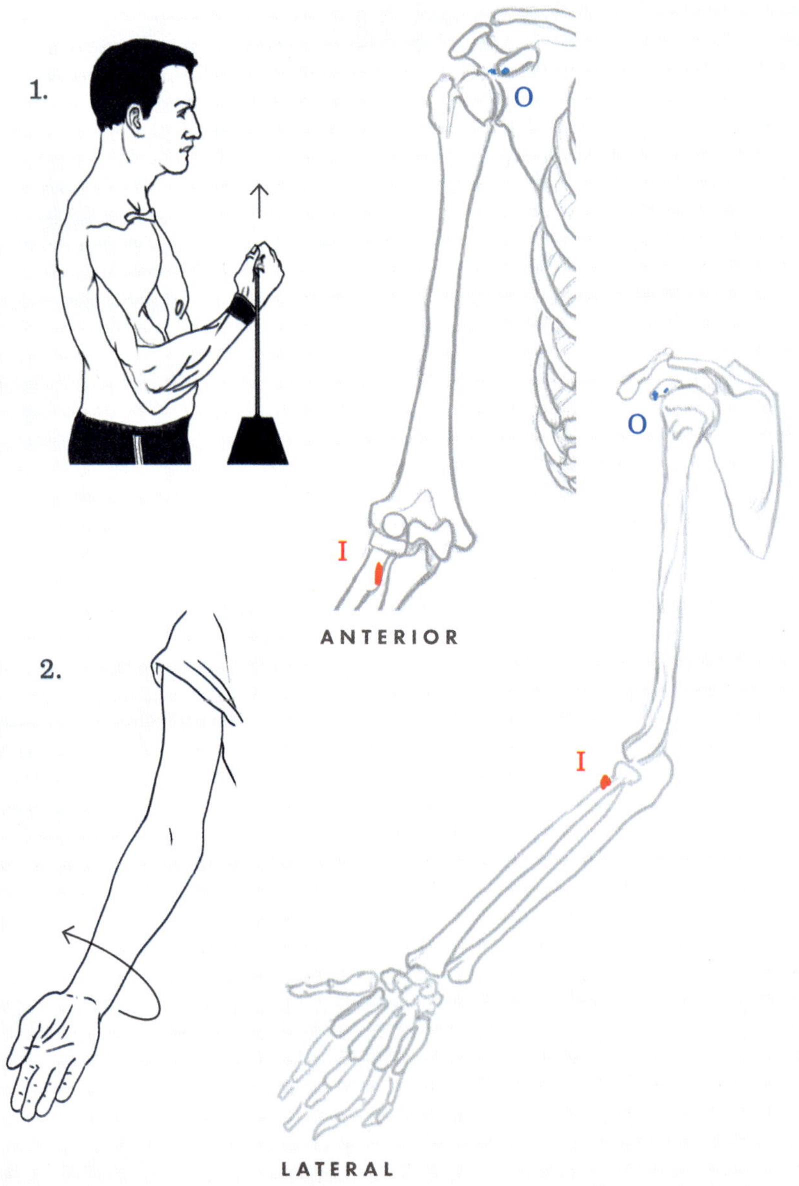

1. Flexes the forearm; 2. Supinates the forearm

CHECKLIST

O Brachialis

O Biceps brachii

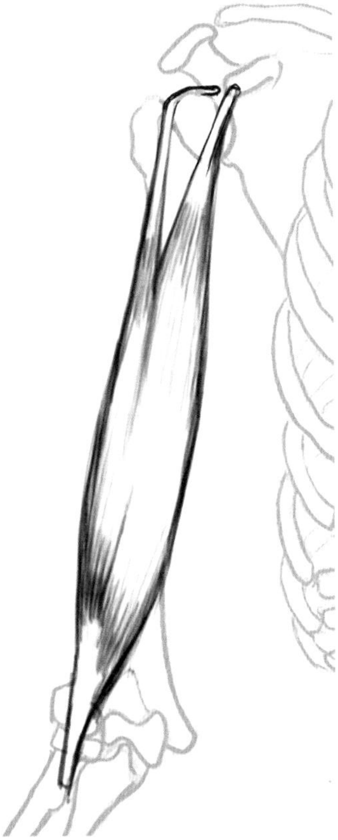

ANTERIOR

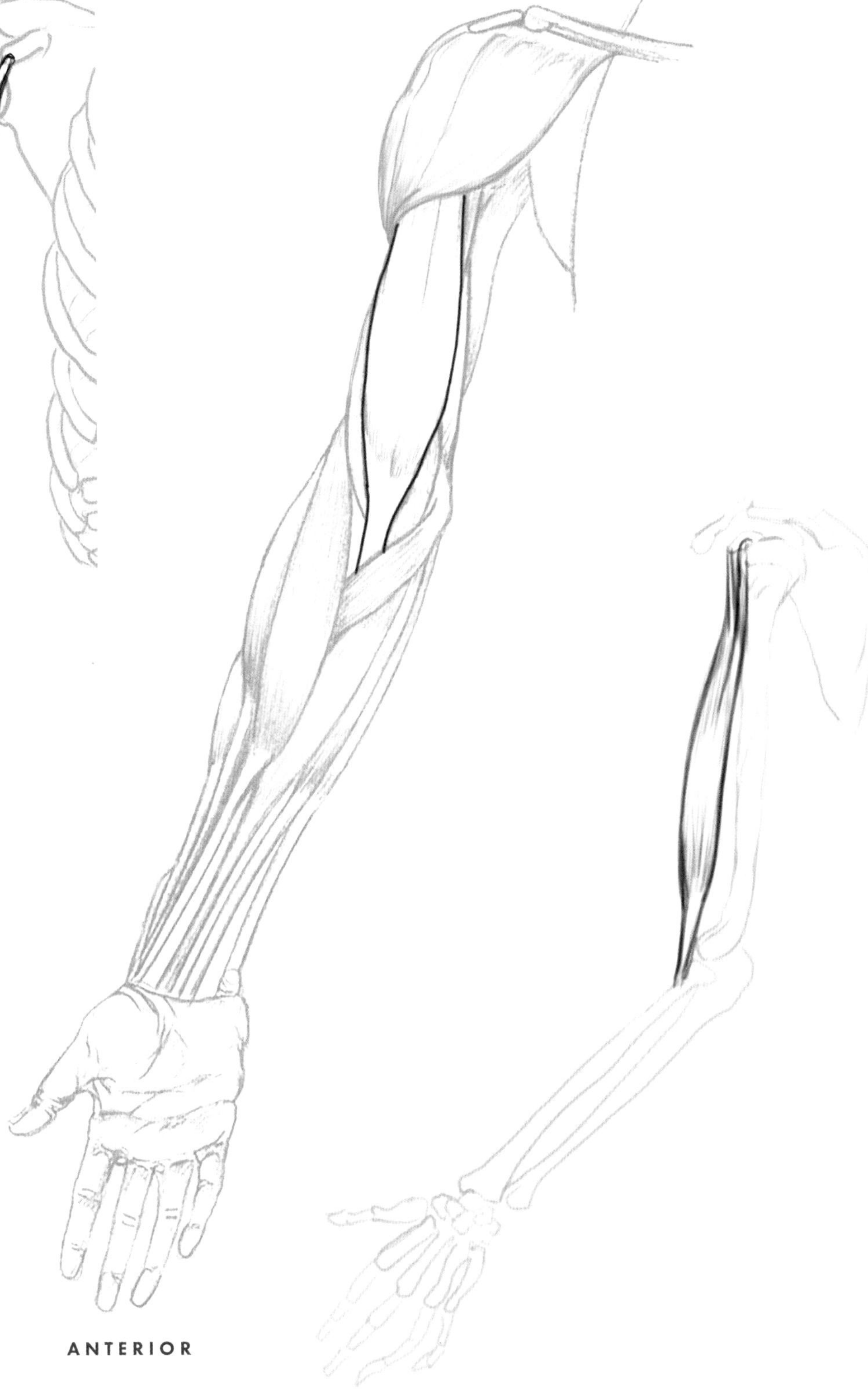

ANTERIOR

LATERAL

E.3. CORACOBRACHIALIS

STRUCTURE

The coracobrachialis is a cylindrical muscle resembling a small version of the biceps brachii.

ORIGIN

The coracoid process of the scapula.

INSERTION

The inside edge of the humerus at around the halfway point.

ACTION

Adducts and flexes the shoulder joint (1).

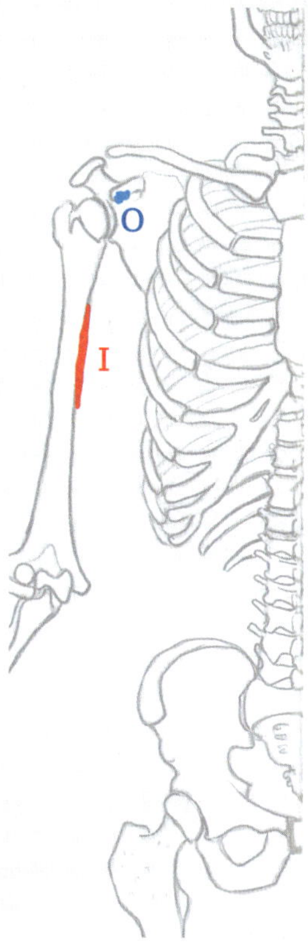

ANTERIOR

1.

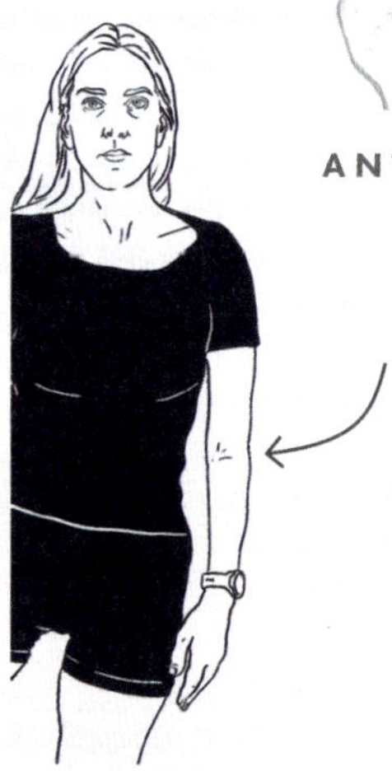

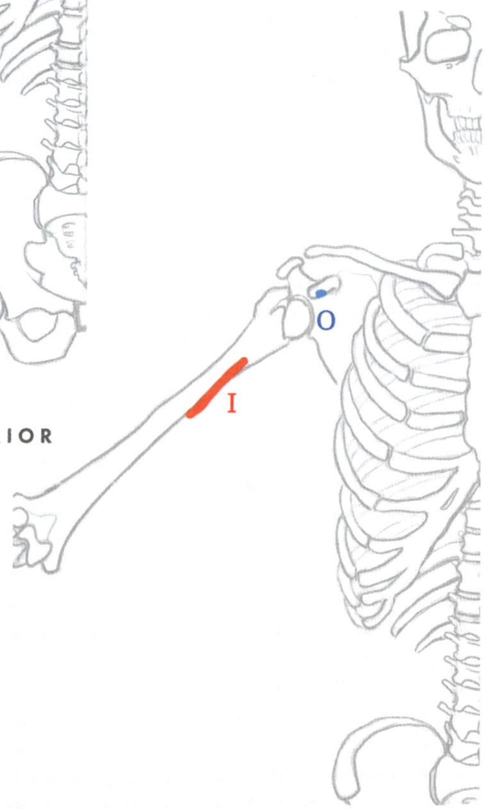

ANTERIOR

1. Adducts and flexes the shoulder joint

CHECKLIST

O Brachialis

O Biceps brachii

O Coracobrachialis

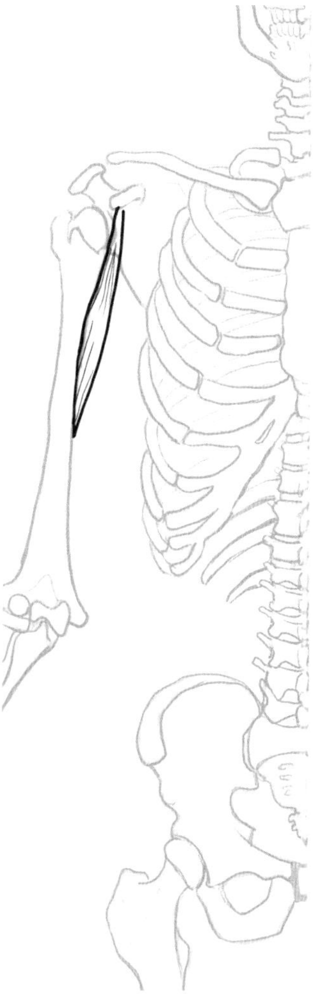

ANTERIOR

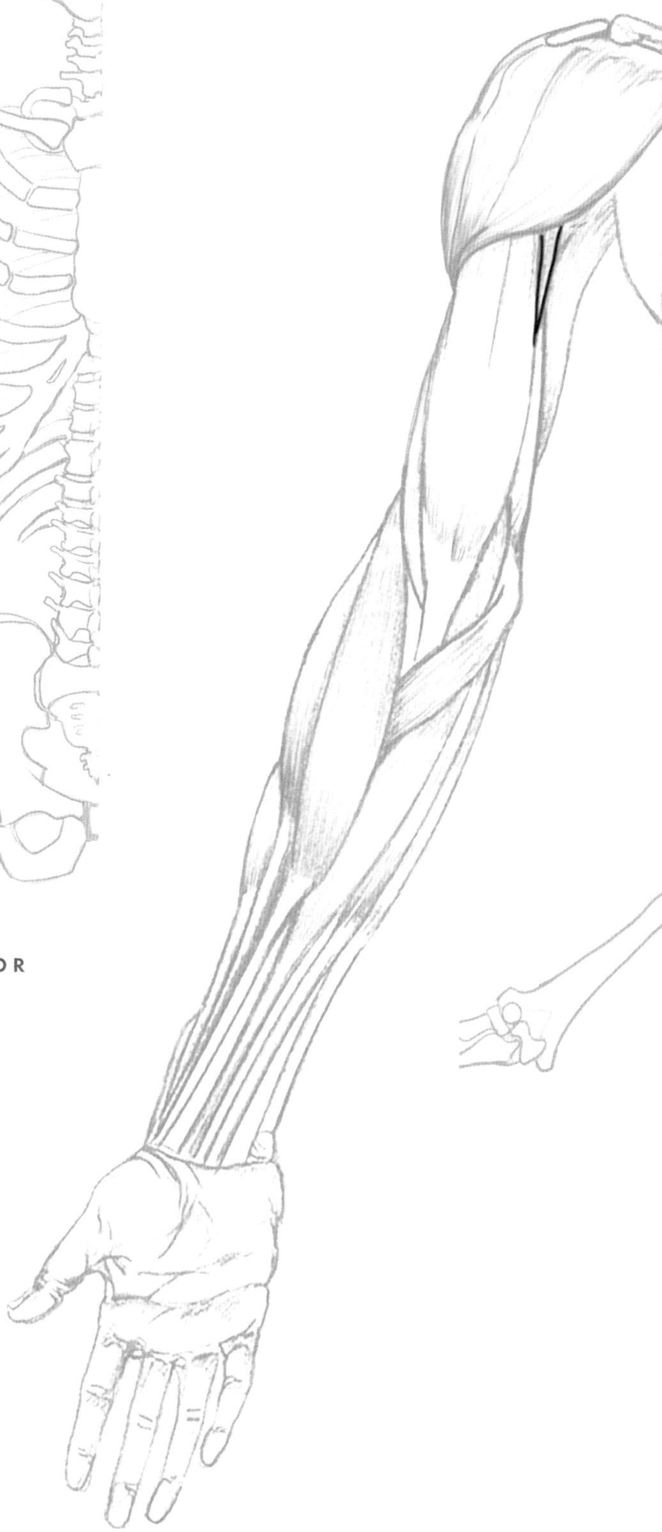

ANTERIOR

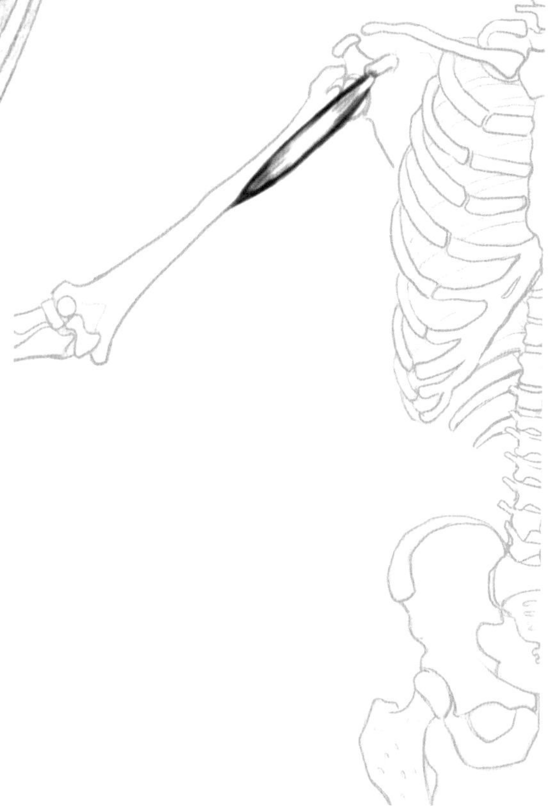

ANTERIOR

E4. TRICEP MEDIAL HEAD

STRUCTURE

The tricep medial head is like a large, compressed teardrop shape. Most of it lies under the other two tricep heads, so what you mainly see is the portion that is exposed medially, such as when the arm is abducted (out to the side).

ORIGIN

A large strip of the humerus on the back and medial area.

INSERTION

The common triceps tendon that inserts onto the olecranon (elbow) of the ulna.

ACTION

Extends the forearm (1).

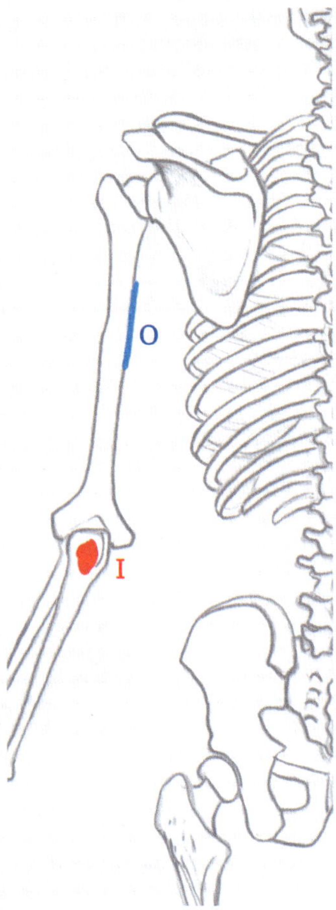

POSTERIOR

1.

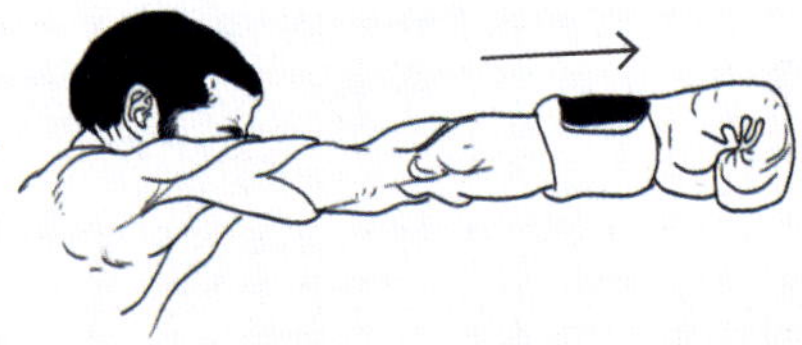

1. Extends forearm

CHECKLIST

- O Brachialis
- O Biceps brachii
- O Coracobrachialis
- O Tricep medial head

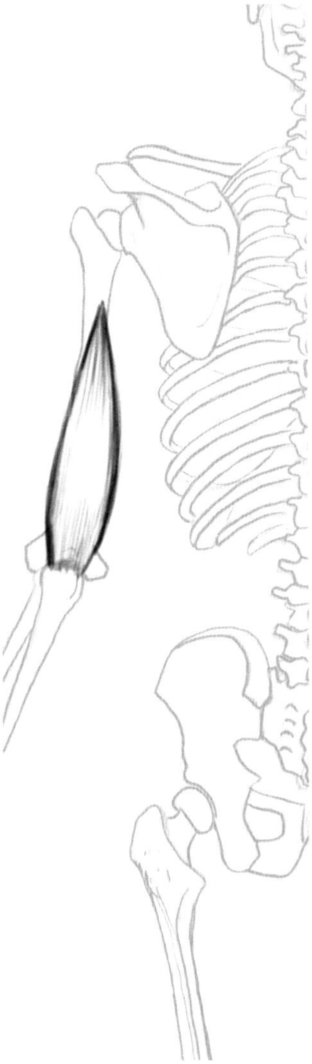

POSTERIOR

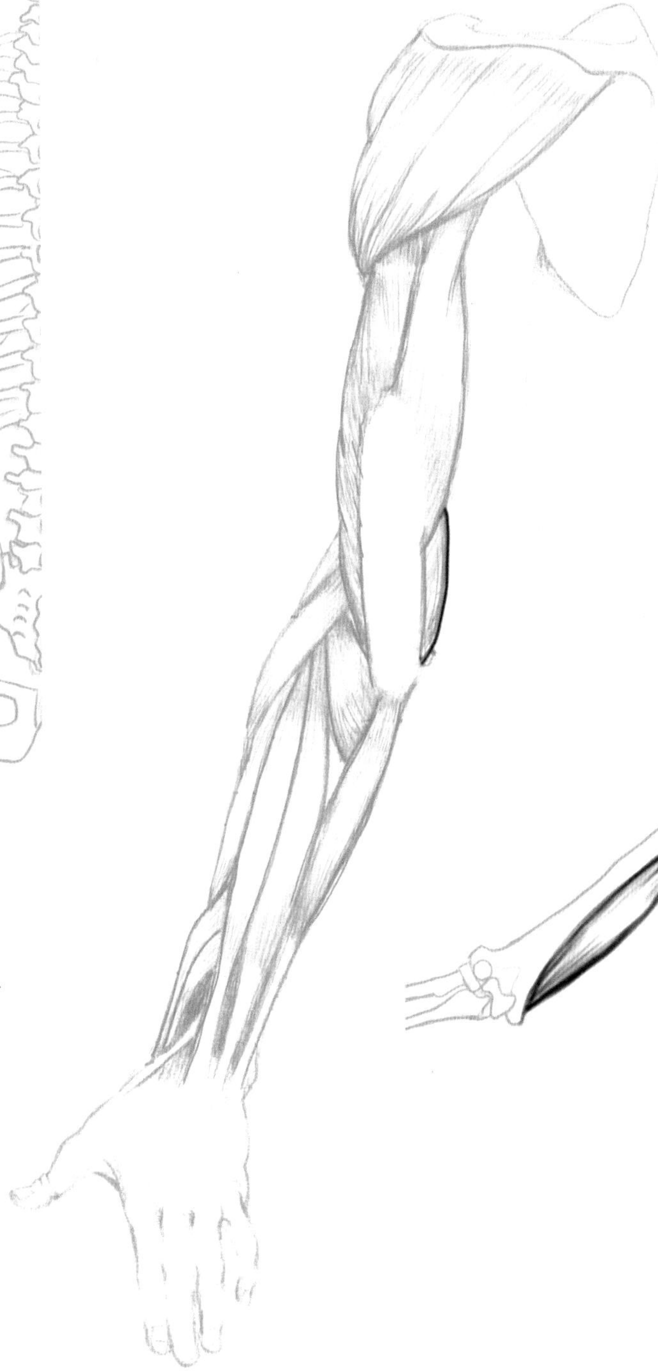

POSTERIOR

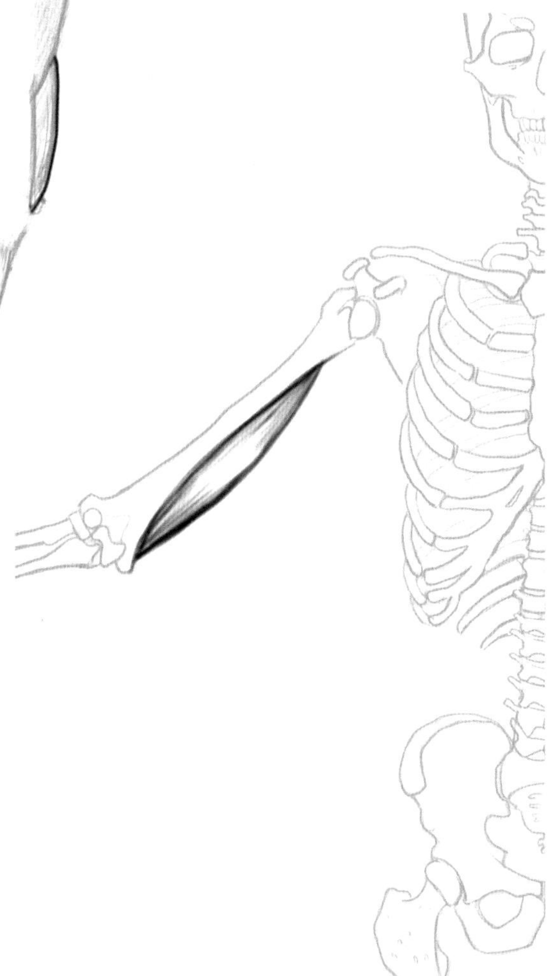

ANTERIOR

E.5. TRICEP LONG HEAD

STRUCTURE

The tricep long head is the largest of the three heads. At the top it is a band of muscle that is attached to the scapula, then it flares out into a large teardrop shape, very much like the gastrocnemius medial head of the lower leg.

ORIGIN

Just below the glenoid fossa (the shallow socket of the scapula) on the lateral edge. It's the only one of the three triceps that attaches to the scapula.

INSERTION

The common tricep tendon that inserts onto the olecranon (elbow) of the ulna.

ACTION

Extends the elbow (1).

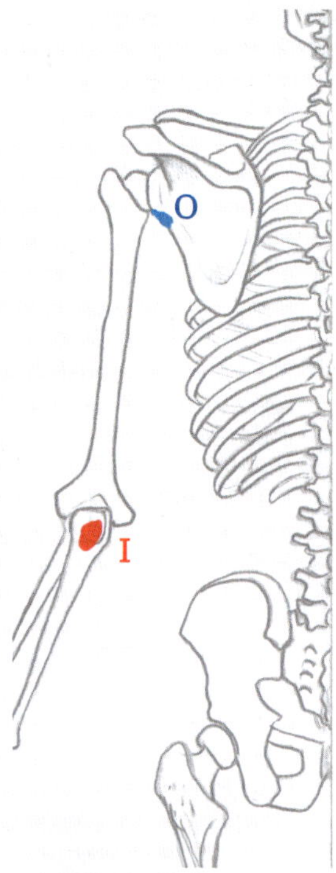

POSTERIOR

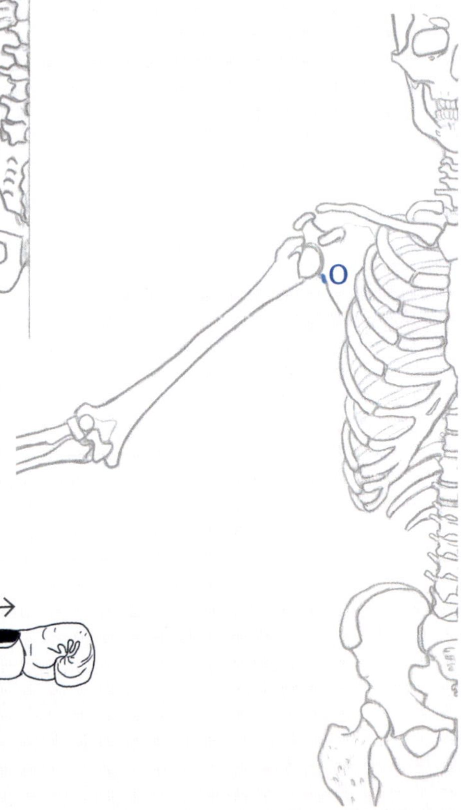

ANTERIOR

1.

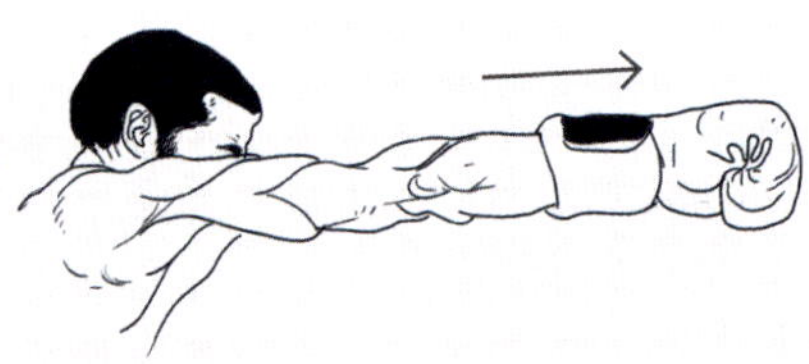

1. Extends the elbow

CHECKLIST

- O Brachialis
- O Biceps brachii
- O Coracobrachialis
- O Tricep medial head
- O Tricep long head

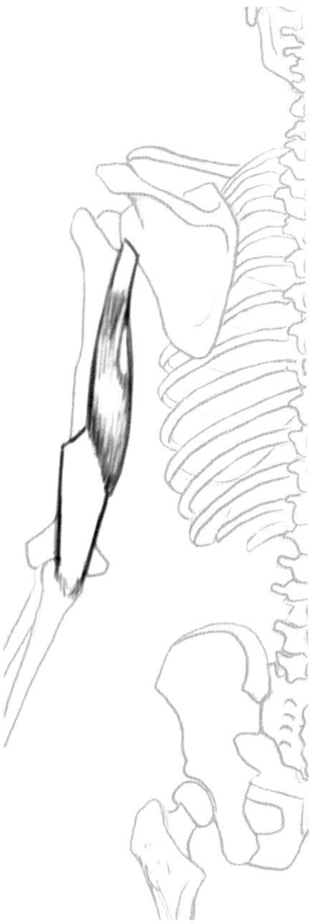

POSTERIOR

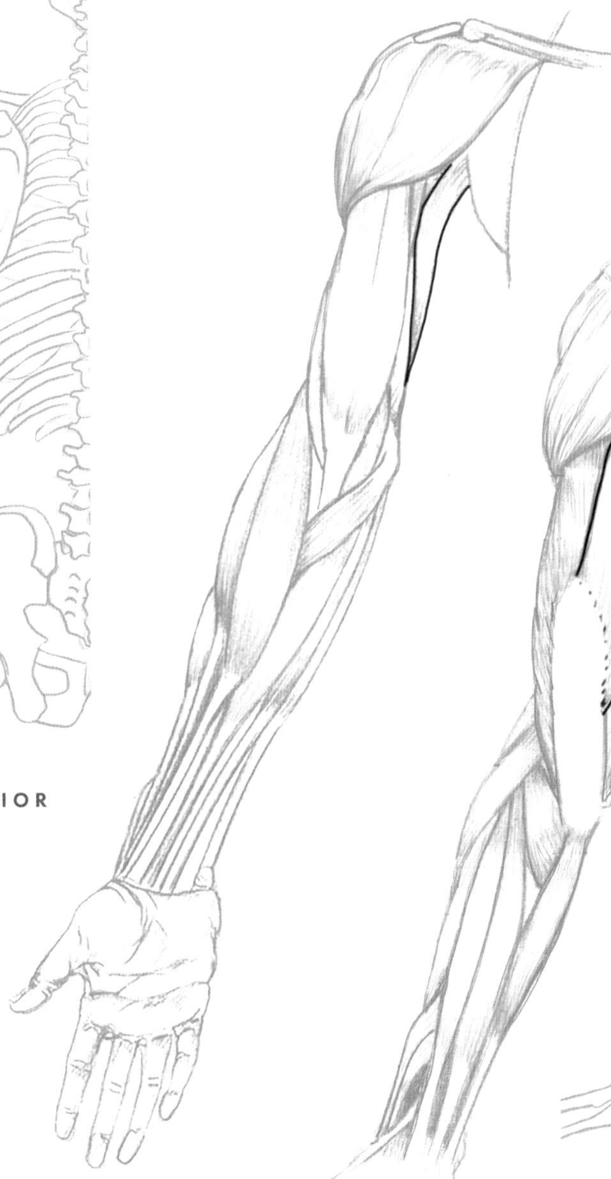

ANTERIOR

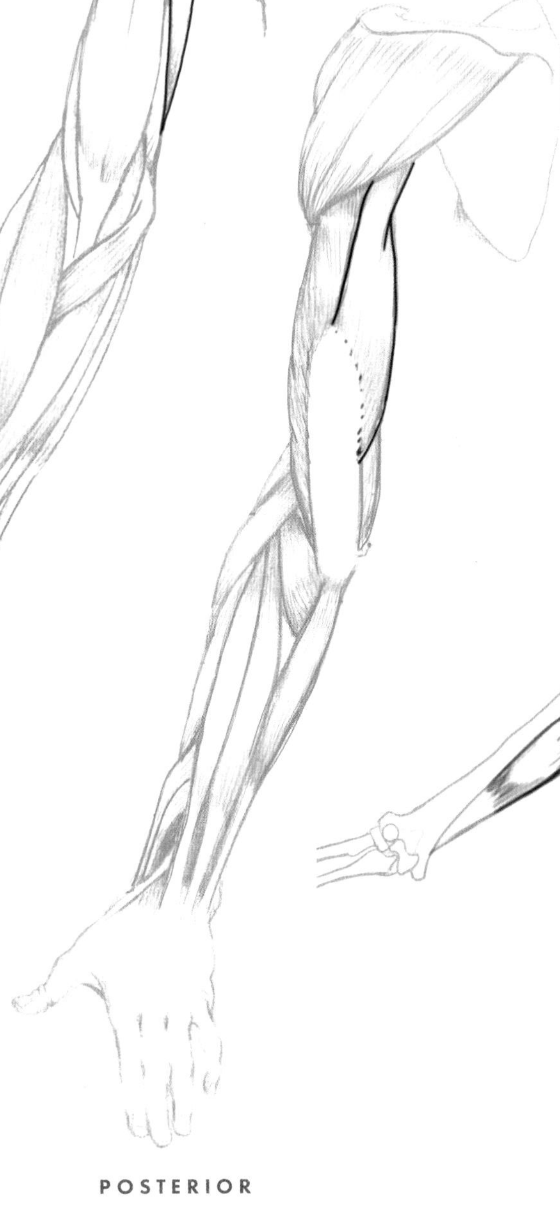

POSTERIOR

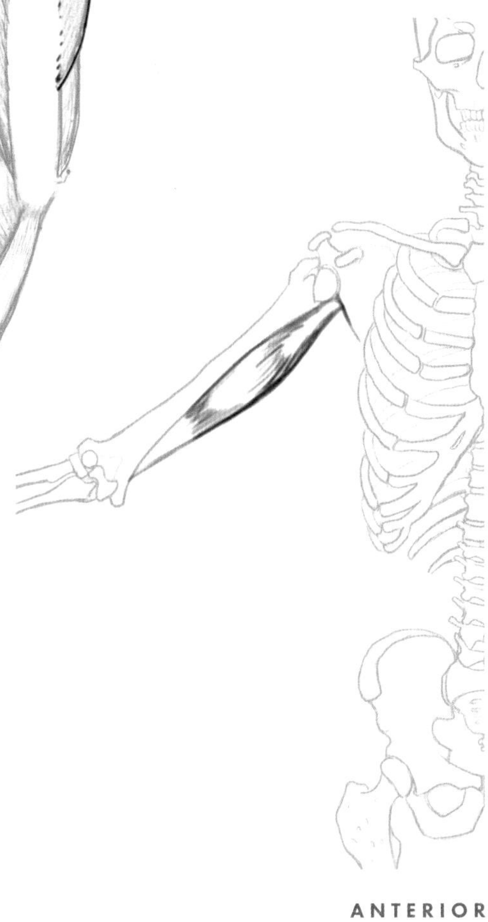

ANTERIOR

E.6. TRICEP LATERAL HEAD

STRUCTURE

The tricep lateral head is a tear-drop-shaped muscle, but it appears to have a "tail" of thin muscle as it drops down toward the elbow.

ORIGIN

Upper two-thirds of the upper lateral edge of the humerus.

INSERTION

The common tricep tendon that inserts onto the olecranon (elbow) of the ulna.

ACTION

Extends the elbow (1).

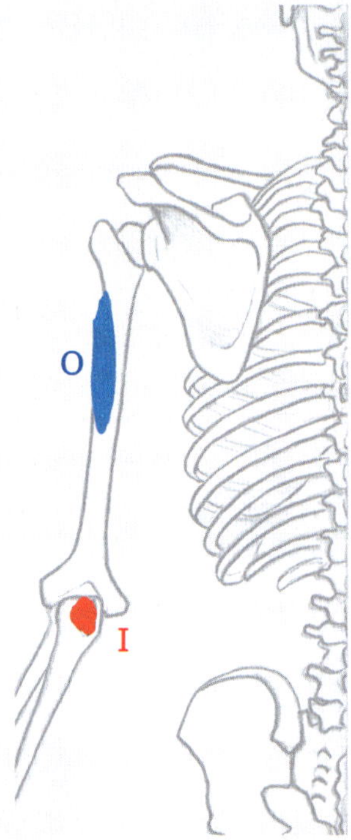

POSTERIOR

1.

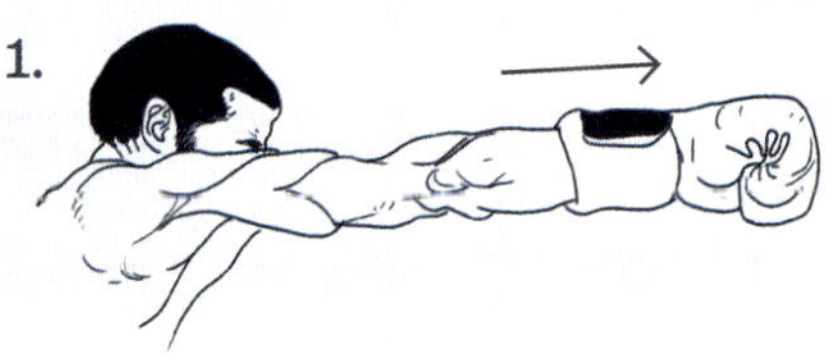

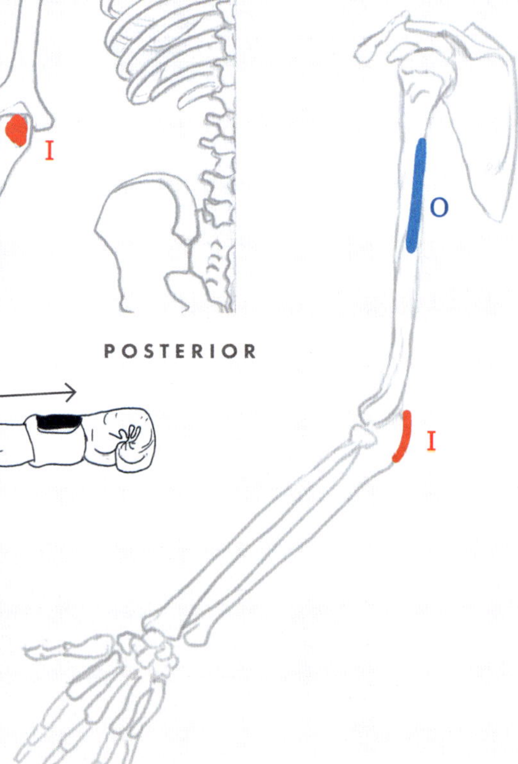

LATERAL

1. Extends the elbow

CHECKLIST

- O Brachialis
- O Biceps brachii
- O Coracobrachialis
- O Tricep medial head
- O Tricep long head
- O Tricep lateral head

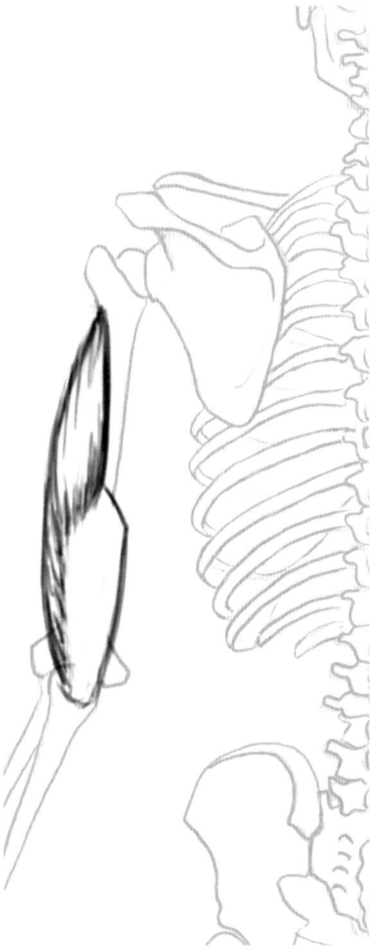

POSTERIOR

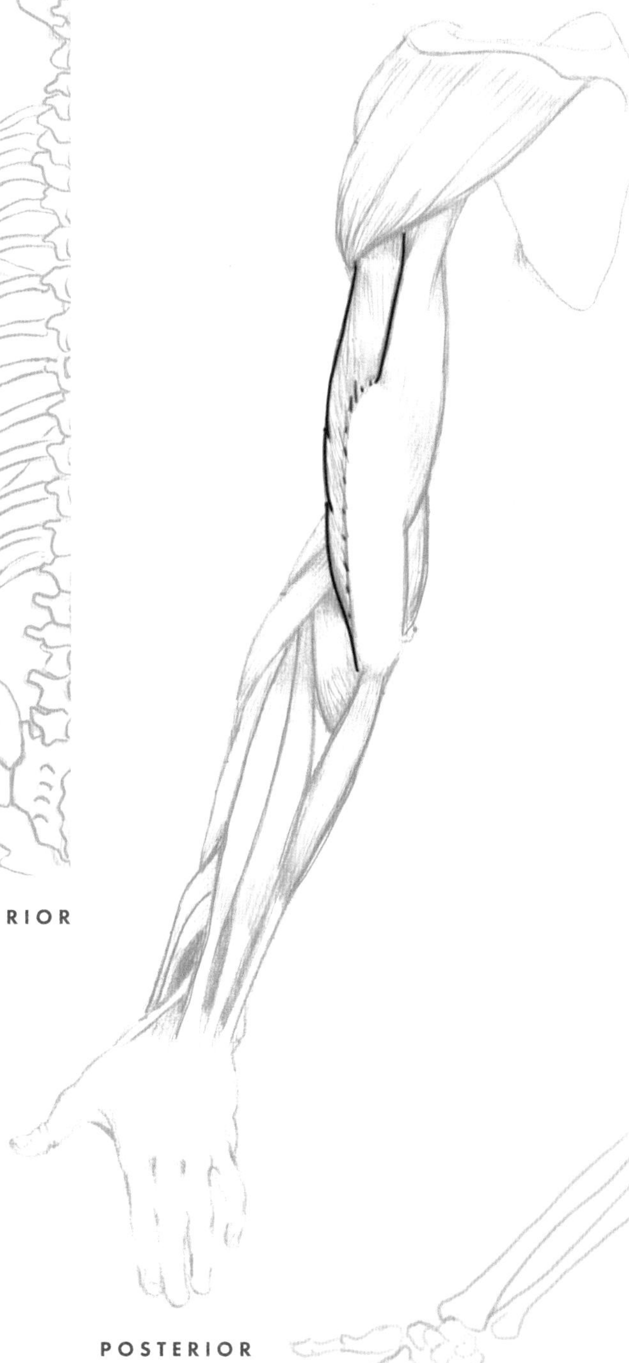

POSTERIOR

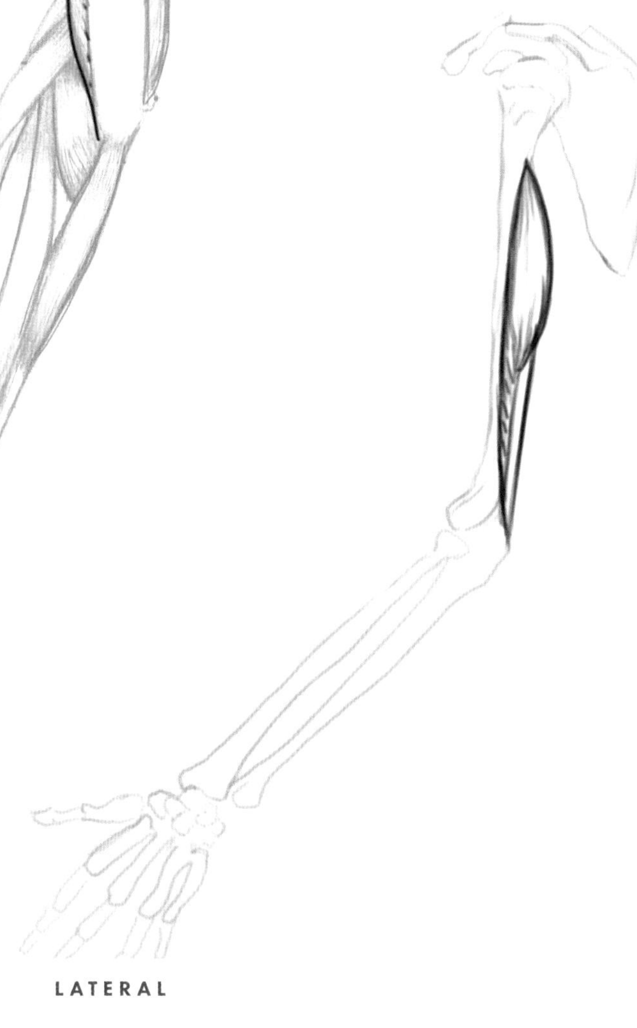

LATERAL

E.7. DELTOID

STRUCTURE

The deltoid is a large triangular muscle that comes to a point at the deltoid tuberosity, halfway down the side of the humerus. Remember that the brachialis starts at this spot.

ORIGIN

This muscle is divided into three portions. The rear, scapular portion originates far into the underneath area of the spine of the scapula. The front, clavicular portion originates a third of the way under the clavicle, the same distance as the trapezius just above it over the clavicle. The center section of the deltoid is called the acromial portion and it cups around the lateral side of the shoulder.

INSERTION

The deltoid tuberosity of the humerus, at the halfway point laterally.

ACTION

The front, clavicular portion helps raise the arm forward (1 and 1b); the back, scapular portion helps bring the arm back (2); and the powerful lateral portion abducts the arm, lifting it outward (3).

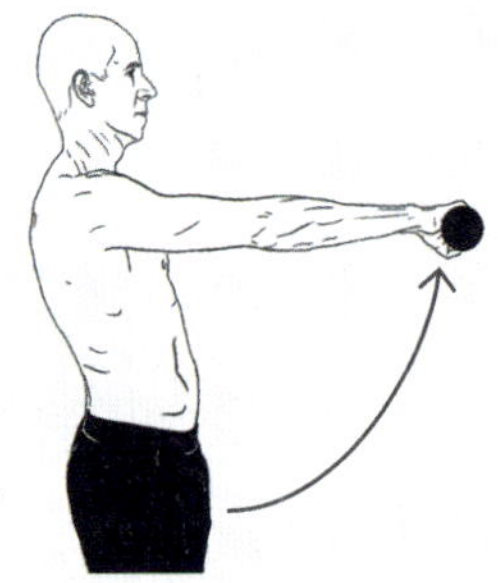
1.

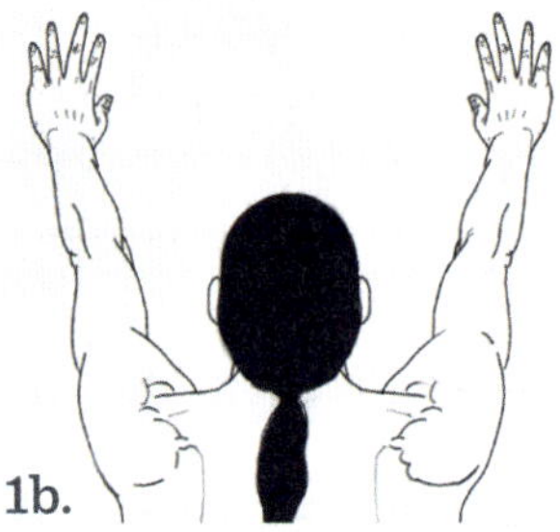
1b.

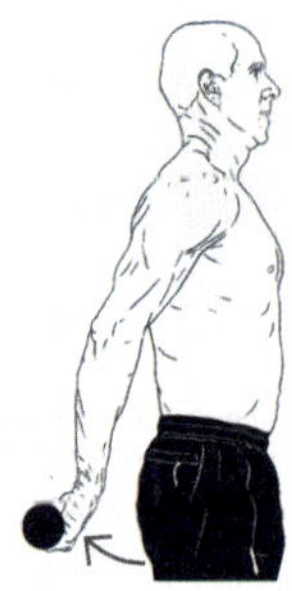
2.

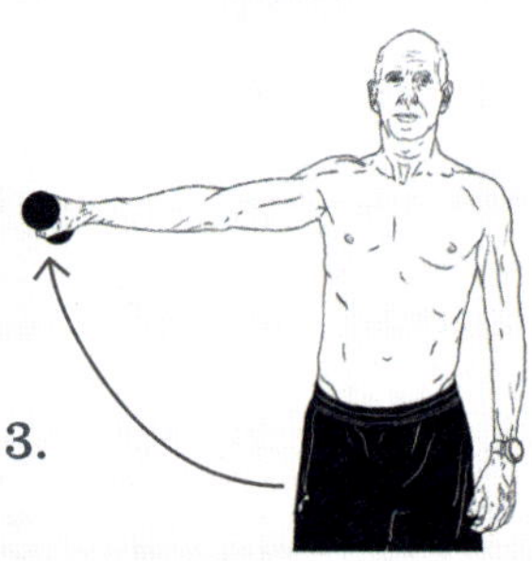
3.

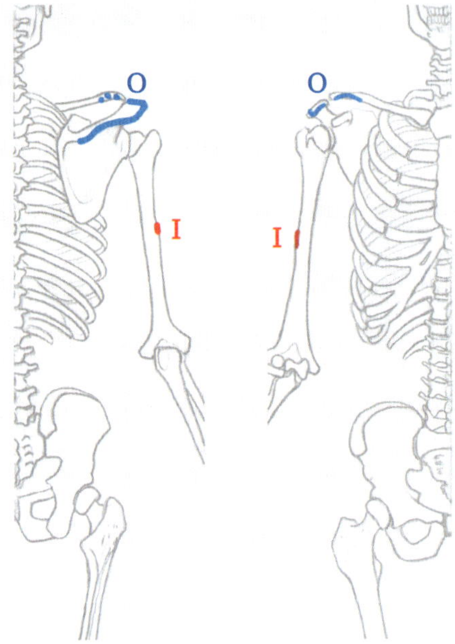

POSTERIOR ANTERIOR

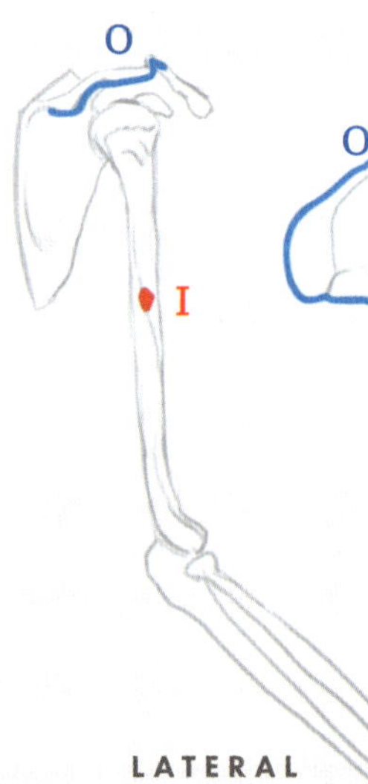

LATERAL

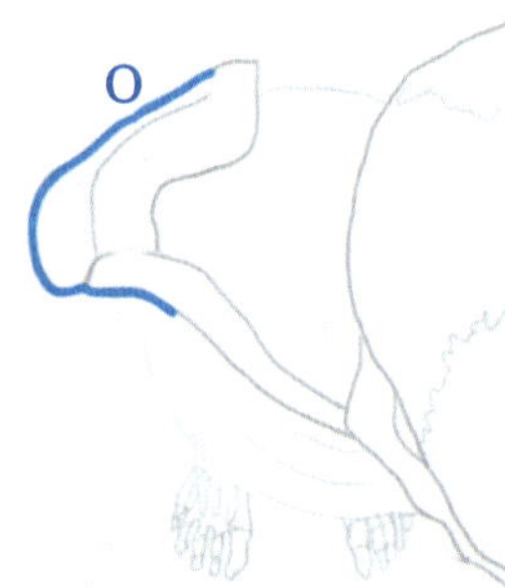

ABOVE

1. Raises arm forward; 2. Brings arm back; 3. Abducts the arm

CHECKLIST

- O Brachialis
- O Biceps brachii
- O Coracobrachialis
- O Tricep medial head
- O Tricep long head
- O Tricep lateral head
- O Deltoid

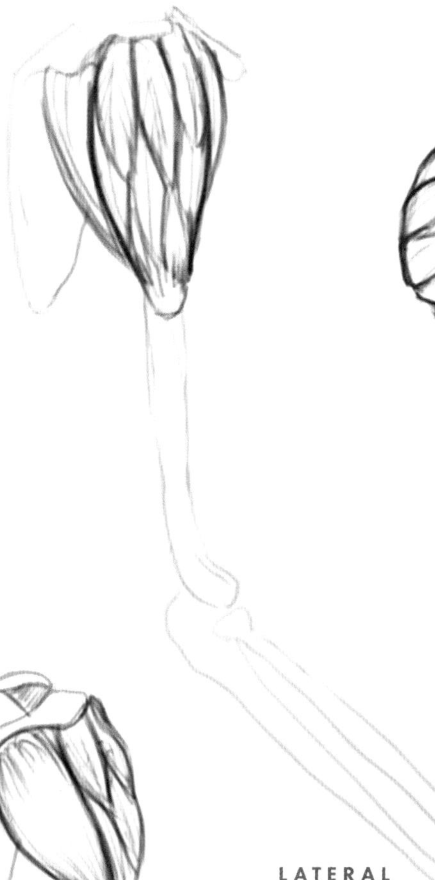

LATERAL

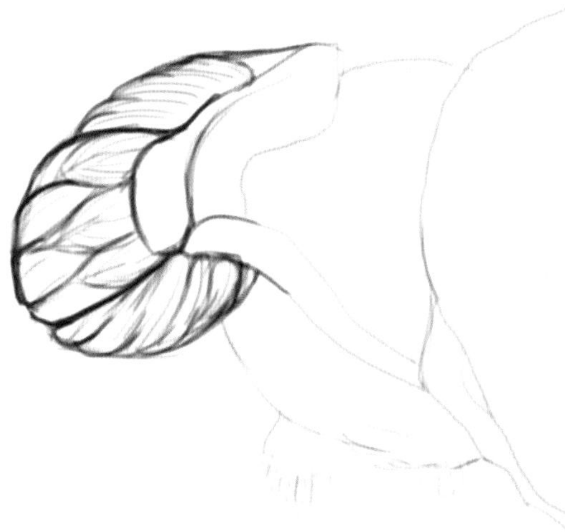

ABOVE

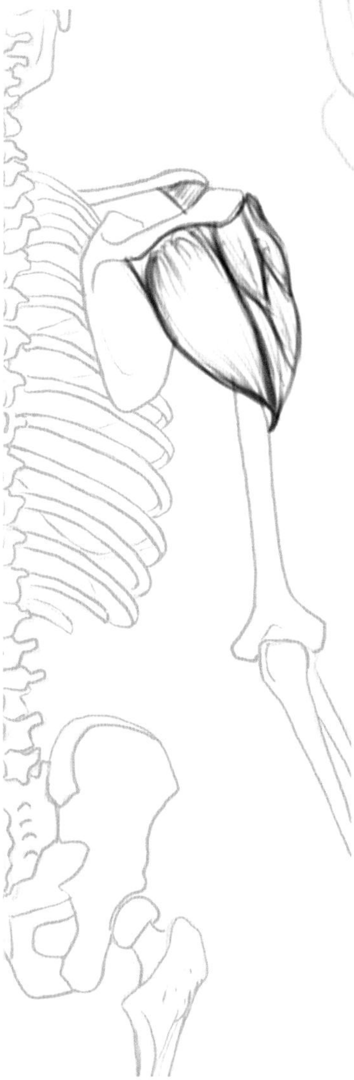

POSTERIOR

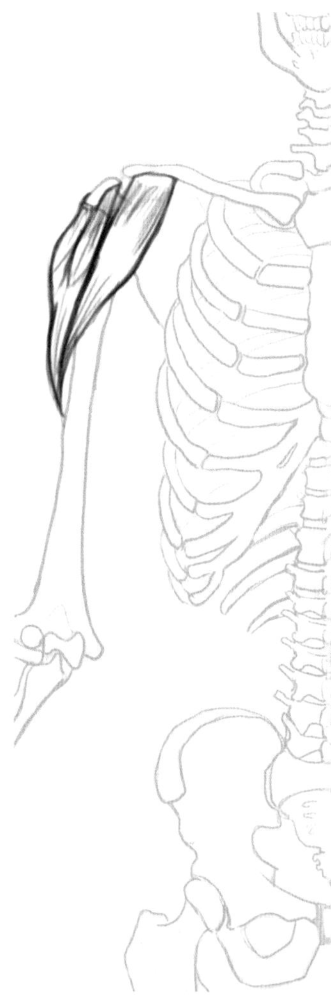

ANTERIOR

E.7. DELTOID

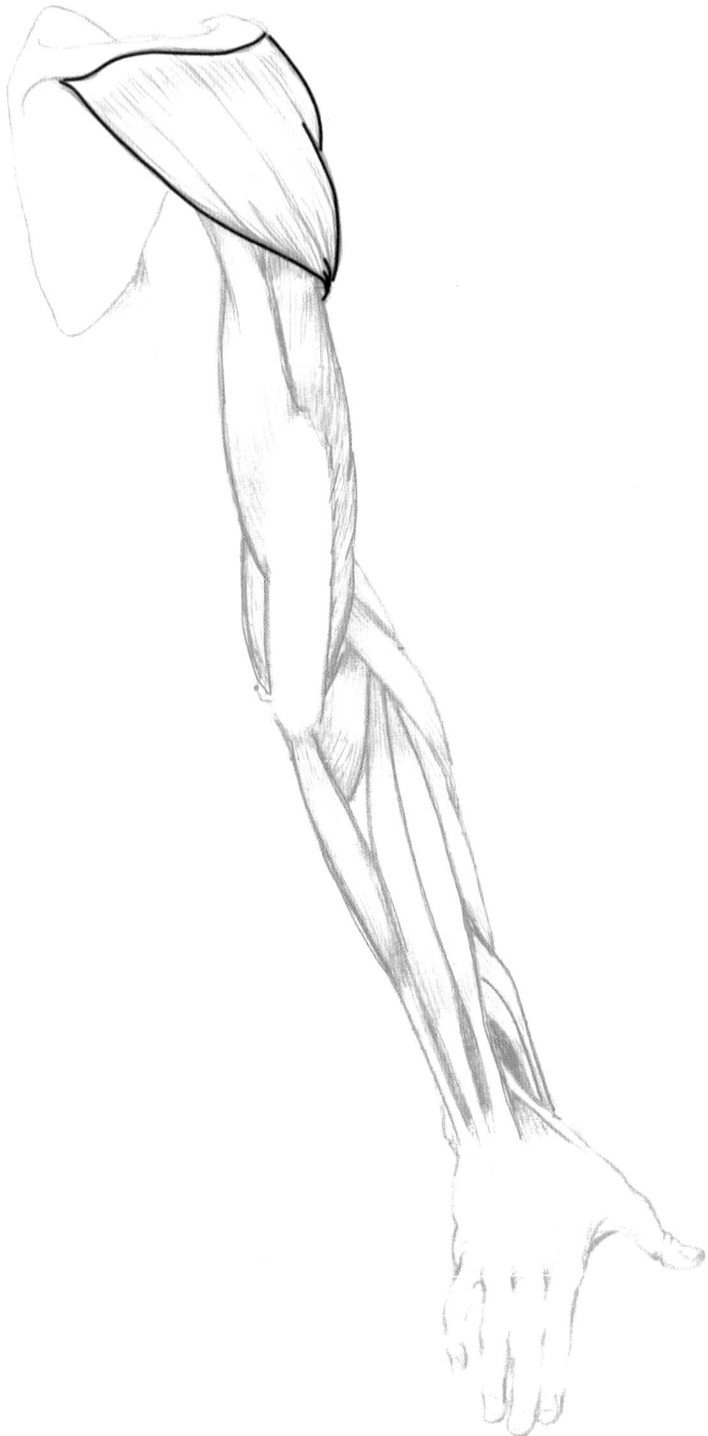

POSTERIOR

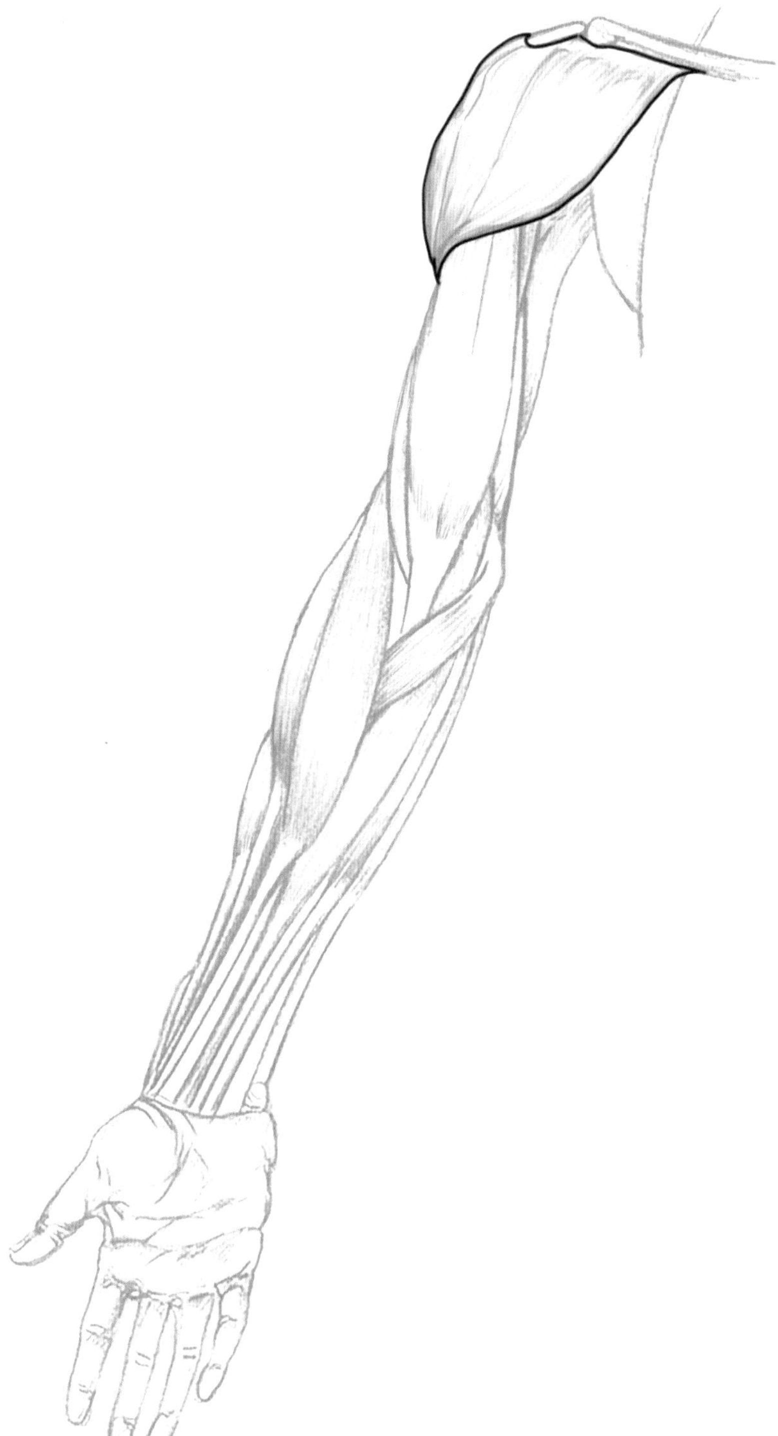

ANTERIOR

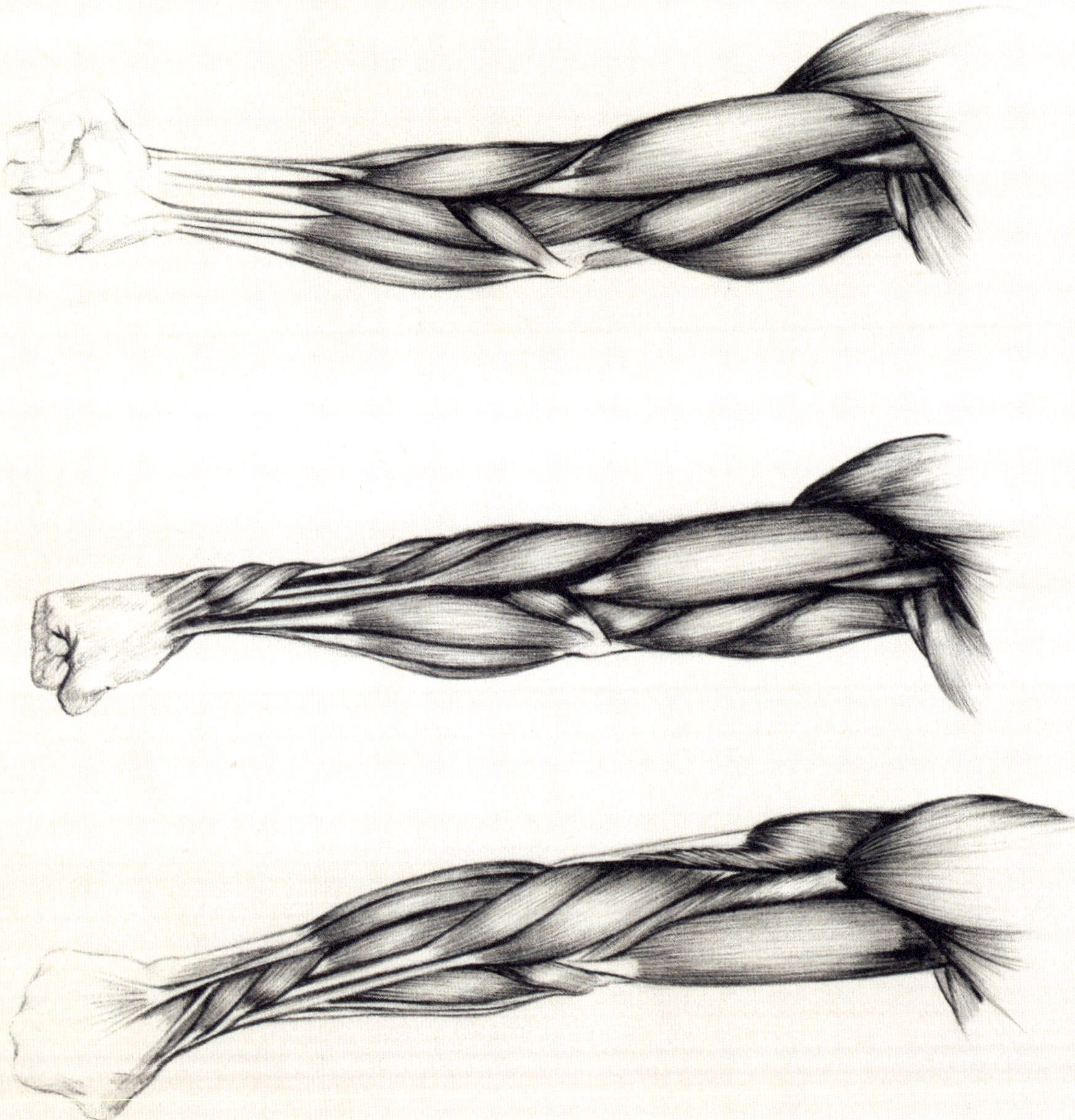

CHAPTER F

THE FOREARM

The forearm muscles provide a wide range of hand and wrist movements. They pronate and supinate the arm (turn the palm down and turn the palm up). The flexors on the front allow for powerful grasping, such as when you're making a fist. The extensors extend your fingers. The forearm muscles are an amazing team that allow you to play the piano or gently take a ladybug off a leaf, but at the same time are strong enough to hold your entire body off the ground by grasping a bar above you.

F.1. PALMARIS LONGUS

STRUCTURE

The palmaris longus is a small, thin, tubular muscle with a long tendon that ends at the palm of the hand as a flat aponeurosis (a flat sheet of fibrous tissue). The muscle can be set aside since you will not see it, but the tendon is very visible at the wrist on the palmar side when you make a fist and move it toward your body. Fun fact, not everyone has a palmaris longus. This is a muscle that is believed to be evolutionarily disappearing. If you do not have one, you will not miss it at all.

ORIGIN

The medial epicondyle ("funny bone") of the humerus. The four "flexors" that are shown in this book all originate at or right by the medial epicondyle.

INSERTION

The palmar aponeurosis of the palm.

ACTION

Weakly helps bring the fist toward the body (1) and flex the wrist.

NOTE: Muscles F.1. through F.4. are the flexors of the forearm. All the forearm muscles have been reduced to the essential muscles for artists.

1.

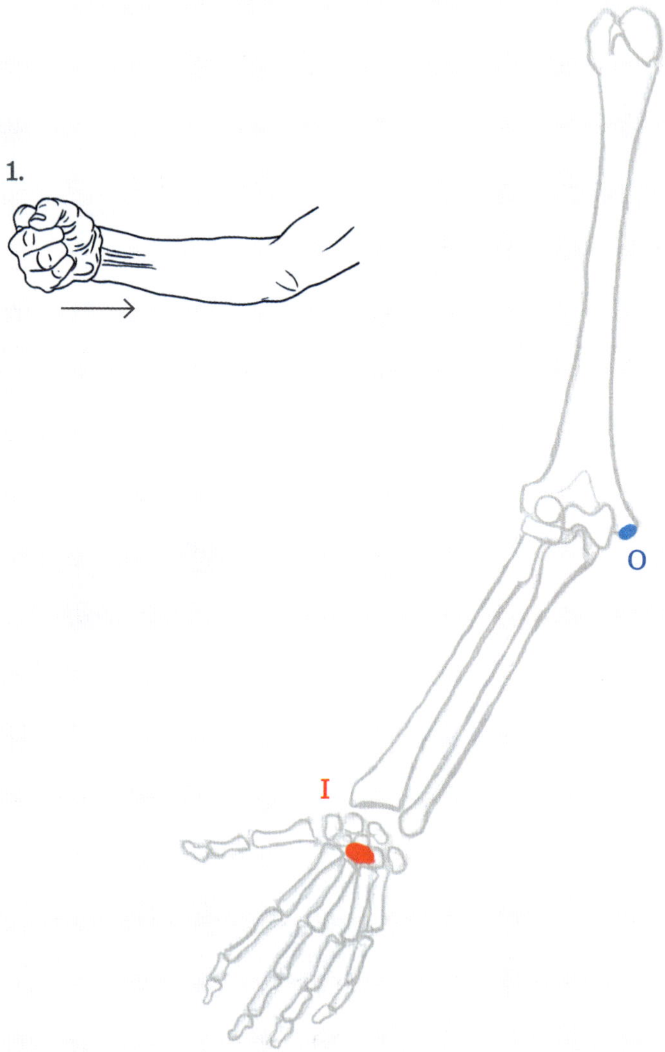

ANTERIOR

1. Helps bring the fist toward the body and flex the fingers

CHECKLIST

O Palmaris longus

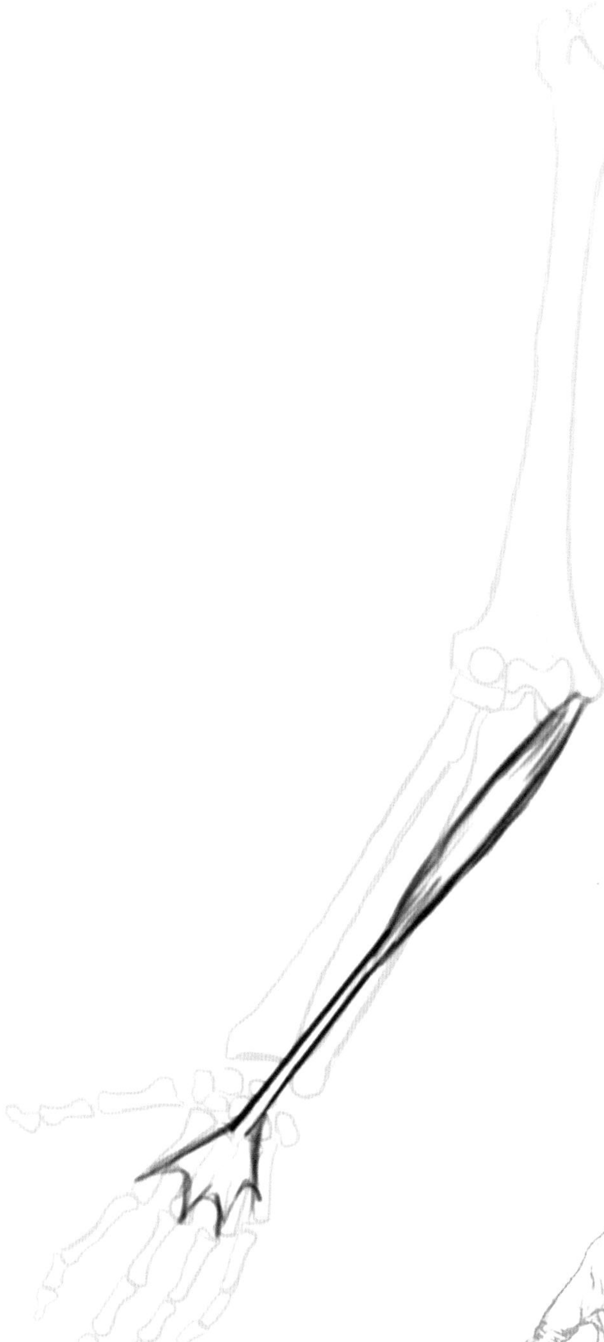

ANTERIOR

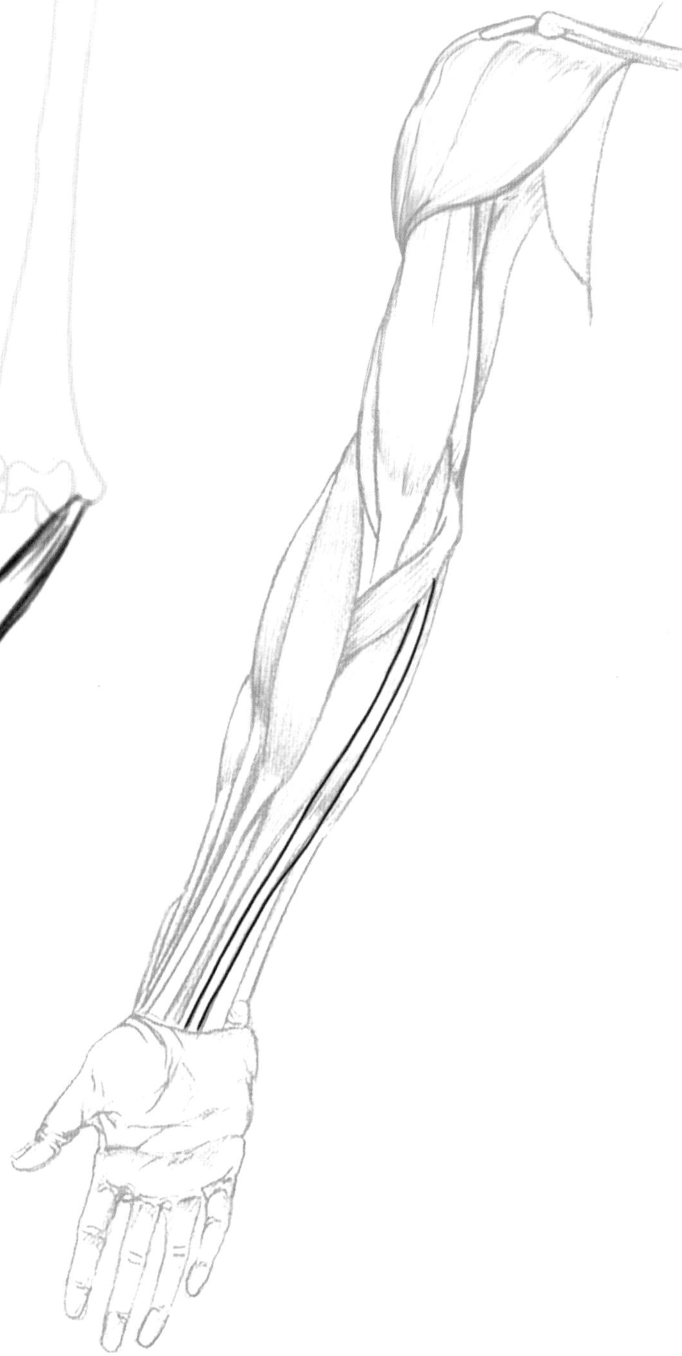

ANTERIOR

F.2. FLEXOR CARPI RADIALIS

STRUCTURE

The flexor carpi radialis is a long, somewhat flat muscle that has a prominent tendon next to the palmaris longus. These two tendons can be easily seen when you make a fist and then bring your fist toward your body. Remember, "carpi" means "wrist," and "radialis" refers to the fact that the direction of this muscle is toward the radius, the thumb side of the forearm.

ORIGIN

The medial epicondyle of the humerus.

INSERTION

The joint between the carpal bones and the metacarpals of the index and middle fingers.

ACTION

Flexes the forearm (1) and helps in radial deviation of the hand, moving the hand outward. That motion is very limited.

1.

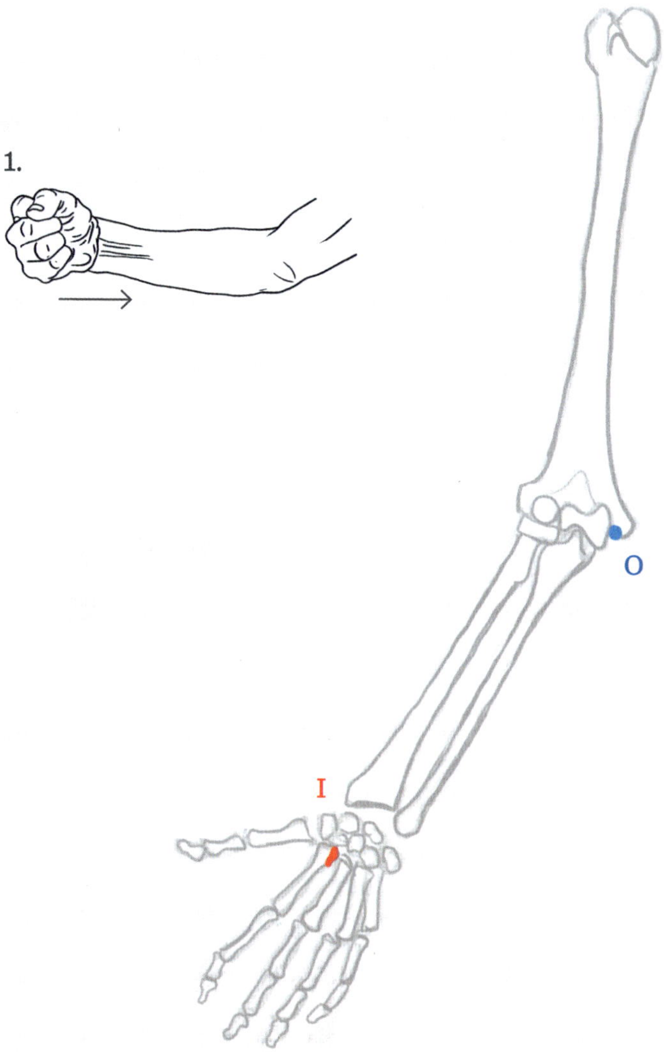

ANTERIOR

1. Flexes the forearm

CHECKLIST

O Palmaris longus

O Flexor carpi radialis

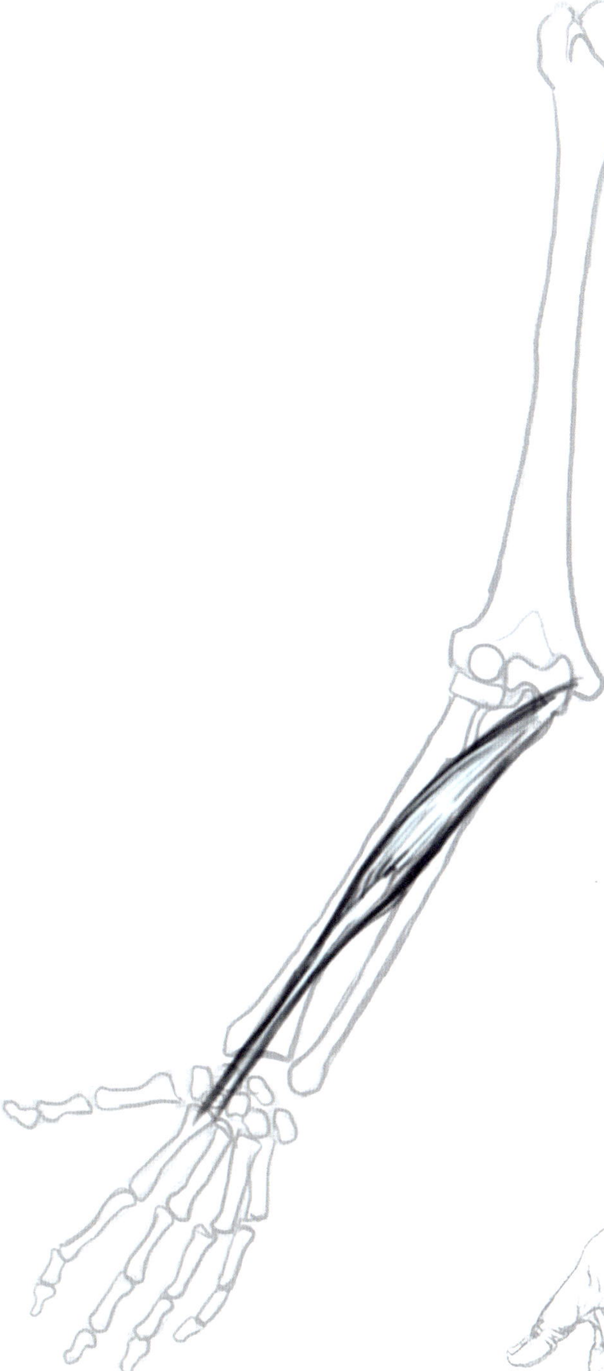

ANTERIOR

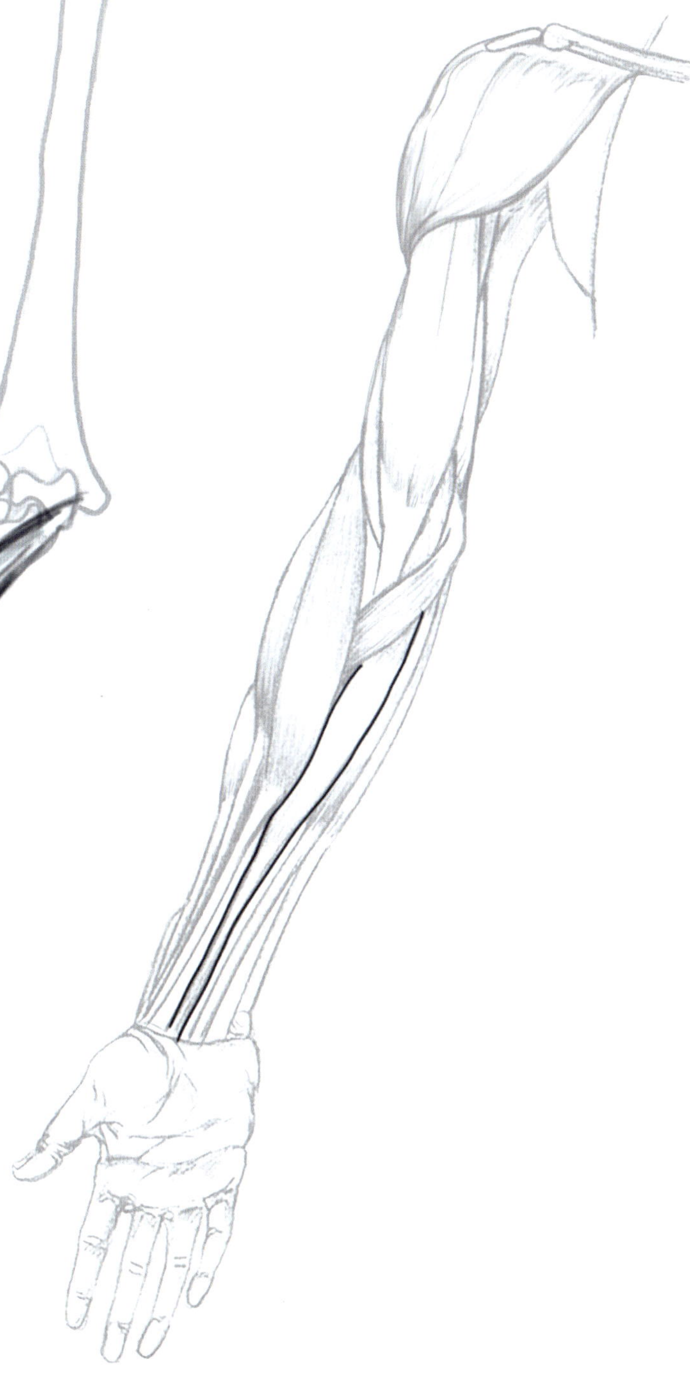

ANTERIOR

F.3. PRONATOR TERES

STRUCTURE

The pronator teres is a short fleshy muscle. Even though this is a "pronator," it is included here with the flexor group.

ORIGIN

The medial epicondyle of the humerus.

INSERTION

The lateral (outside) edge of the radius at the halfway point.

ACTION

Pronates (turns the palm downward; 1) and helps flex the forearm (2).

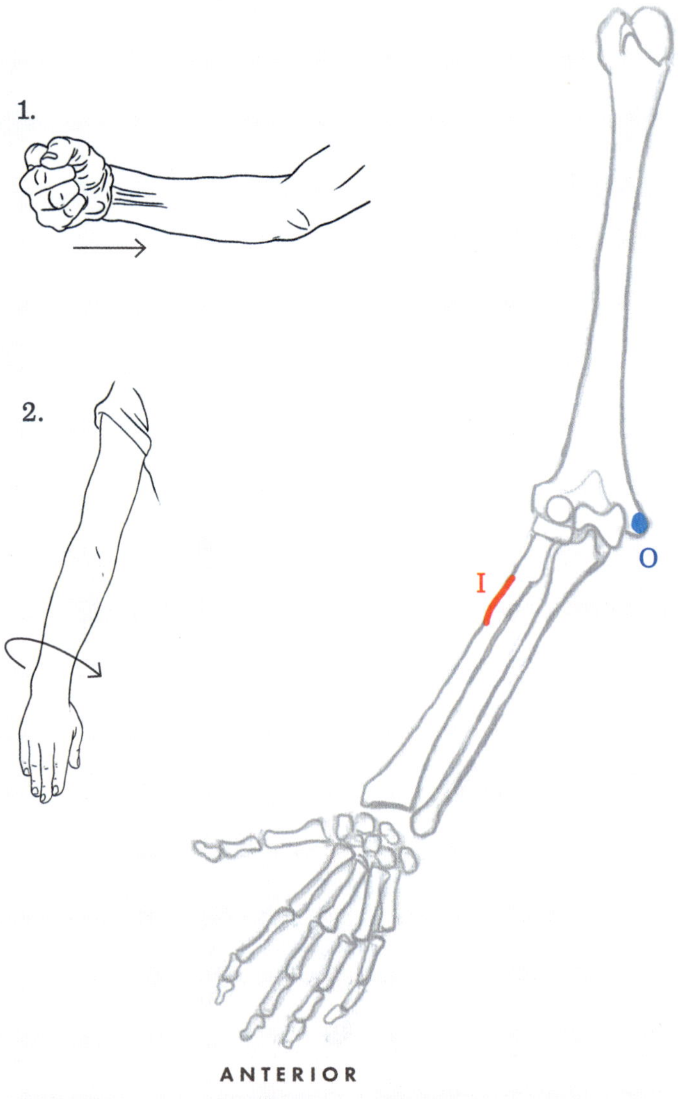

1. Pronates the forearm; 2. Helps flex the forearm

CHECKLIST

- O Palmaris longus
- O Flexor carpi radialis
- O Pronator teres

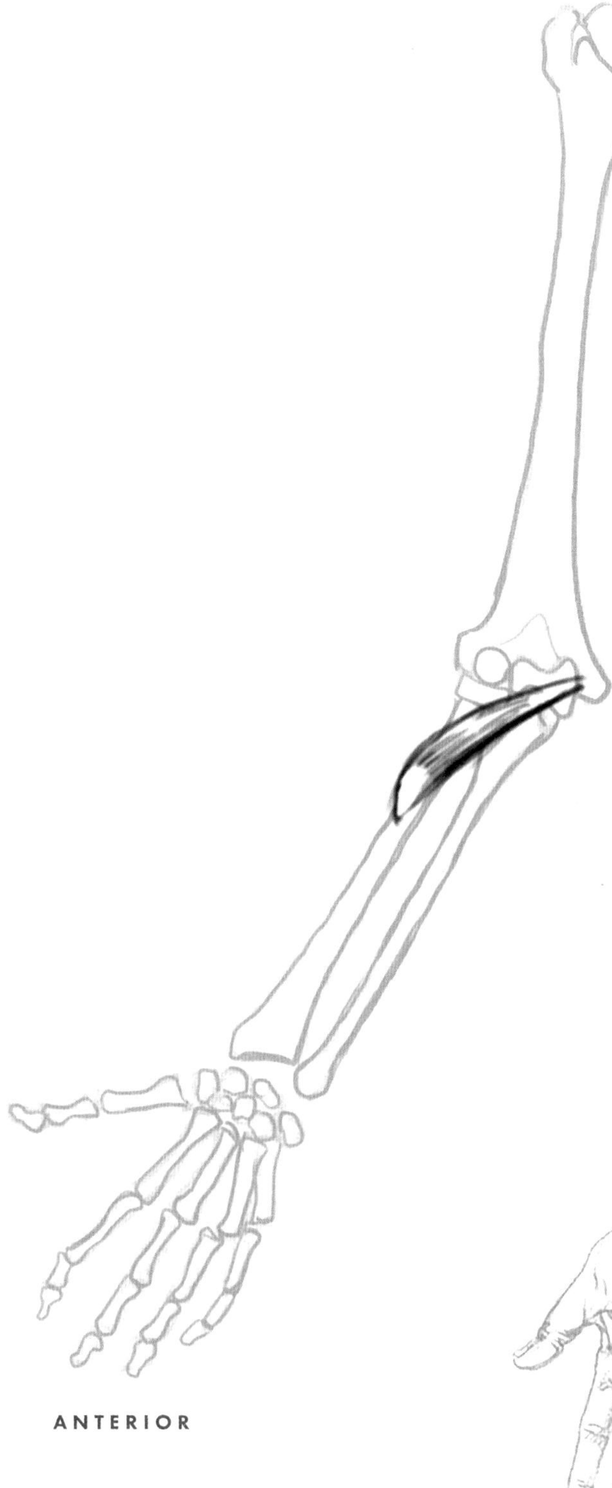

ANTERIOR

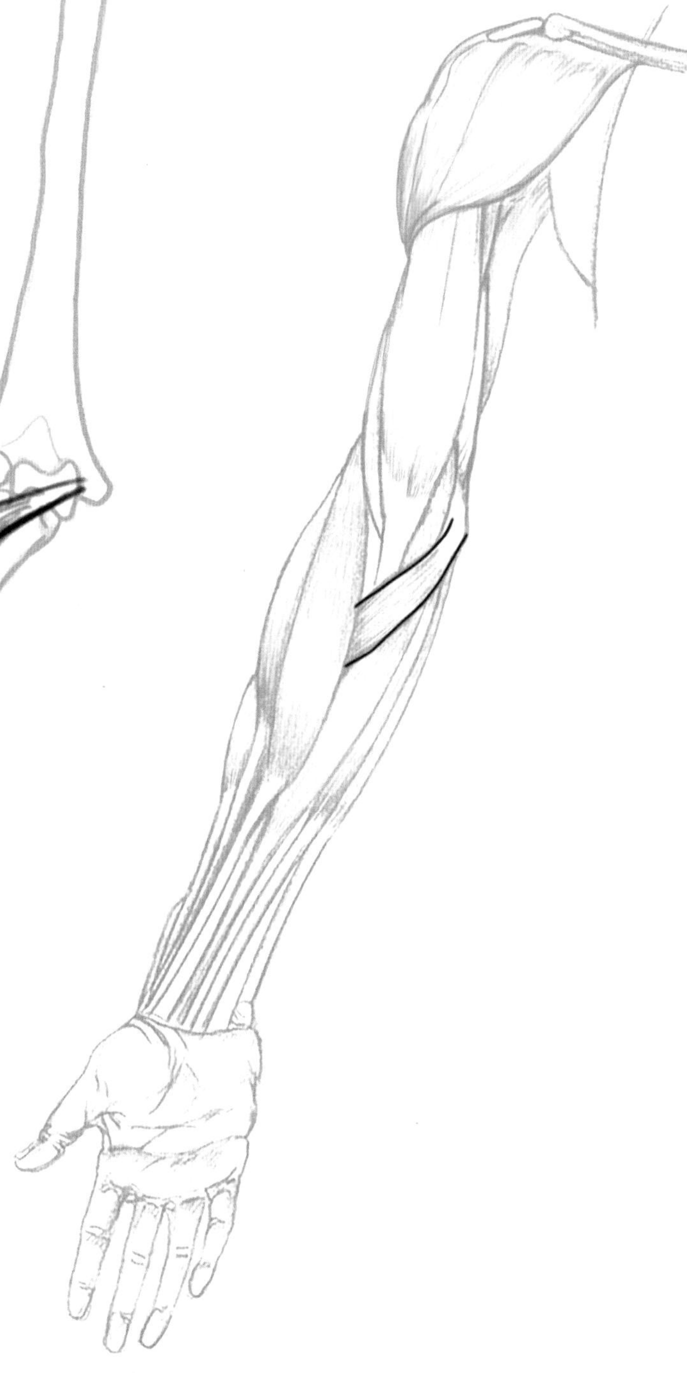

ANTERIOR

F.4. FLEXOR CARPI ULNARIS

STRUCTURE

The flexor carpi ulnaris starts as a broad, flat, canoe-shaped muscle that tapers distally (further from origin). It is an important contour muscle of the forearm. Remember, "carpi" means "wrist," and "ulnar" refers to the ulna, or the little finger side.

ORIGIN

The medial epicondyle of the humerus and also the medial border of the ulna/olecranon and down the crest of the ulna (the ridge).

INSERTION

The protruding wrist bone at the side of the little finger. This little bone is called the pisiform.

ACTION

Flexes and helps with ulnar deviation of the hand (moves the hand toward the little finger; 1).

1.

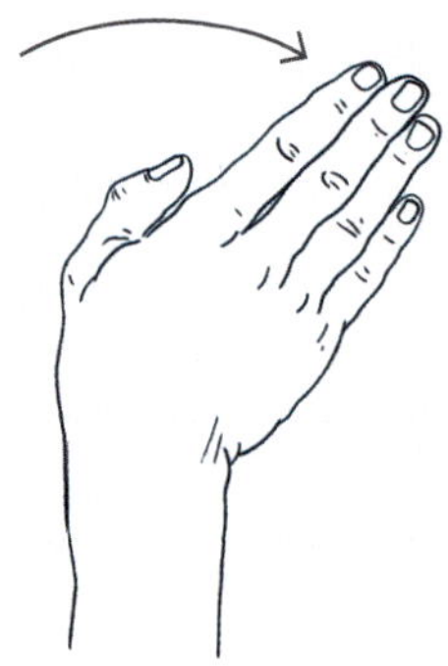

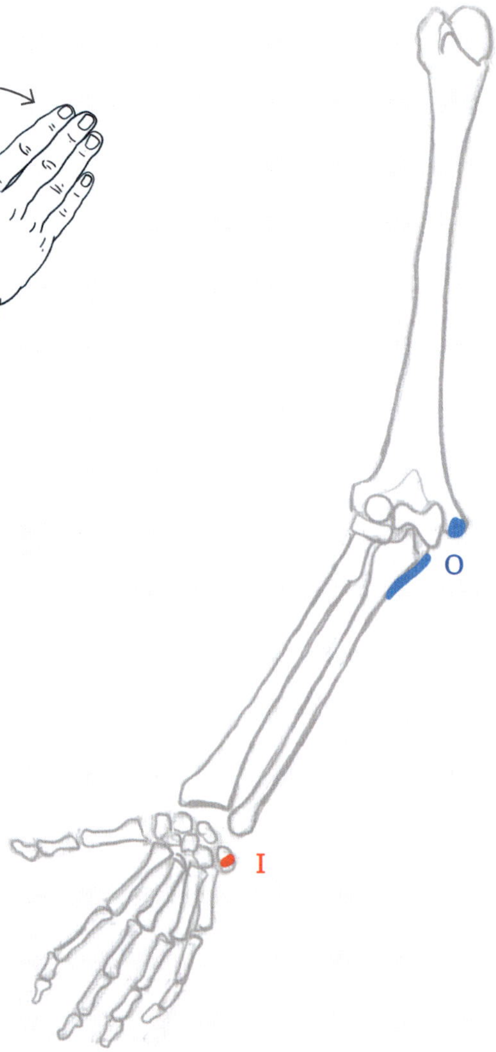

ANTERIOR

1. Moves the hand toward the little finger

CHECKLIST

- O Palmaris longus
- O Flexor carpi radialis
- O Pronator teres
- O Flexor carpi ulnaris

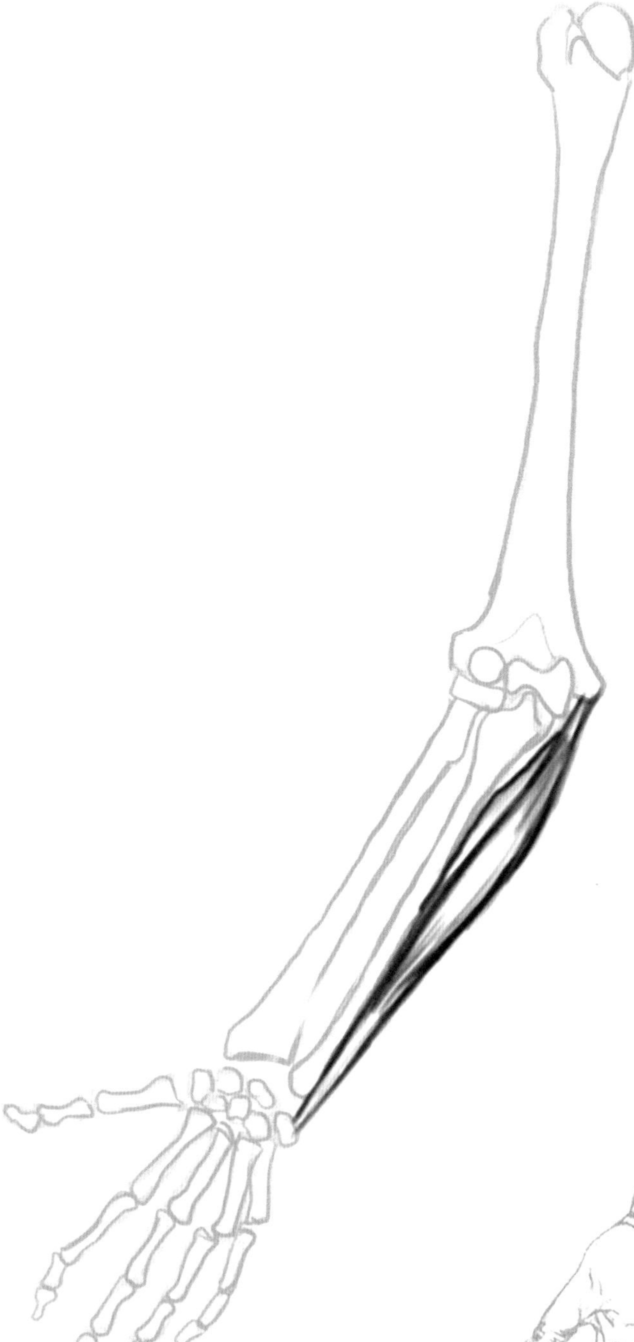

ANTERIOR

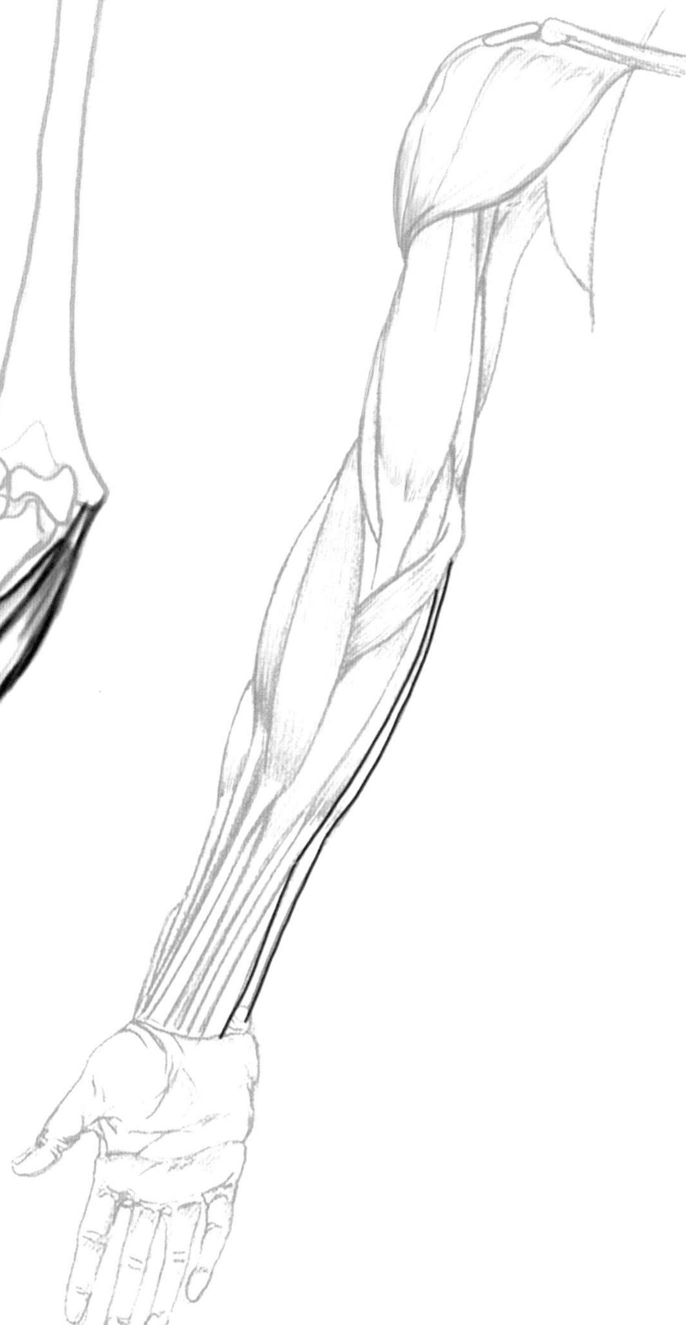

ANTERIOR

F.5. EXTENSOR CARPI RADIALIS BREVIS

STRUCTURE

The extensor carpi radialis brevis (ECRB) is long and plump muscle squeezed in between the extensor carpi radialis longus and the extensor digitorum. You will be able to see the middle belly pop out.

ORIGIN

The lateral epicondyle of the humerus. Remember that the flexors are on the other side of the humerus at the medial epicondyle. The four extensors included here are at the lateral epicondyle.

INSERTION

The dorsal (top) surface of the third metacarpal bone (middle finger).

ACTION

Extends and helps radially deviate the hand (moves the hand toward the thumb; 1).

NOTE: Muscles F.5. through F.8. are the four muscles that in this book make up the extensor group.

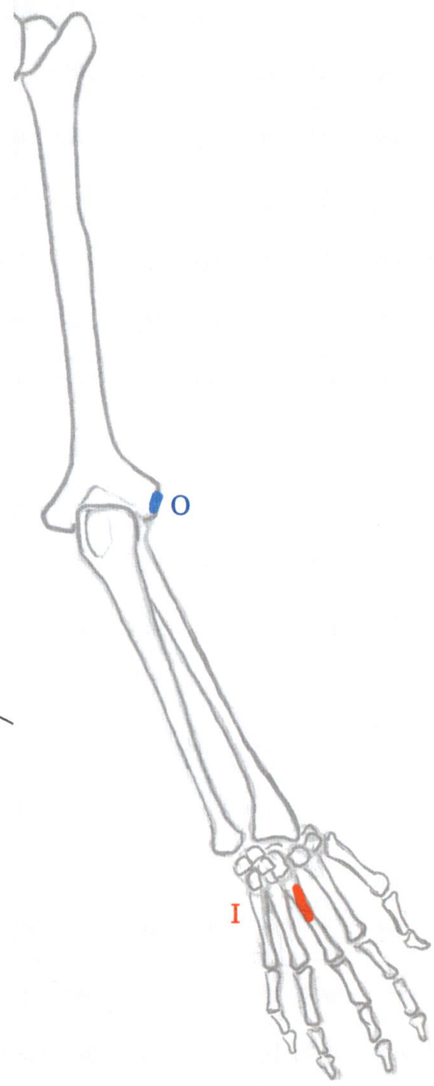

1.

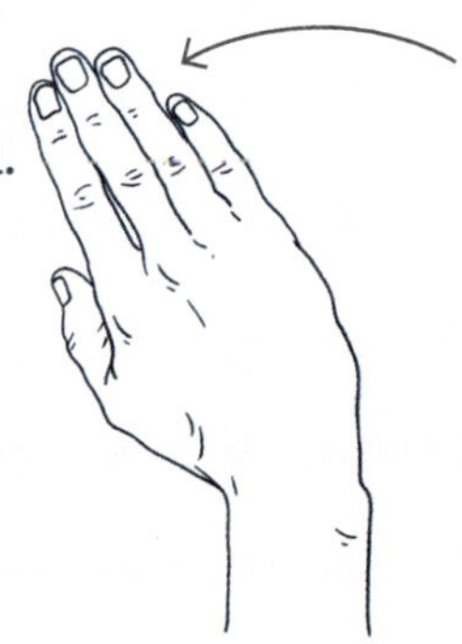

1. Extends and helps radially deviate the hand

CHECKLIST

- O Palmaris longus
- O Flexor carpi radialis
- O Pronator teres
- O Flexor carpi ulnaris
- O Extensor carpi radialis brevis

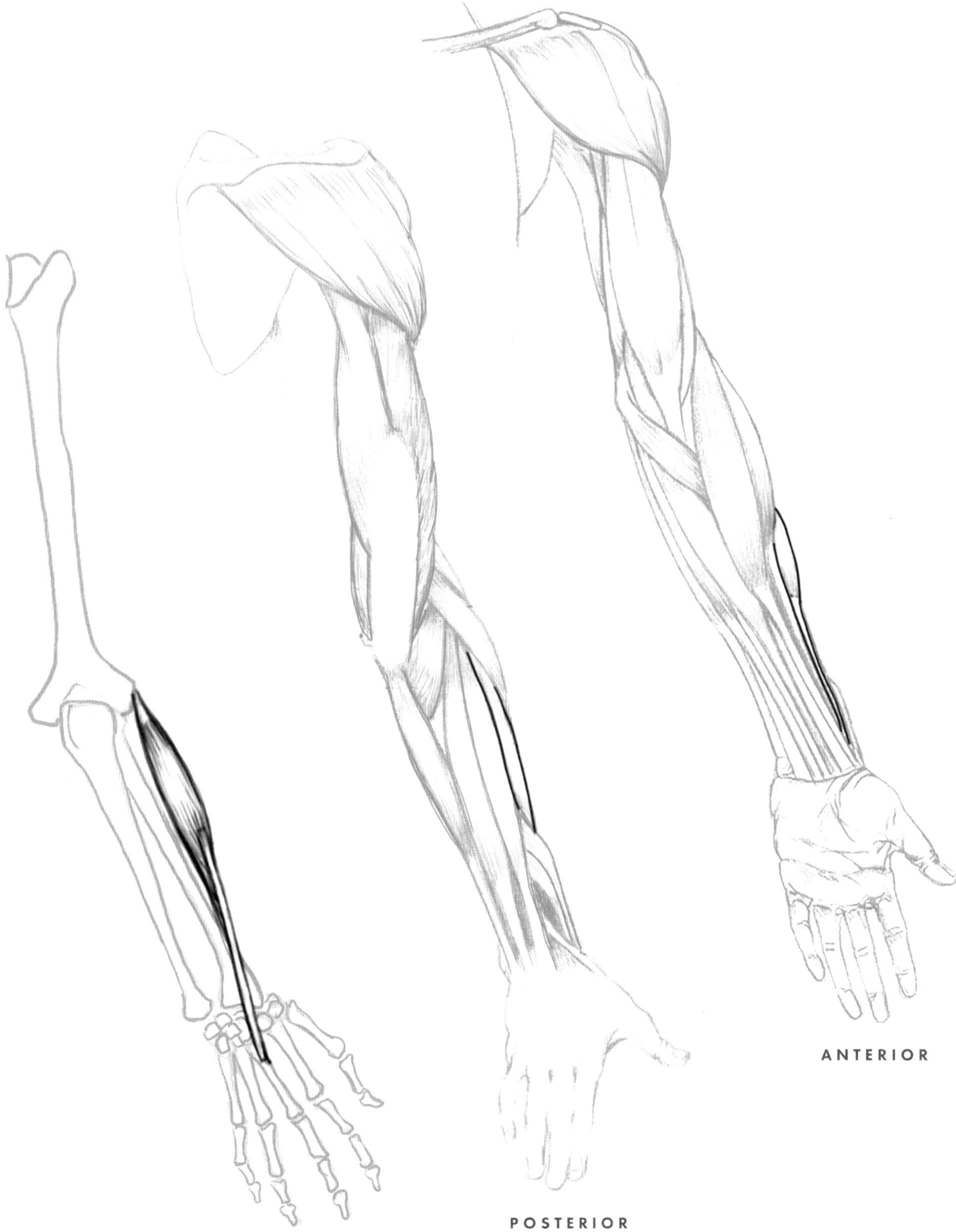

POSTERIOR

POSTERIOR

ANTERIOR

F.6. EXTENSOR DIGITORUM (AND THE EXTENSOR DIGITI MINIMI)

STRUCTURE

The extensor digitorum is a long, broad muscle that is made up of segments that taper toward the hand. The extensor digiti minimi is sometimes included as a blended muscle and sometimes separated. It is included here because it can be seen as a separate form that is very thin and tubular.

ORIGIN

The lateral epicondyle of the humerus.

INSERTION

Three tendons insert at the dorsal (top) of the middle and ends of the index, middle, and ring fingers. The extensor digiti minimi attaches to the middle and end of the little finger.

ACTION

The group extends the fingers (1), and the extensor digiti minimi can extend the little finger all by itself, like when you're having a cup of tea.

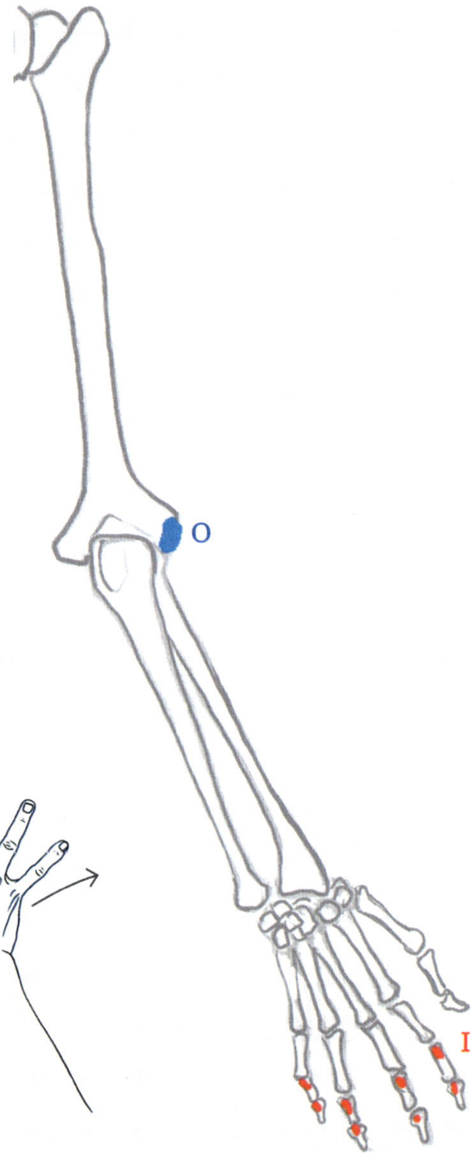

POSTERIOR

1.

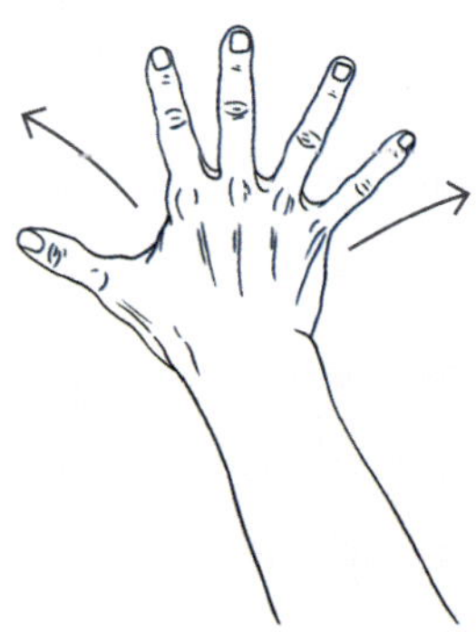

1. *Extends the fingers*

CHECKLIST

- O Palmaris longus
- O Flexor carpi radialis
- O Pronator teres
- O Flexor carpi ulnaris
- O Extensor carpi radialis brevis
- O Extensor digitorum and extensor digiti minimi

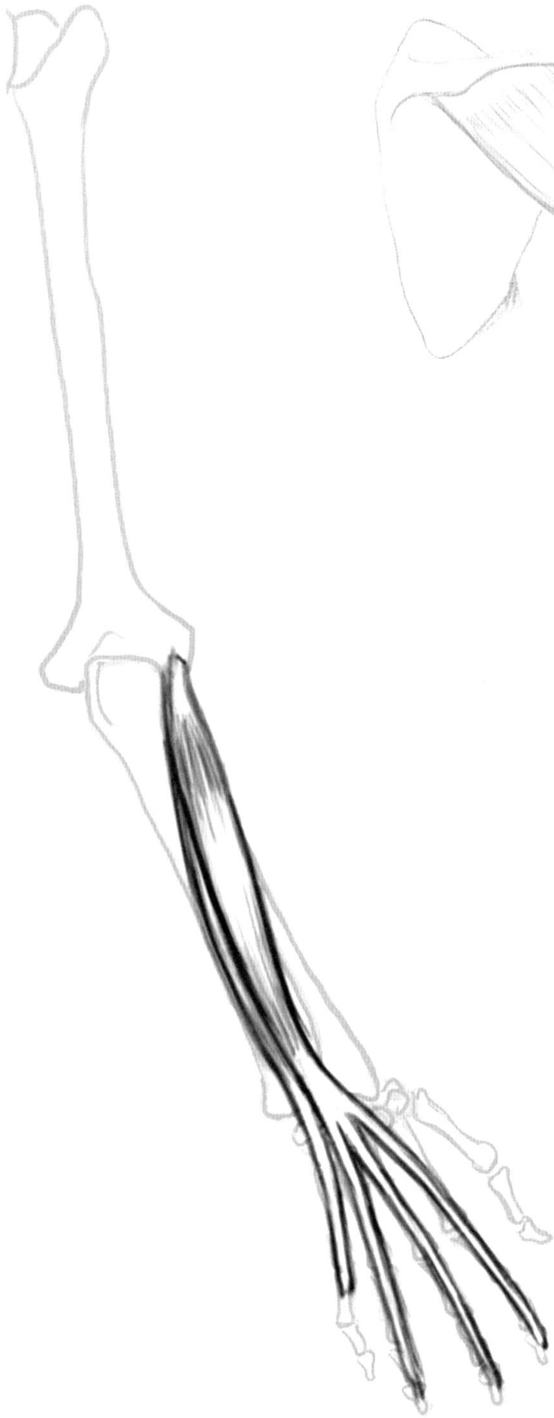

POSTERIOR

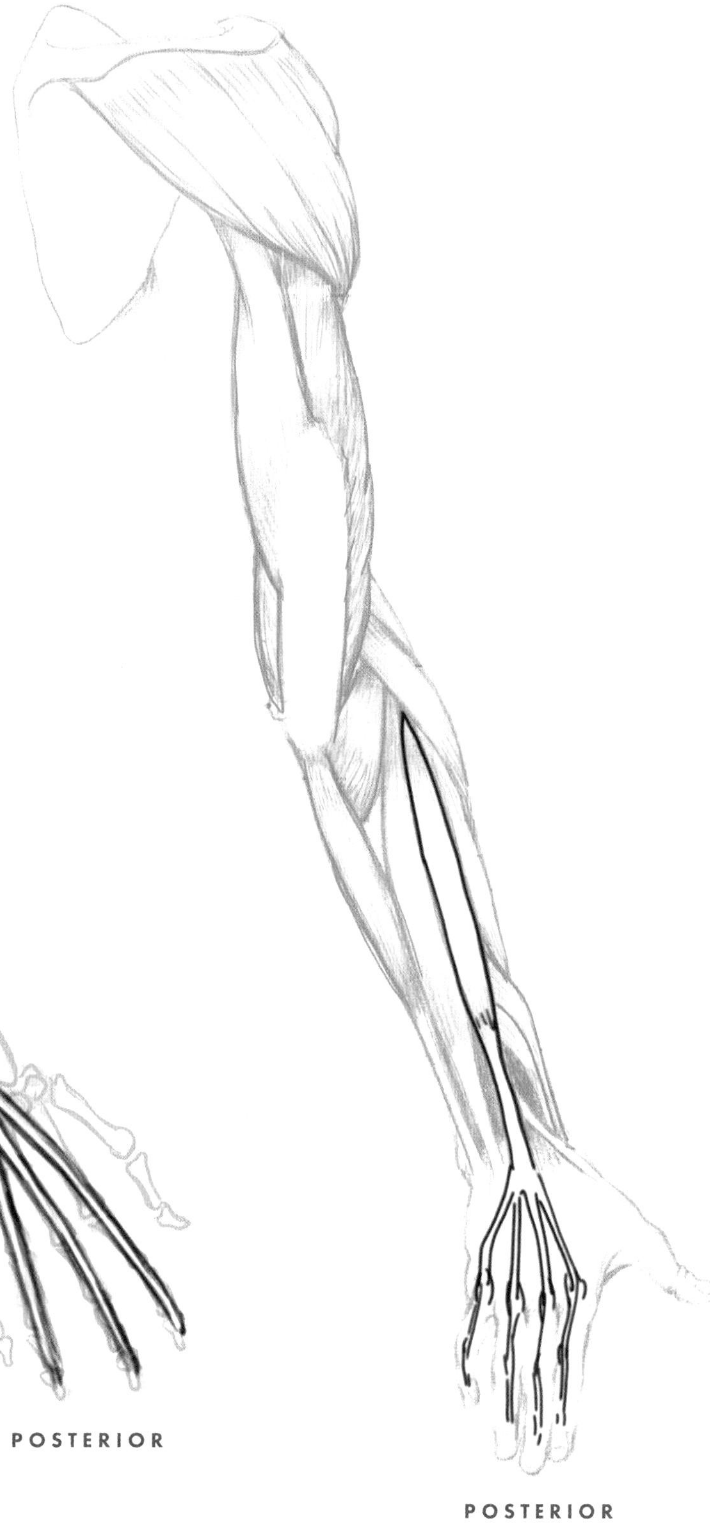

POSTERIOR

F.7. EXTENSOR CARPI ULNARIS

STRUCTURE

The extensor carpi ulnaris is a long, flat muscle. Its tendon can often be clearly seen toward the little finger by the wrist.

ORIGIN

The lateral epicondyle of the humerus.

INSERTION

On the tubercle (bony bump) on the base of the fifth metacarpal bone, the little finger side.

ACTION

Extends and helps with ulnar deviation of the hand (moves the hand toward the little finger; 1).

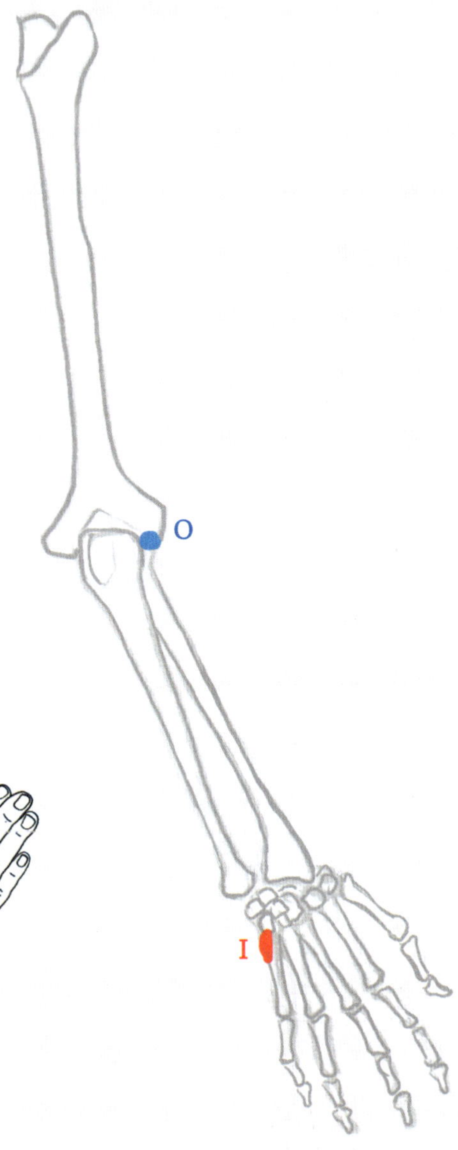

1.

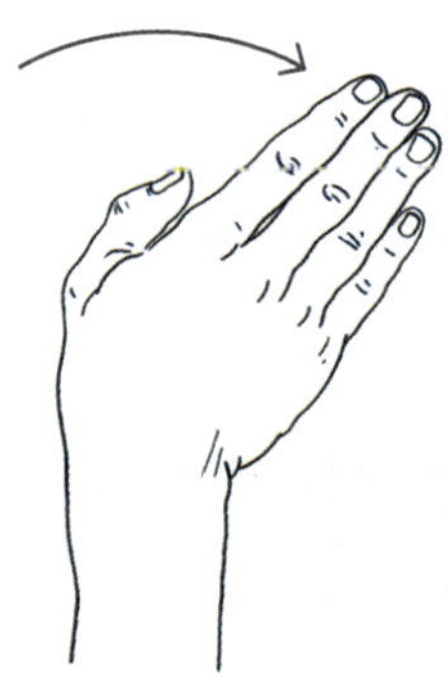

1. *Extension and ulnar deviation of the hand*

CHECKLIST

- O Palmaris longus
- O Flexor carpi radialis
- O Pronator teres
- O Flexor carpi ulnaris
- O Extensor carpi radialis brevis
- O Extensor digitorum and extensor digiti minimi
- O Extensor carpi ulnaris

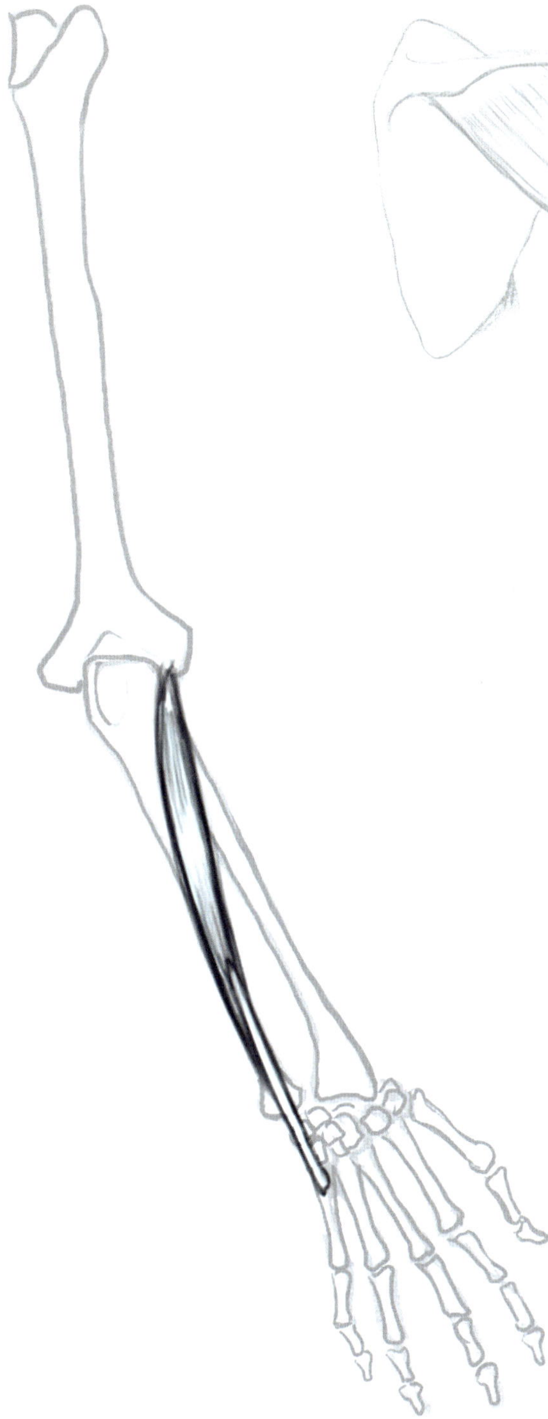

POSTERIOR

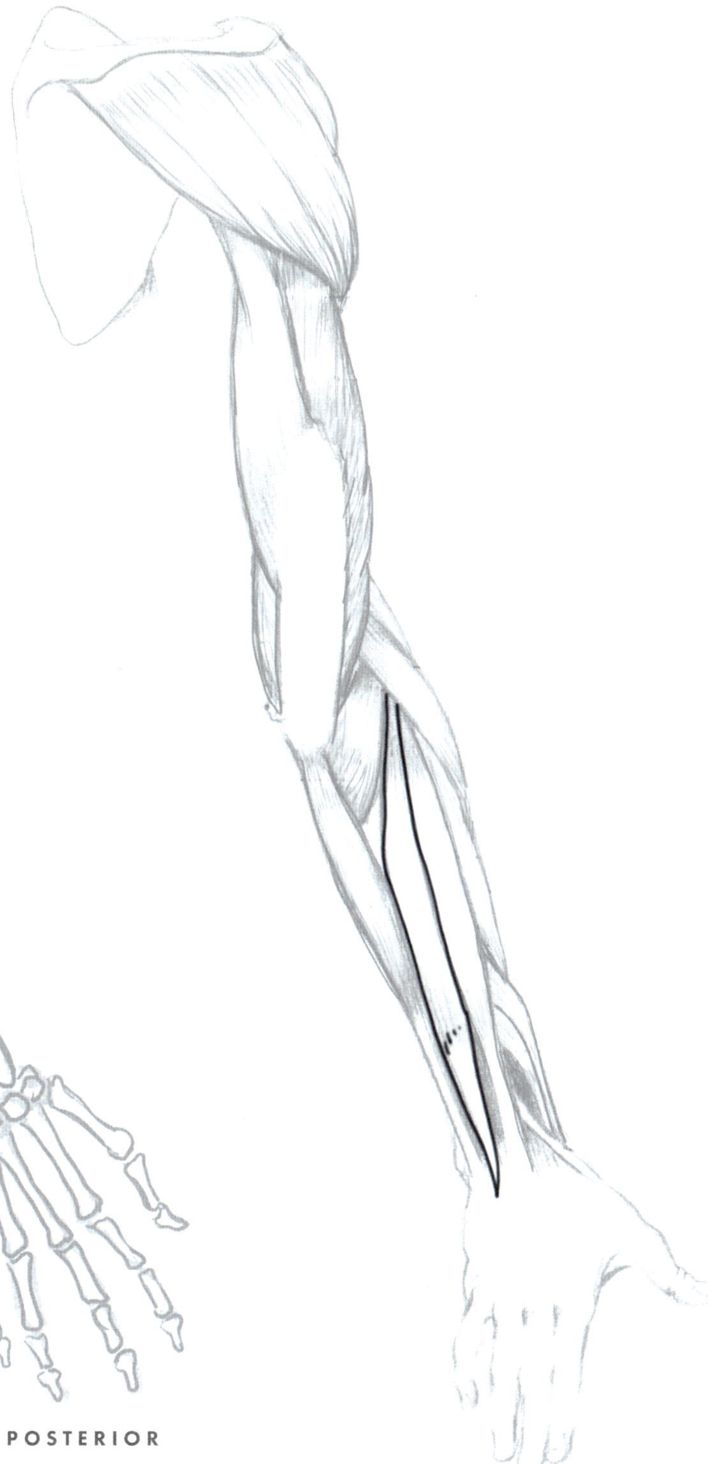

POSTERIOR

F.8. ANCONEUS

STRUCTURE

The anconeus is a triangular muscle that I refer to as the "Dorito." It is plump and easily seen when the arm is fully extended. It is just below the elbow and will overflow over the crest of the ulna.

ORIGIN

The lateral epicondyle of the humerus.

INSERTION

At the olecranon of the ulna, elbow, and down the back edge of the ulna about a fourth of the way down.

ACTION

Extends the elbow and helps stabilize the elbow joint (1).

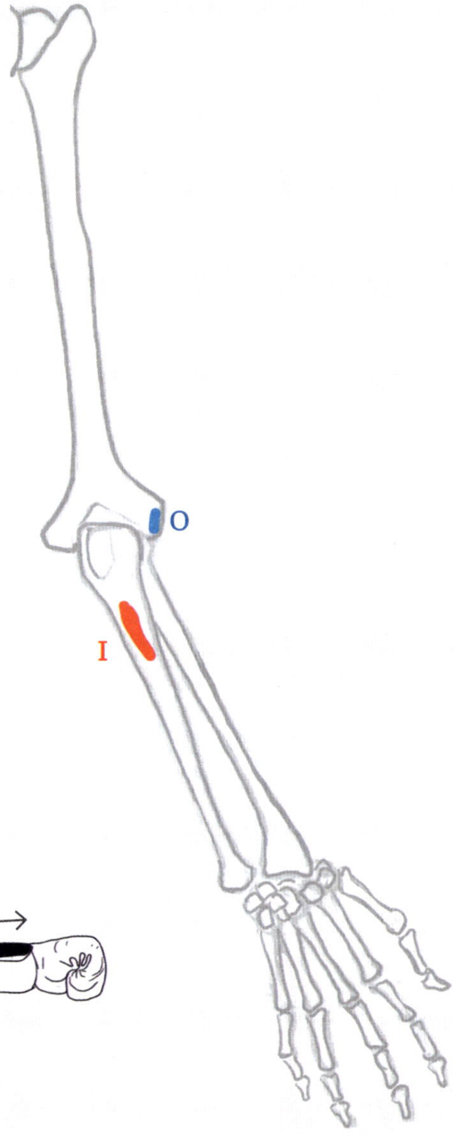

POSTERIOR

1.

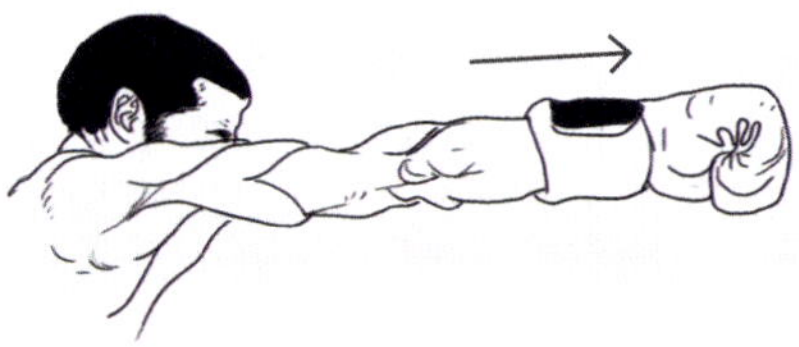

1. Extends and helps stabilize elbow

CHECKLIST

- O Palmaris longus
- O Flexor carpi radialis
- O Pronator teres
- O Flexor carpi ulnaris
- O Extensor carpi radialis brevis
- O Extensor digitorum and extensor digiti minimi
- O Extensor carpi ulnaris
- O Anconeus

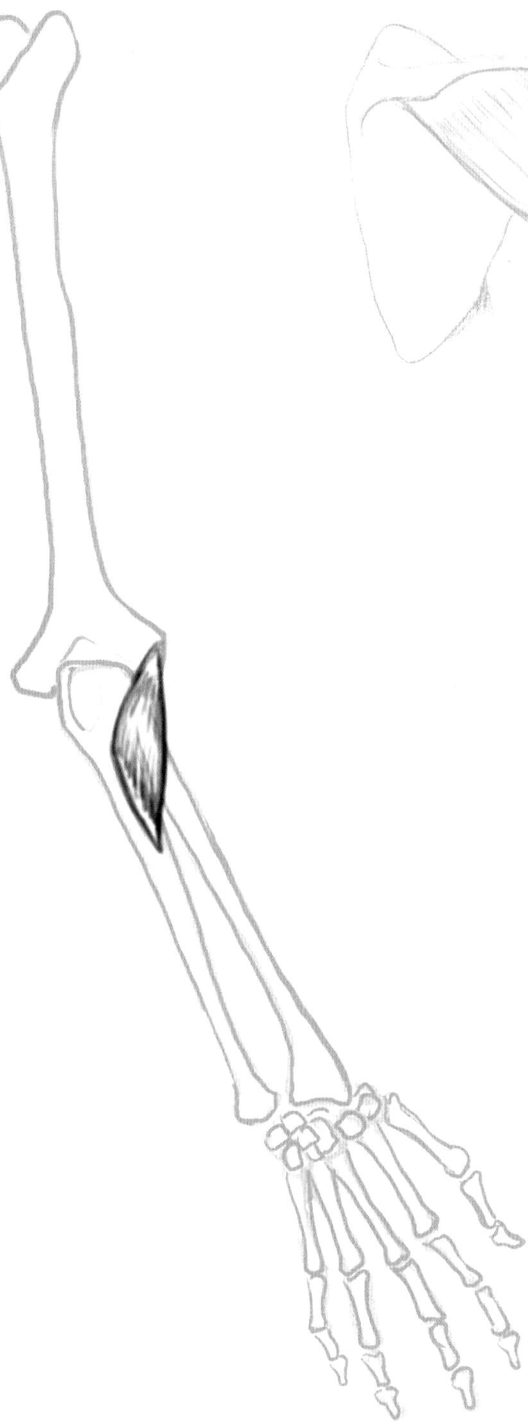

POSTERIOR

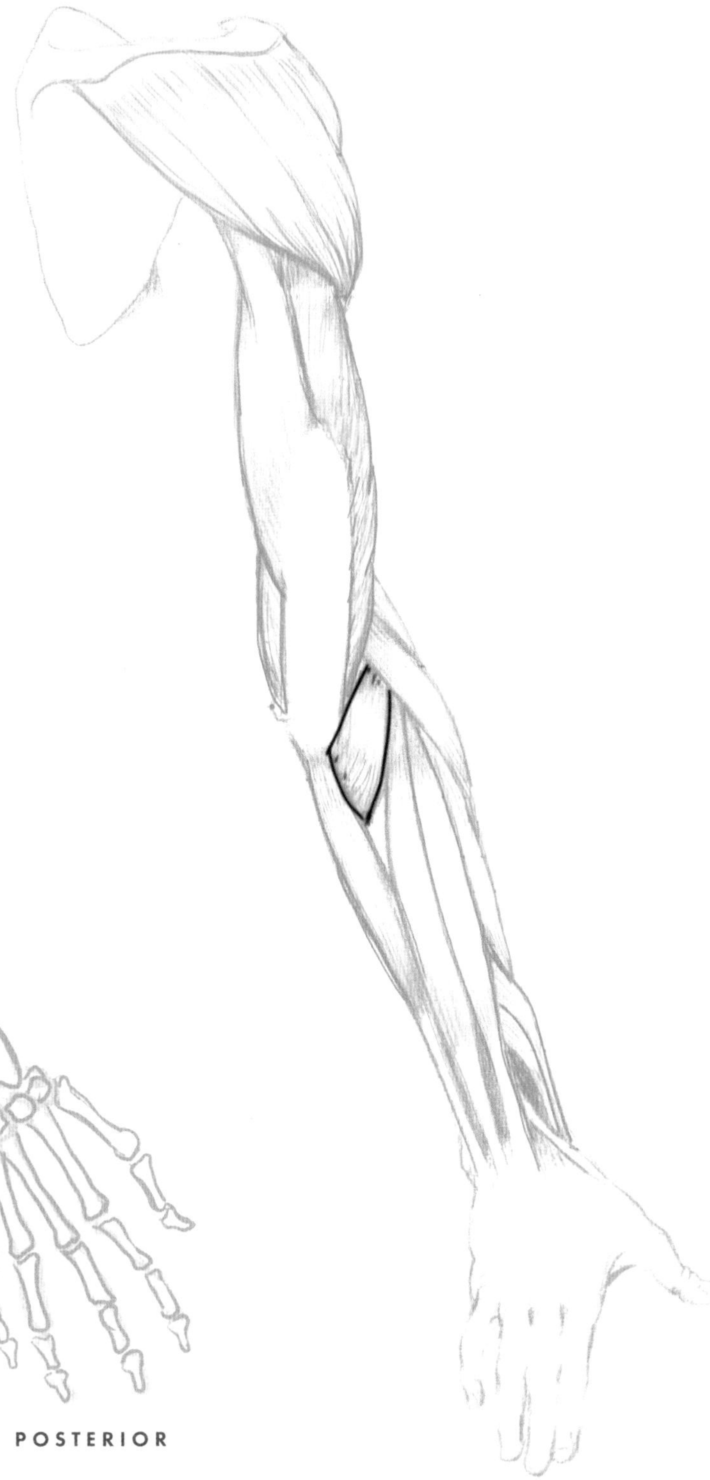

POSTERIOR

F.9. BRACHIORADIALIS & EXTENSOR CARPI RADIALIS LONGUS

STRUCTURE

The brachioradialis starts off flat and large and spins toward the flexor group, then tapers toward the wrist on the thumb side. The extensor carpi radialis longus (ECRL) originates just below the brachialis. It is a short, flat muscle and seems to always follow the brachialis toward the thumb. It has a long and strong tendon. These two muscles are often blended, but on lean individuals you can see the split between them. I call these two "the twins."

ORIGIN

The brachioradialis originates on the side edge of the humerus, high, about a fourth of the way up the bone. The ECRL is attached on the same lateral edge just below the other "twin" the brachioradialis.

INSERTION

The brachioradialis inserts on the end of the lateral distal end of the radius. The ECRL inserts at the dorsal (back of the hand) proximal surface of the second metacarpal (index finger).

ACTION

The brachioradialis flexes the forearm (1), best seen in the handshake position. The ECRL helps flex the forearm and extends and radially deviates the hand (2).

NOTE: I call these "the twins" because they look similar and originate and insert close to each other. The two muscles basically follow the thumb.

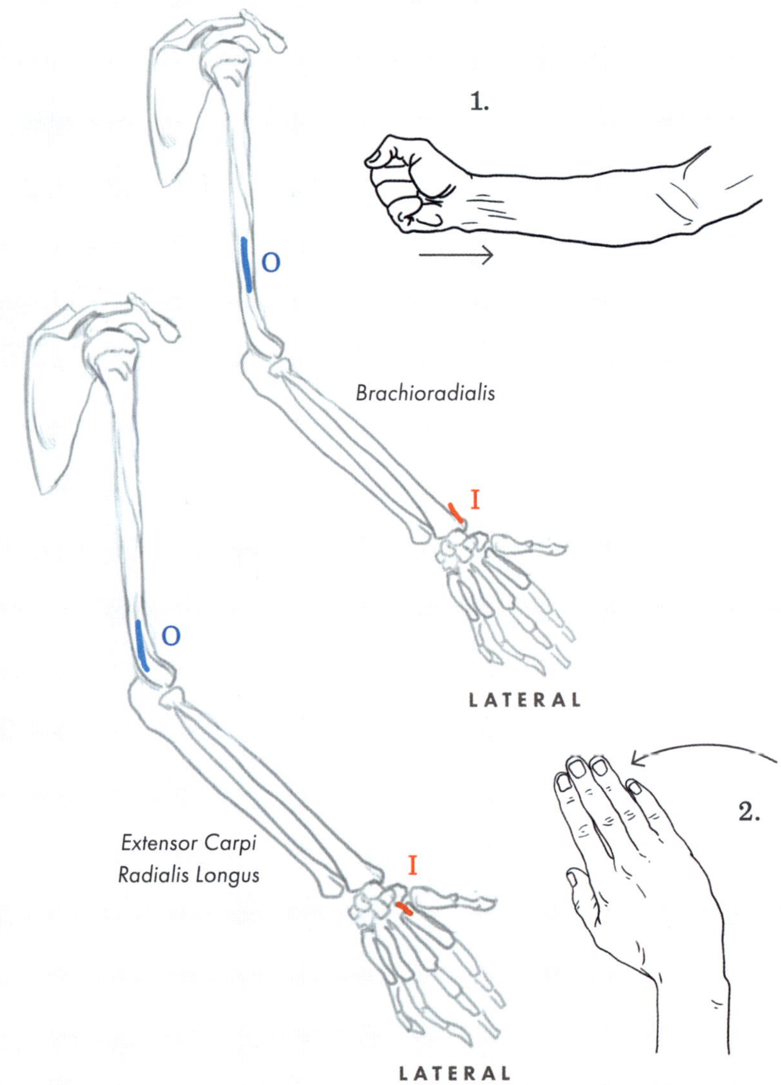

1. Brachioradialis flexes the forearm;

2. ECRL flexes the forearm and extends and radially deviates the hand

CHECKLIST

- O Palmaris longus
- O Flexor carpi radialis
- O Pronator teres
- O Flexor carpi ulnaris
- O Extensor carpi radialis brevis
- O Extensor digitorum and extensor digiti minimi
- O Extensor carpi ulnaris
- O Anconeus
- O Brachioradialis and extensor carpi radialis longus

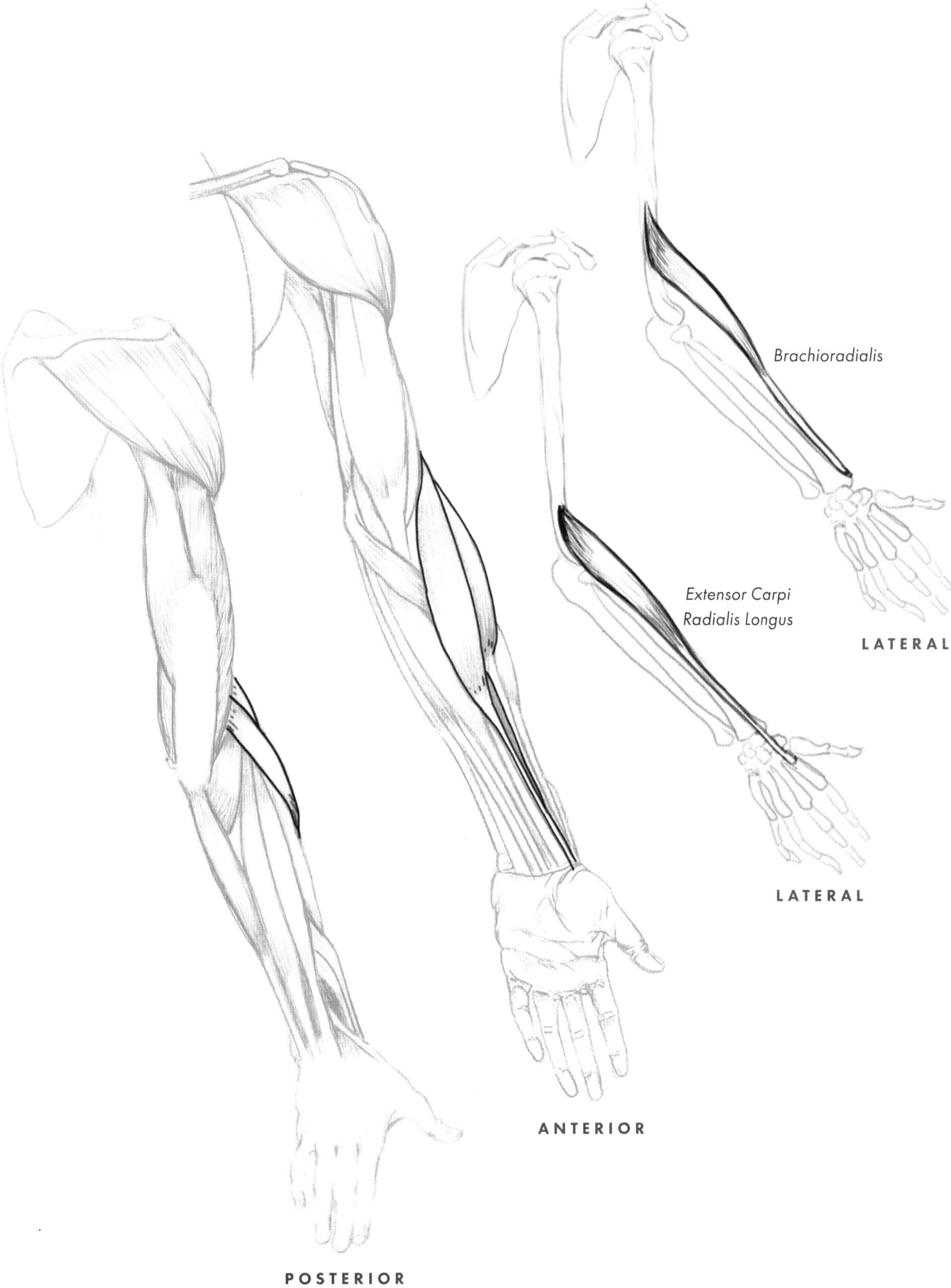
Brachioradialis
Extensor Carpi
Radialis Longus
LATERAL
LATERAL
ANTERIOR
POSTERIOR

F.10. ABDUCTOR POLLICIS LONGUS, EXTENSOR POLLICIS BREVIS & EXTENSOR POLLICIS LONGUS

STRUCTURE

The abductor pollicis longus and extensor pollicis brevis (pollex means thumb in Latin) are both elongated triangular muscles and are therefore called the "mini twins." Mini because they resemble the larger twins, the brachioradialis and the ECRL.

ORIGIN

The abductor pollicis longus (APL) attaches to the back of the ulna. The extensor pollicis brevis (EPB) attaches to the radius and also to a membrane in between the radius and the ulna called the interosseus membrane.

INSERTION

The APL attaches to the base of the first metacarpal (thumb). The EPB attaches to the thumb as well, but farther down at the first phalanx of the thumb.

ACTION

The APL abducts the thumb and the EPB extends the thumb (1).

NOTE: The abductor pollicis longus (APL) and the extensor pollicis brevis (EPB) are the "mini twins," as they resemble a small version of the "twins." Only the tendon of the extensor pollicis longus (EPL) is visible. The space between the tendon of the EPL and the tendons of the APL and EPB is called the "anatomical snuffbox." This hollow is created when the thumb is extended and abducted, like in the thumbs up action.

1.

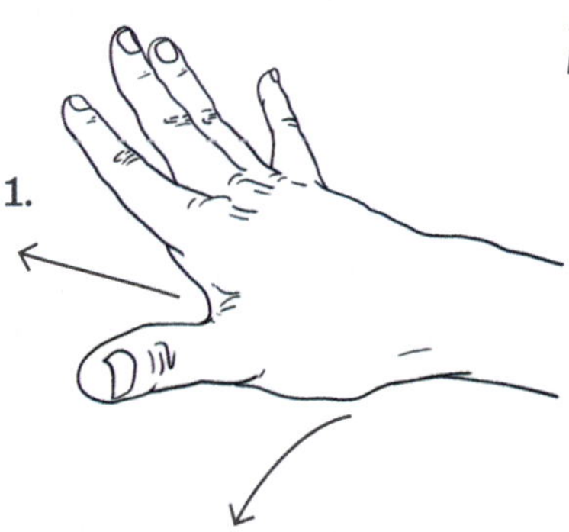

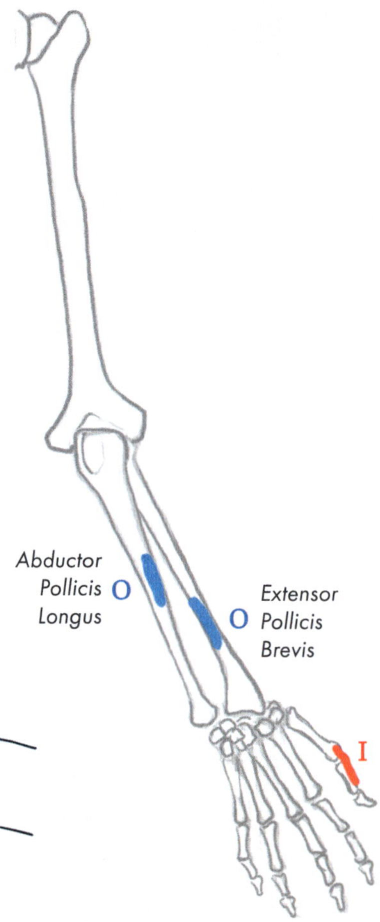

POSTERIOR

1. APL abducts the thumb and EPB extends the thumb

CHECKLIST

- O Palmaris longus
- O Flexor carpi radialis
- O Pronator teres
- O Flexor carpi ulnaris
- O Extensor carpi radialis brevis
- O Extensor digitorum and extensor digiti minimi
- O Extensor carpi ulnaris
- O Anconeus
- O Brachioradialis and extensor carpi radialis longus
- O Abductor pollicis longus, extensor pollicis brevis, and extensor pollicis longus

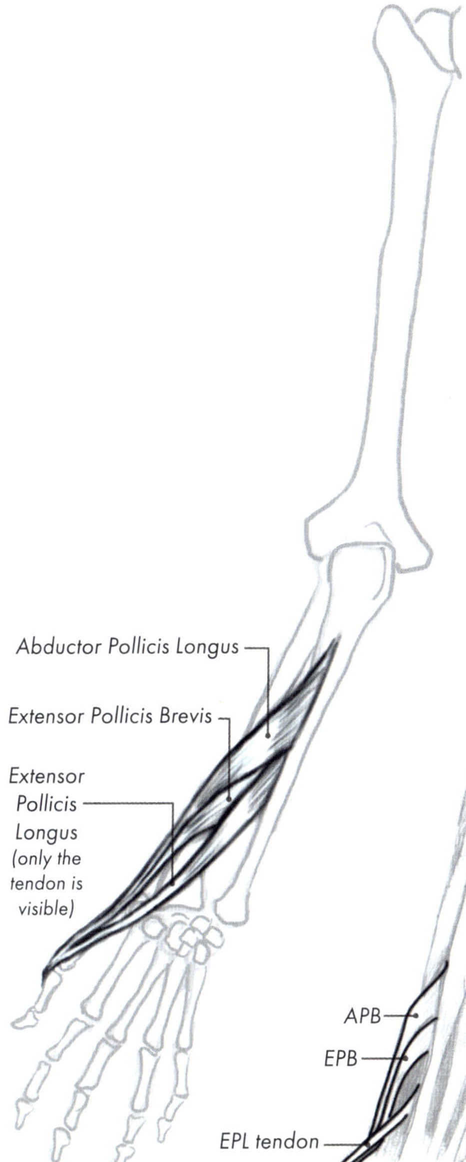

POSTERIOR

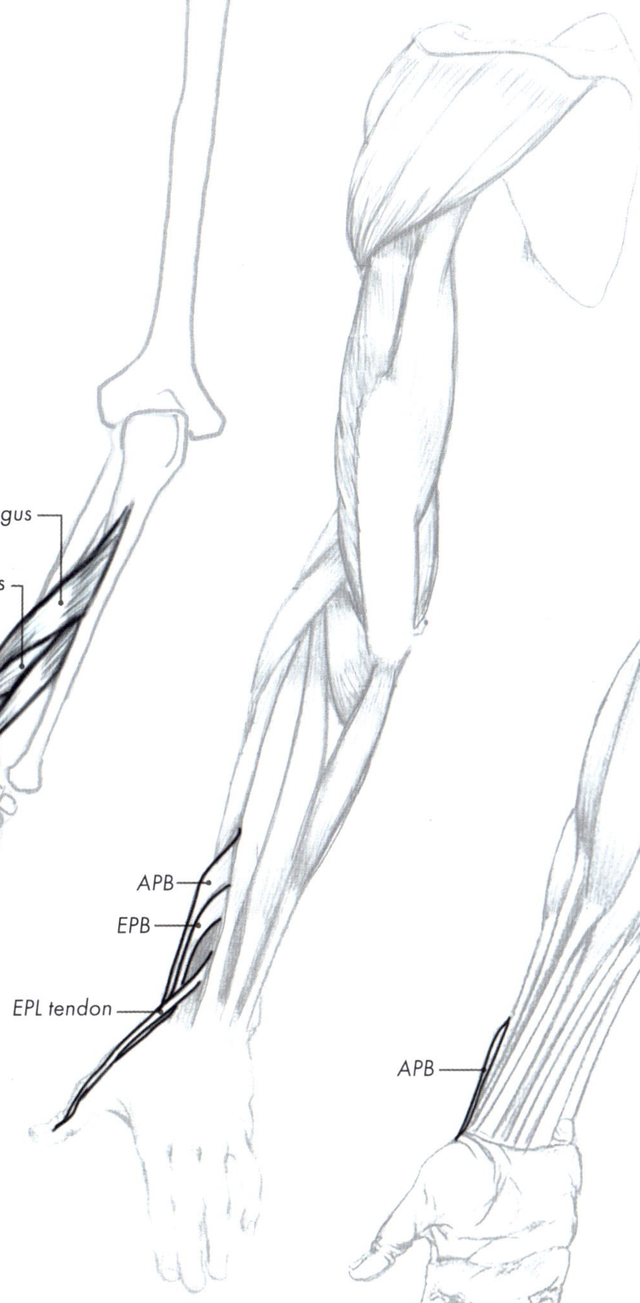

POSTERIOR

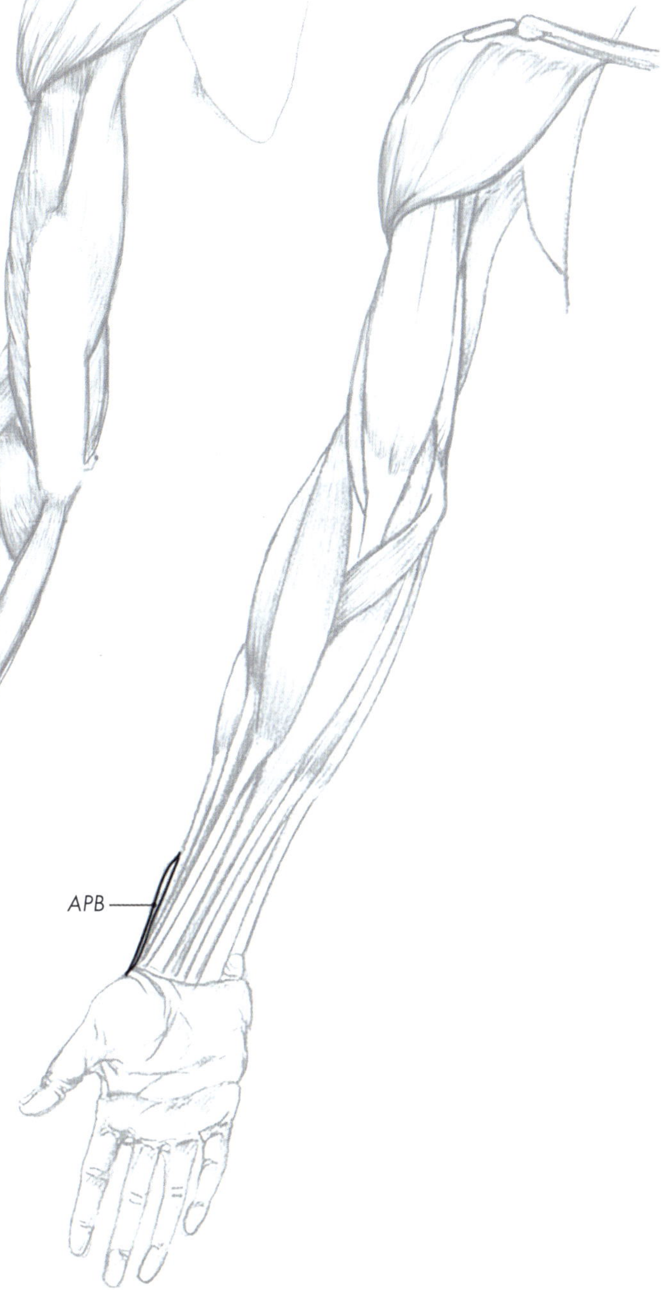

ANTERIOR

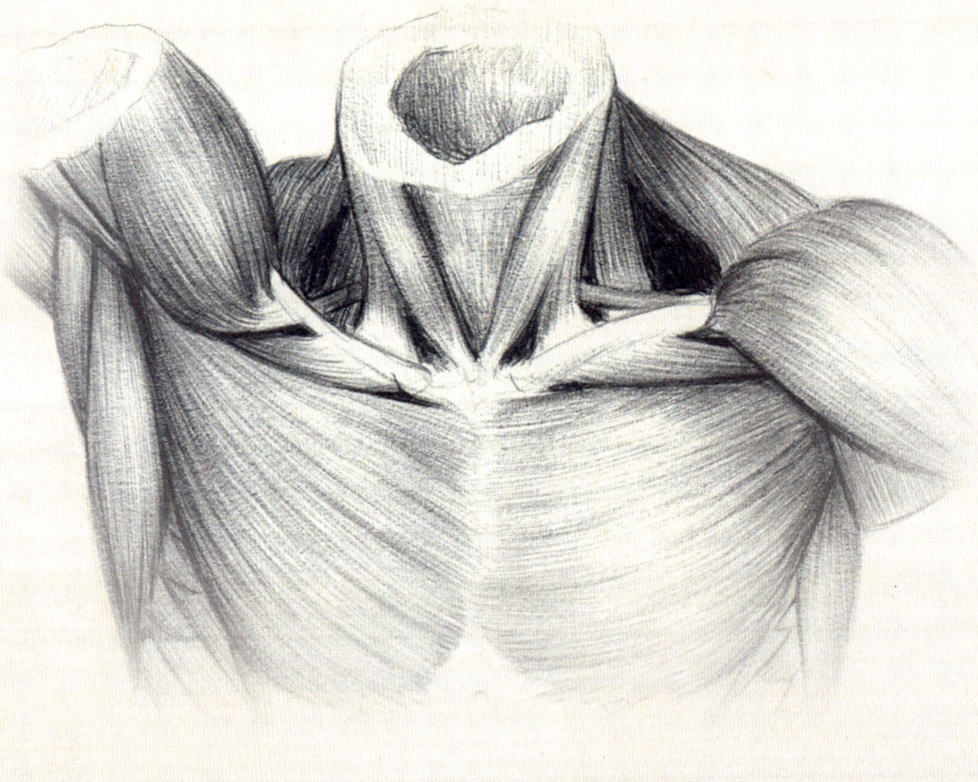

CHAPTER G

THE NECK

The neck muscles help support and facilitate the movement of the head and maintain posture. The lateral muscles, such as scalenus medius, help you move your head side to side. The anterior muscles drop the head down, and the posterior muscles work with the back muscles to hold your head straight and pull it back, as in looking up.

G.1. SEMISPINALIS CAPITIS

STRUCTURE

The semispinalis muscle lies deep under the trapezius. It doesn't show, but it does create a bed for the trapezius, therefore it adds thickness to the back of the neck.

ORIGIN

The muscle has tentacle-like attachments to the cervical vertebrae at the transverse processes (the bony spikes at the sides of each vertebra) from the fourth cervical vertebra down to the sixth or seventh thoracic vertebra, the rib cage vertebrae.

INSERTION

A wide insertion at the base of the skull, not quite to the center line.

ACTION

Extends the head as if looking up (1) and helps rotate the head left and right (2).

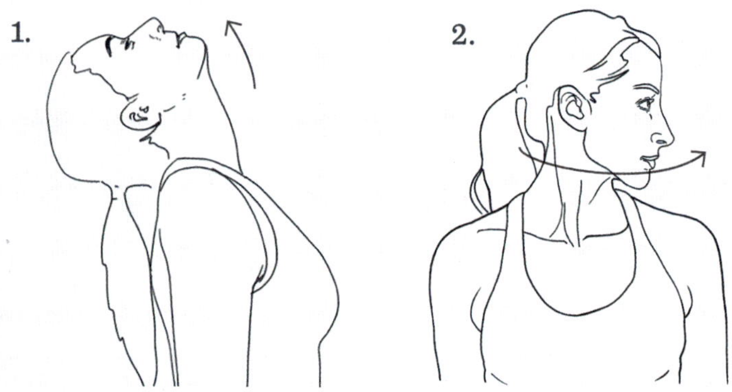

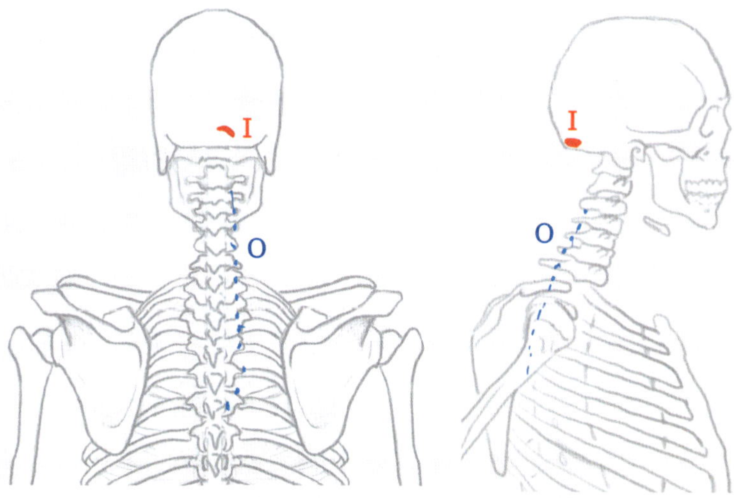

1. Extends head up; 2. Helps rotate the head

CHECKLIST

O Semispinalis capitis

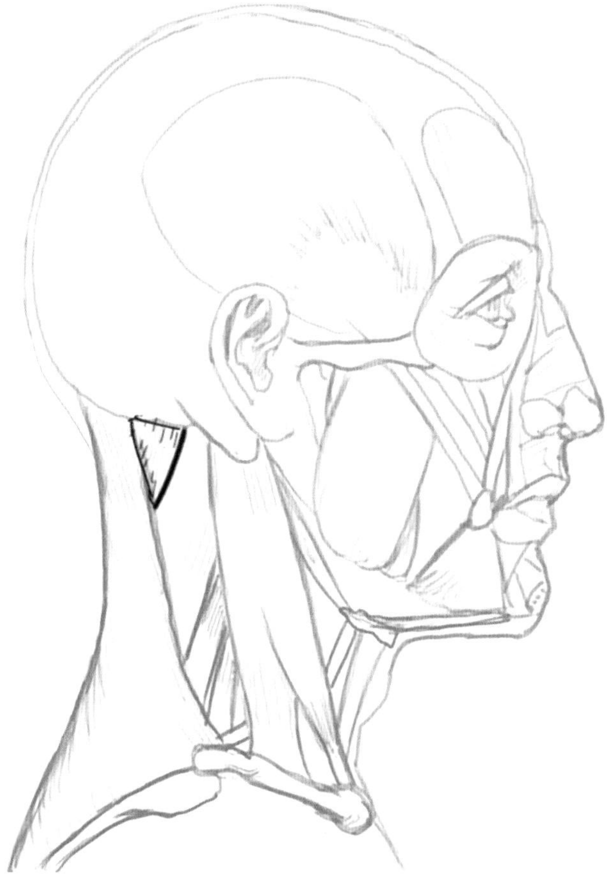

LATERAL

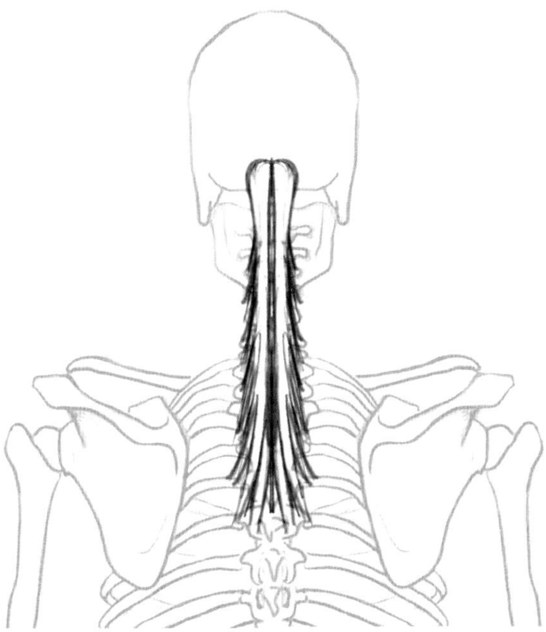

POSTERIOR

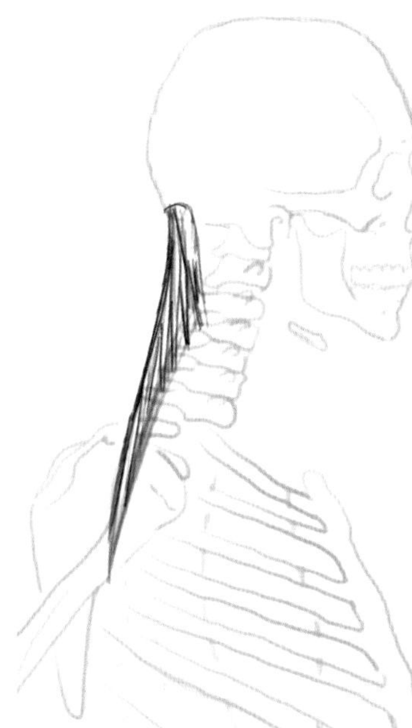

LATERAL

G.2. SPLENIUS CAPITIS

STRUCTURE

The splenius capitis muscle is broad and flat and may pop out closer to the origin by the mastoid process (the bony bump behind the ear).

ORIGIN

The lower part of the nuchal ligament (a ligament that attaches to the base of the skull and down to the seventh cervical vertebra) and the first through fourth thoracic vertebrae.

INSERTION

A broad line at the mastoid process (the bony bump behind the ear) and a little bit toward the rear.

ACTION

Helps rotate the head (1). When contracting together, they help extend the head, as in the looking up movement (2).

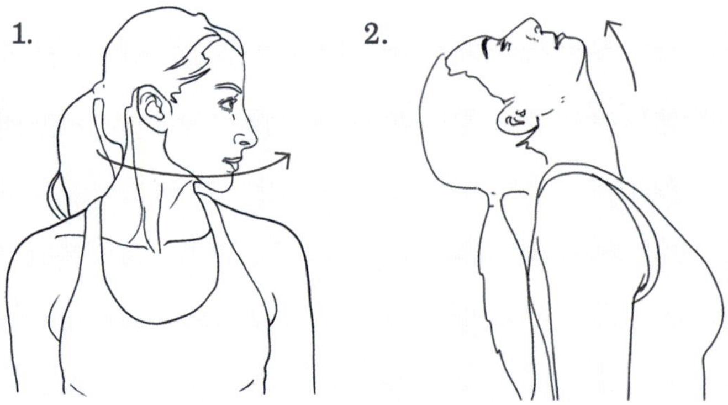

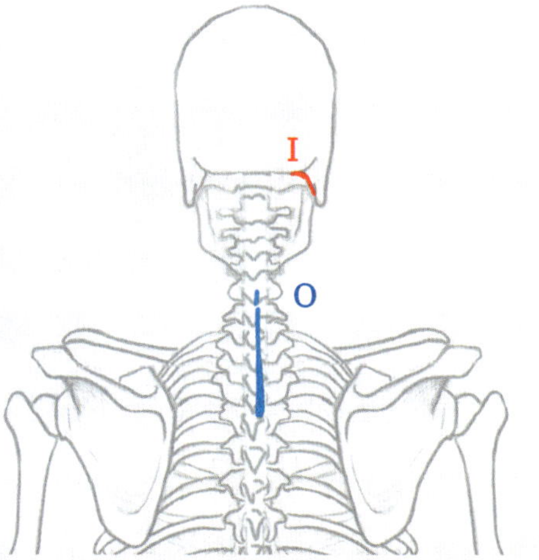

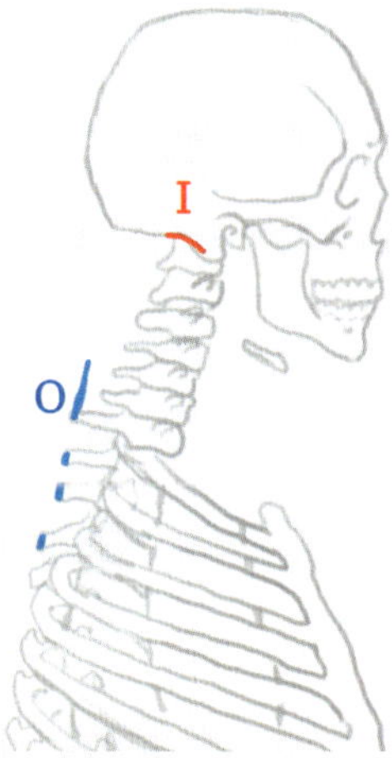

1. Helps rotate the head; 2. Extends the head up

CHECKLIST

○ Semispinalis capitis

○ Splenius capitis

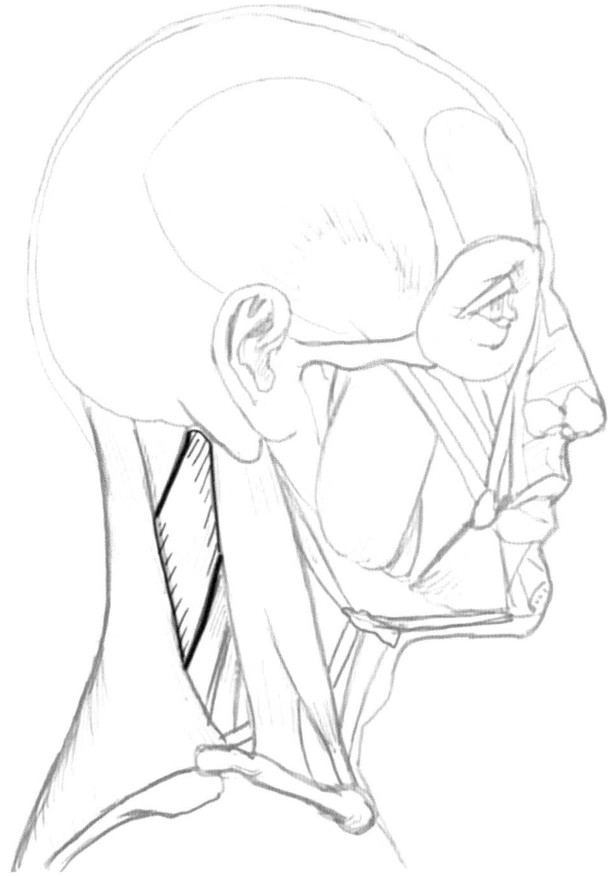

LATERAL

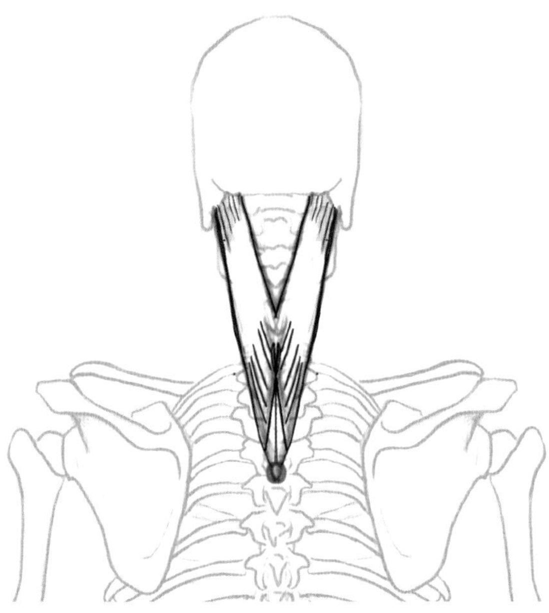

POSTERIOR

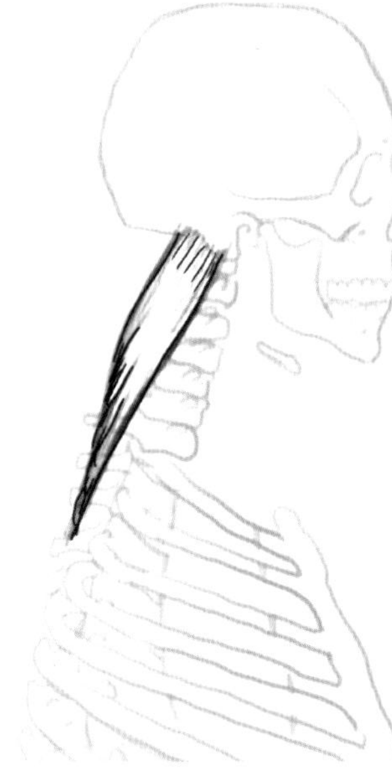

LATERAL

G.3. LEVATOR SCAPULAE

STRUCTURE

The levator scapulae is a deep neck muscle, but it can often be seen on the side of the neck in between the sternocleidomastoid and trapezius muscles. It starts as tentacle-like points and ends as a flat sheet.

ORIGIN

The transverse processes (the bony spikes at the sides of each vertebra) of cervical vertebrae one through four.

INSERTION

The upper edge of the superior aspect of the scapula.

ACTION

As the name implies, the levator scapulae raises the scapula (1). It also pulls it medially (toward the spine).

1.

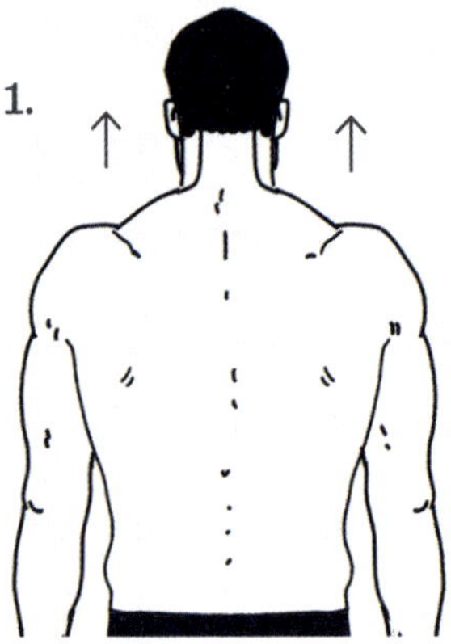

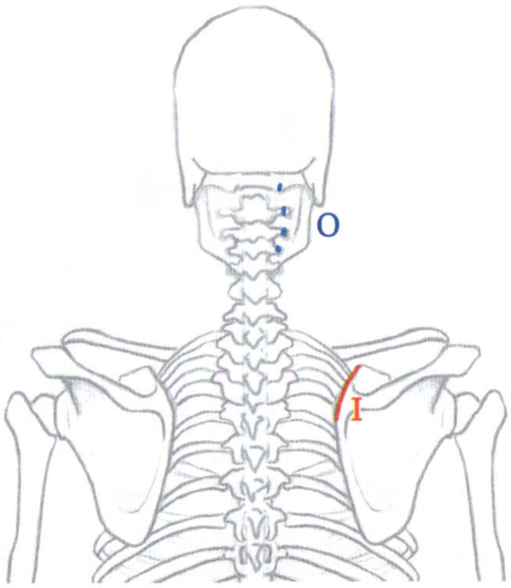

POSTERIOR

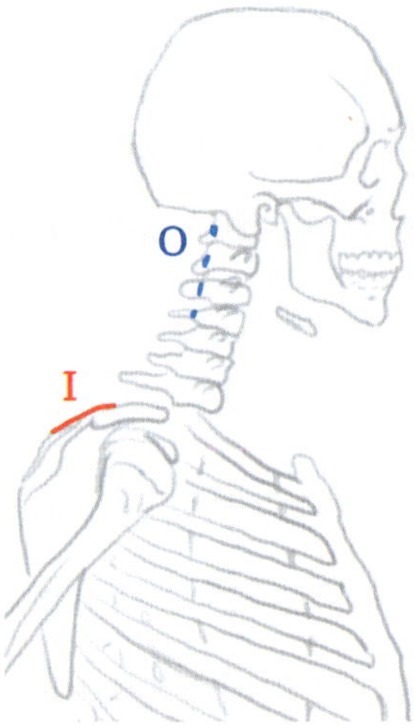

LATERAL

1. Raises the scapula and pulls it medially

CHECKLIST

- O Semispinalis capitis
- O Splenius capitis
- O Levator scapulae

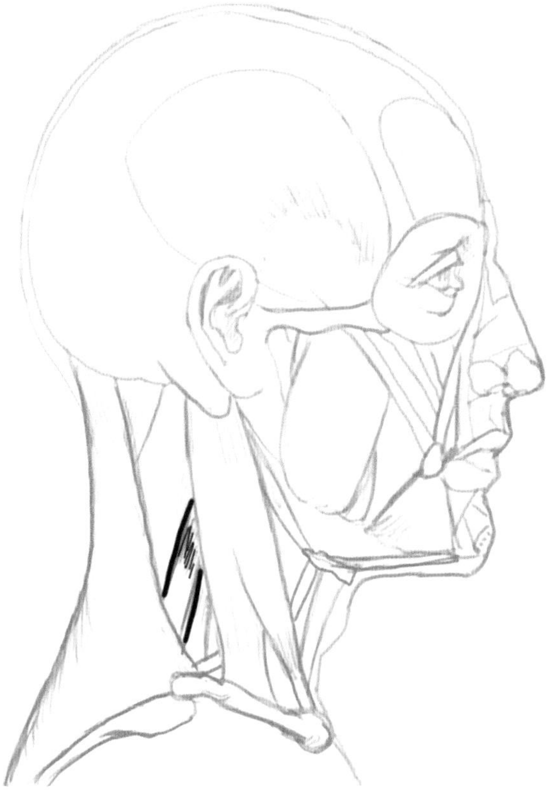

LATERAL

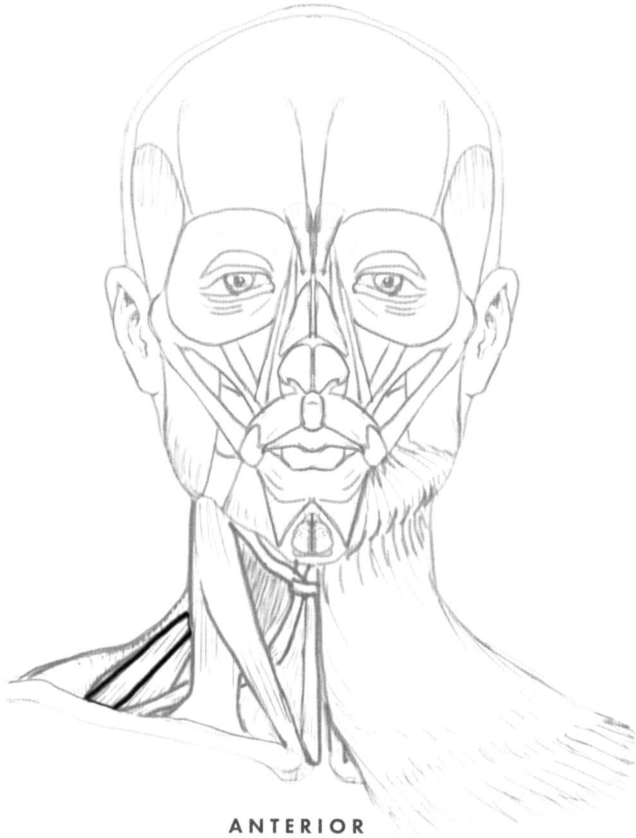

ANTERIOR

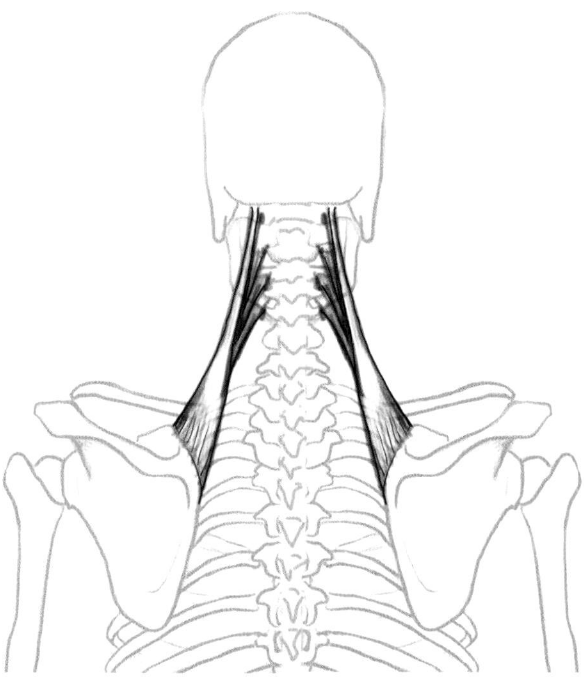

POSTERIOR

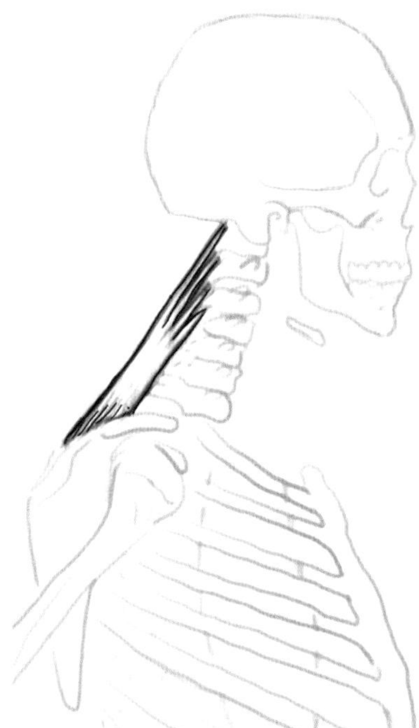

LATERAL

G.4. SCALENE MEDIUS

STRUCTURE

There are three scalene muscles, but the scalene medius is the largest of the three and is the one that is visible on the side of the neck. Like some of the other neck muscles, it has tentacle-like spikes of muscle and tendon that attach to the transverse processes of the second through seventh cervical vertebrae.

ORIGIN

The spinous processes of the second through seventh cervical vertebrae.

INSERTION

The top surface of the first rib.

ACTION

Bends the neck side to side (1).

NOTE: This is one of three scalene muscles, but it is the one that is more easily seen

1.

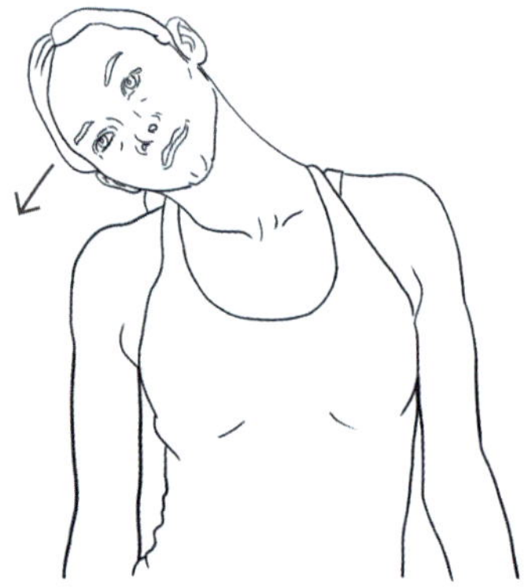

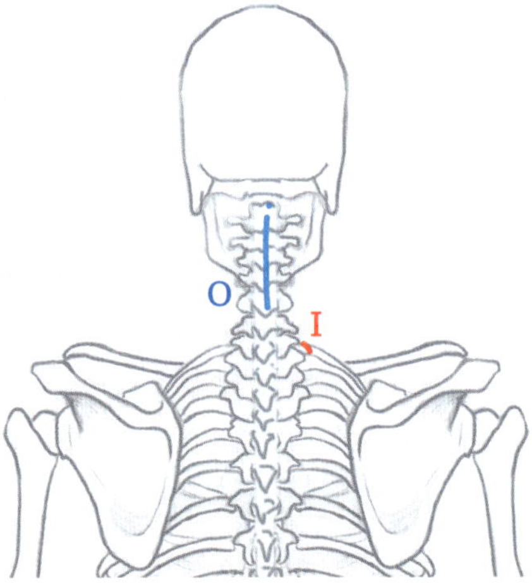

POSTERIOR

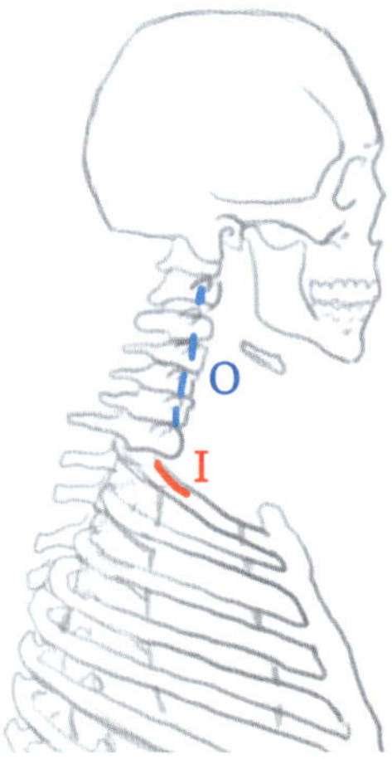

LATERAL

1. Bends the neck side to side

CHECKLIST

- O Semispinalis capitis
- O Splenius capitis
- O Levator scapulae
- O Scalene medius

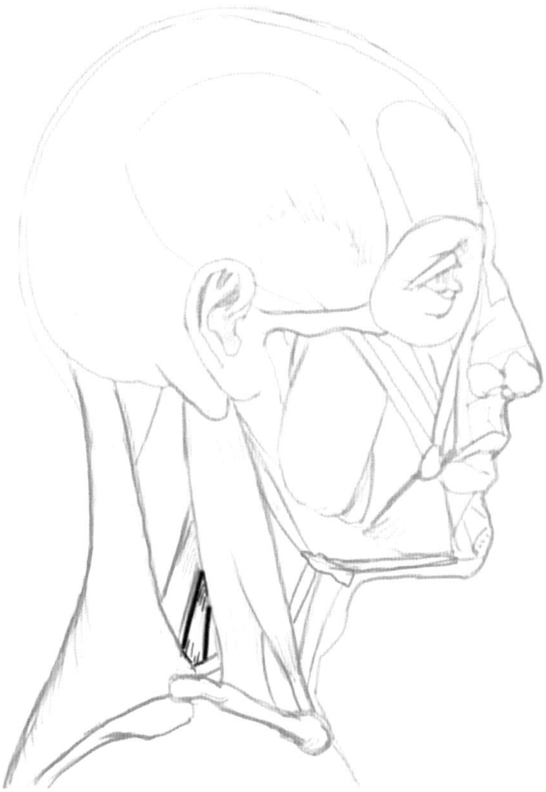

LATERAL

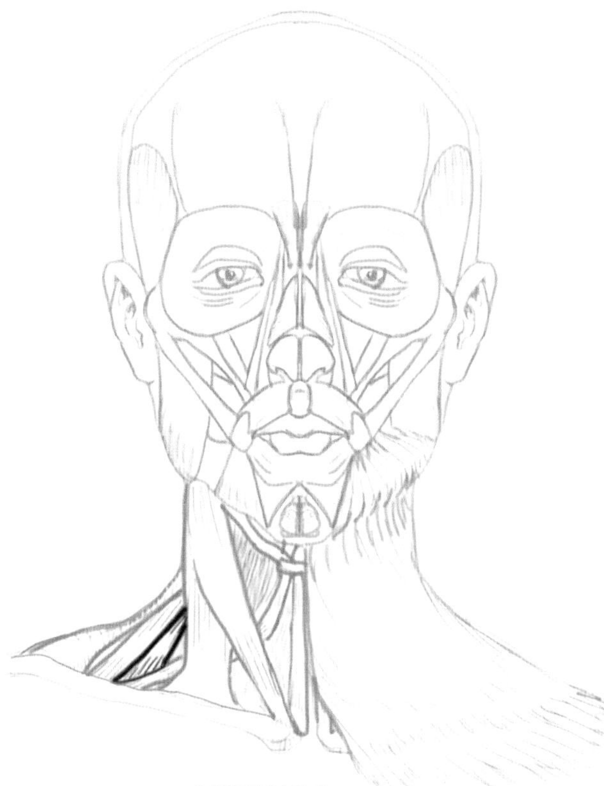

ANTERIOR

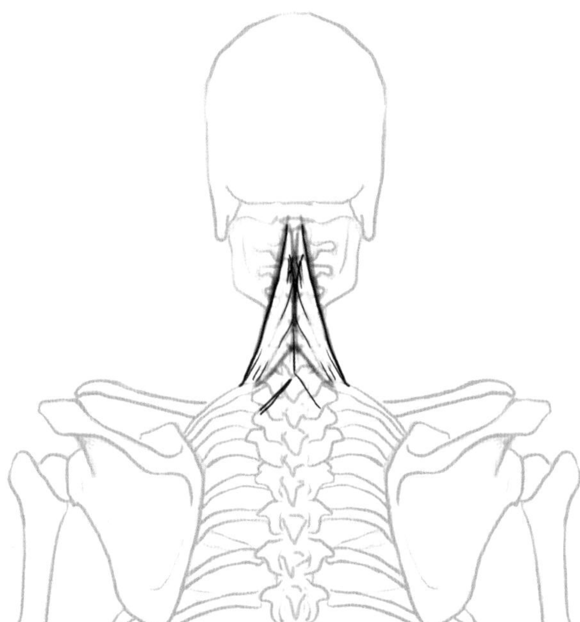

POSTERIOR

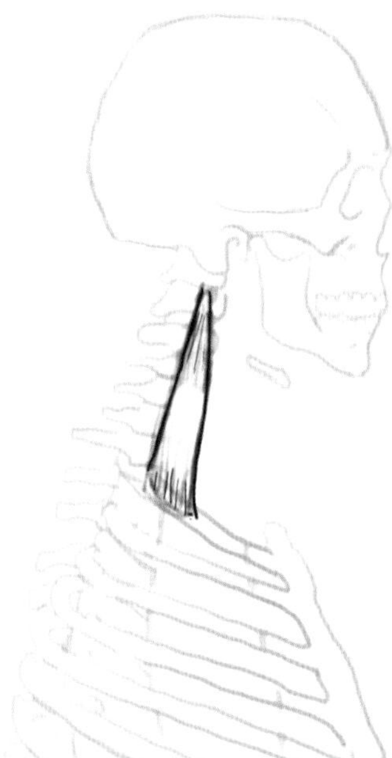

LATERAL

G.5. OMOHYOID

STRUCTURE

The omohyoid has two sections of narrow, cordlike muscles that have a small tendinous connection under the sternocleidomastoid muscle, making it bend.

ORIGIN

On a small spot on the superior aspect of the scapula by the levator scapulae.

INSERTION

On the underside of the hyoid bone of the neck.

ACTION

Pulls the hyoid bone down (1).

1.

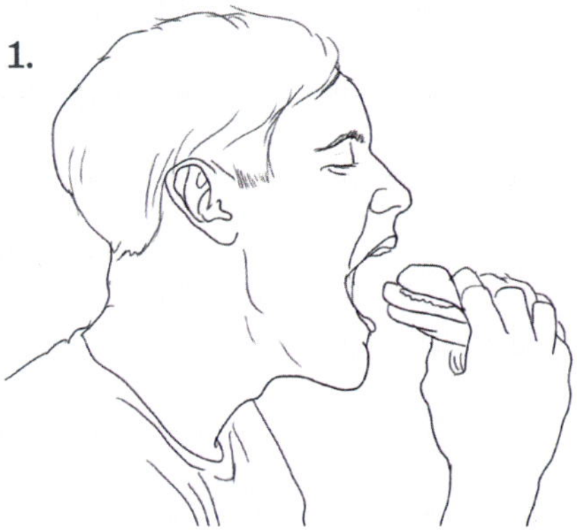

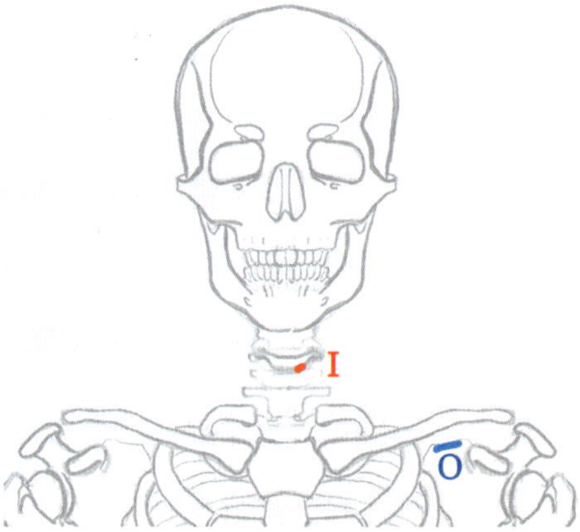

ANTERIOR

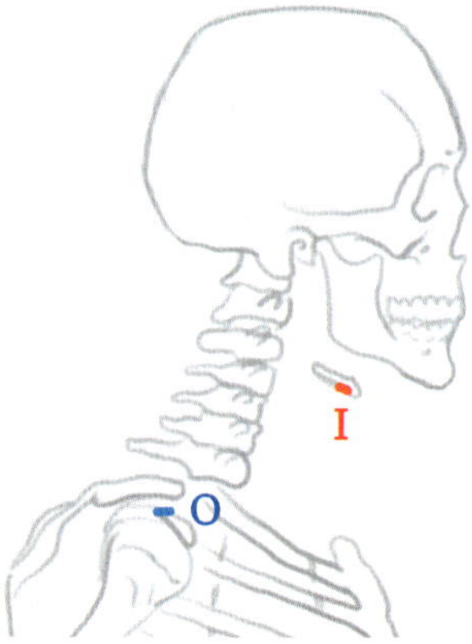

LATERAL

1. Pulls the hyoid bone down

CHECKLIST

- O Semispinalis capitis
- O Splenius capitis
- O Levator scapulae
- O Scalene medius
- O Omohyoid

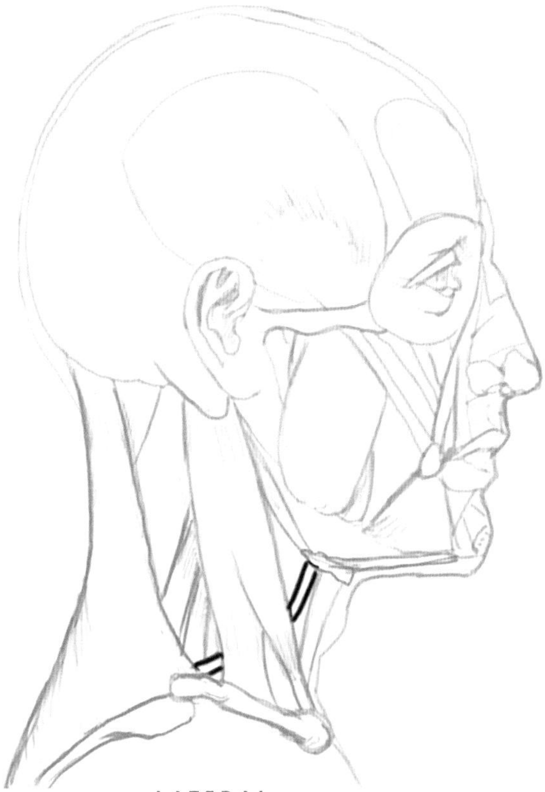

LATERAL

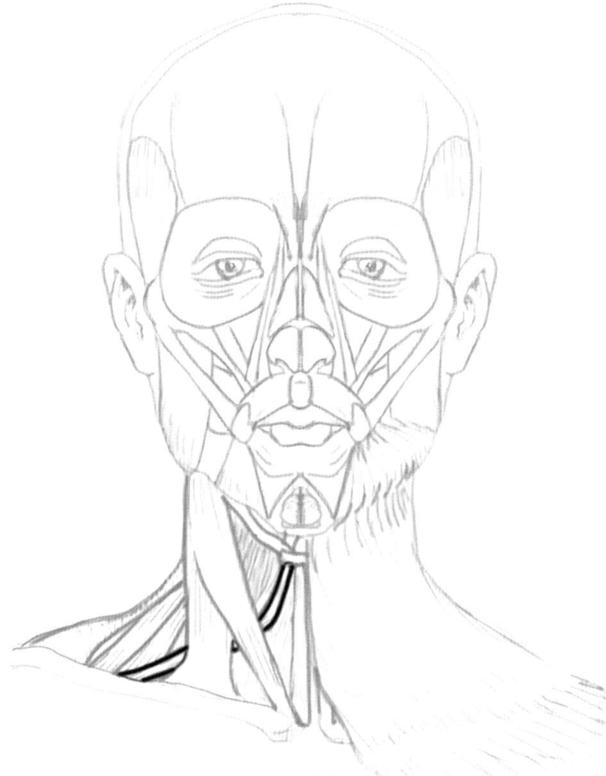

ANTERIOR

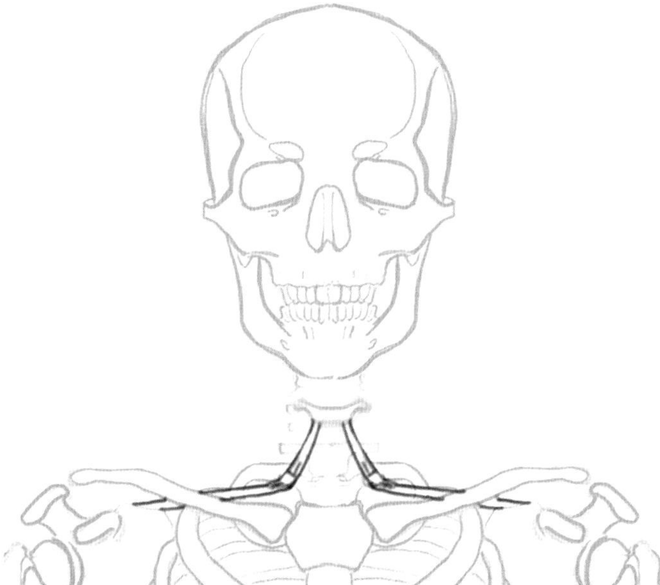

ANTERIOR

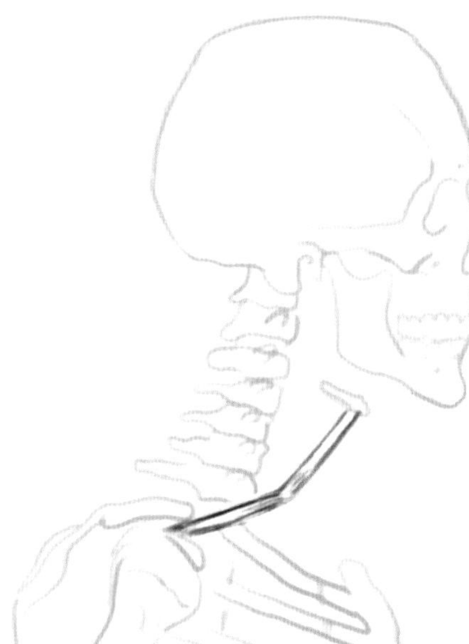

LATERAL

G.6. DIGASTRIC

STRUCTURE

The digastric, like the omohyoid, has two parts, two narrow bellies with a small tendon in the center separating each belly. That little tendon attaches to the hyoid bone, changing the direction of the digastric bellies.

ORIGIN

The mastoid process under the skull, just under the earlobe area.

INSERTION

Just under the mandible (jawbone), not quite at the center of the chin.

ACTION

It opens the mouth and helps in lifting the hyoid bone (1).

1.

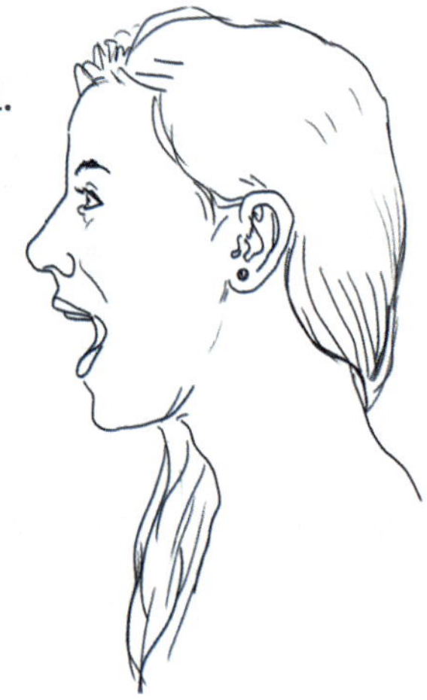

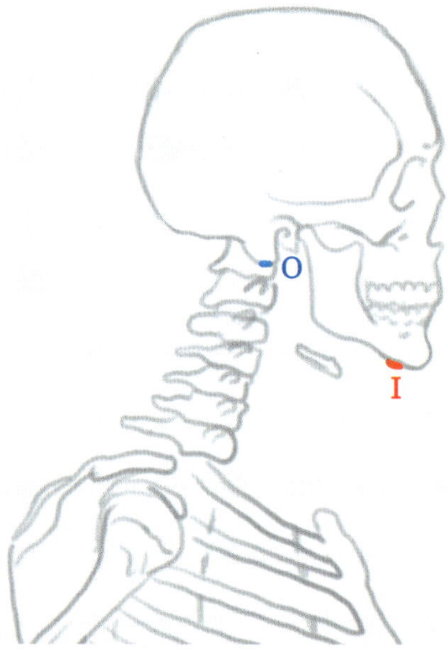

LATERAL

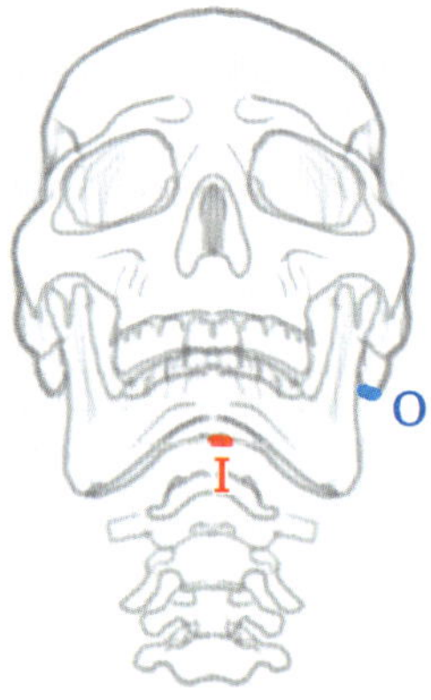

ANTERIOR

1. Opens the mouth and lifts the hyoid bone

CHECKLIST

- O Semispinalis capitis
- O Splenius capitis
- O Levator scapulae
- O Scalene medius
- O Omohyoid
- O Digastric

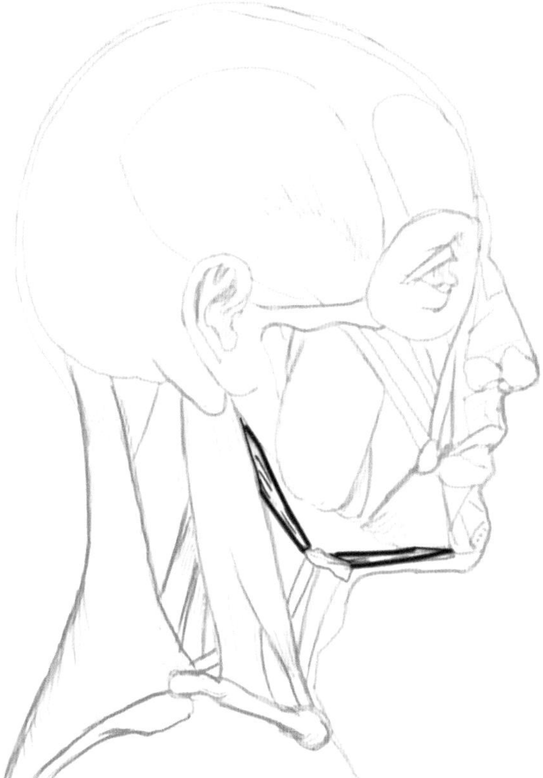

LATERAL

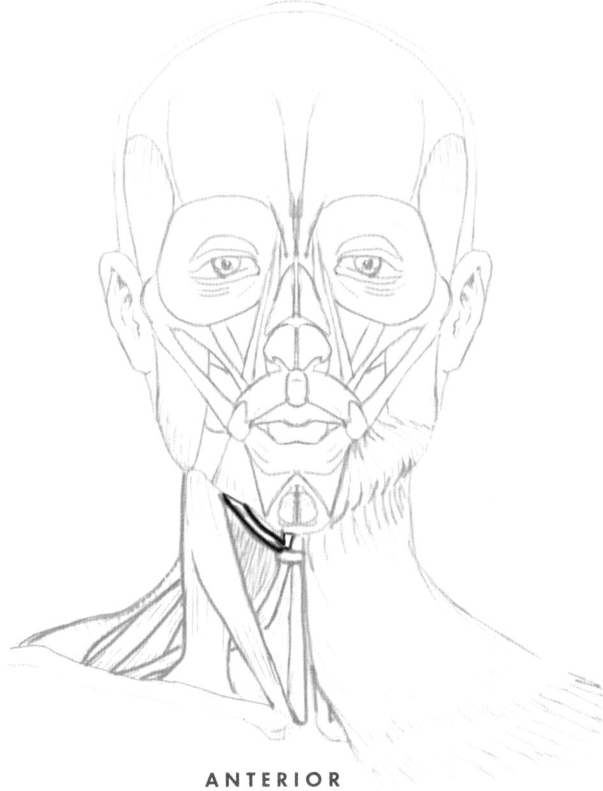

ANTERIOR

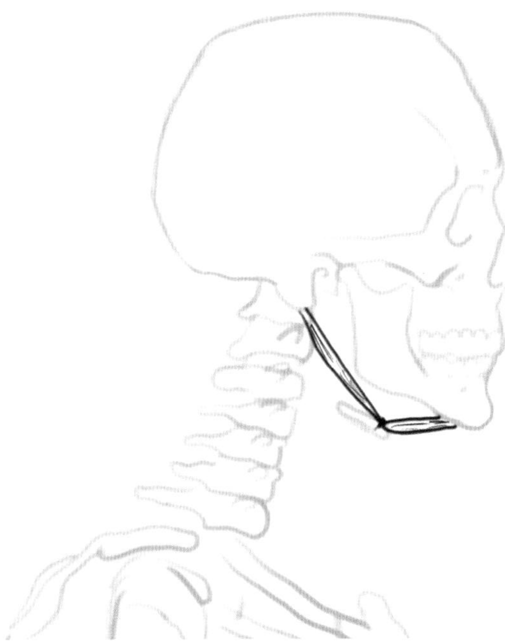

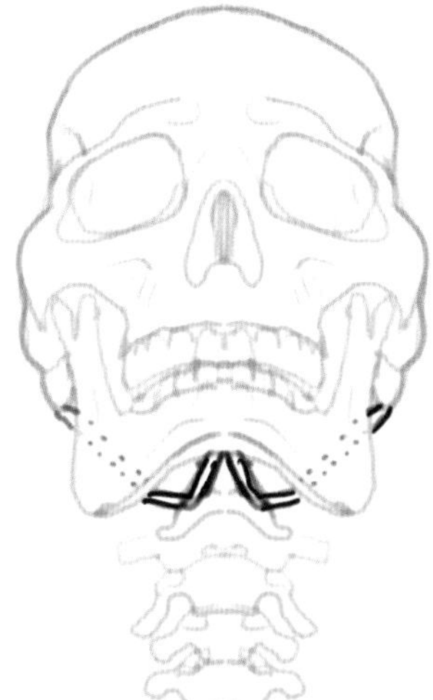

ANTERIOR

LATERAL

G.7. STERNOHYOID

STRUCTURE

The sternohyoid is a thin strap of muscle located and seen at the front of the neck. Together they look like two thin cordlike forms.

ORIGIN

The back area of the clavicle by the pit of the neck.

INSERTION

Under the hyoid bone, just to the side of the center line.

ACTION

Brings the hyoid bone down and helps with swallowing (1).

1.

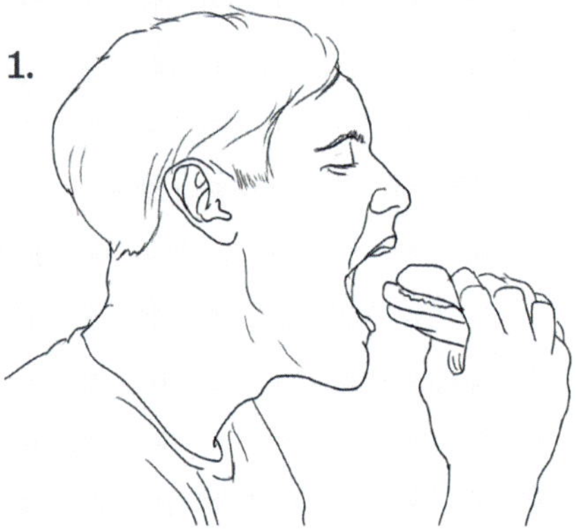

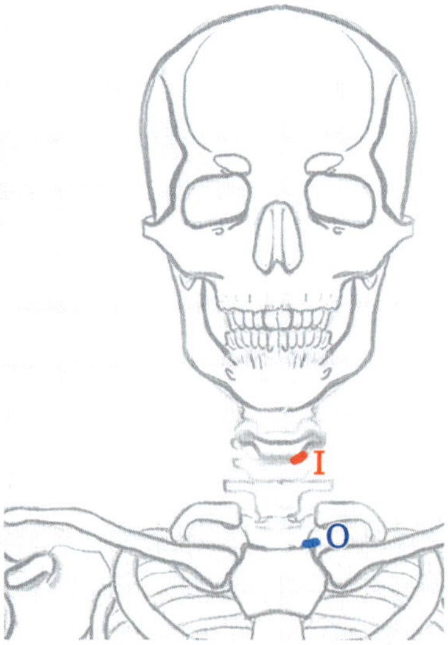

ANTERIOR

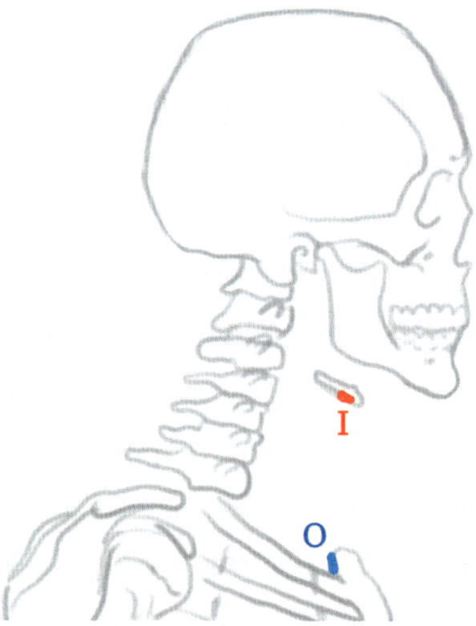

LATERAL

1. Brings the hyoid bone down and helps with swallowing

CHECKLIST

- O Semispinalis capitis
- O Splenius capitis
- O Levator scapulae
- O Scalene medius
- O Omohyoid
- O Digastric
- O Sternohyoid

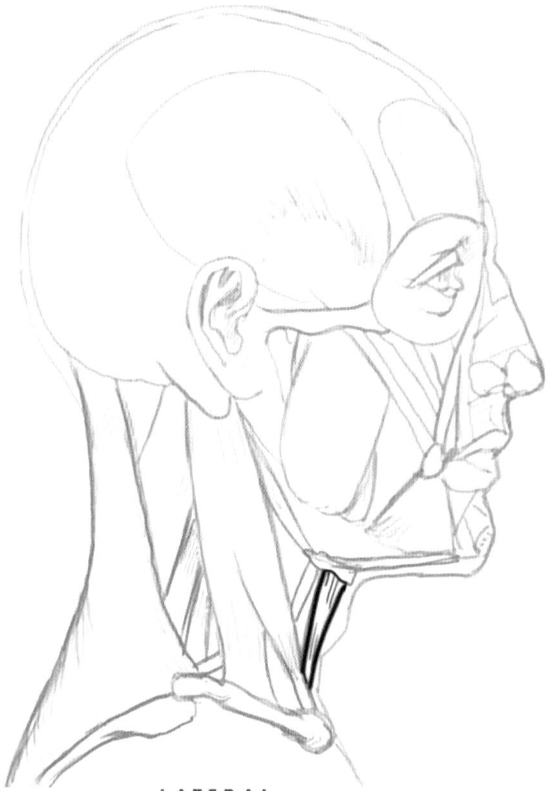

LATERAL

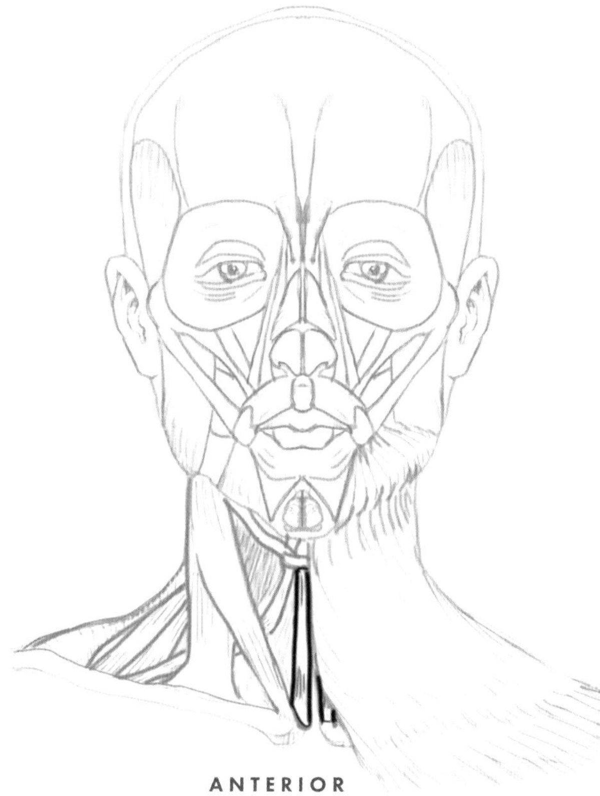

ANTERIOR

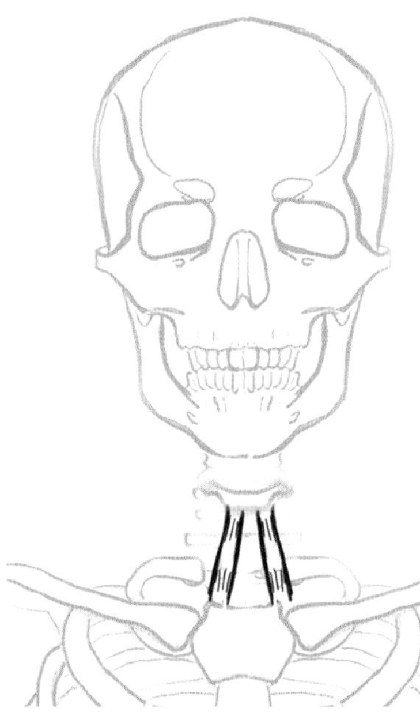

ANTERIOR

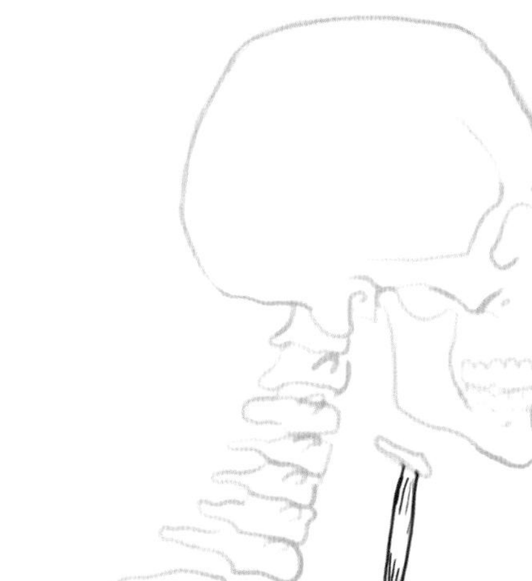

LATERAL

G.8. STERNOCLEIDOMASTOID

STRUCTURE

The sternocleidomastoid (sterno-mastoid, or its long version, sternocleidomastoideus) is broad at the top and splits at the bottom. One of the two heads is tubular and spike-like as it reaches the pit of the neck and can easily be seen, especially when the head is turned to the side. The other is flat and is not always seen. It attaches to the clavicle. The name of this muscle will help you remember it better: *sterno* = sternum, *cleido* = clavicle, and *mastoid* = mastoid process.

ORIGIN

The sternal head attaches to the clavicle and the top part of the sternum, the manubrium. The clavicular head, the flat one, attaches to the upper surface of the clavicle about a third of the way from the proximal end, the part closest to the pit of the neck.

INSERTION

A long line under the occipital bone to the mastoid process.

ACTION

Turns the head side to side (1), and together, the two parts bend the head down (2), as when looking at the feet.

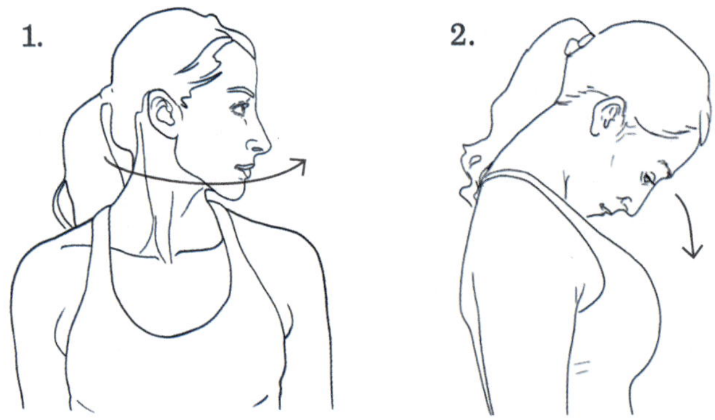

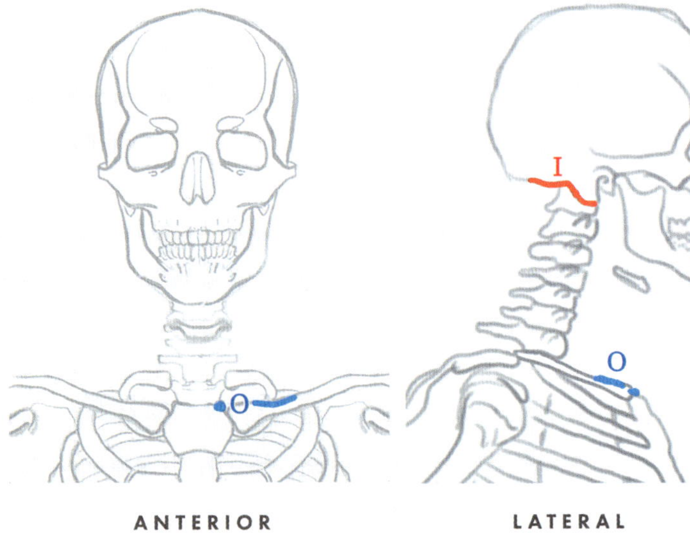

1. Turns the head; 2. Bends the head downward

CHECKLIST

- O Semispinalis capitis
- O Splenius capitis
- O Levator scapulae
- O Scalene medius
- O Omohyoid
- O Digastric
- O Sternohyoid
- O Sternocleidomastoid

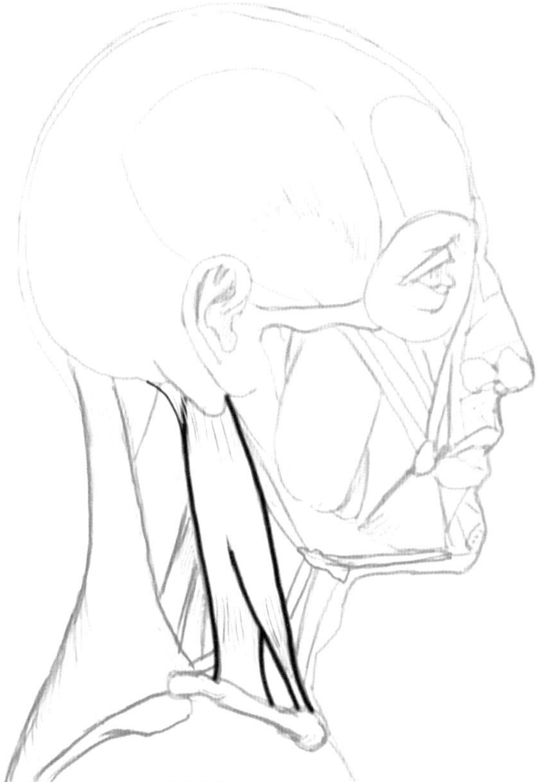

LATERAL

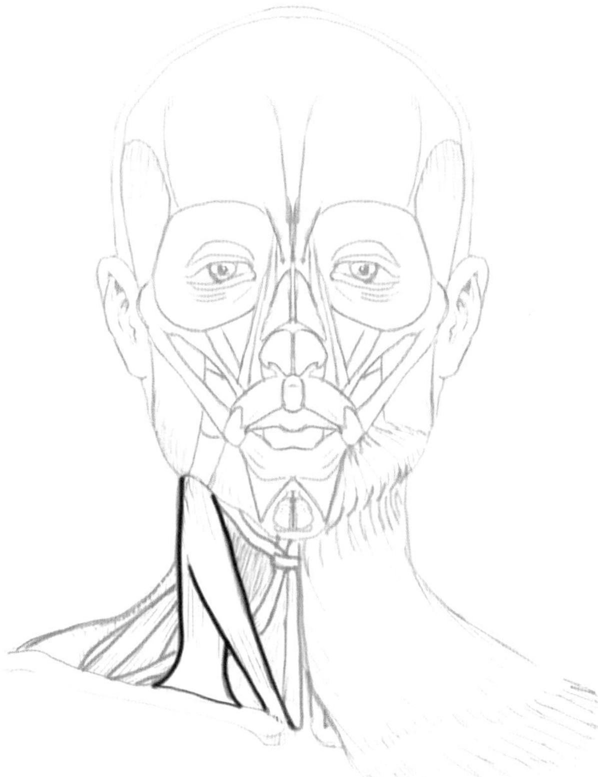

ANTERIOR

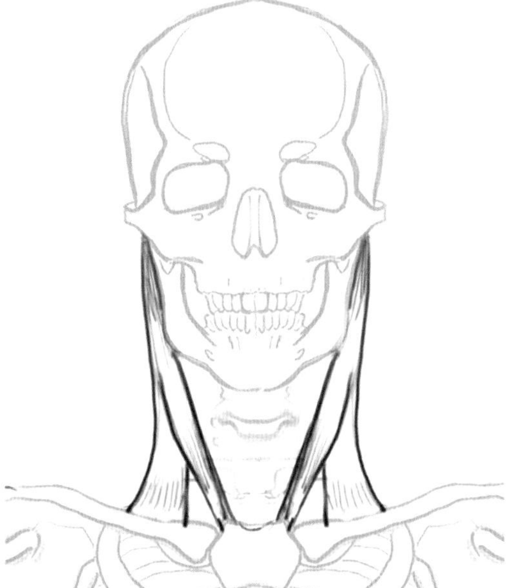

ANTERIOR

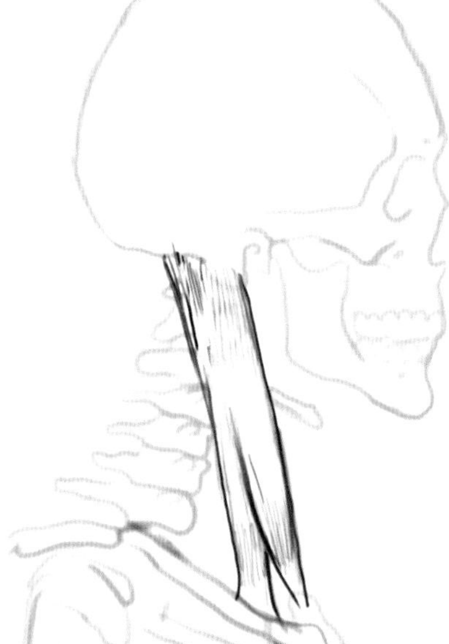

LATERAL

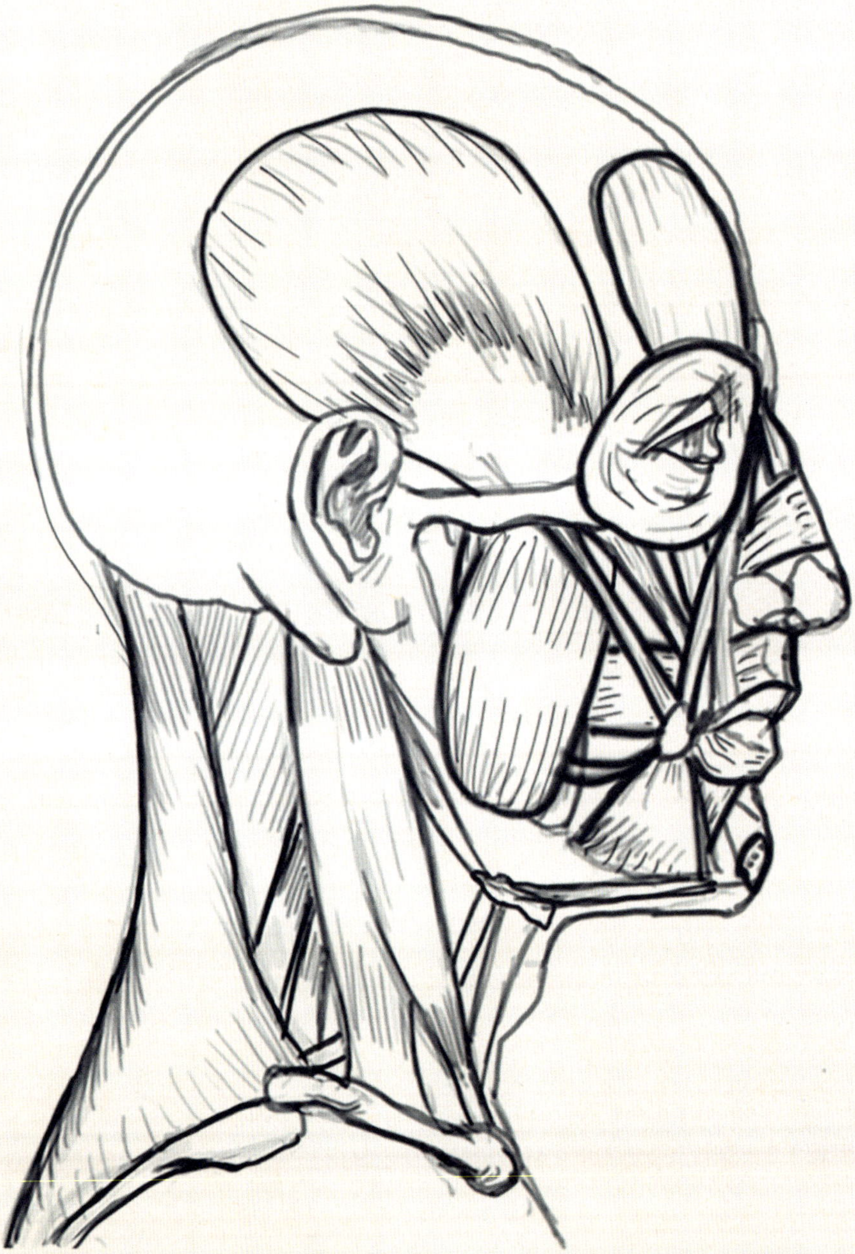

CHAPTER H

THE HEAD AND FACE

I find that it is not always necessary for artists to become experts on every muscle of the head and face, as they are hidden under a healthy abundance of fat. Most of the muscles of the face activate the skin and other muscles to create the countless facial expressions that we are capable of making. Only a few muscles activate bone movement, which is limited to the movement of the mandible.

H.1. TEMPORALIS

STRUCTURE

The temporalis muscle is a pancake-like fan that fits nicely into the temporal fossa (the depression of the temple of the skull). It can be seen in some individuals very clearly and sometimes you can see it when someone is chewing.

ORIGIN

The temporal fossa of the skull.

INSERTION

The coronoid process (the front arm of the mandible) down the ramus (front edge) of the mandible (jawbone).

ACTION

It lifts the mandible, keeps the mouth closed, and helps in chewing (1).

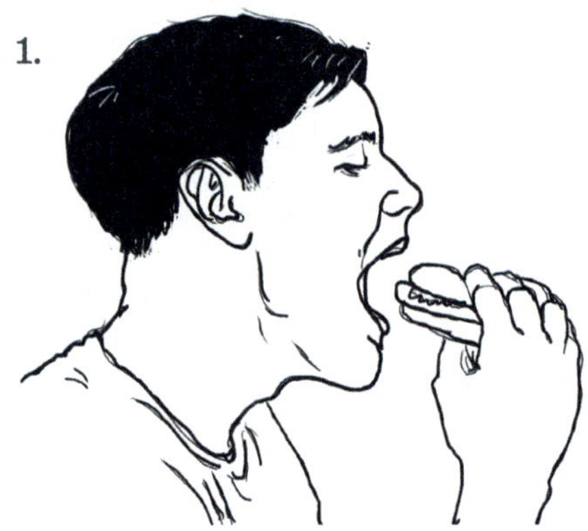

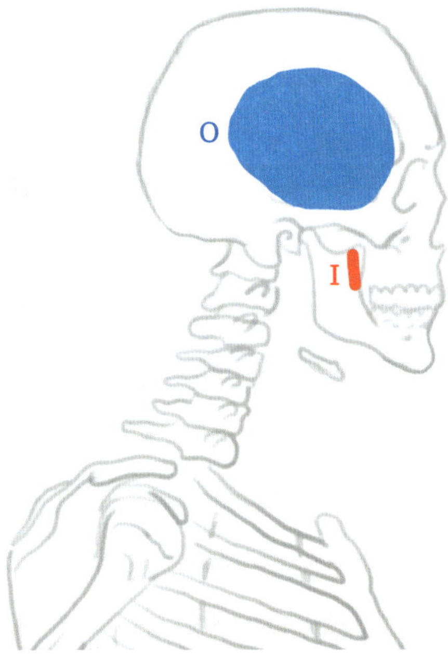

LATERAL

1. *Lifts the mandible*

CHECKLIST

○ Temporalis

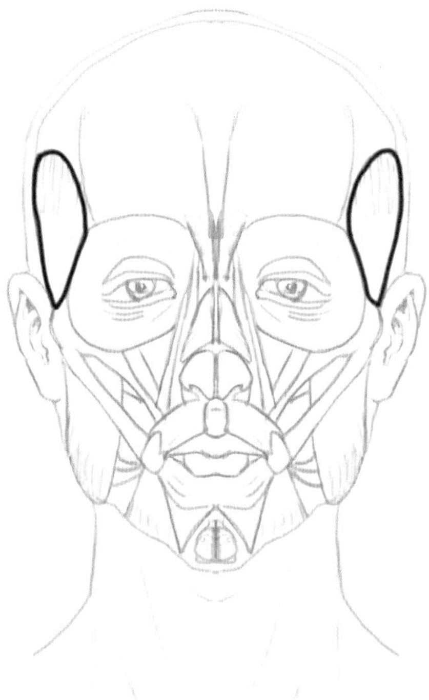

ANTERIOR

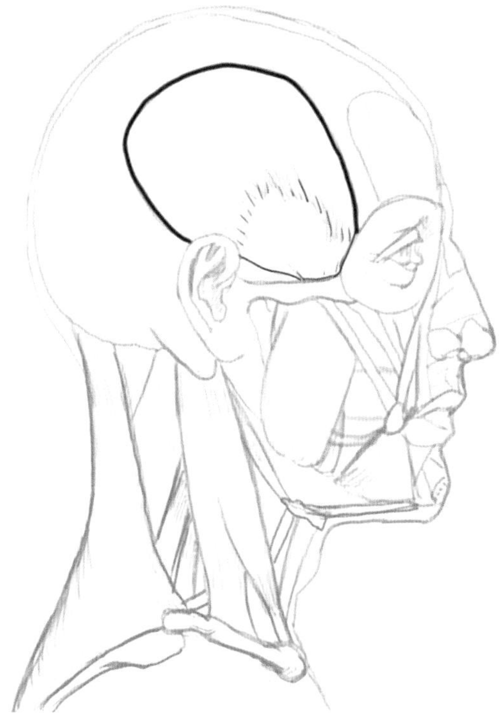

LATERAL

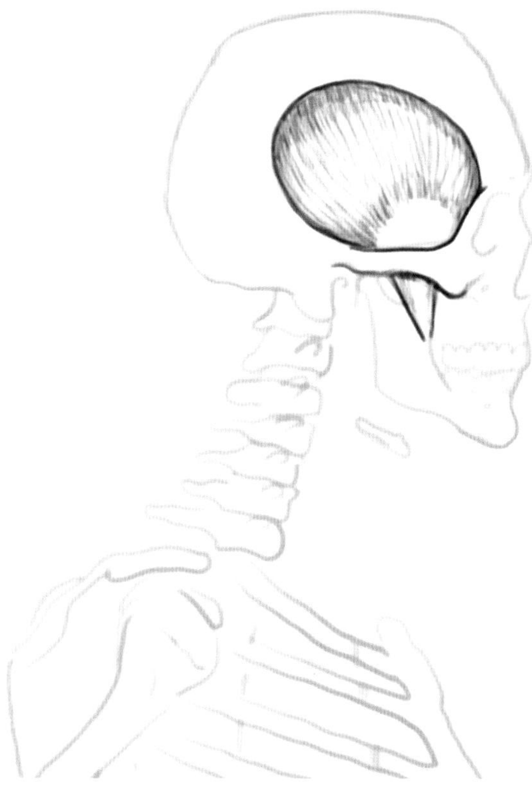

LATERAL

H.2. MASSETER

STRUCTURE

The masseter is a large quadrilateral (four-sided polygon) that is slanted forward.

ORIGIN

Under the edge of the zygomatic arch, the first two thirds and onto the front at the maxilla.

INSERTION

The lateral surface of the ramus of the jaw, the back corner area where the jaw turns.

ACTION

Powerfully closes the mouth as in biting, clenching the jaw, or chewing (1).

1.

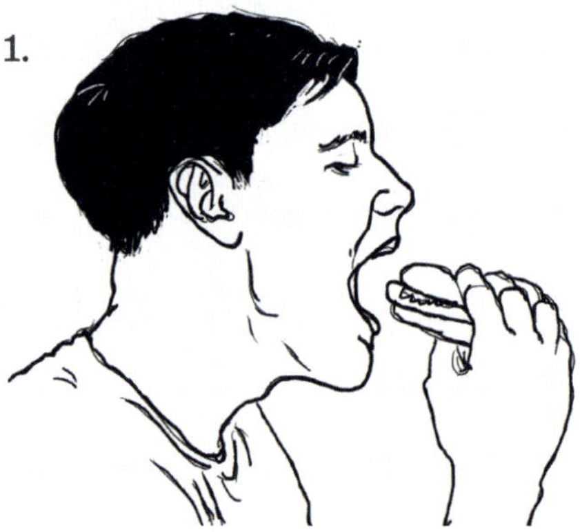

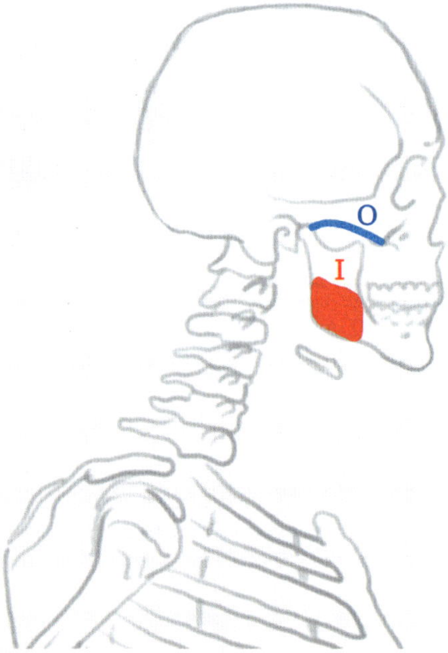

LATERAL

1. Closes the mouth

CHECKLIST

O Temporalis

O Masseter

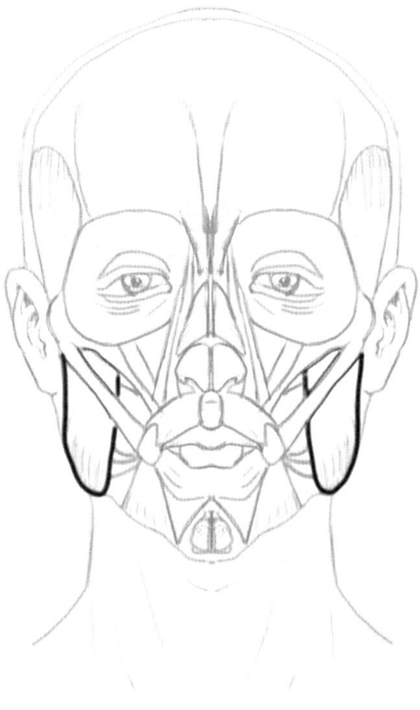

ANTERIOR

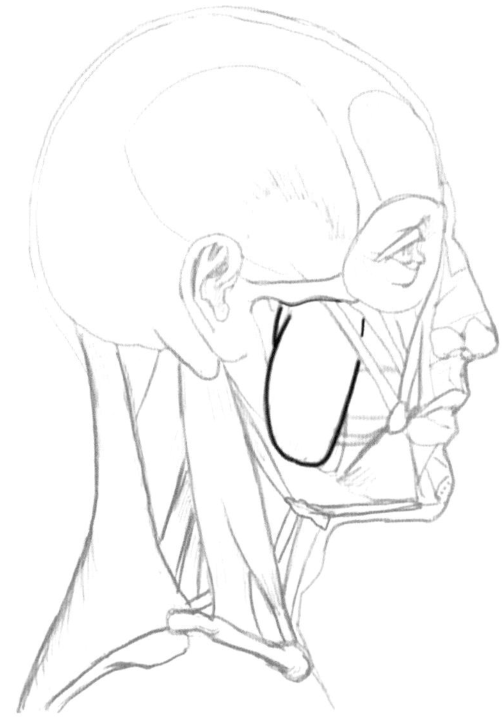

LATERAL

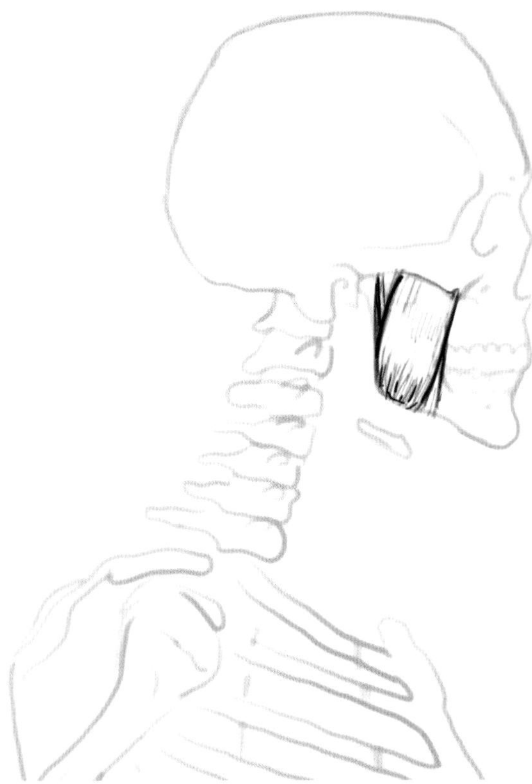

LATERAL

H.3. LEVATOR LABII SUPERIORSIS ALAEQUE NASI (LLSAN)

STRUCTURE

The LLSAN is a three-part muscle composed of three strips of thin muscle that together create movements of disgust or anger. This is easily seen in animals such as cats and dogs when they growl. The nose wrinkles and the teeth show in aggression.

ORIGIN

The three muscles originate on the side of the bridge of the nose.

INSERTION

One of the strips of muscle attaches to the crease that starts at the side of the wing of the nose, the naso-labial furrow (*naso* = nose, *labial* = lip). The second one, the alar strip, attaches to the wing of the nose, and the third, the lip portion, attaches to the skin of the upper lip by the philtrum, the little trough at the center of the upper lip.

ACTION

All three parts contract simultaneously. They raise the lip upward and crinkle the nose at the bridge (1), creating an expression of anger. If raised on only one side, they create a snarl expression.

1.

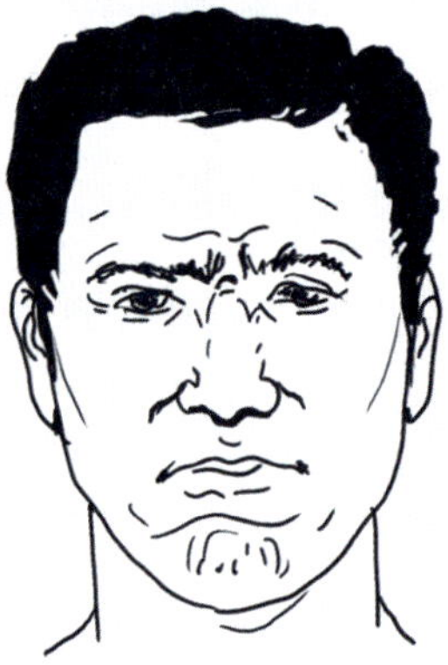

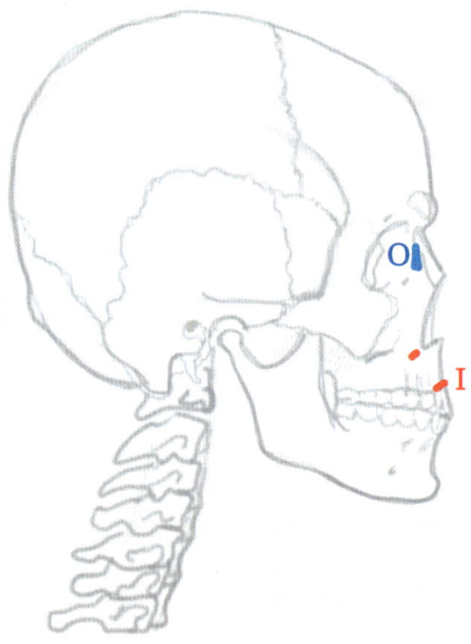

LATERAL

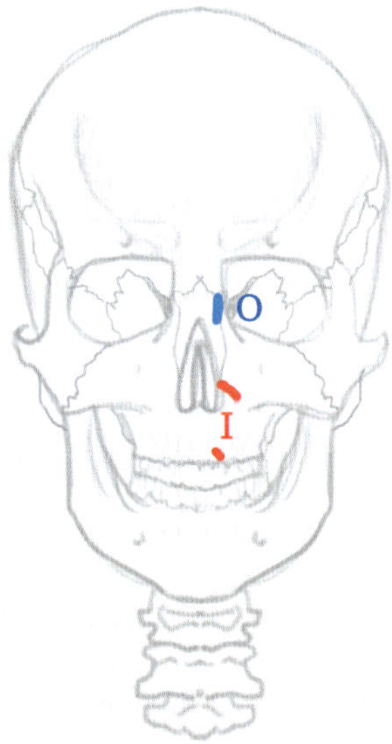

ANTERIOR

1. *Creates expression of anger by raising lip upward and crinkling the nose*

CHECKLIST

- O Temporalis
- O Masseter
- O LLSAN

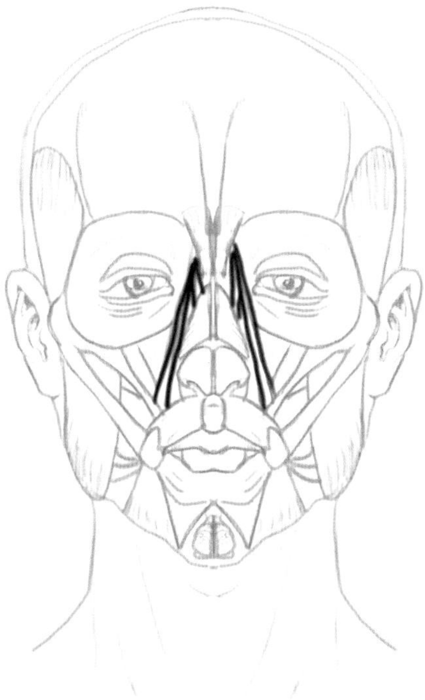

ANTERIOR

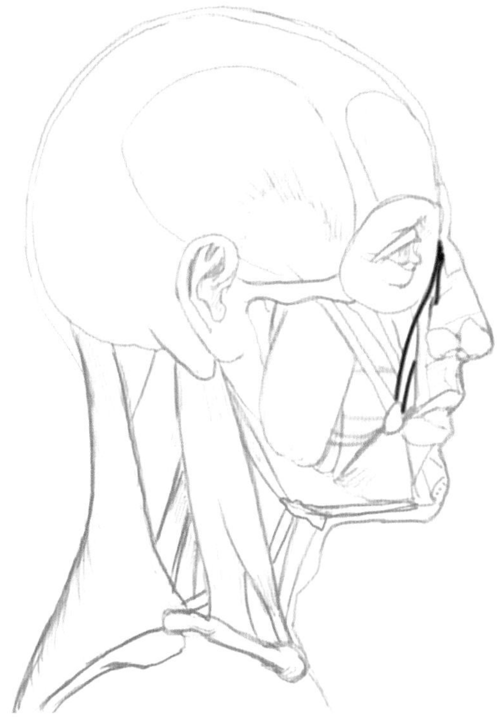

LATERAL

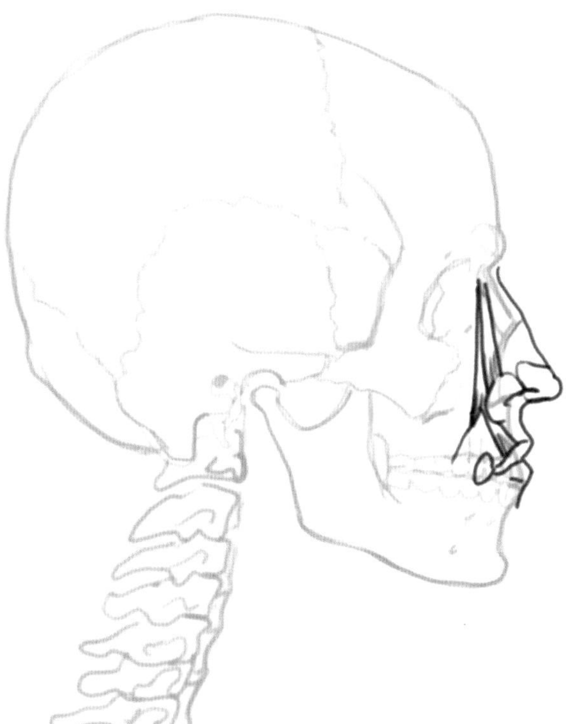

LATERAL

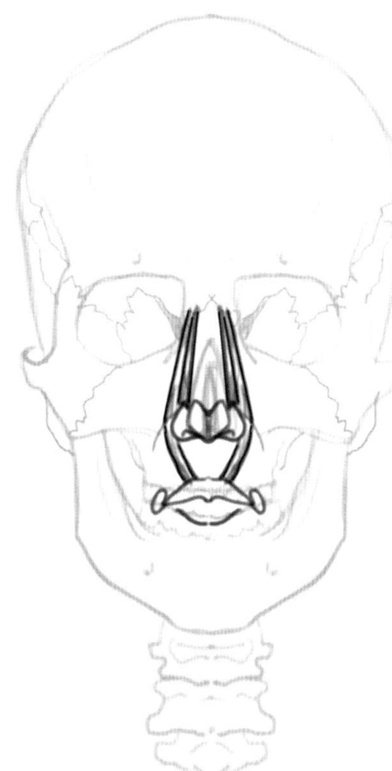

ANTERIOR

H.4. FRONTALIS

STRUCTURE

The frontalis muscle is made up of two separate bodies, one medial and one lateral and larger, but here it is simplified as one form. It is flat and tall, shaped like a slice of bread. They two bodies touch on each side of the forehead but pull away slightly as they ascend. These muscles are not seen, but they create very visible forms on the forehead when contracted.

ORIGIN

The front edge of the epicranial aponeurosis, which is approximately at the hairline.

INSERTION

The skin at the eyebrows and just above the nasal bone.

ACTION

Raises the eyebrows (1), creating the furrows on the forehead.

1.

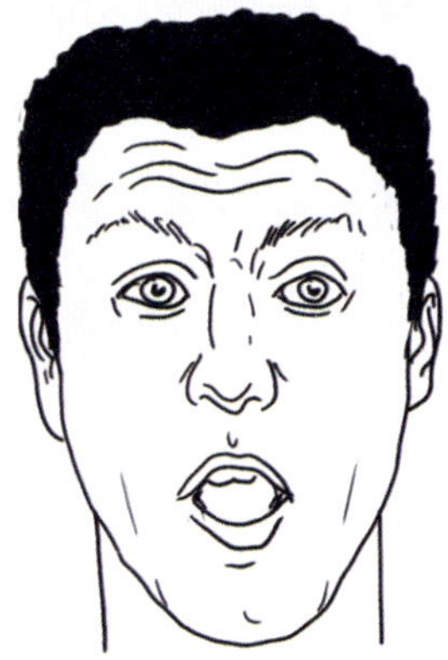

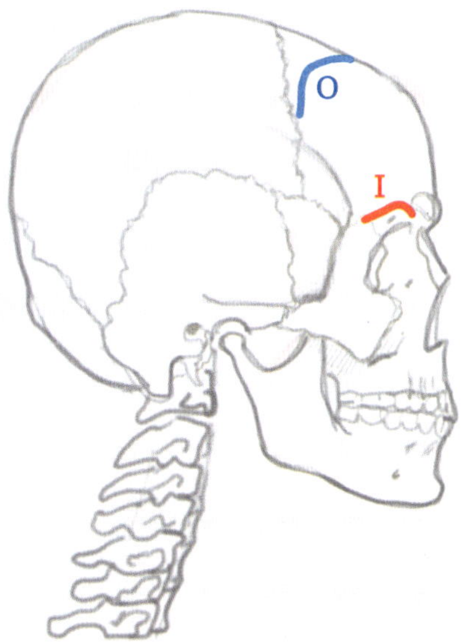

LATERAL

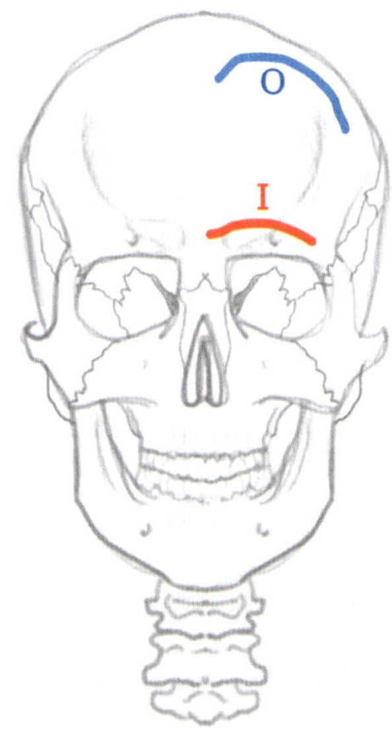

ANTERIOR

1. Raises the eyebrows, creating furrows on the forehead, as in expressions of fear, surprise, and sadness

CHECKLIST

- O Temporalis
- O Masseter
- O LLSAN
- O Frontalis

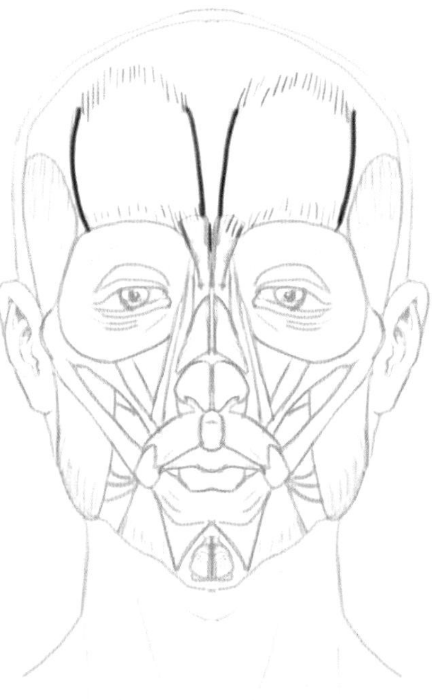

ANTERIOR

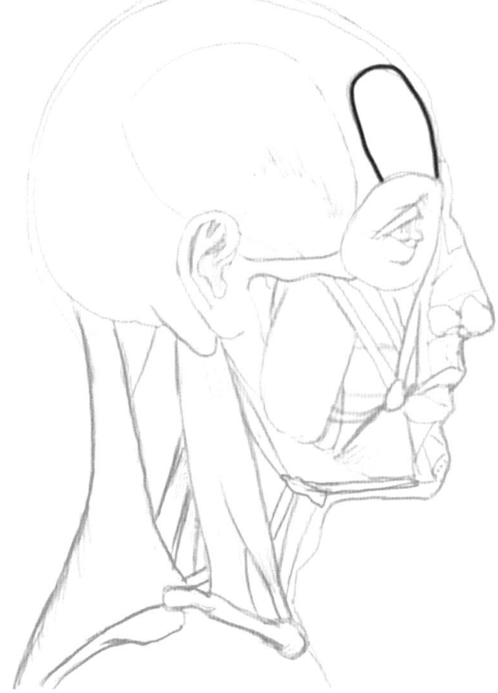

LATERAL

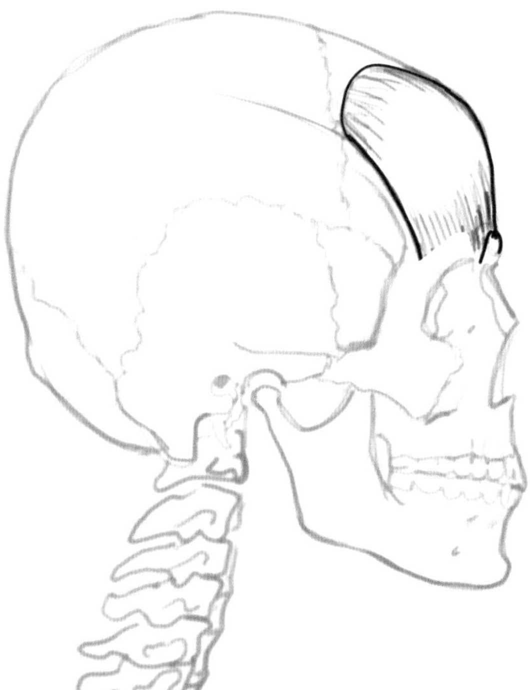

LATERAL

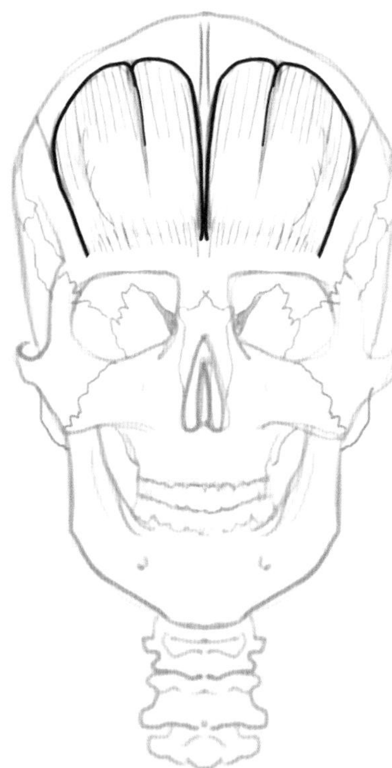

ANTERIOR

H.5. BUCCINATOR ("BUGLER'S MUSCLE")

STRUCTURE

The buccinator is a bilateral (two-sided) muscle that looks like a patch that forms the wall of the cheek.

ORIGIN

The muscle fibers attach in a few spots: the maxilla, inner cheek bone, and mandible on the upper edge.

INSERTION

The "node" of the corner of the mouth, the little jelly bean–shaped fibromuscular form called the modiolus.

ACTION

Pulls the modiolus (the node) inward into the corners of the mouth (1). It also compresses the cheeks, as in playing a bugle, and helps in sucking, as in drinking through a straw. It is one of the first muscles activated and used at birth as a baby suckles. In expression it creates a smirk or expression of annoyance.

1.

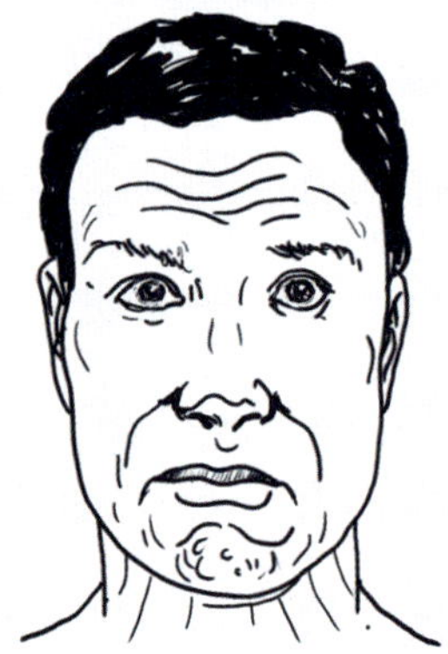

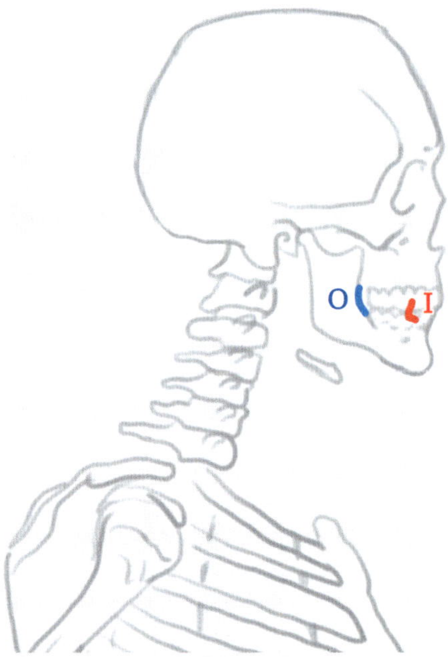

LATERAL

1. Pulls the modiolus inward, compresses the cheeks, and helps in sucking; creates a smirk

CHECKLIST

- O Temporalis
- O Masseter
- O LLSAN
- O Frontalis
- O Buccinator

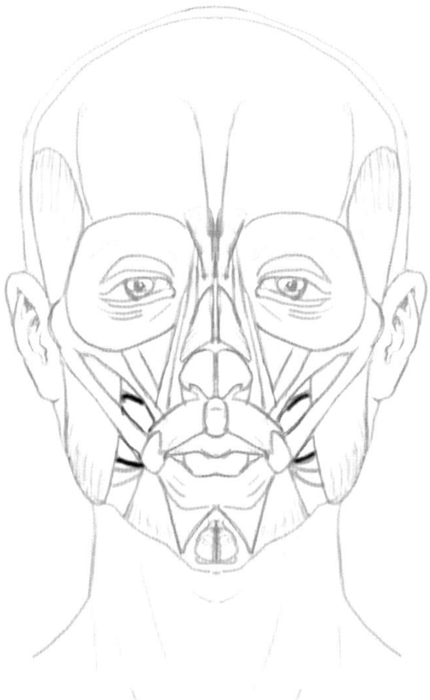

ANTERIOR

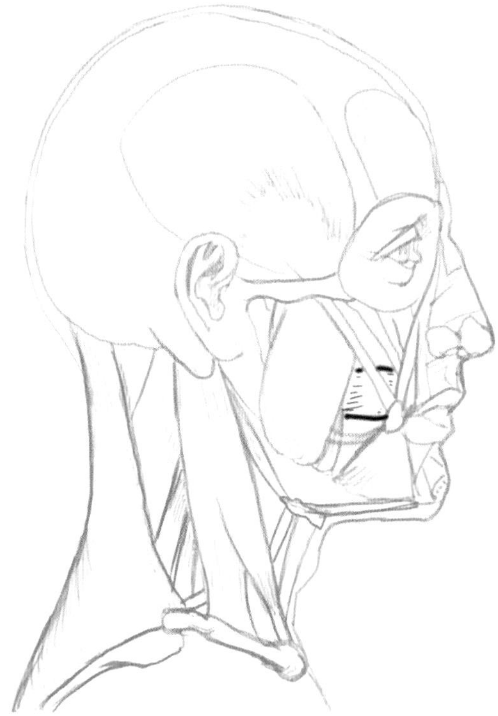

LATERAL

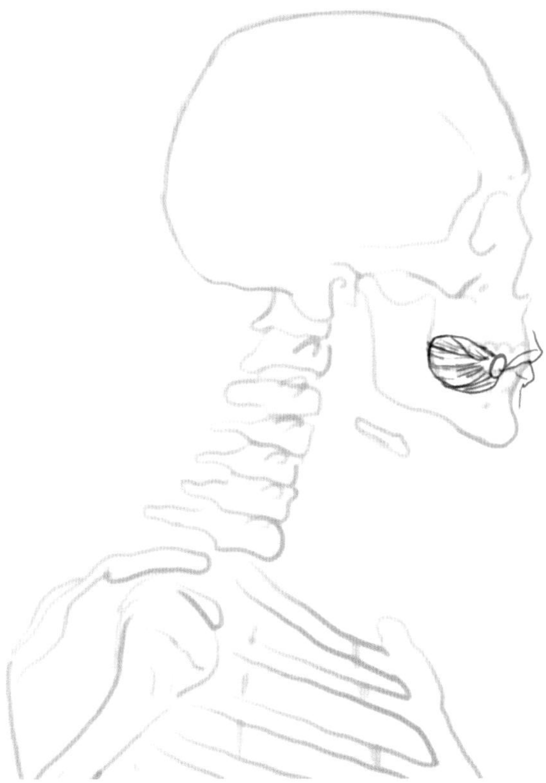

LATERAL

H.6. ZYGOMATICUS MAJOR AND MINOR

STRUCTURE

The zygomatics major and minor are both thin, straplike muscles.

ORIGIN

The zygomaticus major attaches at the zygomatic bone on the corner where it turns from side to front. The zygomaticus minor attaches near the same area as the zygomaticus major, just a tad to the side of it.

INSERTION

The zygomaticus major attaches to the modiolus (node) on the corner of the mouth. The zygomaticus minor attaches to the middle area of the nasolabial furrow and some of it extends down further to the upper lip.

ACTION

The zygomaticus major pulls the angle of the mouth upward, creating a smile (1). The zygomaticus minor pulls the middle portion of the upper lip upward, creating an expression of sadness (2).

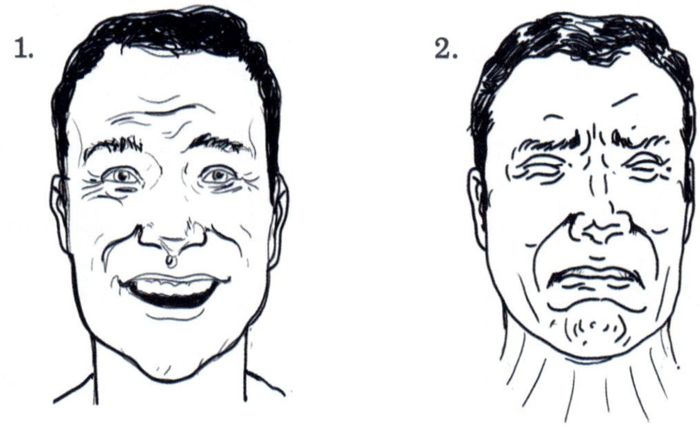

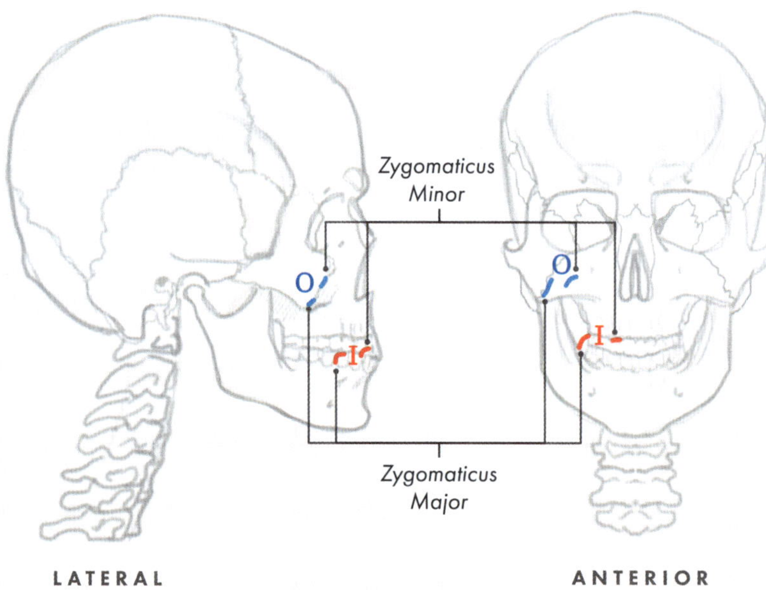

1. Pulls the mouth upward; 2. Pulls the middle part of the upper lip upward

CHECKLIST

- O Temporalis
- O Masseter
- O LLSAN
- O Frontalis
- O Buccinator
- O Zygomaticus major and minor

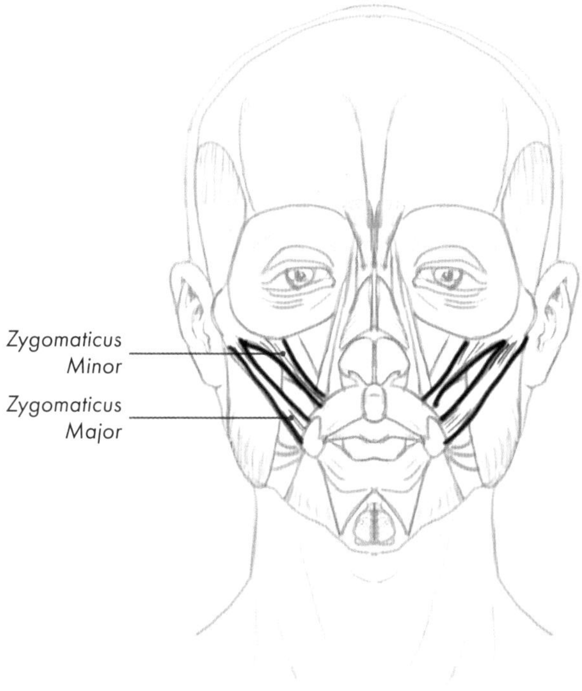

ANTERIOR

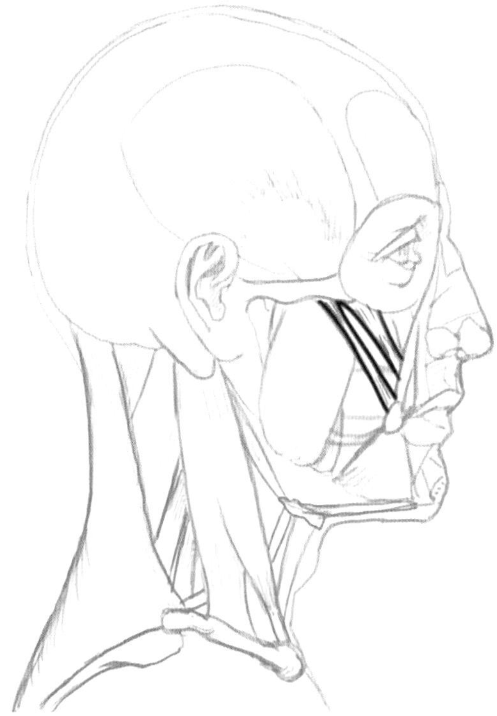

LATERAL

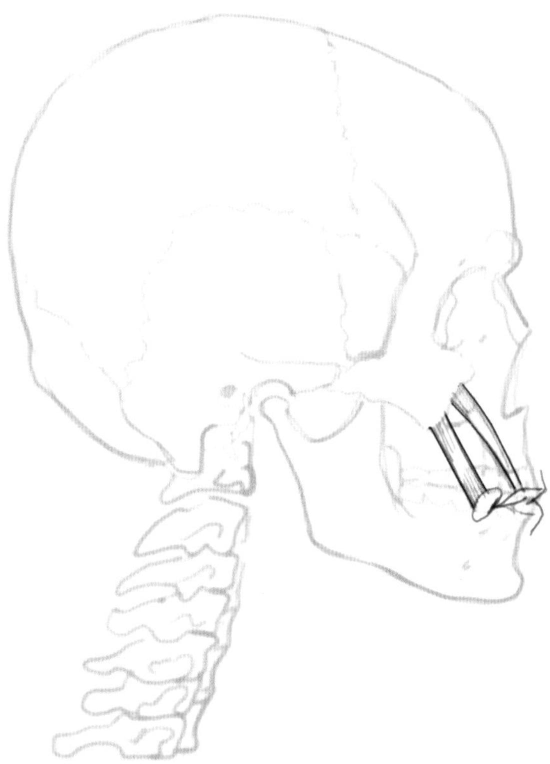

LATERAL

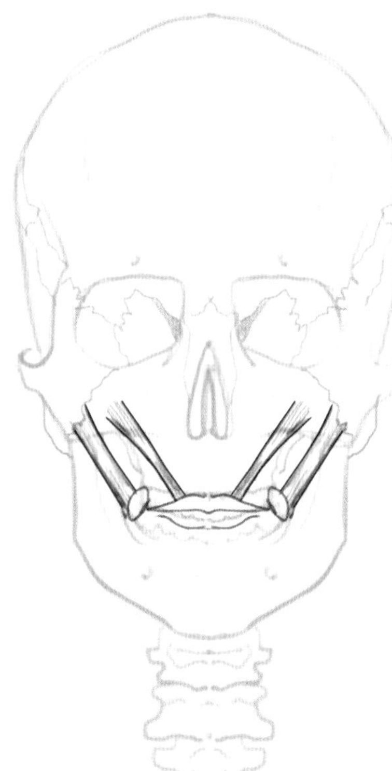

ANTERIOR

H.7. ORBICULARIS ORIS

STRUCTURE

The orbicularis oris (mouth) is a very complex muscle, the most complex of all the facial muscles, allowing for great expression and speech. It includes both the upper and lower red lip.

ORIGIN

The modioli (nodes) at the corners of the mouth.

INSERTION

Horizontal bands of muscle go from the node on one side of the face to the node on the other side, allowing for a vast variety of movement for speech and expression. The insertion is where the origin is since the muscle encircles the mouth.

ACTION

Helps with a wide variety of movements of the mouth for speaking and expression (1).

1.

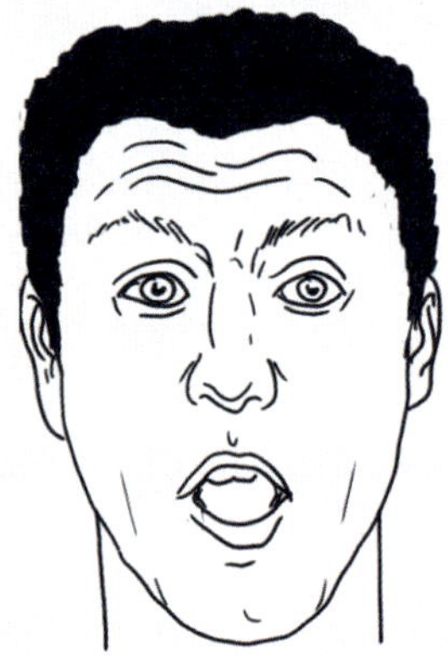

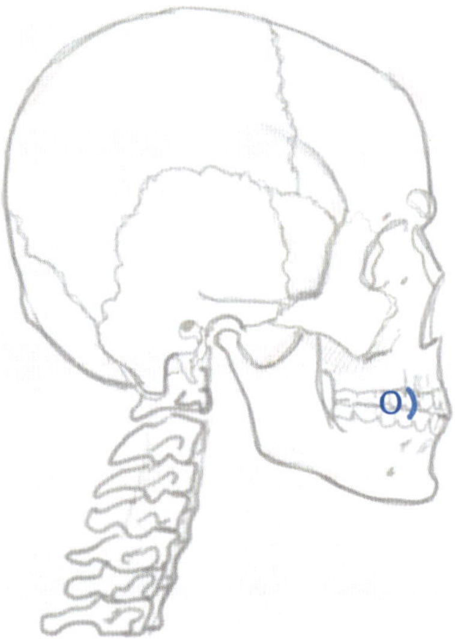

LATERAL

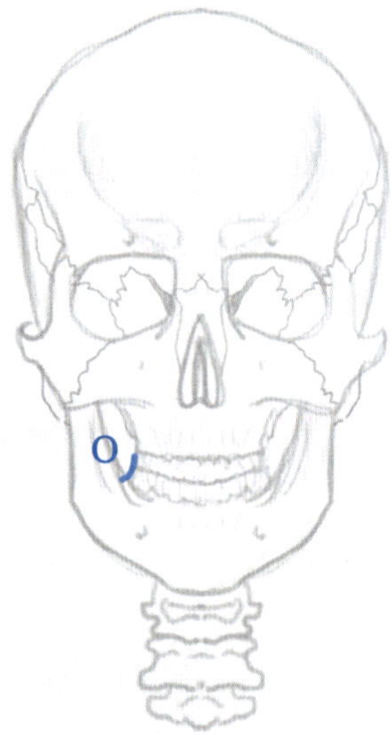

ANTERIOR

1. Moves the mouth

CHECKLIST

- O Temporalis
- O Masseter
- O LLSAN
- O Frontalis
- O Buccinator
- O Zygomaticus major and minor
- O Orbicularis oris

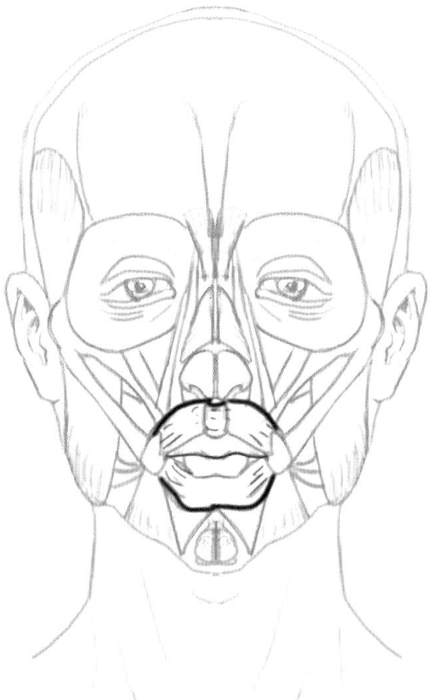

ANTERIOR

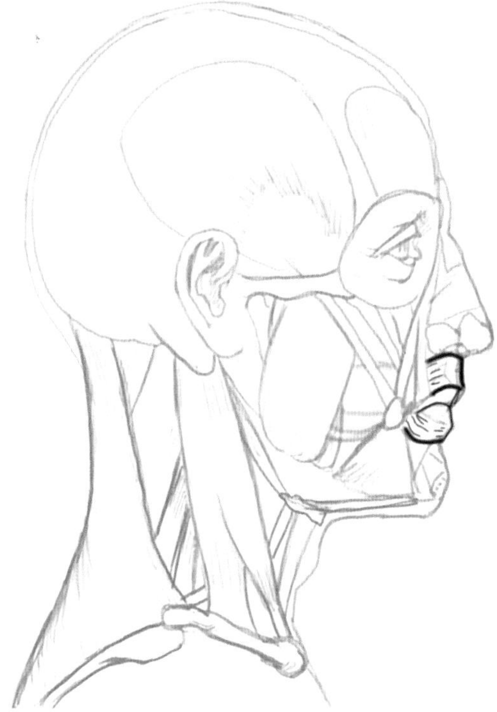

LATERAL

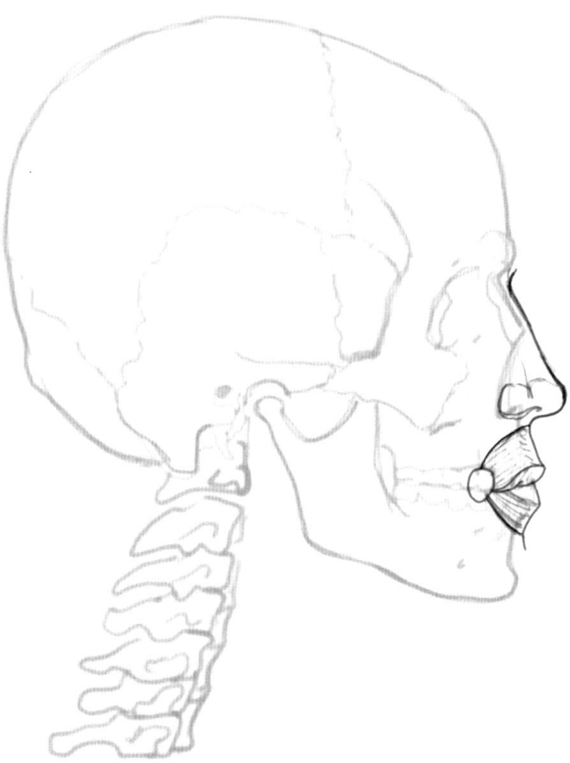

LATERAL

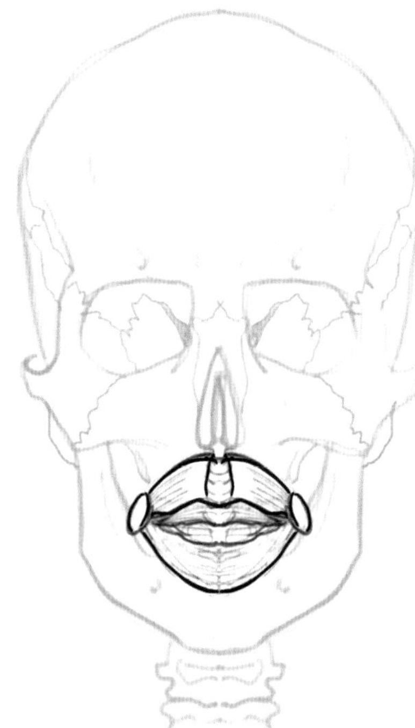

ANTERIOR

H.8. DEPRESSOR ANGULI ORIS

STRUCTURE

The depressor anguli oris is made up of two layers, one under the other. The lower layer is straplike and narrow, and the one on top of it is more of a stretched-out triangle.

ORIGIN

The two parts of the depressor anguli oris attach to the mandible, just to the side of the mental tubercle (chin bone).

INSERTION

The depressor anguli oris inserts into the modiolus (node at the corner of the mouth).

ACTION

Pulls the corners of the lips down (1), such as in sadness.

1.

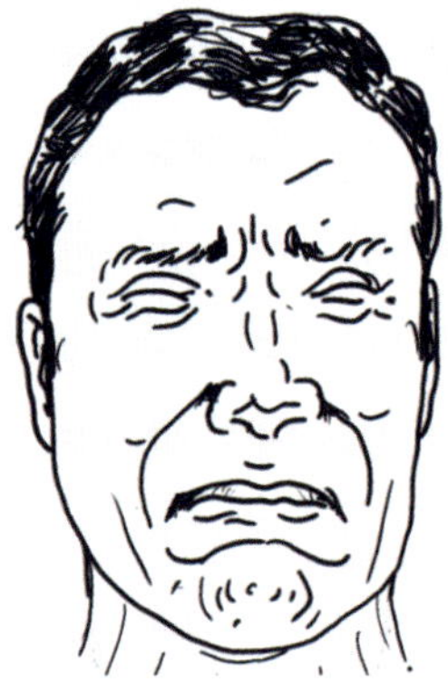

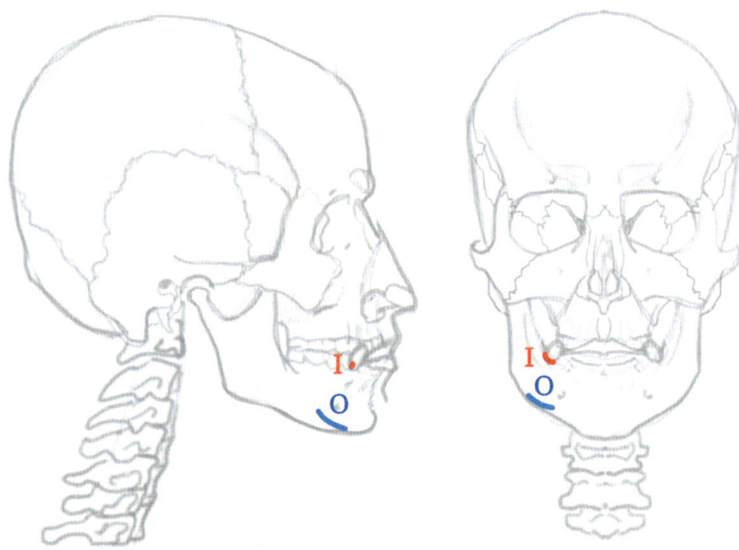

LATERAL

ANTERIOR

1. Pulls the corners of the lips down

CHECKLIST

- O Temporalis
- O Masseter
- O LLSAN
- O Frontalis
- O Buccinator
- O Zygomaticus major and minor
- O Orbicularis oris
- O Depressor anguli oris

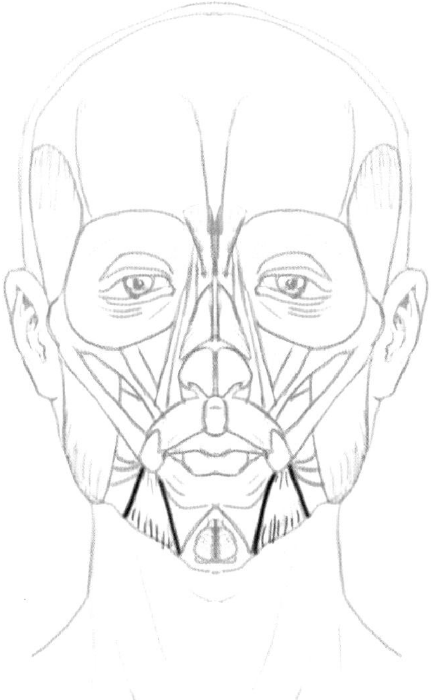

ANTERIOR

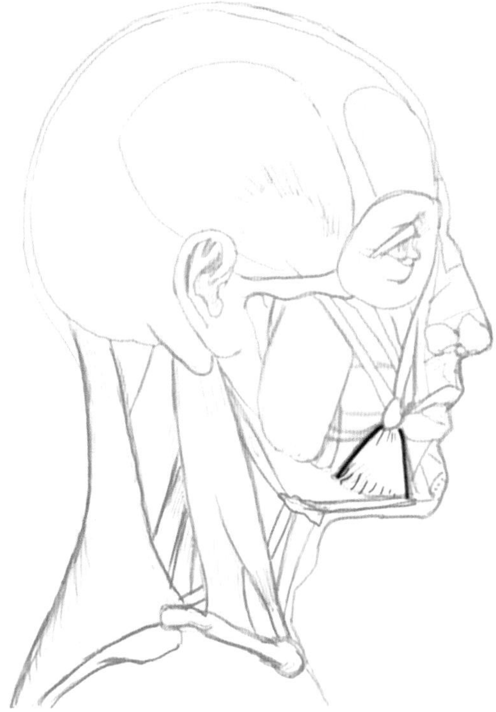

LATERAL

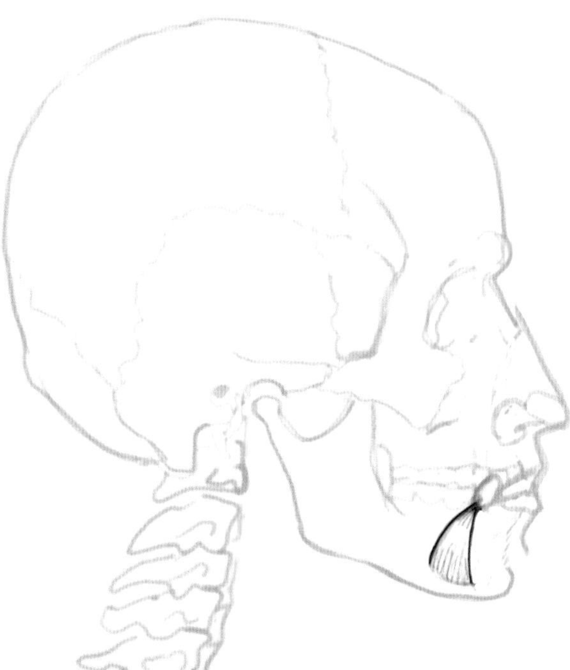

LATERAL

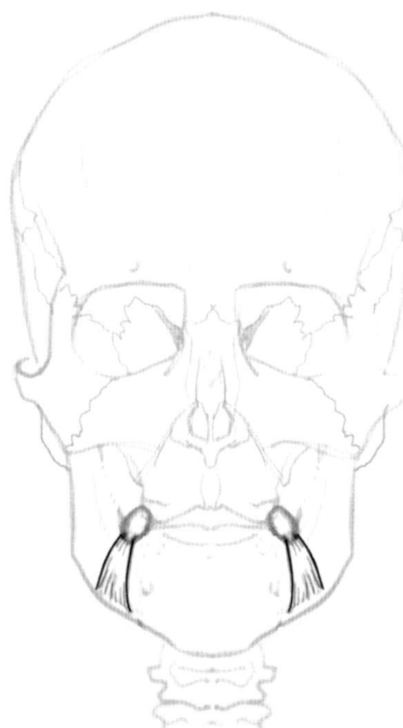

ANTERIOR

H.9. LEVATOR LABII SUPERIORIS

STRUCTURE

The levator labii superioris is a wide band of muscle that narrows as it descends toward the mouth.

ORIGIN

Attaches on a line just below the eye socket.

INSERTION

Attaches to the skin on the nasolabial furrow and down to the red lip and the orbicularis oris.

ACTION

Pulls the lip upward (1), as in snarling.

1.

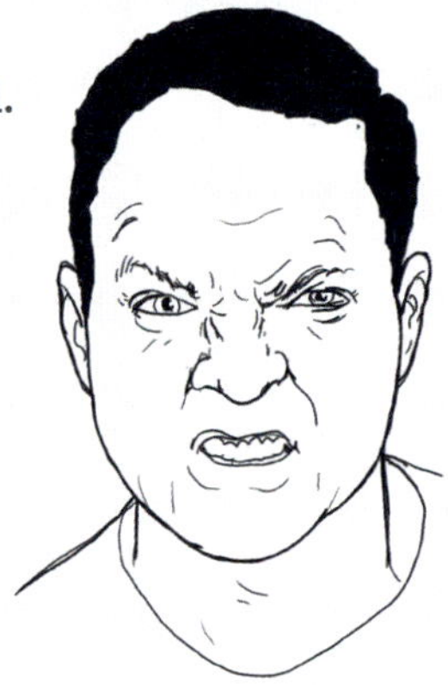

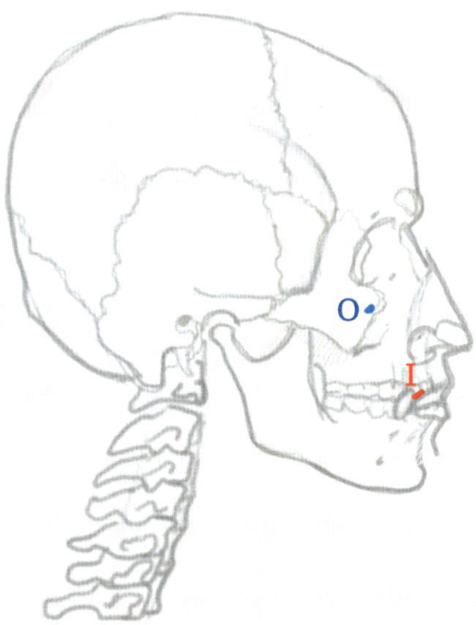

LATERAL

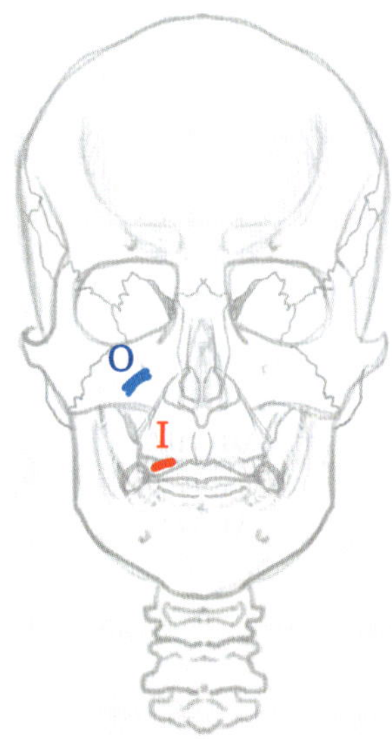

ANTERIOR

1. Pulls the lip upward

CHECKLIST

- O Temporalis
- O Masseter
- O LLSAN
- O Frontalis
- O Buccinator
- O Zygomaticus major and minor
- O Orbicularis oris
- O Depressor anguli oris
- O Levator labii superioris

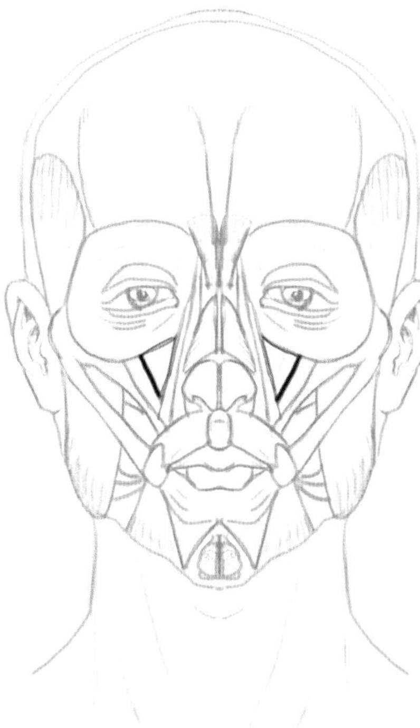

ANTERIOR

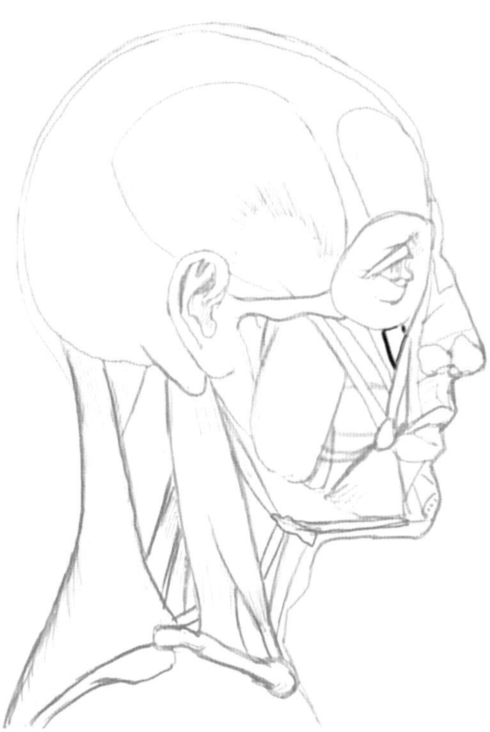

LATERAL

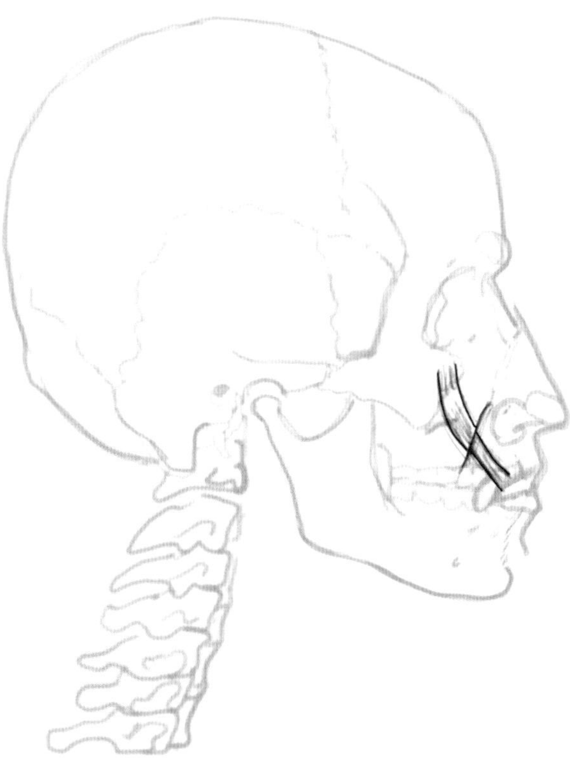

LATERAL

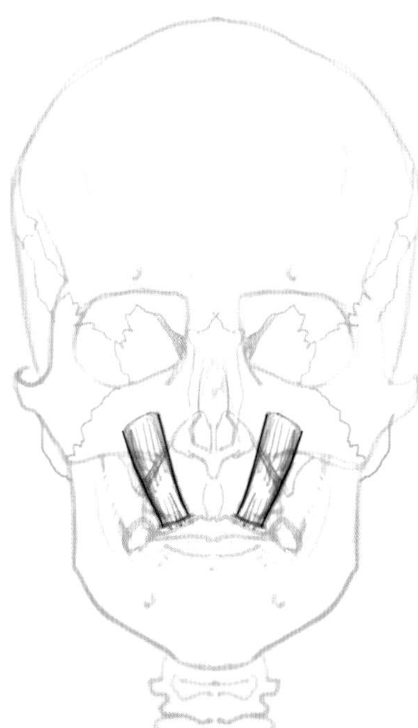

ANTERIOR

H.10. DEPRESSOR LABII INFERIORIS

STRUCTURE

The depressor labii inferioris (*depressor* = brings down, *labii* = lips, and *inferioris* = lower) is a quadrilateral muscle that is rhomboid-shaped and flat. It curves the lip downward and is primarily used for speaking.

ORIGIN

Attaches at a slanted line on the lower edge of the jaw, away from center and flanking the mentalis muscle of the chin.

INSERTION

On the edge of the lower lip.

ACTION

Acting with each side of the chin, the muscles work in unison to pull the lip downward (1), exposing the lower teeth.

1.

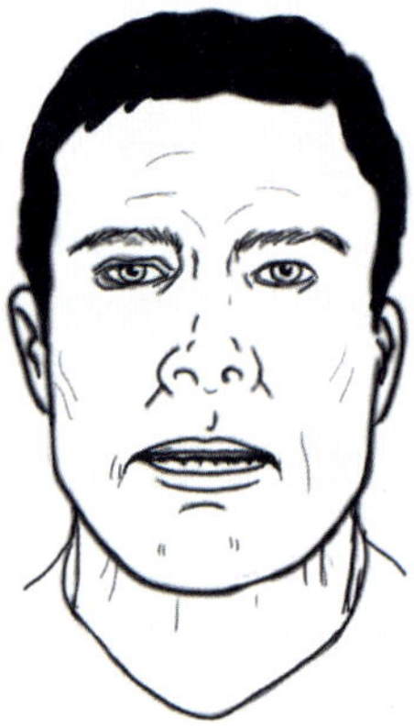

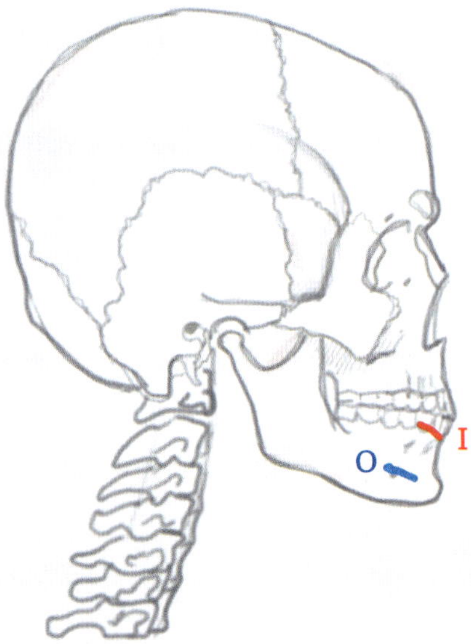

LATERAL

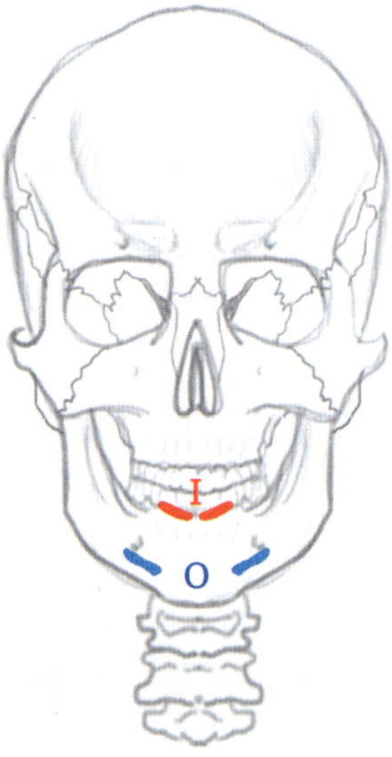

ANTERIOR

1. *Pulls the lip downward*

CHECKLIST

- O Temporalis
- O Masseter
- O LLSAN
- O Frontalis
- O Buccinator
- O Zygomaticus major and minor
- O Orbicularis oris
- O Depressor anguli oris
- O Levator labii superioris
- O Depressor labii inferioris

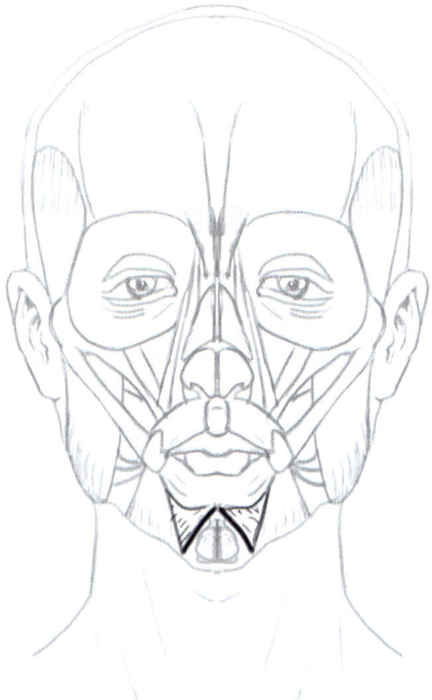

ANTERIOR

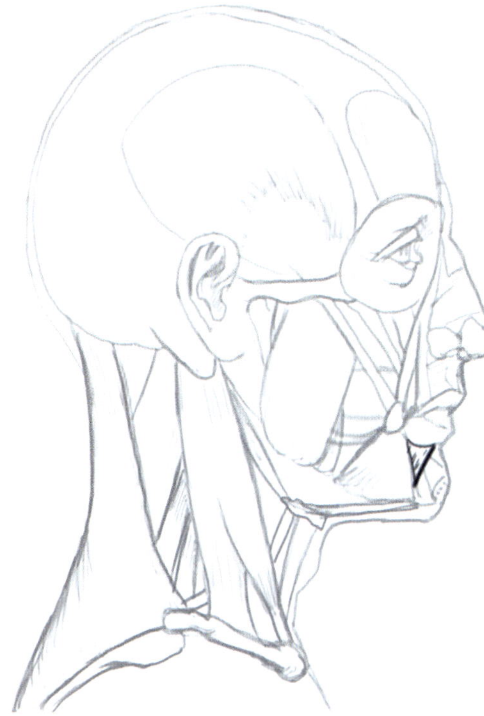

LATERAL

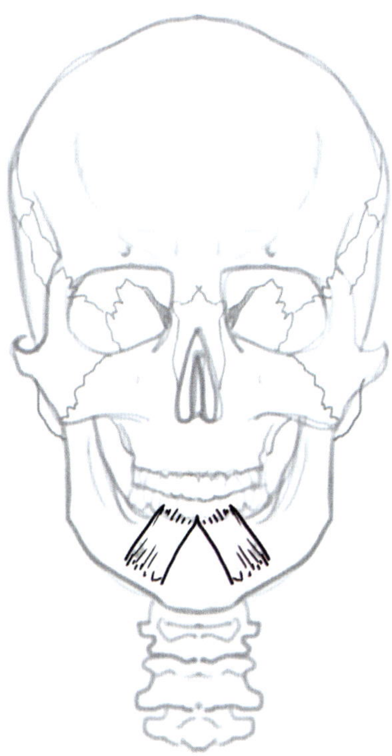

ANTERIOR

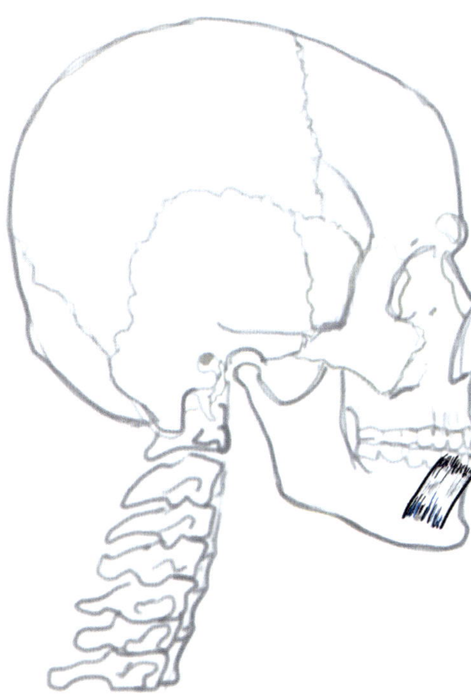

LATERAL

H.11. RISORIUS

STRUCTURE

The risorius is quite variable and some people do not even have this muscle. It can be flat and straplike or it can be thinner and more cablelike.

ORIGIN

The connective tissue of the cheek on the masseter.

INSERTION

Curving to the modiolus (node of the corner of the mouth).

ACTION

Pulls the node and therefore the corners of the mouth outward toward the ear (1). Creates subtle expression, helps in smiling, and moves the nasolabial furrow outward.

1.

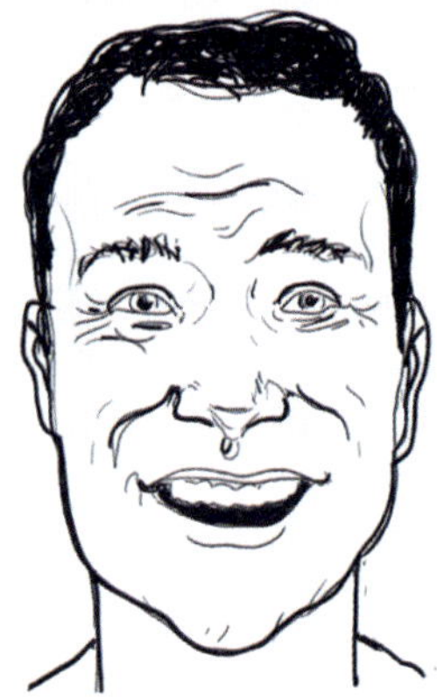

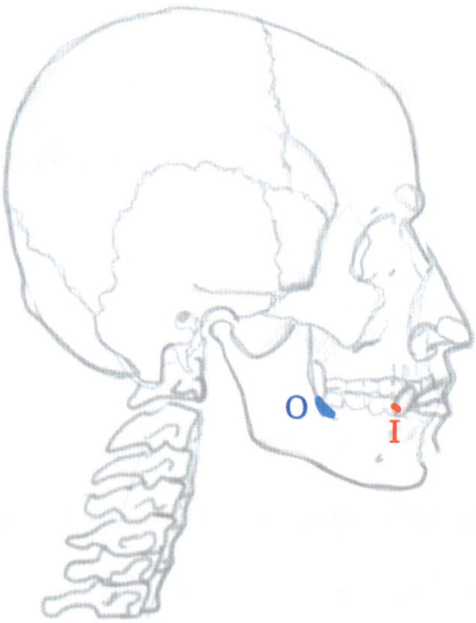

LATERAL

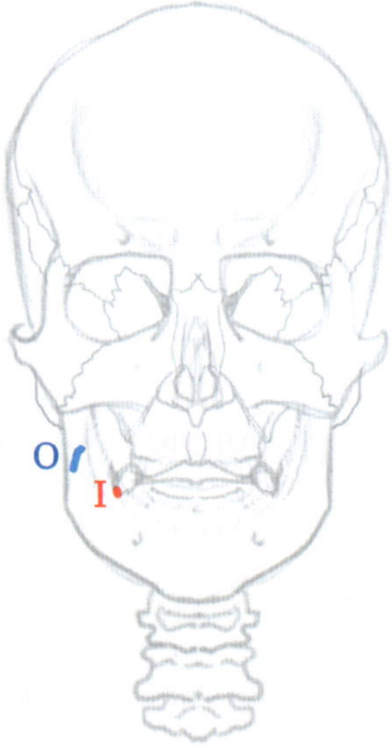

ANTERIOR

1. Pulls the corners of the mouth outward toward the ear and moves the nasolabial furrow outward

CHECKLIST

- O Temporalis
- O Masseter
- O LLSAN
- O Frontalis
- O Buccinator
- O Zygomaticus major and minor
- O Orbicularis oris
- O Depressor anguli oris
- O Levator labii superioris
- O Depressor labii inferioris
- O Risorius

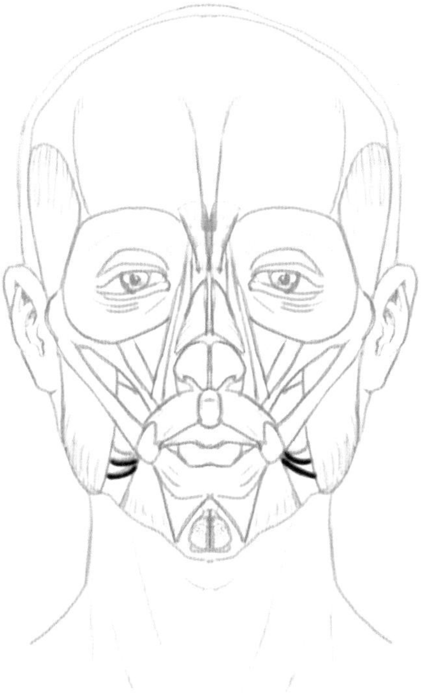

ANTERIOR

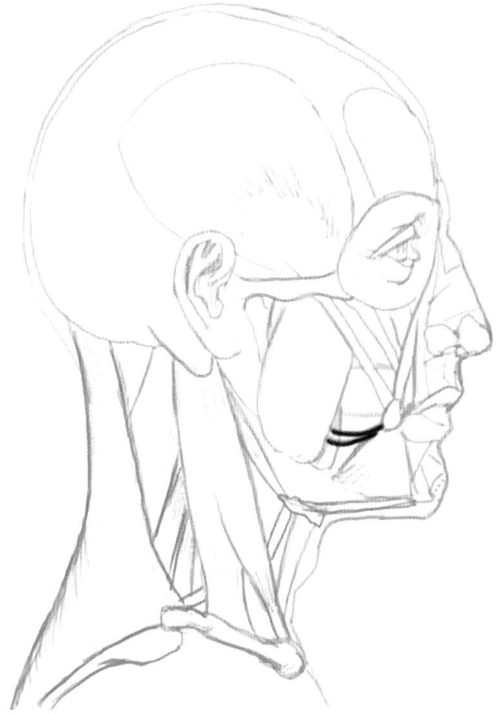

LATERAL

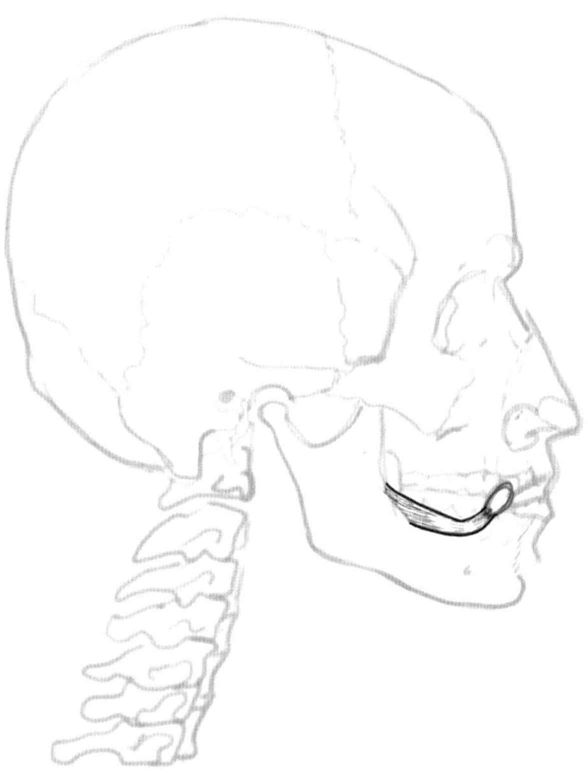

LATERAL

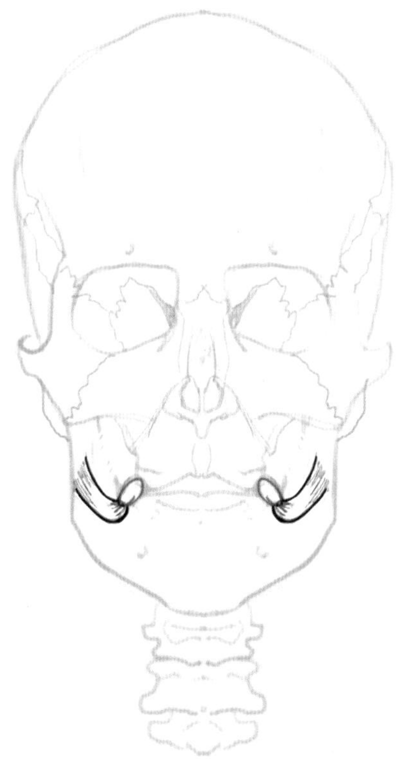

ANTERIOR

H.12. PROCERUS AND NASALIS

STRUCTURE

The procerus is a triangular muscle in between the eyebrows, right at the center. The nasalis is also a small triangular muscle.

ORIGIN

The procerus attaches on the nasal bone. The nasalis attaches to the front of the maxilla.

INSERTION

The procerus attaches on the skin of the glabella (the area between the eyes) and the fibers of the frontalis muscle (H.4.). The nasalis inserts by the nasal cartilage.

ACTION

The procerus pulls down the skin of the middle of the forehead, creating horizontal wrinkles like in anger, pain, or frowning (1). When the lips are pressed together, the alar parts of the nasalis help push the upper lip downward.

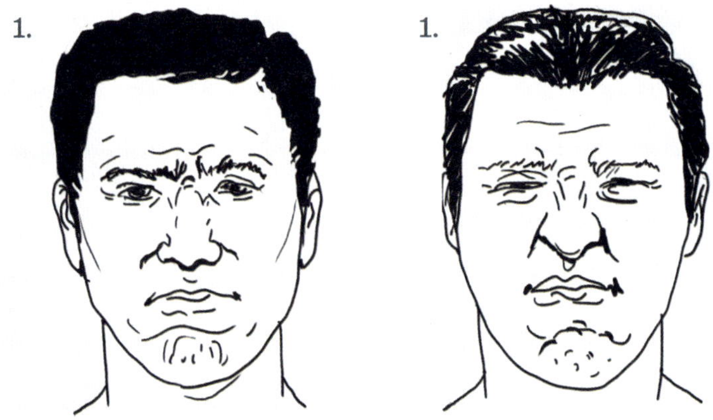

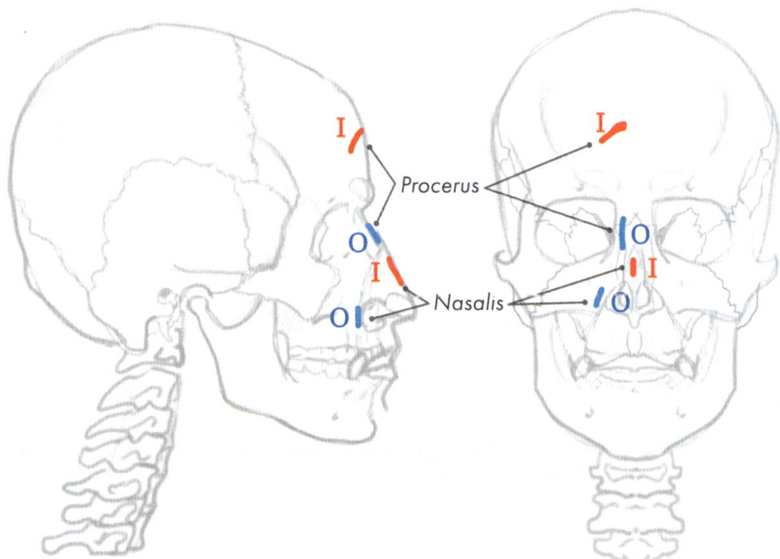

LATERAL

ANTERIOR

1. Pulls down the skin of the middle of the forehead

CHECKLIST

- O Temporalis
- O Masseter
- O LLSAN
- O Frontalis
- O Buccinator
- O Zygomaticus major and minor
- O Orbicularis oris
- O Depressor anguli oris
- O Levator labii superioris
- O Depressor labii inferioris
- O Risorius
- O Procerus and nasalis

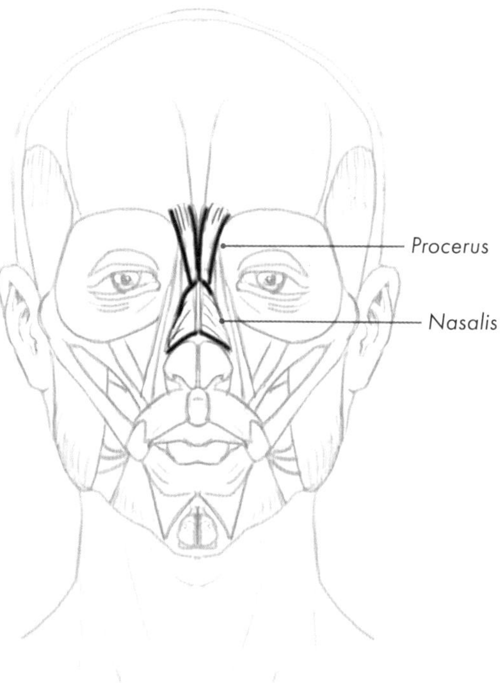

ANTERIOR

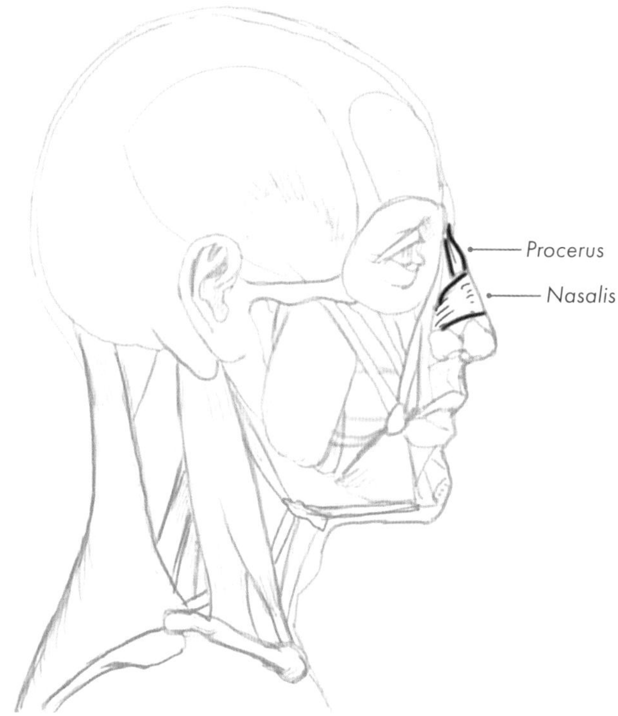

LATERAL

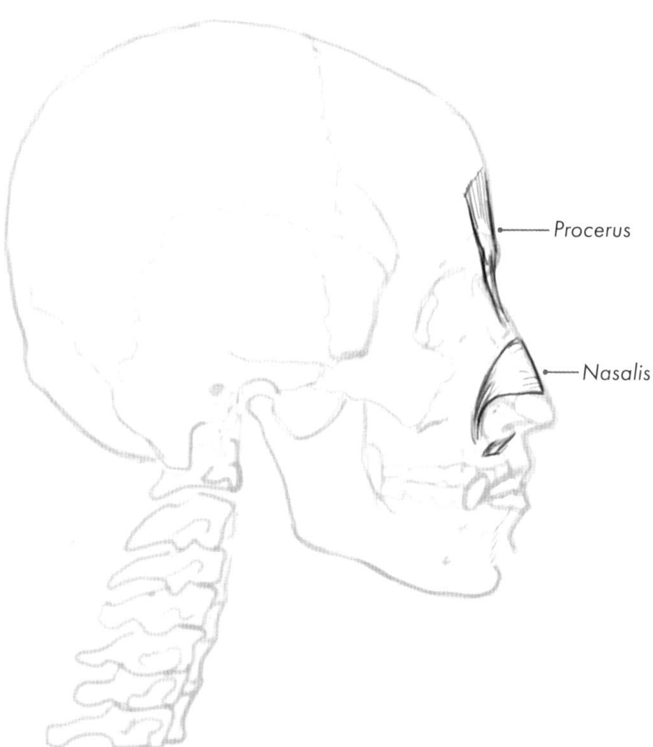

LATERAL

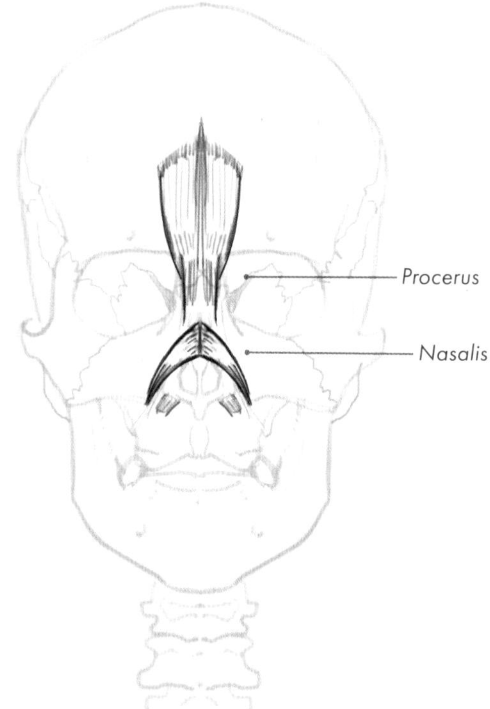

ANTERIOR

H.13. MENTALIS

STRUCTURE

The mentalis is made up of two muscles butted together at the chin. In some people you can easily see the form like a mushroom top protruding out. Each side is made of short, conical forms whose fibers slant downward and end at the skin of the chin.

ORIGIN

On a vertical line just above the mental protuberance (the bump on the front of the jaw that juts out the farthest). The line of origin for each of the muscles is just off the midline. In some cases, these are just a tad further apart, creating a cleft or a dimple on the chin.

INSERTION

The skin of the chin.

ACTION

Raises and wrinkles the skin of the chin (1), pushing up the lower lip and creating a pout.

1.

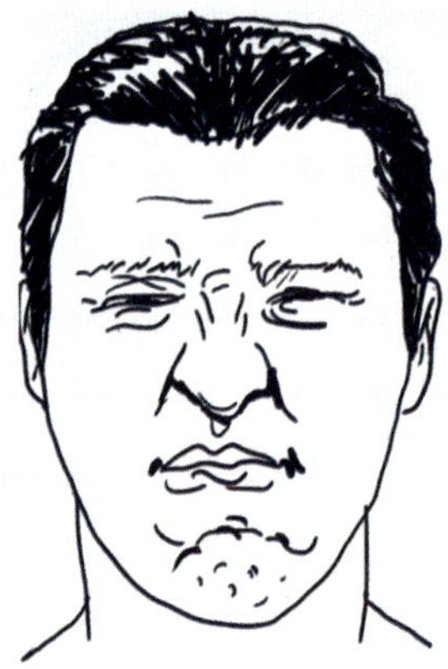

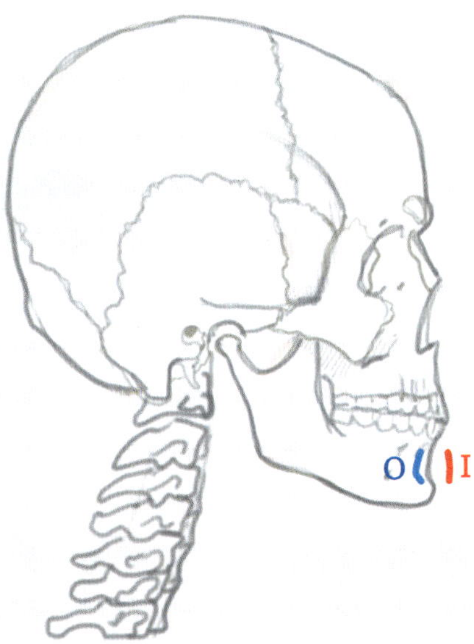

LATERAL

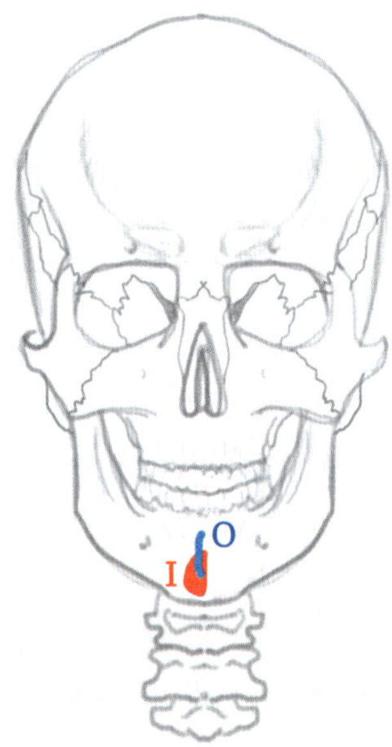

ANTERIOR

1. Raises and wrinkles the skin of the chin and pushes up the lower lip

CHECKLIST

- O Temporalis
- O Masseter
- O LLSAN
- O Frontalis
- O Buccinator
- O Zygomaticus major and minor
- O Orbicularis oris
- O Depressor anguli oris
- O Levator labii superioris
- O Depressor labii inferioris
- O Risorius
- O Procerus and nasalis
- O Mentalis

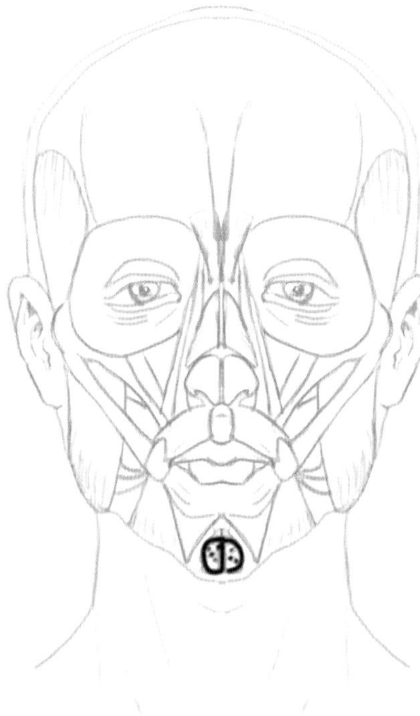

ANTERIOR

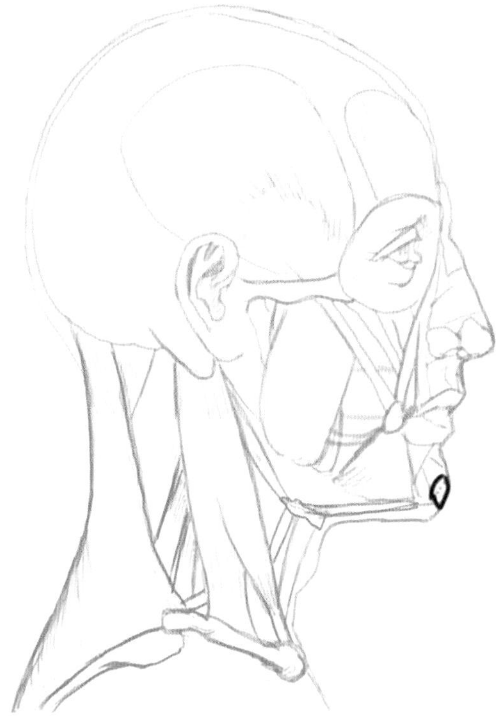

LATERAL

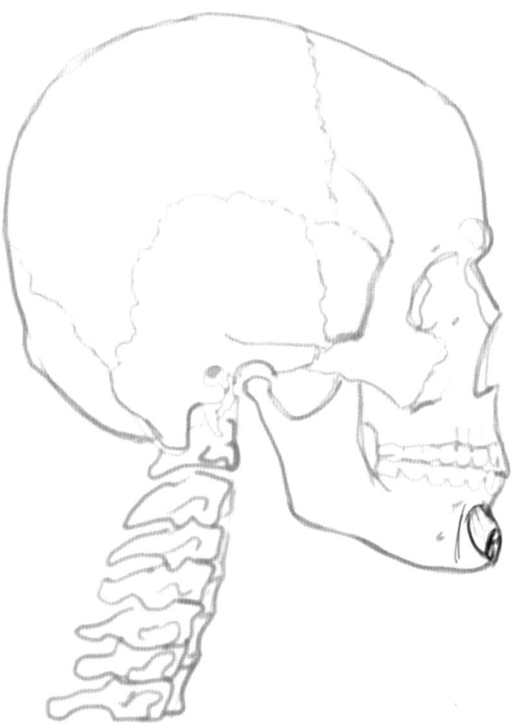

LATERAL

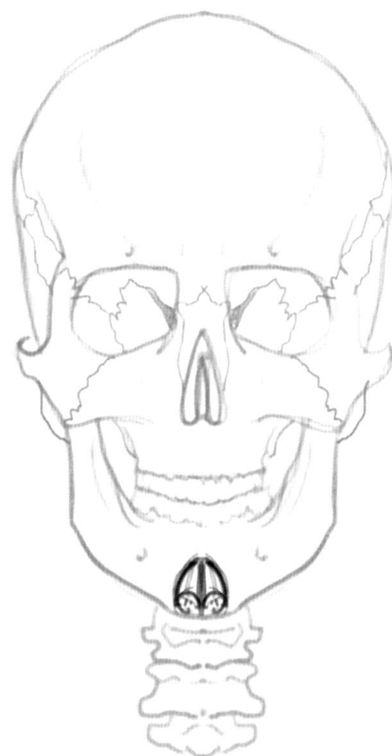

ANTERIOR

H.14. ORBICULARIS OCULI

STRUCTURE

The orbicularis oculi (of the eye) is a flat, oval-shaped muscle that surrounds the eye and is in the eyelids. It is a sphincter muscle (a ring of muscle) arranged in concentric bands around the upper and lower eyelids.

ORIGIN

The orbicularis oculi attaches to the nasal part of the frontal bone, the front of the maxilla. Basically it is like a patch around the eye.

INSERTION

At the side edge of the orbit of the eye socket.

ACTION

Closes the eyelids (1) and helps in pumping out tears.

1.

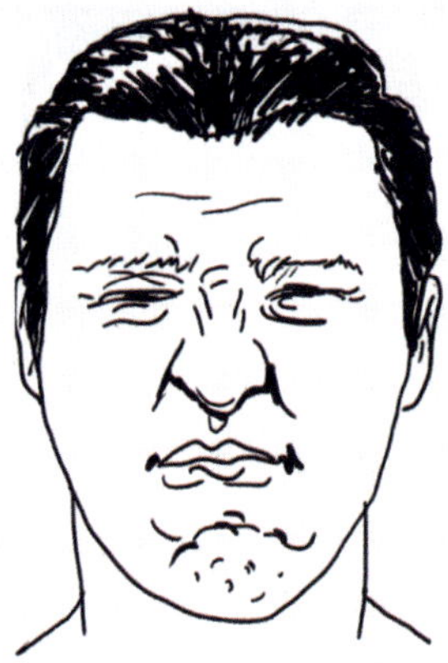

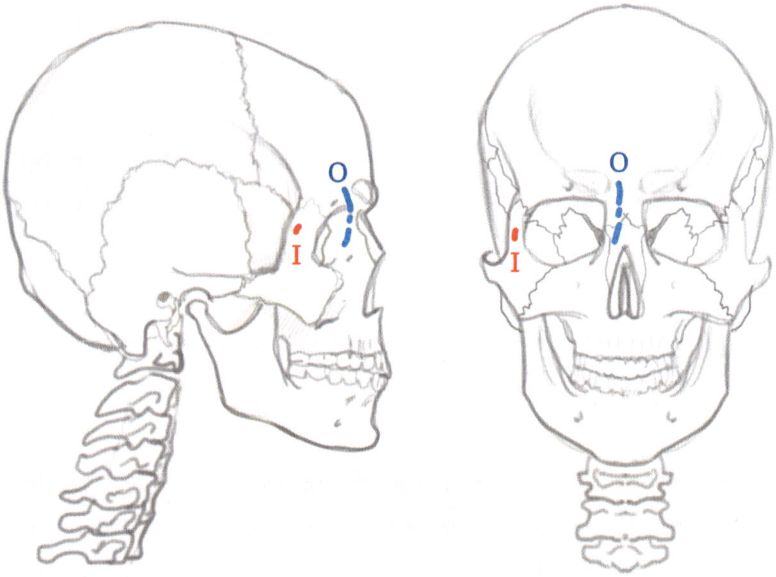

1. Closes the eyelids and helps squeeze out tears

CHECKLIST

- O Temporalis
- O Masseter
- O LLSAN
- O Frontalis
- O Buccinator
- O Zygomaticus major and minor
- O Orbicularis oris
- O Depressor anguli oris
- O Levator labii superioris
- O Depressor labii inferioris
- O Risorius
- O Procerus and nasalis
- O Mentalis
- O Orbicularis oculi

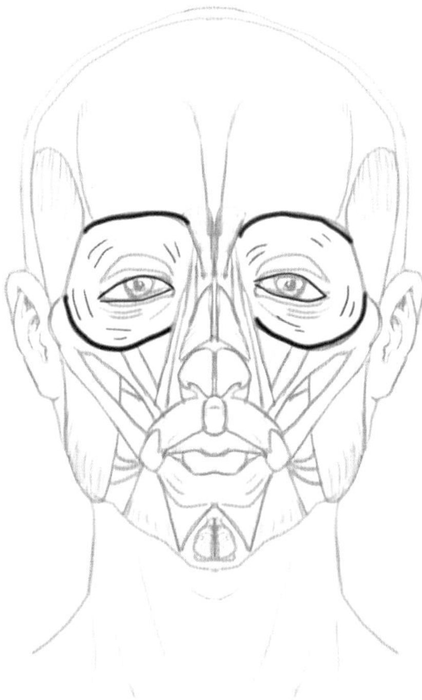

ANTERIOR

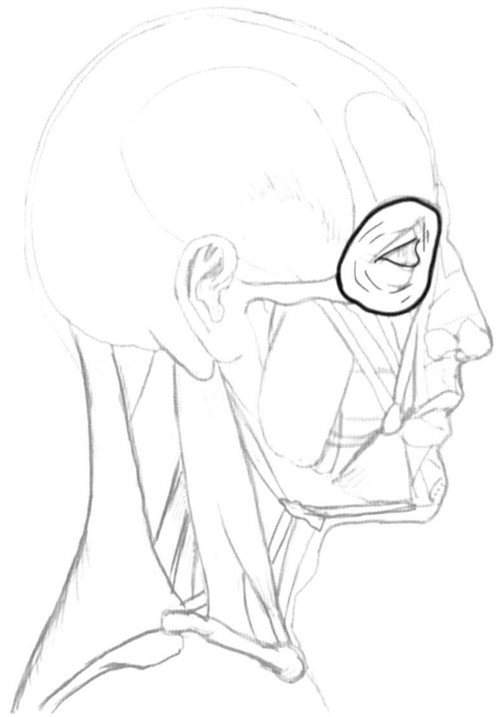

LATERAL

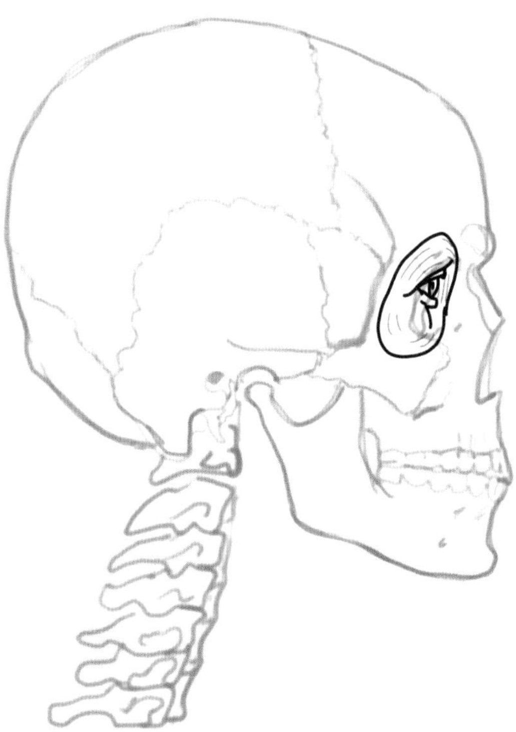

LATERAL

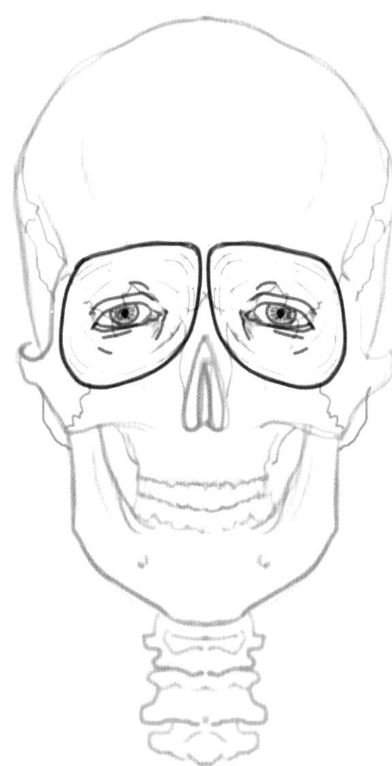

ANTERIOR

H.15. PLATYSMA

STRUCTURE

The platysma is a thin sheet of muscle that roughly resembles a turtleneck sweater halfway around the front of the neck, over the clavicles, and draped over the top portion of the pectorals. When the corners of the mouth are pulled down you can easily see the stringy fibers of the muscle form along the front and sides of the neck.

ORIGIN

Superficial fascia over the pectorals, deltoid, and trapezius.

INSERTION

The lower portion of the mandible, the skin of the lower part of the face, and up to the corners of the mouth.

ACTION

Pulls down the mandible (jaw) and the corners of the mouth (1).

1.

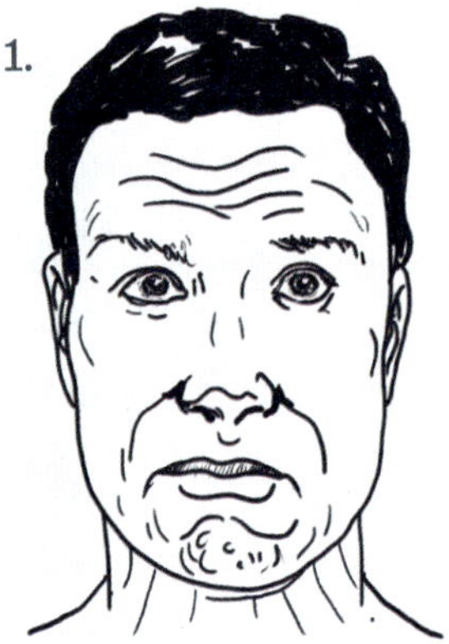

1.

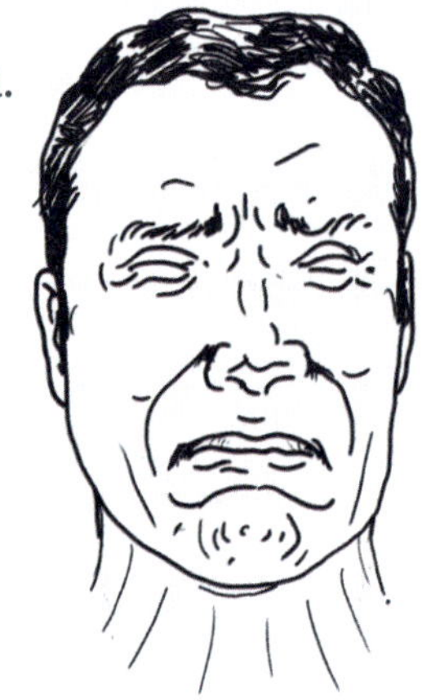

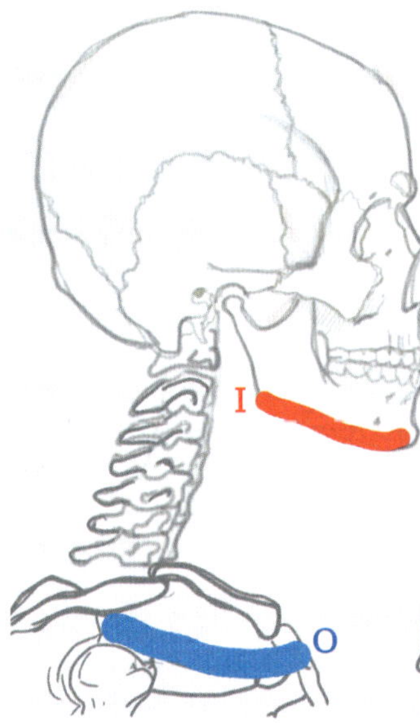

LATERAL

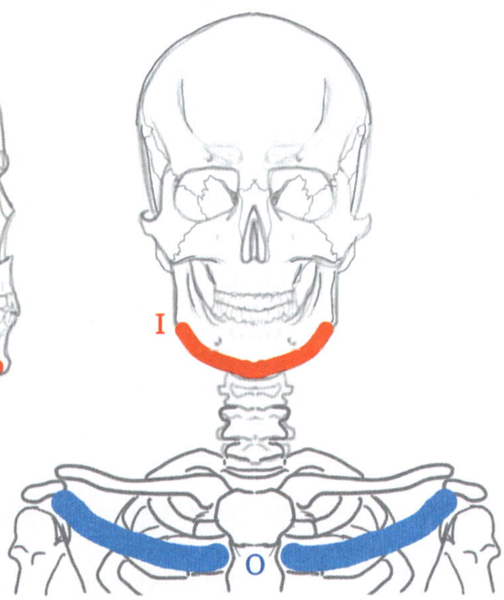

ANTERIOR

1. Pulls down the mandible and the corners of the mouth

CHECKLIST

- O Temporalis
- O Masseter
- O LLSAN
- O Frontalis
- O Buccinator
- O Zygomaticus major and minor
- O Orbicularis oris
- O Depressor anguli oris
- O Levator labii superioris
- O Depressor labii inferioris
- O Risorius
- O Procerus and nasalis
- O Mentalis
- O Orbicularis oculi
- O Platysma

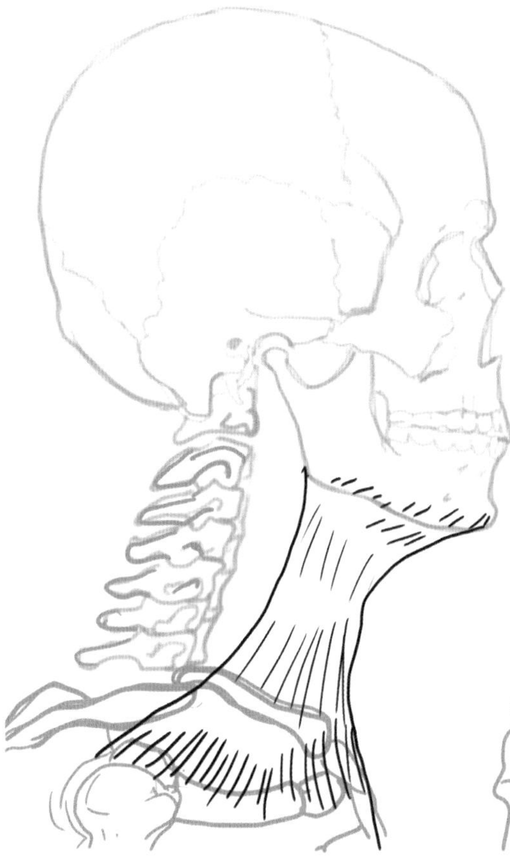

LATERAL

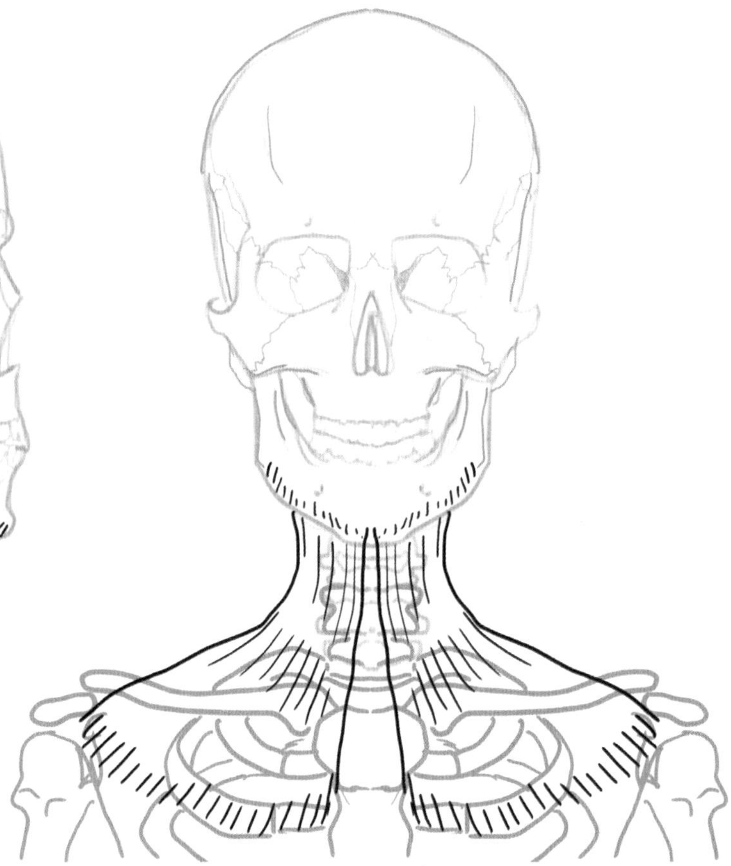

ANTERIOR

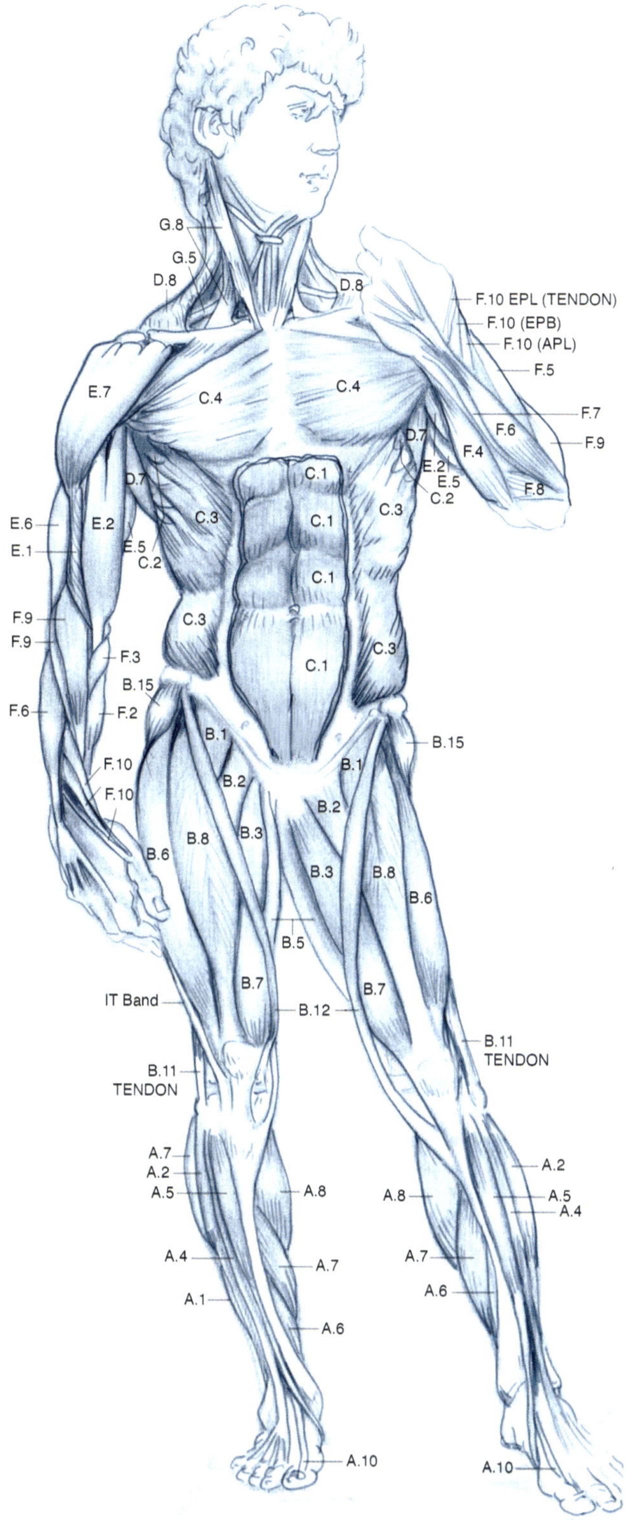

"David" by Michelangelo (*1501*)

G

- O **G.5** Omohyoid
- O **G.8** Sternocleidomastoid

F

- O **F.2** Flexor carpi radialis
- O **F.3** Pronator teres
- O **F.4** Flexor carpi ulnaris
- O **F.5** Extensor carpi radialis brevis
- O **F.6** Extensor digitorum
- O **F.7** Extensor carpi ulnaris
- O **F.8** Anconeus
- O **F.9** Brachioradialis & Extensor carpi radialis longus
- O **F.10** Pollicis muscles of the thumb: *Abductor pollicis longus, extensor pollicis brevis & the extensor pollicis longus tendon—these all create the "Anatomical Snuffbox"*

E

- O **E.1** Brachialis
- O **E.2** Biceps brachii
- O **E.5** Tricep long head
- O **E.6** Tricep lateral head
- O **E.7** Deltoid

D

- O **D.7** Latissimus dorsi
- O **D.8** Trapezius

C

- O **C.1** Rectus abdominis
- O **C.2** Serratus anterior
- O **C.3** External oblique
- O **C.4** Pectoralis major

B

- O **B.1** Iliopsoas
- O **B.2** Pectineus
- O **B.3** Adductor longus
- O **B.5** Gracilis
- O **B.6** Vastus lateralis
- O **B.7** Vastus medialis
- O **B.8** Rectus femoris
- O **B.11** Biceps femoris
- O **B.12** Sartorius
- O **B.15** Tensor fasciae lata

A

- O **A.1** Peroneus brevis
- O **A.2** Peroneus longus
- O **A.4** Extensor digitorum
- O **A.5** Tibialis anterior
- O **A.6** Flexor digitorum longus
- O **A.7** Soleus
- O **A.8** Gastrocnemius
- O **A.10** Extensor hallucis longus (*tendon of the big toe*)

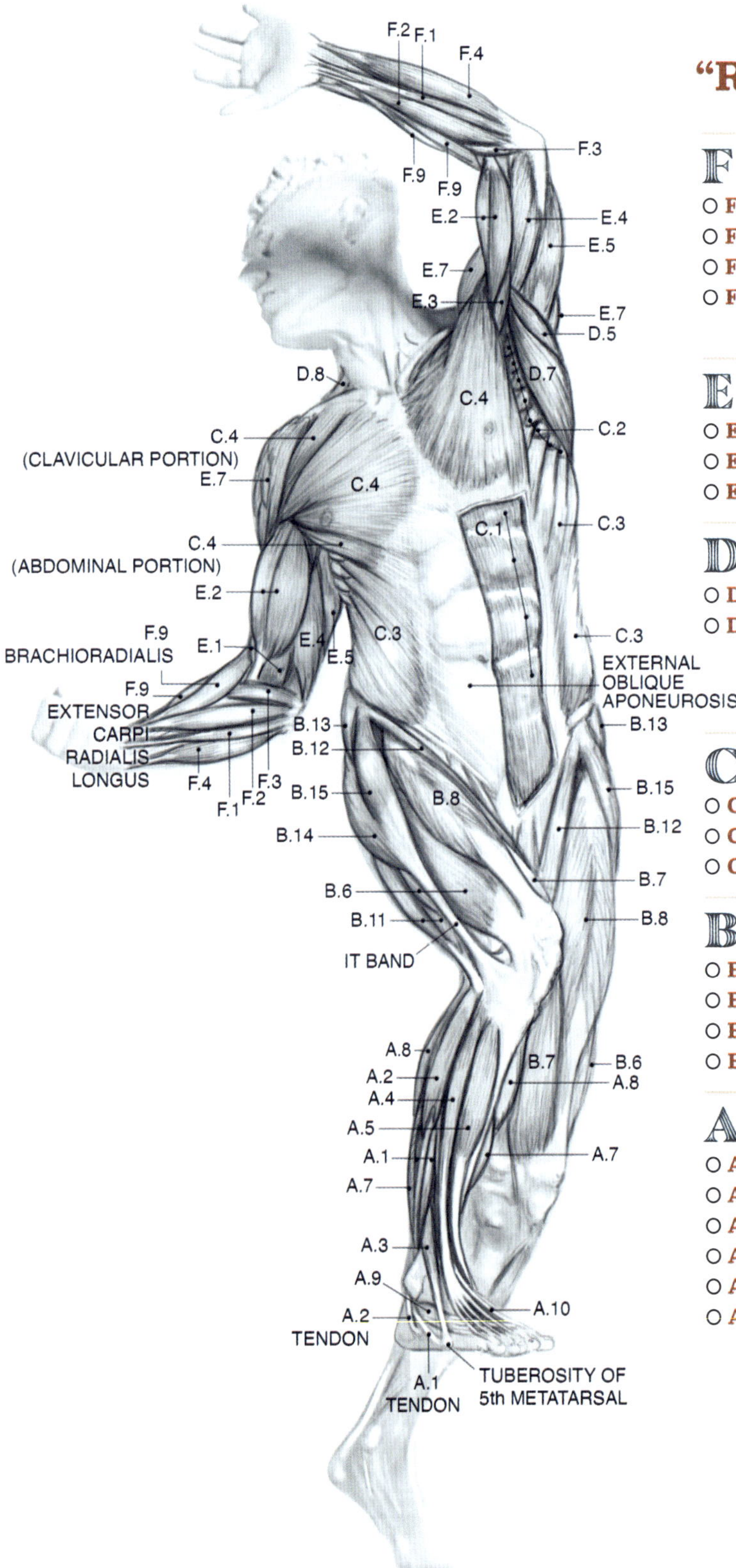

"Rajiv" by Rey Bustos

F

- O **F.1** Palmaris longus
- O **F.2** Flexor carpi radialis
- O **F.3** Pronator teres
- O **F.4** Flexor carpi ulnaris
- O **F.5** Extensor carpi radialis brevis
- O **F.9** Brachioradialis & Extensor carpi radialis longus

E

- O **E.1.** Brachialis
- O **E.2** Biceps brachii
- O **E.3** Coracobrachialis
- O **E.4** Tricep medial head
- O **E.5** Tricep long head
- O **E.7** Deltoid

D

- O **D.5** Teres major
- O **D.7** Latissimus dorsi
- O **D.8** Trapezius

C

- O **C.1** Rectus abdominis
- O **C.2** Serratus anterior
- O **C.3** External oblique
- O **C.4** Pectoralis major (*clavicular & abdominal portions included*)

B

- O **B.6** Vastus lateralis
- O **B.7** Vastus medialis
- O **B.8** Rectus femoris
- O **B.11** Biceps femoris
- O **B.12** Sartorius
- O **B.13** Gluteus medius
- O **B.14** Gluteus maximus
- O **B.15** Tensor fasciae lata

A

- O **A.1** Peroneus brevis
- O **A.2** Peroneus longus
- O **A.3** Pronator teres
- O **A.4** Extensor digitorum
- O **A.5** Tibialis anterior
- O **A.7** Soleus
- O **A.8** Gastrocnemius
- O **A.9** Extensor digitorum brevis
- O **A.10** Extensor hallucis longus

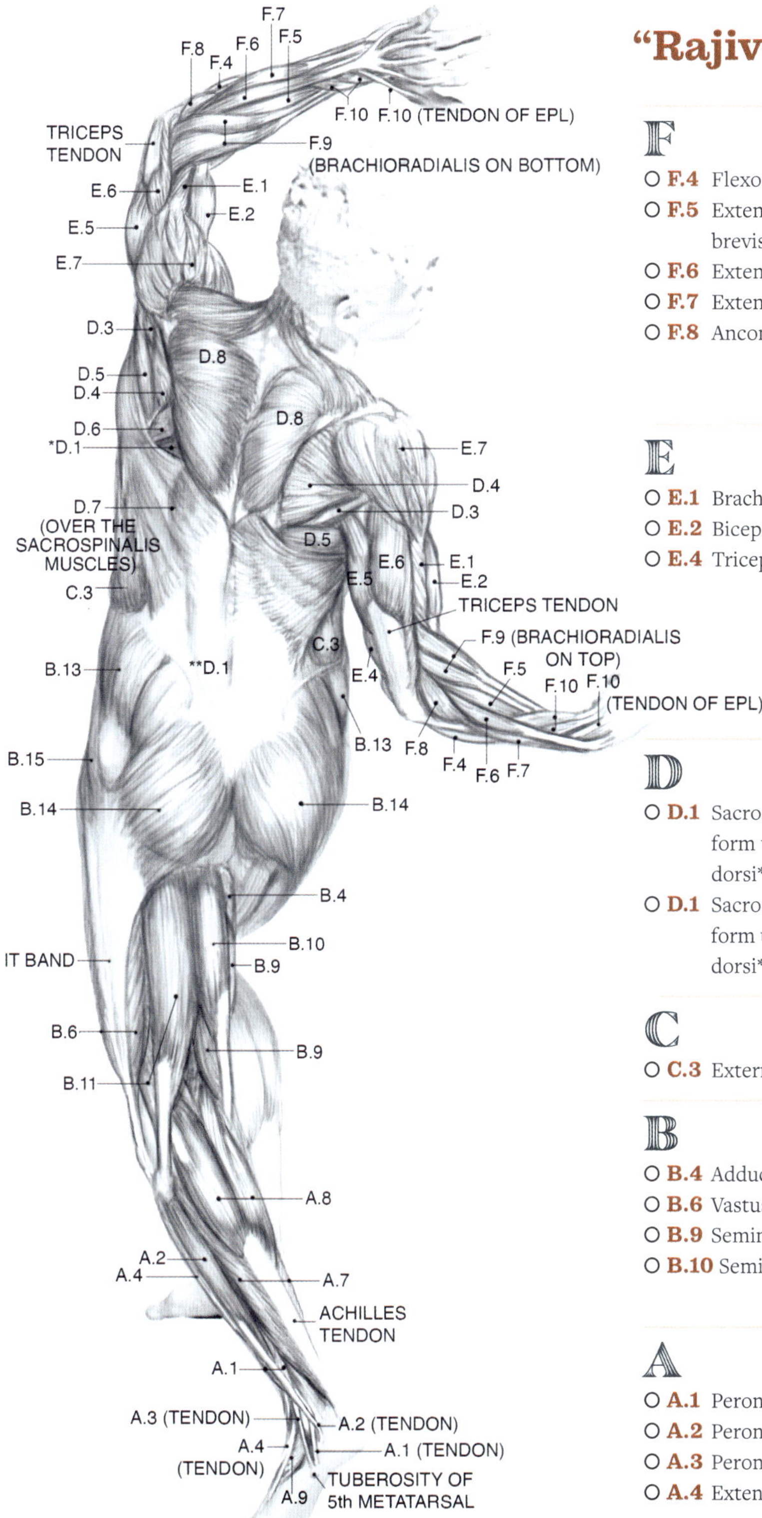

"Rajiv" by Rey Bustos

F

- O **F.4** Flexor carpi ulnaris
- O **F.5** Extensor carpi radialis brevis
- O **F.6** Extensor digitorum
- O **F.7** Extensor carpi ulnaris
- O **F.8** Anconeus
- O **F.9** Brachioriadialis & extensor carpi radialis longus
- O **F.10** Pollicis muscles of the thumb: Abductor pollicis longus, extensor pollicis brevis & the extensor pollicis longus tendon.

E

- O **E.1** Brachialis
- O **E.2** Biceps brachii
- O **E.4** Tricep medial head
- O **E.5** Tricep long head
- O **E.6** Tricep lateral head
- O **E.7** Deltoid

D

- O **D.1** Sacrospinalis lateral form under Latissimus dorsi*
- O **D.1** Sacrospinalis medial form under Latissimus dorsi**
- O **D.3** Teres minor
- O **D.4** Infraspinatus
- O **D.5** Teres major
- O **D.6** Rhomboids
- O **D.7** Latissimus dorsi
- O **D.8** Trapezius

C

- O **C.3** External oblique

B

- O **B.4** Adductor magnus
- O **B.6** Vastus lateralis
- O **B.9** Semimembranosus
- O **B.10** Semitendinosus
- O **B.11** Biceps femoris *(short head, small one)*
- O **B.13** Gluteus medius
- O **B.14** Gluteus maximus
- O **B.15** Tensor fasciae lata

A

- O **A.1** Peroneus brevis
- O **A.2** Peroneus longus
- O **A.3** Peroneus tertius
- O **A.4** Extensor digitorum
- O **A.7** Soleus
- O **A.8** Gastrocnemius
- O **A.9** Extensor digitorum brevis

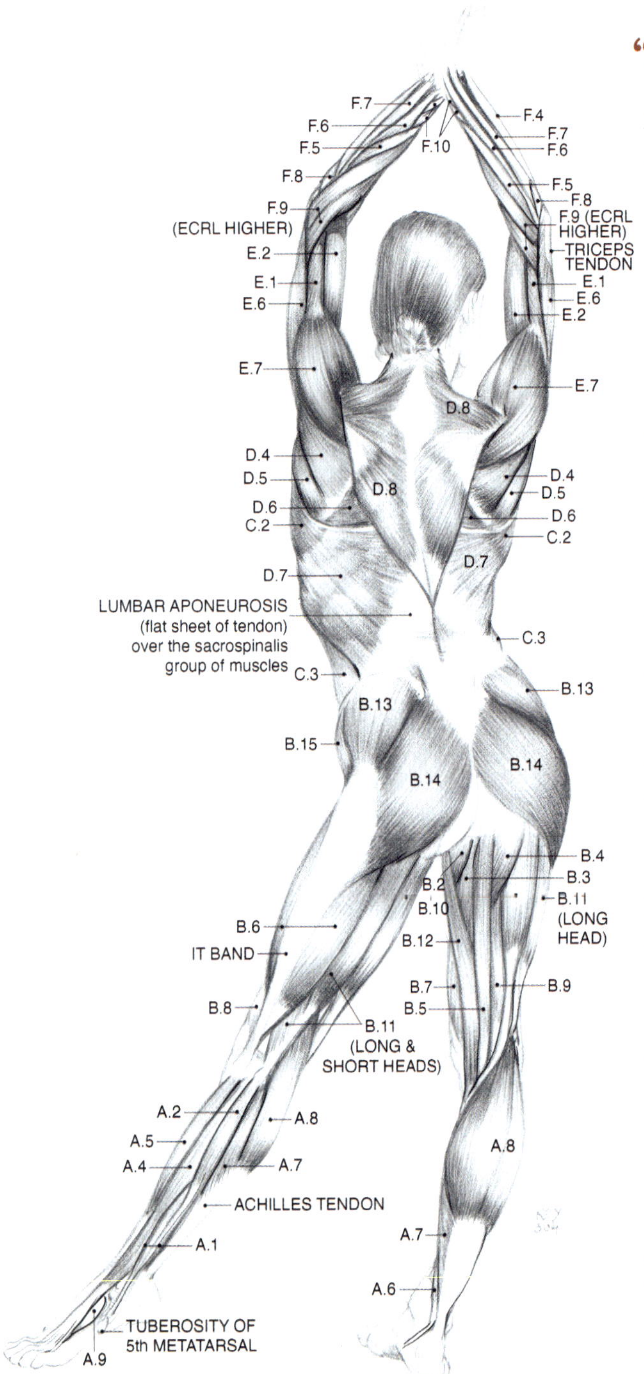

"Sara" by Rey Bustos

F

- O **F.4** Palmaris longus
- O **F.5** Extensor carpi radialis brevis
- O **F.6** Extensor digitorum
- O **F.7** Extensor carpi ulnaris
- O **F.8** Anconeus
- O **F.9** Extensor carpi radialis longus (*higher*) Brachioradialis (*lower on diagram*)
- O **F.10** Abductor pollicis longus, (*lower*) Extensor pollicis brevis (*higher on diagram*)

E

- O **E.1** Brachialis
- O **E.2** Biceps brachii
- O **E.6** Triceps lateral head
- O **E.7** Deltoid

D

- O **D.4** Infraspinatus
- O **D.5** Teres major
- O **D.6** Rhomboids (*inside the triangle of auscultation*)
- O **D.7** Latissimus dorsi
- O **D.8** Trapezius

C

- O **C.2** Serratus anterior (*under the latissimus dorsi*)
- O **C.3** External oblique

B

- O **B.2** Pectineus
- O **B.3** Adductor longus
- O **B.4** Adductor magnus
- O **B.5** Gracilis
- O **B.6** Vastus lateralis
- O **B.7** Vastus medialis
- O **B.8** Rectus femoris
- O **B.9** Semimembranosus
- O **B.10** Semitendinosus
- O **B.11** Biceps femoris (long and short)
- O **B.12** Sartorius
- O **B.13** Gluteus medius
- O **B.14** Gluteus maximus
- O **B.15** Tensor fasciae latae

A

- O **A.1** Peroneus brevis
- O **A.2** Peroneus longus
- O **A.4** Extensor digitorum
- O **A.5** Tibialis anterior
- O **A.6** Flexor digitorum longus
- O **A.7** Soleus
- O **A.8** Gastrocnemius
- O **A.9** Extensor digitorum brevis

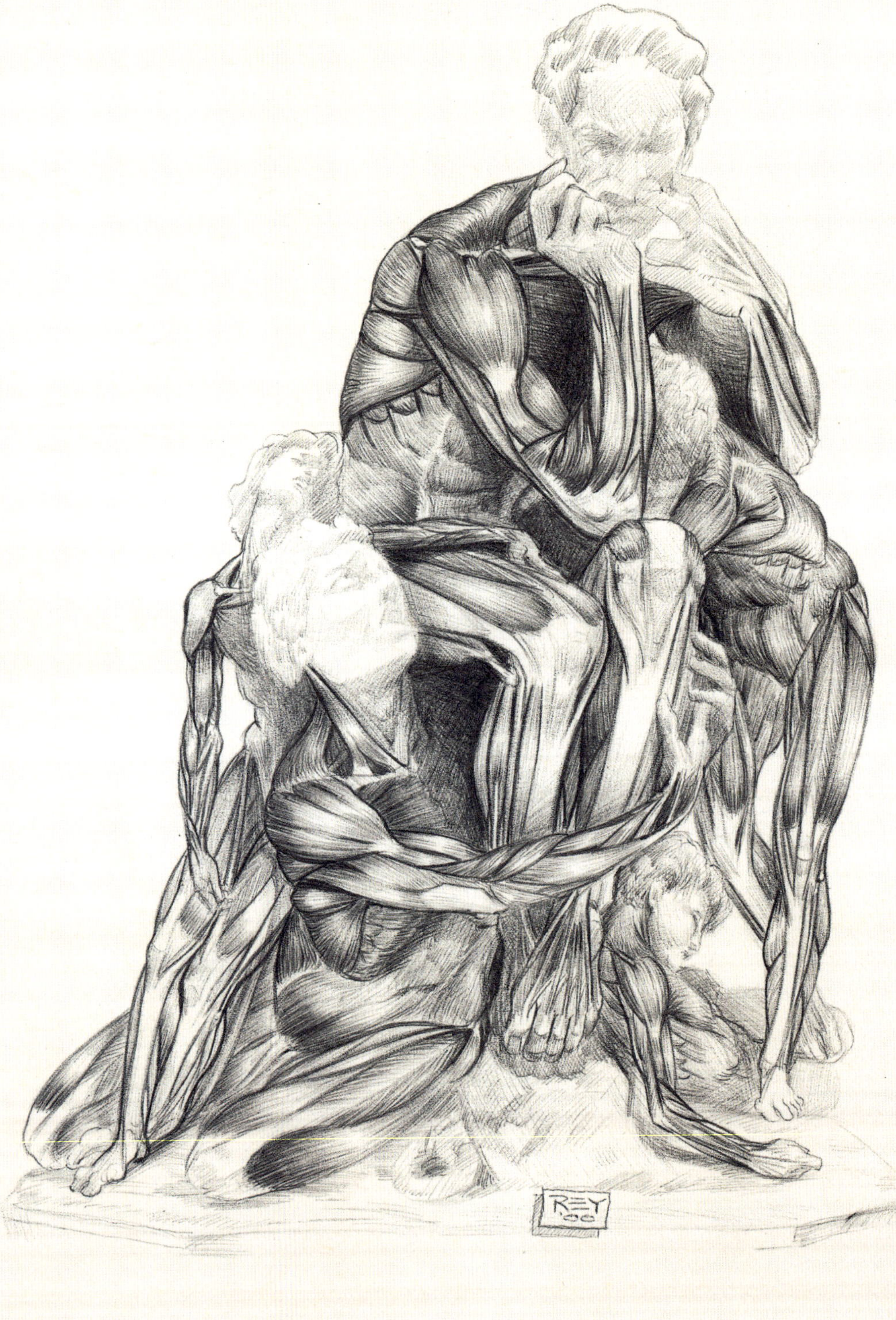
REY
'00

APPENDIX

A THE LEG AND FOOT

A.1. PERONEUS BREVIS

STRUCTURE
The peroneus brevis from the side is a flat fish-shaped muscle. The tendon uses the lateral malleolus—the outside ankle bone (bottom of fibula)—like a pulley. The tendon, along with the tendon of the peroneus longus, is seen clearly by the outside ankle when the heel is off the ground.

ORIGIN
At around halfway down the fibula toward the outside ankle, the lateral malleolus.

INSERTION
The tuberosity of the fifth metatarsal, the bump on the side of the foot.

ACTION
Plantarflexion (lifts the heel off the ground or points the foot) and eversion (pulls the foot outward).

A.2. PERONEUS LONGUS

STRUCTURE
The peroneus longus is an elongated, flat muscle. It lays piggyback over the peroneus brevis. The tendon, along with the tendon of the peroneus brevis, is clearly visible at the ankle, especially when the heel is off the ground.

ORIGIN
Head of the fibula, upper part of the fibula about one-third of the way down the bone.

INSERTION
Under the foot toward the big toe at the medial cuneiform (tarsal), also at the first metatarsal.

ACTION
Plantarflexion (lifts the heel off the ground or points the foot) and eversion (pulls the foot outward).

A.3. PERONEUS TERTIUS

STRUCTURE
The peroneus tertius is a small, somewhat elongated triangular muscle that aids in eversion, pulling the foot outward, and in dorsiflexion, pulling the foot upward toward the head. You will only see the tendon on the side of the foot; the muscle is well tucked in within the group.

ORIGIN
Low down on the anterior aspect of the fibula.

INSERTION
By the tuberosity of the fifth metatarsal.

ACTION
Dorsiflexion (pulls the foot upward) and eversion (pulls the foot outward).

A.4. EXTENSOR DIGITORUM LONGUS

STRUCTURE
The extensor digitorum longus is a long, thin muscle. It is actually four combined muscle bellies with four tendons that attach to four toes—all except the big toe. It is often seen as a blended muscle along with the tibialis anterior.

ORIGIN
A small portion touching the lateral condyle of the tibia, then a long portion down the fibula.

INSERTION
The middle and ends of four toes; not the big toe.

ACTION
Extends, pulls up on all toes except the big one.

A.5. TIBIALIS ANTERIOR

STRUCTURE
The tibialis anterior muscle is a rather large muscle that tapers at the bottom, becoming a strong, thick tendon very visible at the top of the foot. It then disappears into the arch of the foot. It is an important muscle in that it creates the contour of the leg when seen from the side.

ORIGIN
Lateral condyle of the tibia, lateral surface of the upper half of the shaft of the tibia.

INSERTION
The tendon of the tibialis anterior goes down the arch and underneath the foot and is attached to the medial cuneiform bone and into the base of the metatarsal bone toward the big toe.

ACTION
Dorsiflexion (pulls the foot upward) and inversion (pulls the foot inward). In walking, the tibialis anterior keeps your toes from hitting the ground, lifting your foot and toes up toward the face.

A.6. FLEXOR DIGITORUM LONGUS

STRUCTURE
The flexor digitorum longus muscle is deep inside the muscle group underneath the soleus and gastrocnemius on the posterior (backside) of the tibia. The bottom part can sometimes be seen. What you will see on some individuals is the tendon that uses the medial malleolus, or ankle bone of the tibia, as a pulley and it will go underneath the arch of the foot, attaching underneath the foot.

ORIGIN
The back of the shaft of the tibia at about a quarter of the way down from the knee joint to about the three-quarter mark of the length of the tibia.

INSERTION
Underneath the ends of each toe except the big toe.

ACTION
Curls the toes and helps raise the heal.

A.7. SOLEUS

STRUCTURE
The soleus is a very large muscle, almost like a bed of muscle underneath the gastrocnemius heads. From the inside and outside view, it almost looks like a wedge.

ORIGIN
On the posterior, or rear view, the soleus attaches to the head of the fibula a quarter of the way down the shaft of the fibula and on the upper part of the tibia posteriorly.

INSERTION
On the calcaneus. Shares a common tendon, the Achilles tendon, with the gastrocnemius heads.

ACTION
Points and plantarflexes the foot, lifts the heel off the ground.

A.8. GASTROCNEMIUS

STRUCTURE
The gastrocnemius consists of two heads, a medial head and a lateral head. The medial head is lower and larger than the lateral head and is easily seen on the medial (inside) view, along with the soleus.

ORIGIN
Just above the medial condyle of the femur on the flat surface facet of the lower end of the femur. The lateral head is just above the lateral condyle of the femur on the facet at the lower end of the femur on the fibular side.

INSERTION
On the calcaneus along with the soleus, their common tendon, the Achilles tendon.

ACTION
Plantarflexion of the foot (lifts the heel off the ground).

A.9. EXTENSOR DIGITORUM BREVIS

STRUCTURE
The extensor digitorum brevis consists of four slender, flat bellies that pass forward medially over the top of the foot. One of them, the one that goes to the big toe, is actually called the extensor hallucis brevis, but I grouped it as part of the four for simplicity. The combined bellies create a noticeable bulge on the side of the foot, roughly between the lateral malleolus (outside ankle) and the tuberosity of the fifth metatarsal. The belly that goes to the big toe, the extensor hallucis brevis, attaches to bone, and the others attach to other tendons on the second, third, and fourth toes, leaving the little (fifth) toe alone. But remember that the extensor digitorum longus attaches to all except the big toe.

ORIGIN
The upper front portion of the calcaneus.

INSERTION
To the four toes, not the little toe, as follows: The extensor hallucis brevis attaches to the big toe onto

the base of the proximal phalanx. This is the only one that attaches to bone. The others attach to the sides of the tendons of the extensor digitorum longus.

ACTION
Extends the toes. The extensor hallucis brevis helps the extensor hallucis longus pull up on the big toe. Hallux refers to the big toe.

A.10. EXTENSOR HALLUCIS LONGUS

STRUCTURE
The extensor hallucis (big toe) is long and flat but is unseen. What is important for the artist is its tendon, which attaches to the big toe.

ORIGIN
Center section of the shaft of the fibula.

INSERTION
The distal (furthest toe bone) phalanx of the big toe.

ACTION
Lifts the big toe upward.

A.11. ABDUCTOR DIGITI MINIMI

STRUCTURE
The abductor digiti minimi is an elongated, thin muscle that is not seen due to the fatty pad of the side of the foot. However, it is important to know since it pulls the little toe outward.

ORIGIN
Bottom left aspect of the calcaneus.

INSERTION
The proximal phalanx of the little toe.

ACTION
Abducts, or pulls away, the little toe.

A.12. ABDUCTOR HALLUCIS

STRUCTURE
The abductor hallucis (big toe) starts wide and then tapers toward the big toe.

ORIGIN
On the inside aspect of the calcaneus.

INSERTION
The side of the proximal phalanx of the big toe.

ACTION
Abducts, or pulls away, the big toe.

B THE THIGH AND GLUTES

B.1. ILIOPSOAS

STRUCTURE
The iliopsoas is comprised of two muscles: the iliacus and the psoas major. (There is also a third muscle, the psoas minor, not included.) The iliacus is flat and pressed up against the ilium of the pelvis and tapers toward the common insertion with the psoas major. The psoas major is conical and tapers toward the same insertion as the iliacus.

ORIGIN
The psoas major attaches to the five transverse processes of the five lumbar vertebrae. The iliacus attaches to the ilium and a bit to the top corner of the sacrum.

INSERTION
Both parts of the iliopsoas attach to the lesser trochanter of the femur.

ACTION
Very strong flexor of the hip joint. It is also a powerful flexor of the trunk, such as in doing a sit-up.

B.2. PECTINEUS

STRUCTURE
The pectineus is a flattened rectangular muscle.

ORIGIN
The pectineal line of the pubis.

INSERTION
The posterior (back) midline of the femur.

ACTION
Adducts (helps to bring the knees together) and flexes the hip joint.

B.3. ADDUCTOR LONGUS

STRUCTURE
The adductor longus is a long triangular muscle with a very strong tendon at the groin area.

ORIGIN
At the front of the pubic bone.

INSERTION
At a long area at the center line (linea aspera) of the back of the femur.

ACTION
Adducts, flexes, and medially rotates the thigh.

B.4. ADDUCTOR MAGNUS

STRUCTURE
The adductor magnus is a huge muscle, but only one form shows, and that is on the rear inside of the thigh, high up by the butt cheek. It is broad at the top and pointier at the bottom. The bottom splits, with one section attaching to the back of the femur and the other, shaped like a sharp cone, tapering and becoming a strong tendon.

ORIGIN
Ischial tuberosity ("sit bone") of the pelvis and a portion toward the medial edge.

INSERTION
Down the midline of the femur on the back by the linea aspera (linear ridge on the back of the femur) and another section that splits and attaches to the medial edge of the femur.

ACTION
A strong adductor, it pulls the thighs and knees together.

B.5. GRACILIS

STRUCTURE
The gracilis is a long, belt-like muscle that is flat and broad at the top and tapered at the bottom. It is located by the inside of the knee, close to the back of the knee, with a long tendon that attaches at the inside of the tibia. I call it the "inseam" muscle because it approximates where the inseam of a pair of pants would be.

ORIGIN
Ischium by the pubic arch.

INSERTION
Top, medial surface of the tibia.

ACTION
It adducts the thighs and helps flex and medially rotate the leg.

B.6. VASTUS LATERALIS

STRUCTURE
The vastus lateralis is a very large quadricep muscle that is shaped like a large fish. It is on the side of the thigh but also wraps around to the front above the knee.

ORIGIN
The greater trochanter of the femur and the linea aspera on the back of the femur.

INSERTION
The quadriceps tendon, which covers the patella. This is the common tendon for the quadriceps. (The rectus femoris and vastus medialis are the other two quadriceps muscles shown in the following sections. The vastus internus has been left out of this book since it is not seen.) Below the patella, the quadriceps tendon becomes known as the patellar ligament. This is because a tendon connects muscle to bone, and a ligament connects bone to bone. The patellar ligament inserts at the tibial tuberosity.

ACTION
Extends the leg at the knee.

B.7. VASTUS MEDIALIS

STRUCTURE
The vastus medialis is a large teardrop-shaped muscle. It is the lowest of the quadriceps and it rests on the patella.

ORIGIN
By the linea aspera, the midline on the back of the femur, and a small section on the top-front of the femur.

INSERTION
The tibial tuberosity by way of the quadriceps tendon along with the other "quads."

ACTION
Extends the knee and helps balance the action of the vastus lateralis.

B.8. RECTUS FEMORIS

STRUCTURE
The rectus femoris is a strong, straight (rectus means straight) muscle that has a noticeable groove down the center with muscle fibers that look like arrowheads pointing upward. It is tapered at the top and bottom, making it look like a trout on the top of the front of the thigh. It is also the only quadricep that crosses over two joints: the hip, since it is attached to the pelvis, and the knee, since it attaches to the tibia along with the other quadriceps.

ORIGIN
The anterior inferior iliac spine of the pelvis.

INSERTION
At the tibial tuberosity along with the other "quads."

ACTION
It extends the knee and flexes the hip.

B.9. SEMIMEMBRANOSUS

STRUCTURE
The semimembranosus is large and full and has an interesting shape. The tendon at the top is more off to the side, and the lower one is at the inside of the knee, so it almost zigzags. The semimembranosus muscle is one of the three muscles that make up the hamstrings. The other two are the biceps femoris long head and the semitendinosus. The hamstrings all originate at the ischial tuberosity of the pelvis.

ORIGIN
At the ischial tuberosity ("sit bone") of the pelvis.

INSERTION
The top of the tibia, at the top inside corner.

ACTION
Flexes and medially rotates the knee joint (points the foot inward). Extends the thigh at the hip joint.

B.10. SEMITENDINOSUS

STRUCTURE
The semitendinosus is a long muscle tapered at both its origin and insertion. It is one of the three muscles that make up what is called the hamstrings. The other two muscles are the semimembranosus and the biceps femoris long head.

ORIGIN
The ischial tuberosity of the pelvis.

INSERTION
The upper medial aspect of the tibia.

ACTION
Flexes and medially rotates the lower leg (points the foot inward). Extends the thigh at the hip joint.

B.11. BICEPS FEMORIS, LONG AND SHORT HEADS

STRUCTURE
The biceps femoris has two heads. One is long and tapered at both ends, and the other is like a flat knife blade.

ORIGIN
The long head attaches on the ischial tuberosity. It is the third of the three hamstring muscles. The short head attaches on the back of the femur at the linea aspera.

INSERTION
Both heads insert at the head of the fibula with a common tendon, the biceps femoris tendon, which is very prominent on the lateral side of the leg when bent. It becomes a groove when the leg is straight, like the semitendinosus.

ACTION
Both heads flex the knee joint and rotate it laterally, pointing the foot outward. The long head extends the thigh at the hip join.

B.12. SARTORIUS

STRUCTURE
The sartorius is the longest muscle of the human body. It resembles a belt that spirals from the pelvis point to the inside of the knee and it separates the adductors from the quadriceps. It creates an indentation on the inside of the leg, but when the leg is contracted or scissored, it can pop out and can be seen as a convex form. It's called the "tailor's muscle," from the Latin root word for tailor, or "one who patches." Tailors often sat in lotus position when hemming garments and used this muscle to make all of the movements listed to be in that position.

ORIGIN
Just below the anterior superior iliac spine (ASIS) of the pelvis, the pointy, protruding part of the pelvis just under one's beltline.

INSERTION
On the top inside of the tibia, close to the tibial tuberosity, the "nose" of the tibia.

ACTION
The sartorius is rather weak, but it helps other muscles do a variety of things. It flexes, abducts, and laterally rotates the hip at the ball of the femur/acetabulum. It is a relatively strong flexor of the lower leg. When someone sits in "lotus" position, the sartorius is responsible for all of those actions.

B.13. GLUTEUS MEDIUS

STRUCTURE
The gluteus medius is a large fanlike muscle.

ORIGIN
The ilium of the pelvis.

INSERTION
The greater trochanter of the femur.

ACTION
A strong abductor, it pulls the thigh outward like when doing the splits.

B.14. GLUTEUS MAXIMUS

STRUCTURE
The gluteus maximus is a huge, strong muscle that has almost a tire-like shape surrounding the side of the hip.

ORIGIN
Part of the ilium and sacrum.

INSERTION
The bottom border blends into the iliotibial (IT) band, which inserts into the side of the tibia. There is a small part that inserts into the upper back side of the femur, just below the greater trochanter.

ACTION
Extends the thigh and laterally rotates it as well. The upper fibers help abduct the thigh, and the lower fibers of the muscle help in adduction.

B.15. TENSOR FASCIAE LATA (PLURAL: LATAE)

STRUCTURE
The tensor fasciae lata (often referred to as the TFL) is a tear-drop-shaped muscle inside the fascia (thin sheet of connective material) that is part of the iliotibial (IT) band. The iliotibial band is a strong, thick sheet of connective tissue that surrounds the thigh, but on the side it is so much thicker than the rest of the sheath (like a sausage casing) that it is the only important part for the artist to know. It's broad at the top, attaches to the ilium of the pelvis, and narrows toward the outside of the tibia, thus its name: ilio = ilium, and tibial = tibia.

ORIGIN
By the anterior superior iliac spine (ASIS).

INSERTION
Attached to the iliotibial band (IT band), which inserts on the lateral side of the upper part of the tibia.

ACTION
Flexes, abducts, and medially rotates the thigh (turns the thigh inward). It pulls strongly on the iliotibial band and can often make the band appear to be stringy and tight on the side of the thigh, on top of the vastus lateralis, like tight tape.

C THE FRONT TORSO

C.1. RECTUS ABDOMINIS

STRUCTURE
The rectus abdominis is shaped like the front half of a surfboard. It is flat and has sections of tendinous, fibrous bands that segment into six pads of muscle (a "six pack"). Sometimes there is one or two segments below the navel. Each half of the muscle meets at the center line of the abdomen called the linea alba ("white line").

ORIGIN
The pubic bone and over the pubic symphysis (the cartilage at the pubic area in between both halves of the pelvis).

INSERTION
The cartilage of the ribs at the fifth, sixth, and seventh ribs and the xiphoid process (the small "arrow-head" at the bottom of the sternum, or breastbone).

ACTION
Flexes the trunk, the vertebral column, such as when bowing or doing sit ups.

C.2. SERRATUS ANTERIOR

STRUCTURE
The serratus anterior muscle is made up of nine "fingers" called digitations. The serratus anterior has two sections: The first three digitations are the superior (higher) forms, which are flatter than the inferior (lower) forms, which are fuller. The upper forms are not seen, as they are deep under larger muscles. You can see some of the lower forms, four or five at the most, pop out from under the latissimus dorsi. On a muscular figure they can be quite plump and fanlike, especially when the arms are up.

ORIGIN
Each "finger" attaches to a rib, one through nine. The muscle is fanlike and hugs the rib cage as if holding it up. The serratus anterior meshes (interlocks) with the external oblique.

INSERTION
The front edge (underneath) of the scapula by the medial border, the border that roughly parallels the spine. The muscle is completely underneath the scapula, between it and the rib cage.

ACTION
It protracts the scapula (moves the scapula forward) and helps lift the arm.

C.3. EXTERNAL OBLIQUE

STRUCTURE
The external oblique is a large, slat-like muscle that interdigitates (meshes) with the serratus anterior. There is a fuller, fleshier portion on the ilium (the "love handle").

ORIGIN
The slat-like points (almost like the points of a picket fence) of the muscle attach to ribs five through twelve.

INSERTION
About two-thirds of the front portion of the crest of the ilium, the abdominal aponeurosis (flat sheet of tendon), and the linea alba (center line of the torso), the inguinal ligament that spans from the anterior superior iliac spine (ASIS) of the pelvis and the pubic bone.

ACTION
Bends the trunk laterally, side to side, and also twists the trunk.

C.4. PECTORALIS MAJOR

STRUCTURE
The pectoralis major has three sections. The sternal section is broad and shaped like a home plate in baseball, or like a house. The clavicular portion looks like a kitchen knife and crosses over the sternal portion from the clavicle to the humerus (upper arm bone). There is a smaller portion that is an extension of the sternal portion that is lower and slanted toward the abdominal muscles.

ORIGIN
The sternal portion attaches to the sternum, and the lower portion is attached to the abdominal aponeurosis, just like the external oblique. The clavicular portion attaches to the clavicle from the area close to the pit of the neck to two-thirds on the distal (further) end of the clavicle.

INSERTION
On the humerus close to the lateral area of the bone, below the head of the humerus.

ACTION
Adducts the arms, like in a bear hug, and medially rotates the arms. The clavicular portion helps raise the arms. The lower portion of the sternal section and the abdominal portion help in pulling down the arms.

D THE BACK TORSO AND SHOULDER

D.1. SACROSPINALIS GROUP

(ERECTOR SPINAE GROUP)

STRUCTURE
I decided to keep this complicated group of muscles simple. In the classroom I do this by dividing these deep back muscles into two basic forms: the medial form, which is lower and closer to the spine, and the lateral form, which is higher and fuller. I call the medial form the baguette, like the long, narrow loaf of bread at the bakery. It is tight and easily seen on a lean figure, especially when the arms are extended upward. The lateral form is more like a big French loaf, plump and seen easily on most figures.

ORIGIN
The sacrospinalis group (also called the erector spinae group) starts at the ilium by the posterior superior iliac spine (PSIS) (the protruding bumps on the pelvis that create the dimples on your backside) and continues to the lateral edge of the sacrum, to the midline, and all the way up the spine.

INSERTION
The lateral border of the larger form of the muscle has many tendons that attach to many points, including all twelve ribs, and then it narrows upward to the cervical (neck bones) transverse processes (the protruding spines on the neck bones that point outward), then to the mastoid process of the base of the skull (the bump behind the ear).

ACTION
These muscles extend the spine, the opposite action of the rectus abdominus.

D.2. SUPRASPINATUS

STRUCTURE
The supraspinatus (literally "above the spine") is a teardrop-shaped muscle that lies on its side on the superior aspect of the scapula over the spine of the scapula (the spine resembles a shelf).

ORIGIN
The posterior surface of the scapula, over the spine of the scapula (the shelf), resting on the canoe-shaped furrow of the spine of the scapula.

INSERTION
The top of the humerus on the greater tubercle (bony protrusion). The supraspinatus is one of four muscles that hold the head of the humerus into the glenoid fossa of the scapula (the shallow socket).

ACTION
Helps abduct the arm (moves the arm away from the side of the body), which is the position where it might be seen. Since it is under the large trapezius muscle, it is often hidden.

D.3. TERES MINOR

STRUCTURE
The teres minor is a small, thin, cigar-shaped muscle that is mostly hidden under the other, larger shoulder muscles. It is also one of the four rotator cuff muscles that hold the ball of the humerus in the glenoid fossa of the scapula, its shallow socket.

ORIGIN
Small strip on the lateral border of the scapula close to the glenoid fossa (shallow socket).

INSERTION
On the lateral side of the head of the humerus, but lower than the head of the humerus.

ACTION
The teres minor is a weak little muscle, but it helps hold the head of the humerus in the socket. It helps rotate the humerus laterally.

D.4. INFRASPINATUS

STRUCTURE
The infraspinatus (*infra meaning below/lower; spinatus referring to its placement under the spine of the scapula) is a triangular muscle that fits neatly on the shallow depression on the scapula.*

ORIGIN
Most of the scapula.

INSERTION
By the greater tubercle (bump) of the humerus.

ACTION
The infraspinatus is the third of four muscles that make up the rotator cuff. The fourth, the subscapularis, is hidden under the scapula and is not visible, therefore it is not included in this chapter. The infraspinatus holds the ball of the humerus into the glenoid fossa of the scapula and it laterally rotates the upper arm.

D.5. TERES MAJOR

STRUCTURE
The teres major, meaning round and large, is a tubular muscle that can be clearly seen on most figures in many poses.

ORIGIN
The bottom part of the scapula. The scapula looks like South America, so I named this lower section the "Tierra del Fuego" of the scapula, the area at the bottom of the continent.

INSERTION
On the front of the humerus not too far down from the head of the humerus.

ACTION
The teres major complements the other muscles that rotate the arm laterally (outward), the teres minor and the infraspinatus. The teres major rotates the humerus medially (inward). It also adducts the arm, pulling it toward the body.

D.6. RHOMBOIDS
(MAJOR AND MINOR COMBINED)

STRUCTURE
Both parts of the rhomboids are seen as one, which is why they are referred to as plural. They resemble a rhombus shape. Together with the ones on the other side of the spine, they resemble a chevron.

ORIGIN
Roughly on the seventh cervical vertebra (the protruding neck bone on your back) down to around the seventh thoracic (rib cage) vertebra.

INSERTION
The lateral edge of the scapula, from where the spine of the scapula is located down to the bottom of the edge (by the "Tierra del Fuego").

ACTION
The rhomboids adduct, retract, the scapula (brings the scapula closer to the spine). They also help rotate the scapula.

D.7. LATISSIMUS DORSI

STRUCTURE
The latissimus dorsi is a huge, triangular sheet of muscle with an extended band for attachment to the humerus.

ORIGIN
The lumbar aponeurosis that it is attached to runs along the spine and all the way down into the sacrum and to around a third of the rear of the ilium of the pelvis.

INSERTION
The front of the humerus by the insertion of the teres major, but a bit closer to the head of the humerus. When the arm is up and you're viewing the model from the front, this muscle often blends in with the teres major, but on more muscular figures you can easily see them as separate forms. There is a little piece of the latissimus dorsi that attaches to the lower part of the scapula.

ACTION
Adducts (moves inward), extends, and medially rotates (rotates inward) the humerus. It also depresses (pulls down) the scapula and helps rotate it as well.

D.8. TRAPEZIUS

STRUCTURE
The trapezius is so large and has so many muscle fibers that radiate out in different directions that it is almost a group of muscles. Because of that, it performs a variety of actions.

ORIGIN
From the base of the skull, it descends down the spine to the twelfth thoracic (rib cage) vertebra. Some individuals have this attachment higher, making the bottom point of the trapezius closer to the bottom of the scapula. The tendon at the bottom can be at the twelfth vertebra, but the muscle bellies can be higher.

INSERTION
On the front it inserts onto the end of the clavicle about third of the way in from the shoulder. It then wraps around the acromion process of the scapula onto the spine of the scapula. The tendon then wraps underneath the spine by the tubercle (bony bump) of the spine of the scapula.

ACTION
Lifts the scapula, like when holding a suitcase and then shrugging, while the lower fibers of the muscle pull the scapula downward. The center fibers bring together the scapulae along with the rhomboids.

E THE UPPER ARM

E.1. BRACHIALIS

STRUCTURE
The brachialis lies under the biceps brachii like a bed on the outside and front of the humerus where the bend of the elbow is. It can be seen on lean or very muscular people on the lateral side of the arm just below the deltoid. Basically, where the deltoid ends, the brachialis starts. When the elbow is straightened, the brachialis can also be seen right by the medial epicondyle, or the "funny bone" on the medial (inside) side of the arm. It is easily seen and felt as a soft form by the bend of the elbow and just lateral to the biceps brachii. In this section of the upper arm, many muscles have *brach in their names because brachium means "upper arm" in Greek.*

ORIGIN
At the deltoid tuberosity and down the front of the humerus, almost to the bend of the elbow.

INSERTION
At the front, upper part of the ulna.

ACTION
The brachialis flexes the arm.

E.2. BICEPS BRACHII

STRUCTURE
The biceps brachii is made up of two heads, a long head that is lateral, further outward, and a short head that is more medial, inward.

They are spilt at the top, the origin, and blend together as one at the bottom, the insertion. The biceps brachii is large and tubular. It comes out from under the pectoral muscles and deltoid.

ORIGIN
The long head originates over the glenoid fossa (shallow socket of the scapula). The short head originates at the tip of the coracoid process of the scapula (the beaklike bone on the front of the scapula; *coracoid means "bird's beak"*).

INSERTION
The radial tuberosity (the bony bump) of the radius.

ACTION
Flexes and supinates the forearm.

E.3. CORACOBRACHIALIS

STRUCTURE
The coracobrachialis is a cylindrical muscle resembling a small version of the biceps brachii.

ORIGIN
The coracoid process of the scapula.

INSERTION
The inside edge of the humerus at around the halfway point.

ACTION
Adducts and flexes the shoulder joint.

E.4. TRICEP MEDIAL HEAD

STRUCTURE
The tricep medial head is like a large, compressed teardrop shape. Most of it lies under the other two tricep heads, so what you mainly see is the portion that is exposed medially, such as when the arm is abducted (out to the side).

ORIGIN
A large strip of the humerus on the back and medial area.

INSERTION
The common triceps tendon that inserts onto the olecranon (elbow) of the ulna.

ACTION
Extends the forearm.

E.5. TRICEP LONG HEAD

STRUCTURE
The tricep long head is the largest of the three heads. At the top it is a band of muscle that is attached to the scapula, then it flares out into a large teardrop shape, very much like the gastrocnemius medial head of the lower leg.

ORIGIN
Just below the glenoid fossa (the shallow socket of the scapula) on the lateral edge. It's the only one of the three triceps that attaches to the scapula.

INSERTION
The common tricep tendon that inserts onto the olecranon (elbow) of the ulna.

ACTION
Extends the elbow

E.6. TRICEP LATERAL HEAD

STRUCTURE
The tricep lateral head is a tear-drop-shaped muscle, but it appears to have a "tail" of thin muscle as it drops down toward the elbow.

ORIGIN
Upper two-thirds of the upper lateral edge of the humerus.

INSERTION
The common tricep tendon that inserts onto the olecranon (elbow) of the ulna.

ACTION
Extends the elbow.

E.7. DELTOID

STRUCTURE
The deltoid is a large triangular muscle that comes to a point at the deltoid tuberosity, halfway down the side of the humerus. Remember that the brachialis starts at this spot.

ORIGIN
This muscle is divided into three portions. The rear, scapular portion originates far into the underneath area of the spine of the scapula. The front, clavicular portion originates a third of the way under the clavicle, the same distance as the trapezius just above it over the clavicle. The center section of the deltoid is called the acromial portion and it cups around the lateral side of the shoulder.

INSERTION
The deltoid tuberosity of the humerus, at the halfway point laterally.

ACTION
The front, clavicular portion helps raise the arm forward; the back, scapular portion helps bring the arm back; and the powerful lateral portion abducts the arm, lifting it outward.

F THE FOREARM

F.1. PALMARIS LONGUS

Note: Muscles F.1 through F.4 are the flexors of the forearm. All the forearm muscles have been reduced to the essential muscles for artists.

STRUCTURE
The palmaris longus is a small, thin, tubular muscle with a long tendon that ends at the palm of the hand as a flat aponeurosis (a flat sheet of fibrous tissue). The muscle can be set aside since you will not see it, but the tendon is very visible at the wrist on the palmar side when you make a fist and move it toward your body. Fun fact, not everyone has a palmaris longus. This is a muscle that is believed to be evolutionarily disappearing. If you do not have one, you will not miss it at all.

ORIGIN
The medial epicondyle ("funny bone") of the humerus. The four "flexors" that are shown in this book all originate at or right by the medial epicondyle.

INSERTION
The palmar aponeurosis of the palm.

ACTION
Weakly helps bring the fist toward the body and flex the wrist.

F.2. FLEXOR CARPI RADIALIS

STRUCTURE
The flexor carpi radialis is a long, somewhat flat muscle that has a prominent tendon next to the palmaris longus. These two tendons can be easily seen when you make a fist and then bring your fist toward your body. Remember, "carpi" means "wrist," and "radialis" refers to the fact that the direction of this muscle is toward the radius, the thumb side of the forearm.

ORIGIN
The medial epicondyle of the humerus.

INSERTION
The joint between the carpal bones and the metacarpals of the index and middle fingers.

ACTION
Flexes the forearm and helps in radial deviation of the hand, moving the hand outward. That motion is very limited.

F.3. PRONATOR TERES

STRUCTURE
The pronator teres is a short fleshy muscle. Even though this is a "pronator," it is included here with the flexor group.

ORIGIN
The medial epicondyle of the humerus.

INSERTION
The lateral (outside) edge of the radius at the halfway point.

ACTION
Pronates (turns the palm upward) and helps flex the forearm.

F.4. FLEXOR CARPI ULNARIS

STRUCTURE
The flexor carpi ulnaris starts as a broad, flat, canoe-shaped muscle that tapers distally (further from origin). It is an important contour muscle of the forearm. Remember, "carpi" means "wrist," and "ulnar" refers to the ulna, or the little finger side.

ORIGIN
The medial epicondyle of the humerus and also the medial border of the ulna/olecranon and down the crest of the ulna (the ridge).

INSERTION
The protruding wrist bone at the side of the little finger. This little bone is called the pisiform.

ACTION
Flexion and ulnar deviation (bends the hand toward the little finger).

F.5. EXTENSOR CARPI RADIALIS BREVIS

Note: Muscles F.5 through F.8 are the four muscles that in this book make up the extensor group.

STRUCTURE
The extensor carpi radialis brevis (ECRB) is long and plump muscle squeezed in between the extensor carpi radialis longus and the extensor digitorum. You will be able to see the middle belly pop out.

ORIGIN
The lateral epicondyle of humerus. Remember that the flexors are on the other side of the humerus at the medial epicondyle. The four extensors included here are at the lateral epicondyle.

INSERTION
The dorsal (top) surface of the third metacarpal bone (middle finger).

ACTION
Extends and helps radially deviate the hand (moves the hand outward toward the thumb).

F.6. EXTENSOR DIGITORUM

(AND THE EXTENSOR DIGITI MINIMI)

STRUCTURE
The extensor digitorum is a long, broad muscle that is made up of segments that taper toward the hand. The extensor digiti minimi is sometimes included as a blended muscle and sometimes separated. It is included here because it can be seen as a separate form that is very thin and tubular.

ORIGIN
The lateral epicondyle of the humerus.

INSERTION
Three tendons insert at the dorsal (top) of the middle and ends of the index, middle, and ring fingers. The extensor digiti minimi attaches to the middle and end of the little finger.

ACTION
The group extends the fingers, and the extensor digiti minimi can extend the little finger all by itself, like when you're having a cup of tea.

F.7. EXTENSOR CARPI ULNARIS

STRUCTURE
The extensor carpi ulnaris is a long, flat muscle. Its tendon can often be clearly seen toward the little finger by the wrist.

ORIGIN
The lateral epicondyle of the humerus.

INSERTION
On the tubercle (bony bump) on the base of the fifth metacarpal bone, the little finger side.

ACTION
Extension and ulnar deviation of the hand (moving the hand outward).

F.8. ANCONEUS

STRUCTURE
The anconeus is a triangular muscle that I refer to as the "Dorito." It is plump and easily seen when the arm is fully extended. It is just below the elbow and will overflow over the crest of the ulna.

ORIGIN
The lateral epicondyle of the humerus.

INSERTION
At the olecranon of the ulna, elbow, and down the back edge of the ulna about a fourth of the way down.

ACTION
Extends the elbow and helps stabilize the elbow joint.

F.9. BRACHIORADIALIS & EXTENSOR CARPI RADIALIS LONGUS

Note: I call these "the twins" because they look similar and originate and insert close to each other. The two muscles basically follow the thumb.

STRUCTURE
The brachioradialis starts off flat and large and spins toward the flexor group, then tapers toward the wrist on the thumb side. The extensor carpi radialis longus (ECRL) originates just below the brachialis. It is a short, flat muscle and seems to always follow the brachialis toward the thumb. It has a long and strong tendon. These two muscles are often blended, but on lean individuals you can see the split between them. I call these two "the twins."

ORIGIN
The brachioradialis originates on the side edge of the humerus, high, about a fourth of the way up the bone. The ECRL is attached on the same lateral edge just below the other "twin" the brachioradialis.

INSERTION
The brachioradialis inserts on the end of the lateral distal end of the radius. The ECRL inserts at the dorsal (back of the hand) proximal surface of the second metacarpal (index finger).

ACTION
The brachioradialis flexes the forearm, best seen in the handshake position. The ECRL helps flex the forearm and extends and radially deviates the hand.

F.10. ABDUCTOR POLLICIS LONGUS, EXTENSOR POLLICIS BREVIS & EXTENSOR POLLICIS LONGUS

Note: The abductor pollicis longus (APL) and the extensor pollicis brevis (EPB) are the "mini twins," as they resemble a small version of the "twins." Only the tendon of the extensor pollicis longus (EPL) is visible. The space between the tendon of the EPL and the tendons of the APL and EPB is called the "anatomical snuffbox." This hollow is created when the thumb is extended and abducted, like in the thumbs up action.

STRUCTURE
The abductor pollicis longus and extensor pollicis brevis (pollex means thumb in Latin) are both elongated triangular muscles and are therefore called the "mini twins." Mini because they resemble the larger twins, the brachioradialis and the ECRL.

ORIGIN
The abductor pollicis longus (APL) attaches to the back of the ulna. The extensor pollicis brevis (EPB) attaches to the radius and also to a membrane in between the radius and the ulna called the interosseus membrane.

INSERTION
The APL attaches to the base of the first metacarpal (thumb). The EPB attaches to the thumb as well, but farther down at the first phalanx of the thumb.

ACTION
The APL abducts the thumb and the EPB extends the thumb.

G THE NECK

G.1 SEMISPINALIS CAPITIS

STRUCTURE
The semispinalis muscle lies deep under the trapezius. It doesn't show, but it does create a bed for the trapezius, therefore it adds thickness to the back of the neck.

ORIGIN
The muscle has tentacle-like attachments to the cervical vertebrae at the transverse processes (the bony spikes at the sides of each vertebra) from the fourth cervical vertebra down to the sixth or seventh thoracic vertebra, the rib cage vertebrae.

INSERTION
A wide insertion at the base of the skull, not quite to the center line.

ACTION
It extends the head as if looking up and it helps rotate the head left and right.

G.2. SPLENIUS CAPITIS

STRUCTURE
The splenius capitis muscle is broad and flat and may pop out closer to the origin by the mastoid process (the bony bump behind the ear).

ORIGIN
The lower part of the nuchal ligament (a ligament that attaches to the base of the skull and down to the seventh cervical vertebra) and the first through fourth thoracic vertebrae.

INSERTION
A broad line at the mastoid process (the bony bump behind the ear) and a little bit toward the rear.

ACTION
Helps rotate the head. When contracting together, they help extend the head, as in the looking up movement.

G.3. LEVATOR SCAPULAE

STRUCTURE
The levator scapulae is a deep neck muscle, but it can often be seen on the side of the neck in between the sternocleidomastoid and trapezius muscles. It starts as tentacle-like points and ends as a flat sheet.

ORIGIN
The transverse processes (the bony spikes at the sides of each vertebra) of cervical vertebrae one through four.

INSERTION
The upper edge of the superior aspect of the scapula.

ACTION
As the name implies, the levator scapulae raises the scapula. It also pulls it medially (toward the spine).

G.4. SCALENE MEDIUS

Note: This is one of three scalene muscles, but it is the one that is more easily seen.

STRUCTURE
There are three scalene muscles, but the scalene medius is the largest of the three and is the one that is visible on the side of the neck. Like some of the other neck muscles, it has tentacle-like spikes of muscle

and tendon that attach to the transverse processes of the second through seventh cervical vertebrae.

ORIGIN
The spinous processes of the second through seventh cervical vertebrae.

INSERTION
The top surface of the first rib.

ACTION
Bends the neck side to side.

G.5. OMOHYOID

STRUCTURE
The omohyoid has two sections of narrow, cordlike muscles that have a small tendinous connection under the sternocleidomastoid muscle, making it bend.

ORIGIN
On a small spot on the superior aspect of the scapula by the levator scapulae.

INSERTION
On the underside of the hyoid bone of the neck.

ACTION
Pulls the hyoid bone down.

G.6. DIGASTRIC

STRUCTURE
The digastric, like the omohyoid, has two parts, two narrow bellies with a small tendon in the center separating each belly. That little tendon attaches to the hyoid bone, changing the direction of the digastric bellies.

ORIGIN
The mastoid process under the skull, just under the earlobe area.

INSERTION
Just under the mandible (jawbone), not quite at the center of the chin.

ACTION
It opens the mouth and helps in lifting the hyoid bone.

G.7. STERNOHYOID

STRUCTURE
The sternohyoid is a thin strap of muscle located and seen at the front of the neck. Together they look like two thin cordlike forms.

ORIGIN
The back area of the clavicle by the pit of the neck.

INSERTION
Under the hyoid bone, just to the side of the center line.

ACTION
Brings the hyoid bone down and helps with swallowing

G.8. STERNOCLEIDOMASTOID

STRUCTURE
The sternocleidomastoid (sterno-mastoid, or its long version, sternocleidomastoideus) is broad at the top and splits at the bottom. One of the two heads is tubular and spike-like as it reaches the pit of the neck and can easily be seen, especially when the head is turned to the side. The other is flat and is not always seen. It attaches to the clavicle. The name of this muscle will help you remember it better: *sterno = sternum, cleido = clavicle, and mastoid = mastoid process.*

ORIGIN
The sternal head attaches to the clavicle and the top part of the sternum, the manubrium. The clavicular head, the flat one, attaches to the upper surface of the clavicle about a third of the way from the proximal end, the part closest to the pit of the neck.

INSERTION
A long line under the occipital bone to the mastoid process.

ACTION
Turns the head side to side, and together, the two parts bend the head down, as when looking at the feet.

H THE HEAD AND FACE

H.1. TEMPORALIS

STRUCTURE
The temporalis muscle is a pancake-like fan that fits nicely into the temporal fossa (the depression of the temple of the skull). It can be seen in some individuals very clearly and sometimes you can see it when someone is chewing.

ORIGIN
The temporal fossa of the skull.

INSERTION
The coronoid process (the front arm of the mandible) down the ramus (front edge) of the mandible (jawbone).

ACTION
It lifts the mandible, keeps the mouth closed, and helps in chewing.

H.2. MASSETER

STRUCTURE
The masseter is a large quadrilateral (four-sided polygon) that is slanted forward.

ORIGIN
Under the edge of the zygomatic arch, the first two thirds and onto the front at the maxilla.

INSERTION
The lateral surface of the ramus of the jaw, the back corner area where the jaw turns.

ACTION
Powerfully closes the mouth as in biting, clenching the jaw, or chewing.

H.3. LEVATOR LABII SUPERIORSIS ALAEQUE NASI *(LLSAN)*

STRUCTURE
The LLSAN is a three-part muscle composed of three strips of thin muscle that together create movements of disgust or anger. This is easily seen in animals such as cats and dogs when they growl. The nose wrinkles and the teeth show in aggression.

ORIGIN
The three muscles originate on the side of the bridge of the nose.

INSERTION
One of the strips of muscle attaches to the crease that starts at the side of the wing of the nose, the nasolabial furrow (*naso = nose, labial = lip*). *The second one, the alar strip, attaches to the wing of the nose, and the third, the lip portion, attaches to the skin of the upper lip by the philtrum, the little trough at the center of the upper lip.*

ACTION
All three parts contract simultaneously. They raise the lip upward and crinkle the nose at the bridge, creating an expression of anger. If raised on only one side, they create a snarl expression.

H.4. FRONTALIS

STRUCTURE
The frontalis muscle is made up of two separate bodies, one medial and one lateral and larger, but here it is simplified as one form. It is flat and tall, shaped like a slice of bread. They two bodies touch on each side of the forehead but pull away slightly as they ascend. These muscles are not seen, but they create very visible forms on the forehead when contracted.

ORIGIN
The front edge of the epicranial aponeurosis, which is approximately at the hairline.

INSERTION
The skin at the eyebrows and just above the nasal bone.

ACTION
Raises the eyebrows, creating the furrows on the forehead.

H.5. BUCCINATOR *("BUGLER'S MUSCLE")*

STRUCTURE
The buccinator is a bilateral (two-sided) muscle that looks like a patch that forms the wall of the cheek.

ORIGIN
The muscle fibers attach in a few spots: the maxilla, inner cheek bone, and mandible on the upper edge.

INSERTION
The "node" of the corner of the mouth, the little jelly bean–shaped fibromuscular form called the modiolus.

ACTION
Pulls the modiolus (the node) inward into the corners of the mouth. It also compresses the cheeks, as in playing a bugle, and helps in sucking, as in drinking through a straw. It is one of the first muscles activated and used at birth

as a baby suckles. In expression it creates a smirk or expression of annoyance.

H.6. ZYGOMATICUS MAJOR AND MINOR

STRUCTURE
The zygomatics major and minor are both thin, straplike muscles.

ORIGIN
The zygomaticus major attaches at the zygomatic bone on the corner where it turns from side to front. The zygomaticus minor attaches near the same area as the zygomaticus major, just a tad to the side of it.

INSERTION
The zygomaticus major attaches to the modiolus (node) on the corner of the mouth. The zygomaticus minor attaches to the middle area of the nasolabial furrow and some of it extends down further to the upper lip.

ACTION
The zygomaticus major pulls the angle of the mouth upward, creating a smile. The zygomaticus minor pulls the middle portion of the upper lip upward, creating an expression of sadness.

H.7. ORBICULARIS ORIS

STRUCTURE
The orbicularis oris (mouth) is a very complex muscle, the most complex of all the facial muscles, allowing for great expression and speech. It includes both the upper and lower red lip.

ORIGIN
The modioli (nodes) at the corners of the mouth.

INSERTION
Horizontal bands of muscle go from the node on one side of the face to the node on the other side, allowing for a vast variety of movement for speech and expression.

ACTION
A wide variety of movements of the mouth for speaking and expression.

H.8. DEPRESSOR ANGULI ORIS

STRUCTURE
The depressor anguli oris is made up of two layers, one under the other. The lower layer is straplike and narrow, and the one on top of it is more of a stretched-out triangle.

ORIGIN
The two parts of the depressor anguli oris attach to the mandible, just to the side of the mental tubercle (chin bone).

INSERTION
The depressor anguli oris inserts into the modiolus (node at the corner of the mouth).

ACTION
Pulls the corners of the lips down, such as in sadness.

H.9. LEVATOR LABII SUPERIORIS

STRUCTURE
The levator labii superioris is a wide band of muscle that narrows as it descends toward the mouth.

ORIGIN
Attaches on a line just below the eye socket.

INSERTION
Attaches to the skin on the nasolabial furrow and down to the red lip and the orbicularis oris.

ACTION
Pulls the lip upward, as in snarling.

H.10. DEPRESSOR LABII INFERIORIS

STRUCTURE
The depressor labii inferioris (*depressor* = brings down, *labii* = lips, and *inferioris* = lower) is a quadrilateral muscle, rhomboid-shaped and flat. It curves the lip downward and is primarily used for speaking.

ORIGIN
Attaches at a slanted line on the lower edge of the jaw, away from center and flanking the mentalis muscle of the chin.

INSERTION
On the edge of the lower lip.

ACTION
Acting with each side of the chin, the muscles work in unison to pull the lip downward, exposing the lower teeth.

H.11. RISORIUS

STRUCTURE
The risorius is quite variable and some people do not even have this muscle. It can be flat and straplike or it can be thinner and more cablelike.

ORIGIN
The connective tissue of the cheek on the masseter.

INSERTION
Curving to the modiolus (node of the corner of the mouth).

ACTION
Pulls the node and therefore the corners of the mouth outward toward the ear. Creates subtle

expression, helps in smiling, and moves the nasolabial furrow outward.

H.12. PROCERUS AND NASALIS

STRUCTURE
The procerus is a triangular muscle in between the eyebrows, right at the center. The nasalis is also a small triangular muscle.

ORIGIN
The procerus attaches on the nasal bone. The nasalis attaches to the front of the maxilla.

INSERTION
The procerus attaches on the skin of the glabella (the area between the eyes) and the fibers of the frontalis muscle (H.4.). The nasalis inserts by the nasal cartilage.

ACTION
The procerus pulls down the skin of the middle of the forehead, creating horizontal wrinkles like in anger, pain, or frowning. When the lips are pressed together, the alar parts of the nasalis help push the upper lip downward.

H.13. MENTALIS

STRUCTURE
The mentalis is made up of two muscles butted together at the chin. In some people you can easily see the form like a mushroom top protruding out. Each side is made of short, conical forms whose fibers slant downward and end at the skin of the chin.

ORIGIN
On a vertical line just above the mental protuberance (the bump on the front of the jaw that juts out the farthest). The line of origin for each of the muscles is just off the midline. In some cases, these are just a tad further apart, creating a cleft or a dimple on the chin.

INSERTION
The skin of the chin.

ACTION
Raises and wrinkles the skin of the chin, pushing up the lower lip and creating a pout.

H.14. ORBICULARIS OCULI

STRUCTURE
The orbicularis oculi (of the eye) is a flat, oval-shaped muscle that surrounds the eye and is in the eyelids. It is a sphincter muscle (a ring of muscle) arranged in concentric bands around the upper and lower eyelids.

ORIGIN
The orbicularis oculi attaches to the nasal part of the frontal bone, the front of the maxilla. Basically it is like a patch around the eye.

INSERTION
At the side edge of the orbit of the eye socket.

ACTION
Closes the eyelids and helps in pumping out tears.

H.15. PLATYSMA

STRUCTURE
The platysma is a thin sheet of muscle that roughly resembles a turtleneck sweater halfway around the front of the neck, over the clavicles, and draped over the top portion of the pectorals. When the corners of the mouth are pulled down you can easily see the stringy fibers of the muscle form along the front and sides of the neck.

ORIGIN
Superficial fascia over the pectorals, deltoid, and trapezius.

INSERTION
The lower portion of the mandible, the skin of the lower part of the face, and up to the corners of the mouth.

ACTION
Pulls down the mandible (jaw) and the corners of the mouth.

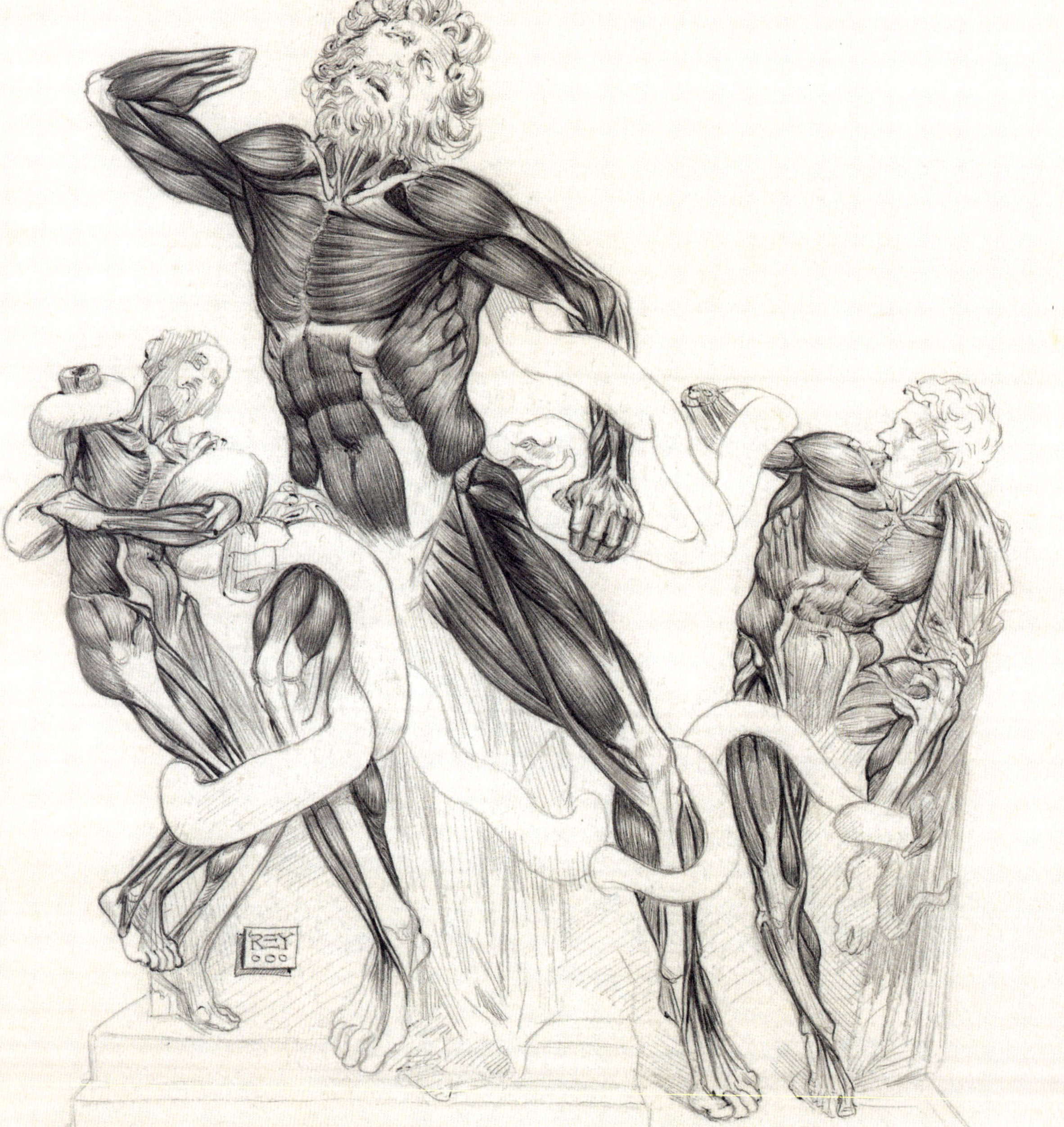
REY

GLOSSARY

Abduct (*ab-duct*): To move away from midline.

Abduction (*ab-duct-shun*): The action of moving away from midline.

Abductor (*ab-duct-tor*): A muscle that moves a body part away from midline.

Abductor hallucis longus (*ab-duct-tor hah-loo-siss long-us*): A muscle that brings the big toe up toward the head.

Abductor pollicis longus (*ab-duct-tor pol-i-siss long-us*): A thumb muscle that pulls the thumb out, as in the hitchhiker position. This is part of the "Anatomical Snuffbox" group.

Acetabulum (*ass-eh-tah-be-ū-lum*): The hip socket on the pelvis into which the head of the femur fits.

Achilles tendon (*ah-kill-ees*): The large tendon that attaches the calf muscles (gastrocnemius) and soleus to the calcaneus (heel).

Acromion process of the scapula (*ah-krow-mee-un*): The bony mass of bone at the end of the spine of the scapula. This is where the shoulder muscle, the deltoid, surrounds the spine of the scapula.

Adduct (*ah-duct*): To bring closer to midline.

Adduction (*ah-duct-shun*): The action of bringing closer to midline.

Adductor group (*Ah-duct-tor*): The group of muscles on the inner thigh that brings the legs together. The adductor muscles covered in this book are the adductor magnus, adductor longus, pectineus, and gracilis; not included is the adductor brevis. The iliopsoas was listed here as part of this group only because it fits nicely in the same area and is easier to be seen as a part of this when seeing it as an area of the thigh.

Adductor longus (*ah-duct-tor long-us*): A large, flat, triangular muscle that helps bring the thigh closer to the midline of the body, bringing the knees together.

Adductor magnus (*ah-duct-tor mag-nus*): The largest of the adductor group, but not easily seen. It is at the inner part of the thigh and is located under other muscles, making it difficult to point out on a model.

Anatomical snuffbox: A hollow at the top of the wrist just before the thumb created by three tendons: the abductor pollicis longus, extensor pollicis brevis, and extensor pollicis longus. Fun fact, this is where, in the distant past, people would place snuff (powdered tobacco) and sniff it into their noses.

Anconeus (*an-koh-nee-us*): A triangular muscle close to the elbow that helps in extending the arm.

Anterior: Front or toward the front.

Anterior superior iliac spine, or ASIS: These are the pointy and protruding tips of the pelvis at the beltline. These are at the front ends of the ilia of the pelvis.

Axilla (*ack-silla*): The name of the armpit created by the walls of the latissimus dorsi and the pectoralis major.

Axis (*ack-siss*): The imaginary center line running vertically through the body or form.

Belly of muscle: The fleshy center part of a muscle made of contractile tissue.

Biceps brachii (*bi-seps bray-kee-eye*): A prominent two-headed muscle that lies at the front of the arm. It flexes and supinates the arm.

Biceps femoris (*bi-seps fem-or-iss*): A two-headed muscle of the hamstring group or thigh flexors. It helps bend the knee.

Bipennate muscle (*bi-pen-ate*): A muscle with a fiber arrangement where the fibers are attached at an angle from two different directions, resembling a feather. *Penna* means "feather" in Latin.

Body types: *see* ectomorph, endomorph, and mesomorph.

Bone: Hard tissue made of collagen and calcium phosphate. There are approximately 206 bones in the human adult, whereas at birth, there are about 270 because many of these bones are not fully finished fusing together.

Bony landmark: Areas on the body where a bone or part of a bone lies close to the surface of the skin and can be felt or seen.

Brachialis (*bray-kee-ah-liss*): A flat muscle of the upper arm that creates a bed for the biceps brachii and helps flex the elbow.

Brachioradialis (*bray-kee-oh-ray-dee-ah-liss*): A prominent muscle that starts at the side of the upper arm and spirals toward the thumb. It helps flex the elbow and supinates the forearm.

Bridge (*of the nose*): The bony ridge of bone that protrudes in some individuals.

Brow ridges: The two bony protruding bones over the eyebrow. These are usually more prominent on men.

Calcaneus (*kal-kay-nee-us*): The large heel bone of the tarsal group of the ankle.

Canon of the body: The mathematical proportional system used to measure the body.

Carpal bones: The eight bones that make up the wrist bones. These are the capitate, hamate, lunate, pisiform, scaphoid, trapezium, trapezoid, and triquetral bone.

Carpal tunnel: An area at the palmar side of the wrist that has a strong strap, the retinaculum ligament, that creates a passageway for the many flexor tendons of the forearm. This area can become aggravated from misuse and create pain in an individual.

Cartilage (*kar-tih-lij*): Connective tissue found in joints to act as a shock absorber or tissue that creates the shapes of the ear and nose or acts like bone in protecting the organs when attached to the ribs.

Cervical vertebrae (*sir-vi-kull ver-teh-bray*): The seven neck bones.

Clavicle (*klah-vi-kull*): The two long bones that are commonly called the collar bones.

Coccyx (*kock-six*): The four small tail bones at the bottom of the sacrum of the pelvis.

Concha (*kong-ka*): The bowl-shaped area of the ear.

Condyle (*kon-dīl*): Round prominence at the end of a bone. *Condyle* means "knuckle."

Connective tissue: Tissue that holds, supports, or connects various structures of the body. These include bone, cartilage, ligaments, tendons, aponeuroses, fascia, and subcutaneous fat.

Contraction: When a muscle tenses, it can shorten (concentric contraction) or remain the same length (isometric contraction). In both cases, the muscle becomes more defined, which is of interest to the artist.

Deltoid (*dell-toyd*): The shoulder muscle shaped like a triangle. This muscle is broken up into three parts: the rear, or scapular, portion; the front, or clavicular, section; and the center, or acromial, portion.

Digastric muscles (*die-gas-trick*): These thin, straplike muscles are important in this book because they help in drawing the underneath area of the neck (see "The Head and Neck").

Digit (*dih-jit*): A finger or toe.

Distal: Further away from the origin or attachment of a limb or bone.

Dorsal (*dor-sull*): A location term referring to the back surface of an anatomical area or surface. It is also used to describe the top of the foot.

Dorsiflexion (*dor-si-fleck-shun*): The action of the foot flexing at the ankle and pointing toward the head.

Ectomorph (*ek-toe-morf*): One of the three main body types. Characterized as thin, bony, and light with noticeable skeletal protrusions.

Endomorph (*en-doh-morf*): One of the three main body types. Characterized by a variation of shapes ranging from slightly plump to portly and stout to obese.

Epicanthic fold (*epi-can-thick*) or epicanthal fold: This is the fold of skin that covers the inner corner of the eye. This is typically a feature of Asian people but can also be seen on some people of other races, although rare. It is also seen on people with Down Syndrome.

Epicondyle (*ep-ih-con-dial*): A small projection on a bone by a joint. The word *epicondyle* means "little knuckle," as opposed to *condyle* which means "knuckle."

Eversion (*ee-ver-zhun*): The action of moving the foot outward.

Extend: To straighten an area like the torso, limb, finger, or toe from a bent or flexed position.

Extensor (*ex-ten-sor*): A muscle that causes straightening.

Extensor carpi radialis brevis (*ex-ten-sor karp-eye ray-dee-ah-liss breh-viss*): One of the extensors of the wrist.

Extensor carpi radialis longus (*ex-ten-sor karp-eye ray-dee-ah-liss long-us*): One of the extensors of the wrist, and in this book, one of the "twins," along with the brachioradialis.

Extensor hallucis longus (*ex-ten-sor hal-loo-siss long-us*): The prominent tendon that pulls up on the big toe. *Hallux* is Latin for the big toe.

Facet (*fah-set*): The flat area of a bone or a visualization of an area that can be seen as flat areas or planes to show the major changes of a form or forms.

Fascia (*fah-shia*): Thin, fibrous connective tissue that surrounds muscles and muscle groups.

Femur (*fee-mur*): The thigh bone and the longest bone of the human body. This is the major bone in determining a person's height. The forensic formula is length of the femur X 2.5 + 23″.

Fibula (*fib-yoo-lah*): The thinner of the two bones of the lower leg, the tibia (shin bone) being the larger bone.

Flexion (*fleck-shun*): The action of bending an area, limbs, fingers, or toes.

Flexor carpi radialis (*fleck-sor karp-eye ray-dee-ah-liss*): One of the muscles on the anterior side of the forearm.

Foramen (*foh-ray-men*): An opening on a bone. Foramina is the plural.

Fossa (*foss-ah*): A shallow depression on a bone, but it can also be on the body's surface.

Frontalis (*frun-tay-liss*): The muscle on the forehead.

Gastrocnemius (*gas-trok-nee-mee-us*): The calf muscle.

Glabella (*glah-bell-ah*): The small area just above the nasal bone, sometimes referred to as the keystone.

Glenoid fossa (*glee-noyd foss-ah*): The shallow socket on the scapula where the head of the humerus attaches.

Gluteal cleft (*gloo-tee-ul*): The vertical division between the two gluteus maximus muscles. Sometimes called the "plumber's cleft."

Gluteal fold (*gloo-tee-ul*): The prominent horizontal fold at the bottom of the gluteus maximus.

Gluteal muscles (*gloo-tee-ul*): There are three major muscles that make up this group: the gluteus medius, gluteus maximus, and tensor fasciae latae.

Gluteus maximus (*gloo-tee-us mack-sih-muss*): The very large muscle of the gluteal group that extends the thigh backward and helps maintain an upright posture.

Gluteus medius (*gloo-tee-us mee-dee-us*): Large abductor on the side of the gluteal group.

Gracilis (*grah-sill-liss*): Long belt-like muscle that is basically at the inseam of a pair of pants. It is one of the adductor muscles.

Great trochanter or **greater trochanter** (*trow-kan-ter*): The large prominent and protruding process of the upper femur.

Hallux (*hay-luks* or *hah-luks*): Big toe in Latin.

Hamstring group: Also called the thigh flexors, these are the muscles of the back of the thigh that bend the knee joint.

Head of the femur (*fee-mur*): The round ball that fits into the socket of the pelvis, the acetabulum.

Head of the fibula (*fib-yoo-luh*): The expanded part of the top of the fibula.

Head of the humerus (*hume-er-us*): The ball of the upper part of the humerus that articulates with the glenoid fossa of the scapula.

Humerus (*hume-er-us*): The upper arm bone.

Hyoid bone (*hy-oyd*): The U-shaped bone that is just above the Adam's Apple under the jaw.

Iliac crest (*ill-ee-ak*): The top curved edge of the pelvis.

Iliotibial band (*ill-ee-oh-tib-ee-ul*): A strong, flat fascia strap that attaches from the gluteal muscles all of the way up to the ilium, down to the upper lateral area of the tibia.

Ilium (*ill-ee-um*): The large dish-like part of the pelvis.

Inferior: Below or closer to foot.

Infraclavicular fossa (*in-frah-clav-ih-cue-lur foss-uh*): Literally means "Shallow depression below the clavicle." This is a small dip or depression under the clavicle and in between the deltoid and the clavicular portion of the pectoralis major.

Infraspinatus (*in-frah-spin-ay-tuss*): The large muscle on the scapula attached under the spine of the scapula—hence its name, which means "under the spine."

Inguinal ligament (*in-gwee-nul*): The strappy, fibrous band that spans from the anterior superior iliac spine (ASIS) to the public bone.

Insertion of a muscle: The attachment of a muscle at the end where it moves.

Inversion (*in-ver-zhion*): The movement of the foot turning inward, or medially.

Iris: The colored area of the eye that identifies eye color.

Ischial tuberosity (*iss-kee-ul too-ber-oss-ity*): The part of the ischium that is at the bottom and sometimes referred to as the "sit bone." The hamstring muscles attach here.

Ischium (*iss-kee-um*): The lower portion or loops of the pelvis.

Joint: The connection point of two bones, where they meet.

Lacrimal caruncle (*lah-krim-ul ka-ran-kul*): The pinkish, fleshy tear duct on the inner corner of the eye.

Lateral malleolus (*mah-lee-oh-luss*): The outside ankle, the distal or bottom end of the fibula.

Latissimus dorsi (*lah-tiss-ih-muss dor-sigh*): The broad triangular muscle on the back and side of the torso that helps in extending the arm and in medial rotation.

Leg: In anatomy, this is the area between the knee to the foot; the shin and calves.

Lesser trochanter (*trow-kan-ter*): This is the small protruding bone on the inside top of the femur.

Ligament (*lig-uh-ment*): Connective tissue that binds bone to bone.

Linea alba (*lih-nee-uh*): The center line of the front torso from the bottom of the sternum to the pubic bone.

Linea aspera (*lih-nee-uh ahs-per-ah*): The ridge on the back of the femur.

Lumbar vertebrae (*lum-bar ver-teh-bray*): The five spinal bones of the lower back between the thorax and the pelvis.

Mandible (*man-deh-bul*): The lower jaw.

Manubrium (*mah-noo-bree-um*): The upper part of the sternum.

Masseter (*mass-eh-ter*): The prominent chewing muscle on the side of the jaw.

Mastoid process (*mass-toyd prah-sess*): The prominent bony protrusion behind the ear at the base of the skull.

Medial: Closer to midline.

Medial malleolus (*mah-lee-oh-luss*): The bony inside ankle; the lower inside end of the tibia.

Median line: The imaginary center line of the body or limb.

Meniscus (*meh-niss-kuss*): A crescent-shaped cartilage pad in between the tibia and femur. Menisci is the plural.

Mentalis (*men-tay-liss*): A small muscle at the chin that pushes out the lip in a pout-like fashion and raises the chin. Often you can see little dimples, such as when biting a lemon.

Mental protuberance: The chin area of the mandible. Humans are the only primates that have this, therefore humans are the only primates with a chin.

Mesomorph (*mez-oh-morf*): One of the three main body types. Characterized by a naturally athletic build.

Metacarpal bones: These are the bones of the body of the hand. *Meta* means "beyond" and *carpal* refers to the wrist; therefore, this literally means "beyond the wrist" bones.

Metacarpophalangeal articulation (*met-uh-kar-poh-fuh-lan-jee-ul*): Literally this means the joint between the body of the hand and the fingers. The common name is the knuckles of the hand.

Metatarsal bones (*met-ah-tar-sul*): The bones of the top of the foot.

Multipennate muscle (*mull-tee-pen-ate*): Muscle with multiple tendon branches with muscle fibers attached along both sides of each tendon. The side of the deltoid has this and it is very clearly seen on a cadaver.

Muscle: Soft tissue made up of contractile cells.

Nasal bones: The bones on the face that form the bridge of the nose.

Nasolabial fold (*nay-zo-lay-bee-ul*): The crease seen off of the nostril wings and lateral to the mouth. *Naso* = nose, *labial* = lips.

Navel (*nay-vul*): Belly button. Also called the umbilicus.

Nose: The external bony and cartilaginous structure over the nasal cavity.

Nostrils: The two small openings formed by the cartilage of the wings of the nose.

Nuchal ligament (*new-kull*): This is the strong ligament that attaches at the base of the skull and down along the spinous processes of the cervical vertebrae of the neck. You can feel this by placing your finger on the back of your neck then dropping your head down to your chest. The nuchal ligament will be felt very easily as if it were a cable stretching down the center of the back of your neck.

Oblique (*oh-bleek*): In anatomy, this means at a slant or diagonal.

Occipital bone (*ocks-sih-pih-tul*): The bone of the back of the skull.

Olecranon (*ole-lek-rah-non*): The proximal, prominent bump on the ulna; the elbow.

Orbicularis oris (*or-bih-cue-lair-iss oh-riss*): The large, flat muscle that surrounds the mouth.

Palm: The anterior surface of the hand.

Palmaris longus (*pahl-mair-iss*): One of the flexor muscles of the forearm that originates at the medial epicondyle (funny bone) to the palm.

Parotid gland (*pah-rot-id*): The largest of the salivary glands. Because it sits on top of the masseter (chewing muscle) by the ear, it softens the jawline by the earlobe.

Patella (*pah-tell-ah*): The largest of the sesamoid bones; the kneecap.

Patellar ligament (*pah-tell-ar*): This is the prominent ligament that connects the patella to the tibial tuberosity.

Pectineus (*peck-tih-nee-us*): The relatively rectangular adductor muscle of the inner thigh.

Pectoralis major (*peck-tor-ah-liss*): The large muscle of the chest. In this book it is divided into the two parts, the pectoralis major sternal head and the clavicular head.

Pelvic brim: The large opening in the pelvis basin.

Pelvis: The main bony structure of the lower torso. In Latin the word means "basin."

Pennate muscle (*pen-ate*): A muscle arrangement that has muscle fibers coming at an oblique or slanted angle. *Penna* means "feather" in Latin. *See also* bipennate and multipennate muscles.

Peroneus brevis (*peh-row-nee-us breh-viss*): The muscle on the lateral side of the leg by the ankle. The tendon is very prominent, as it uses the lateral malleolus of the fibula as a pulley and then inserts at the tuberosity of the fifth metatarsal on the side of the foot.

Peroneus longus (*peh-row-nee-us long-us*): This muscle partners with the peroneus brevis on the fibular side of the leg to help plantarflex (move down) and evert (move outward) the foot.

Pes anserinus (*pez ahn-sir-eye-niss*): Means "goose foot." This is the tendinous bundle that creates a large mound on the inside of the knee.

Phalanx (*fay-lanks* or *fay-links*): Finger or toe; phalanges is the plural. It means a "row of soldiers" in Greek.

Philtrum (*fill-trum*): The vertical depression or trough above the upper lip, just below the septum of the nose.

Pit of the neck: This is the hollow created between the proximal ends of the clavicles and above the sternum. It is also called the suprasternal notch, meaning the notch above the sternum.

Plantarflexion (*plan-tar-flecks-shun*): The action of the foot at the ankle joint moving the foot down, pointing the foot.

Posterior (*poss-teer-ee-or*): On the back or the back surface of the body or body part.

Posterior superior iliac spine, or PSIS (*ill-ee-ak*): The protruding bony bumps on the back of the pelvis that create the two dimples on the rear of the lower torso.

Process: A bony projection on a bone that can often be seen or felt.

Pronate: Turning the hand with the palm down towards the ground.

Pronator teres (*pro-nate-or teh-reez*): This muscle is on the flexor area or the forearm and originates at the medial epicondyle (funny bone) in the same area as the major flexors of the arm. It is obliquely placed and pronates the arm as it inserts onto the lateral aspect of the ulna.

Protuberance (*pro-too-bur-ants*): A bony bump or outgrowth on a bone.

Proximal (*procks-ih-mull*): Closer to the beginning or origin of a limb or bone.

Pubic arch: The space between the ischia on the pelvis that is a good indicator of the sex of the person. It resembles the angle of a capital A on a male and it is wider on a woman, at a 90-degree angle or more. The male and female genitals lie in the area.

Pubic bone (*pyoo-bik*): The bridge of bone at the front of the pelvis.

Pubic symphysis (*pyoo-bik sim-fih-siss*): The joint in between the pubic bones. A fibrocartilage pad lies in this space.

Pupil (*pyoo-pill*): The small black opening or aperture of the iris of the eye.

Pyramidalis (*pir-ah-my-dah-liss* or *pir-ah-my-day-liss*): The small triangular muscle just above the pubic bone and on top of the lower end of the rectus abdominus.

Quadriceps group (*kwahd-rih-seps*): The muscles of the front of the thigh. There are four, as *quad* implies, but in this book we refer to only the three that are seen on the model: the vastus medialis, vastus lateralis, and rectus femoris. The one that I am leaving out is the vastus intermedius, which is underneath the rectus femoris.

Radius (*ray-dee-us*): One of the two bones of the forearm. The ulna is the other. The radius basically follows the thumb.

Rectus abdominis (*reck-tuss ab-dom-ih-niss*): The large, flat "six pack" muscle of the abdominal region.

Rectus femoris (*reck-tuss fee-mor-iss* or *reck-tuss fem-or-iss*): The trout-shaped, bipennate muscle of the front of the thigh.

Retinaculum (*reh-tin-ah-cyoo-lum*): Any of the binding bands that hold things like tendons together, such as the ones on the wrists and ankles. They are like nature's duct tape.

Rhomboids (*rom-boyds*): There are two, the rhomboid major and minor. They are both attached to the spine and insert on the inner edge of the scapula. They have an oblique angle, or upward slant. The top edge is at the inner spine of the scapula, toward the seventh cervical vertebra, and can be seen on many models.

Rhombus of Michaelis (*rom-bus of my-kah-liss*): This is an area created by subcutaneous fat on a woman that covers the sacrum, therefore creating a soft diamond-shaped rhombus at the lower back. It makes women's backs look more feminine. Men have the sacral triangle.

Rib cage: The bones and thoracic cartilage that protect the organs. Also called the thorax. There are 14 true ribs, 6 false ribs, and 4 floating ribs, making 24 total ribs.

Sacral triangle (*say-krall*): The triangular area seen at the sacrum of the pelvis.

Sacrospinalis (*say-kro-spih-nay-liss*), also called the erector spinae muscles: A group of nine muscles that create two major forms. The medial form is at the base of the spine and is narrow and tubular. The lateral form is seen at around the bottom of the rib cage on the back and has larger bellies that can be seen all of the way up the spine in some poses but are more pronounced at the base of the rib cage up to the lower part of the scapulae.

Sacrum (*say-krum*): The shieldlike bone on the back, in between the two pelvic halves.

Sartorius (*sar-tor-ee-us*): This is the longest muscle of the human body. It is a long, belt-like muscle that originates at the anterior superior iliac spine (ASIS) of the pelvis, at the beltline, and winds toward the inside of the knee and back to the front at the top and side of the tibia. It is the separator between the quadriceps and the adductors of the thigh.

Scapula (*scap-u-la*): Either of the two flat South America–shaped bones that glide on the back. Commonly known as the shoulder blades.

Sclera (*skleh-rah*): The white of the eye.

Semimembranosus (*sem-eye-mem-bra-noh-sus*): One of the hamstring or flexor muscles of the back of the thigh.

Semitendinosus (*sem-eye-ten-din-oh-sus*): One of the hamstring or flexor muscles of the back of the thigh. The tendon is very prominent on the inside of the back of the knee.

Septum: A wall of connective tissue that divides an area of the body into two sections.

Serratus anterior (*sir-ray-tus*): A fingerlike and fan-shaped muscle with eight or nine paw-like fingers that originate on the front under the nipple and insert at the underneath edge of the scapula.

Sesamoid bone (*sess-ah-moyd*): A pebble-like bone embedded in a tendon to create mechanical advantage. The patella, the kneecap, is the largest of the sesamoids. There are also a couple behind the joint of the big toe and thumb.

Seventh cervical vertebra (*C-7*): The pronounced and last bone of the neck vertebrae.

Shoulder girdle: The bony ring around the neck area created mostly by the clavicles and the spines of the scapulae.

Skeleton: The bony framework of the body. The human skeleton is made up of 206 bones in the adult, and 270–300 bones at birth. The number lessens as the bones fuse together.

Skull: The entire set of bones that create the head and face of the skeleton.

Soleus (*sol-ee-us*): The large muscle under the two gastrocnemius heads that share the Achilles tendon.

Spine: A sharp, pointy process of a bone. It is also the common name for the vertebral column.

Spine of scapula: The prominent, bony shelf of the scapula. Sometimes I call these the clavicles of the back. They help create the shoulder girdle.

Spinous process (*spy-niss*): The pointy protruding part of each of the vertebrae.

Sternocleidomastoideus (*stir-no-cly-doe-mass-toyd-ee-us*): The prominent muscle of the neck that can be more easily seen when turning the head to one side. It attaches to the sternum, clavicle, and mastoid process, hence its name.

Sternum (*stir-num*): The necktie-looking bone on the front of the chest. Commonly called the breast bone.

Subcutaneous fat (*sub-kyoo-tay-nee-us*): The fat layer under the skin.

Superficial muscles: The muscles closer to the surface of the body creating the visible forms.

Superior: Higher or closer to the head.

Supination (*soo-pih-nay-shun*): The movement of the hand as it rotates to have the palm facing upward.

Symphysis (*sim-fih-siss*): A slightly moveable cartilaginous joint such as the prominent one at the pubis. *See* pubic symphysis.

Tarsal bones: The seven bones that make up the ankle and heel: the calcaneus, talus, navicular, cuboid, and, lastly, the three cuneiform bones.

Temporalis (*tem-poor-ah-liss*): The muscle on the side of the skull on the temple.

Tendon (*ten-din*): Connective tissue that attaches muscle to bone. Ligaments attach bones to other bones.

Tensor fasciae latae (*ten-sor fash-ee-uh lah-tee*): One of the gluteal muscles, it is shaped like a teardrop and is seen at the area of someone's jeans pocket.

Teres major (*teh-reez*): A long, round muscle prominent at the lower tip of the scapula and visually moving toward the underarm.

Teres minor (*teh-reez*): A small, cigar-shaped muscle that is tucked in between the infraspinatus and the teres major. It is not easily seen on most people.

Thigh: The upper leg.

Thoracic vertebrae (*thor-ah-sik ver-teh-bray*): The vertebrae or the part of the spine that holds the 24 ribs, therefore there are 12 thoracic vertebrae.

Thorax (*thor-acks*): The rib cage.

Thumb: The opposable first digit of the hand. The Latin word for the thumb is *hallux*.

Thyroid cartilage: The cartilage that lies at the front of the neck. It is prominent on men and is commonly called the "Adam's apple."

Tibia: The larger of the two bones of the lower leg.

Tibialis anterior (*tib-ee-ah-liss ant-ee-ree-or*): One of the contour muscles of the front of the shin. It helps to raise your foot up toward the head and also to help invert it. The tendon at the foot is very prominent and appears to move toward the arch of the foot.

Tibial tuberosity (*tib-ee-al too-ber-oss-it-ee*): The prominent "nose" of the tibia, just below the patella and where the patellar ligament is attached.

Tip of the nose: The end of the nose that is made up of two pieces of cartilage. Also called the apex of the nose.

Torso: The body without the limbs or head. The torso can also be called the trunk.

Tragus (*tray-gus*): The cartilaginous bump by the ear hole that can be pushed in to shut out sound.

Trapezius (*trap-ee-zee-us*): The large back and shoulder muscle that takes up a major area of the back. Its muscles fibers radiate in many different directions, making this an amazingly active muscle in a large variety of movements.

Triceps brachii (*try-seps bray-kee-eye*): The three heads of the upper arm that extend the forearm. The three heads are the long head, lateral head, and medial head, and all three are attached to the elbow (olecranon) by the triceps tendon.

True ribs: The 14 ribs, 7 pairs, that attach most directly to the sternum. The 3 pairs of false ribs attach to the costal cartilage and the 2 pairs of floating ribs do not attach to anything at the front.

Tubercle (*too-bur-cul*): A bump on a bone or cartilage.

Tuberosity (*too-bur-oss-ih-tee*): A bony protrusion on a bone where a tendon or ligament is attached.

Ulna: One of the two forearm bones, the other being the radius. The ulna follows the pinky finger.

Ulnar furrow: The furrow created by the crest of the ulna due to the attachment of the flexors and extensors, with the crest being the meeting of the two creating a furrow or linear indentation.

Vastus lateralis (*vass-tuss lah-ter-ah-liss*): The largest of the quadricep group of muscles that extends the leg. It runs down the lateral aspect of the thigh and rolls toward the front and close to the knee. It shares the quadriceps tendon with the other three muscles of this group, the vastus medialis, rectus femoris, and the hidden quadricep, the vastus intermedius. The tendon surrounds the patella and becomes the patellar ligament, which attaches to the tibial tuberosity.

Vastus medialis (*vass-tuss mee-dee-ah-liss*): One of four quadriceps, this muscle appears to be tear-drop-shaped. It ends lowest of the group by the patella on the front and inside area of the knee.

Vertebra (*ver-teh-brah*): The singular of the bones that make up the spinal or vertebral column. Vertebrae (ver-teh-bray): Plural of vertebra.

Vertebral column (*ver-teh-brahl*): The spine of the back of the skeleton.

Vomer bone: The wall of bone that separates the nasal bone in the skull into two sections.

Wing of nose: The cartilaginous area flanking the side of the nose and what also creates each nostril.

Wrist bones: *See* **carpal bones.**

Xiphoid process of sternum (*zy-foyd* or *zih-foyd*): The small bone that is at the very bottom of the sternum. *Xiphoid* means "swordlike" in Greek.

Zygomatic arch: The arch on the side of the skull, the cheek bone.

Zygomaticus muscles: Two thin, straplike muscles, major and minor, that attach on the zygomatic arch and the corners of the mouth and upper lip.

ACKNOWLEDGMENTS

I would like to express my deepest gratitude to my many teachers through the years of my youth, especially Mr. Berne Hogarth, who taught my first and only anatomy class way back in 1986 at the Art Center College of Design. As figurative teachers, I am indebted to: Harry Carmean, Lorri Madden, Mark Strickland, and Vern Wilson. Through the years I have also been blessed by my friendship with my mentor and my mentee, Eliot Goldfinger and Yuki Toy, respectively. Eliot has been my go-to man and, more importantly, a great friend. My friend and fellow anatomy lover Yuki Toy has blessed me with her friendship, support, and many art and anatomy conversations through the years.

To Dr. Anthony Friscia, who opened up his UCLA lab for me and my students for over a decade, allowing us to touch, draw, and learn from cadaver specimens. This has been a great part of my own education and I thank you.

To the many schools that I called home: ArtCenter College of Design, where I taught for twenty-three years and reached a position of associate professor; Los Angeles Academy of Figurative Art (LAAFA), where I taught for twenty years; Computer Graphics Masters Academy (CGMA), where I taught online for eleven years; New Masters Academy (NMA), where I still teach online; Disney Feature Animation, where I served as a visiting artist teaching 3D anatomy/écorché as well as running figure drawing workshops; California State University, Los Angeles (Cal State LA), where I taught figure drawing and 3D anatomy/écorché for seven years; and a few other places where I have either taught or for whom I have created online lectures and classes. All of these places represent years of different formats, and different student bodies, all of which added to my joy of passing on my love of and passion for anatomy. I thank all of the places that gave me a room and a blackboard, and more importantly, the students for me to share with.

I am grateful to my parents for bringing us to this wonderful country. We are a melting pot of many peoples and cultures living together and adding to each other's lives and experiences. It is indeed an honor to have become an American citizen.

For the past few years, since around 2005, I have been blessed by being asked to teach online. I do not even own a cell phone, so I was at first very reluctant and admittedly scared to try something so new, but I am so glad that I did. This allowed me to reach well beyond my own community and reach a global community of eager students. I could not have done it alone. I have two major people to thank for helping me with the IT aspects of teaching online: Steve Moore at CGMA, who was a constant aid to me and eased me through many tech glitches and situations, and Peter Henderson, who also made my life so much easier with New Masters Academy. Peter was also my right-hand man when teaching live; he was a partner in many of my classes with NMA and I am so blessed to continue to have his help and friendship. Thank you to Joshua Jacobo, founder and schoolmaster of New Masters Academy, affectionately shortened to NMA. He changed my professional life. He has recorded my lectures and has given me the gift of giving. I can now teach new students even after I am no longer here. We do what we do because of the passion that we both have for passing on such timeless and beautiful information. I have been so blessed by being able to teach with NMA—thank you.

Thank you to my assistants who provided me with technical help and were always will to help their old teacher: Richard Johnson and Peter Henderson. I would also like to thank Sandra Salem, once my student and now my friend. Sandra was able to help me with some of the action drawings in this book when I was having a lot of health and physical problems. She was terrific and helped me with finishing this book.

Finally, sincere thanks to Ted Waitt at Rocky Nook for supporting this project and to my editor, Jocelyn Howell at RN—working with you was a pleasure, we made an excellent team. Despite challenges with my surgeries and losing our Altadena home in the January 2025 Eaton Fire, you were supportive, understanding, and kind.

DEDICATION

To my wife Fiona, I could not have found a better, more loving and supportive partner in life. Thank you for keeping me humble, and yes, when I am done writing this last little section before I finally finish this book, I will empty the dishwasher and take out the trash. To our wonderful daughter Catherine, you are at the heart of everything mom and I do. It's now your turn to go out there and make your own dreams come true.

ABOUT THE AUTHOR

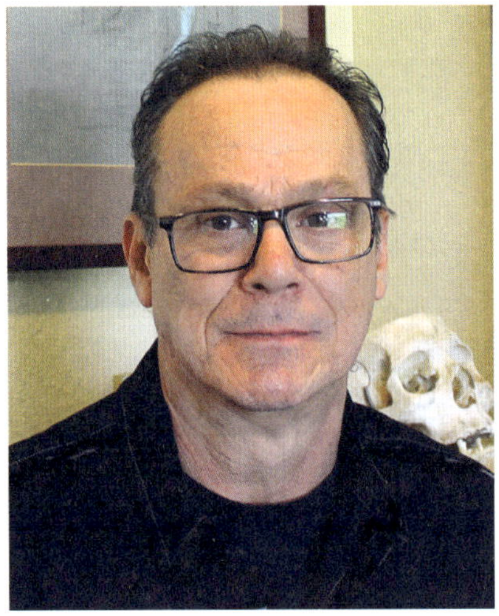

REY BUSTOS is one of the preeminent artistic anatomy teachers in the United States. He is known for his lively and passionate lectures, where his enthusiasm is evident and contagious.

Rey taught at his alma mater, ArtCenter College of Design, in Pasadena, California, for twenty-three years, from 1998 until April 2020. He has also taught at many other schools and online platforms, including the Los Angeles Academy of Figurative Art, Computer Graphics Master Academy, New Masters Academy, and California State University, Los Angeles.

Rey is the author of the book *Rey's Anatomy: Figurative Lessons from the Classroom* (2021). He lives in Altadena, CA, and can be found online at www.reybustos.com.